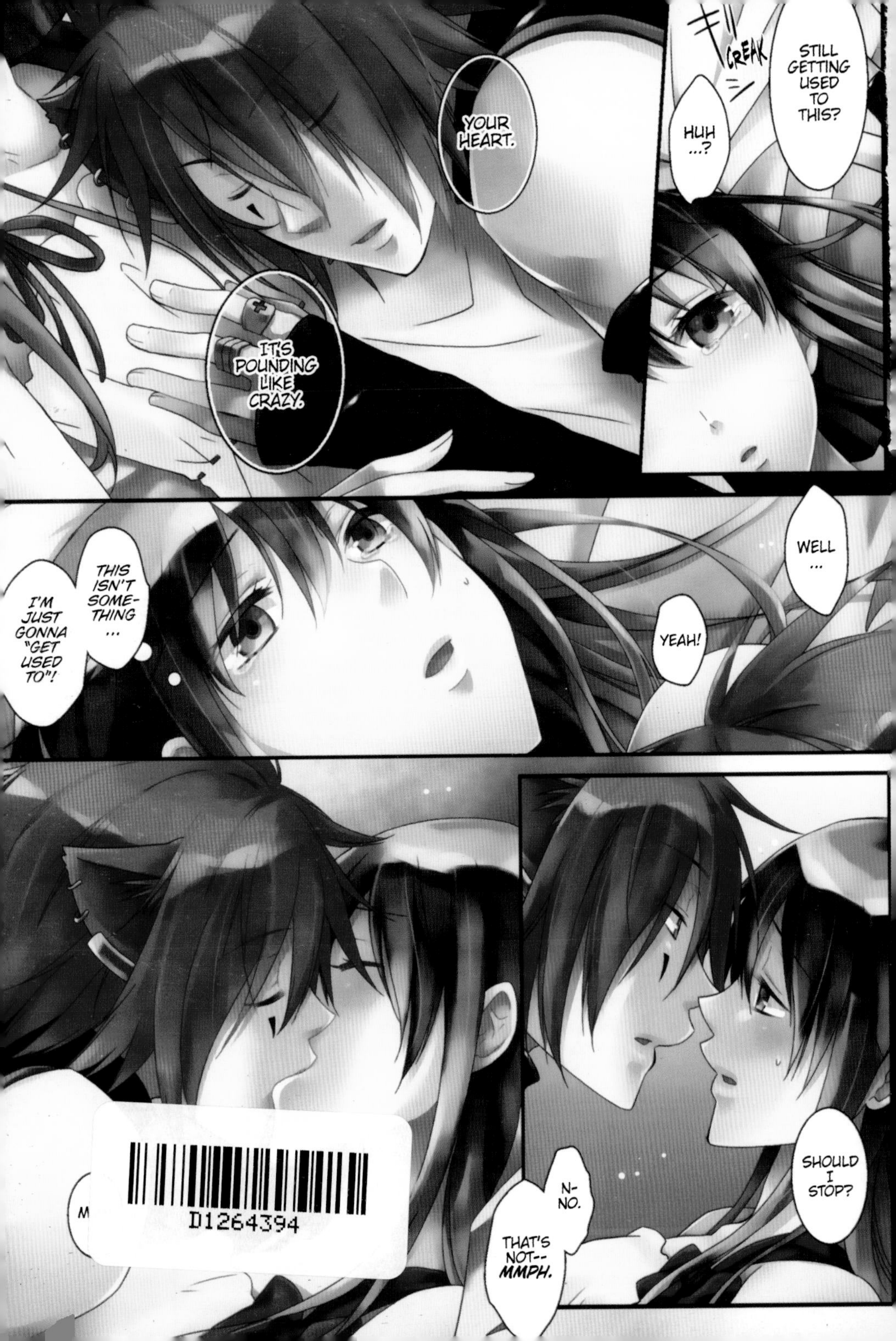
CREAK
STILL GETTING USED TO THIS?
HUH ...?
YOUR HEART.
IT'S POUNDING LIKE CRAZY.
WELL ...
YEAH!
THIS ISN'T SOMETHING ...
I'M JUST GONNA "GET USED TO"!
SHOULD I STOP?
N-NO.
THAT'S NOT-- ***MMPH.***

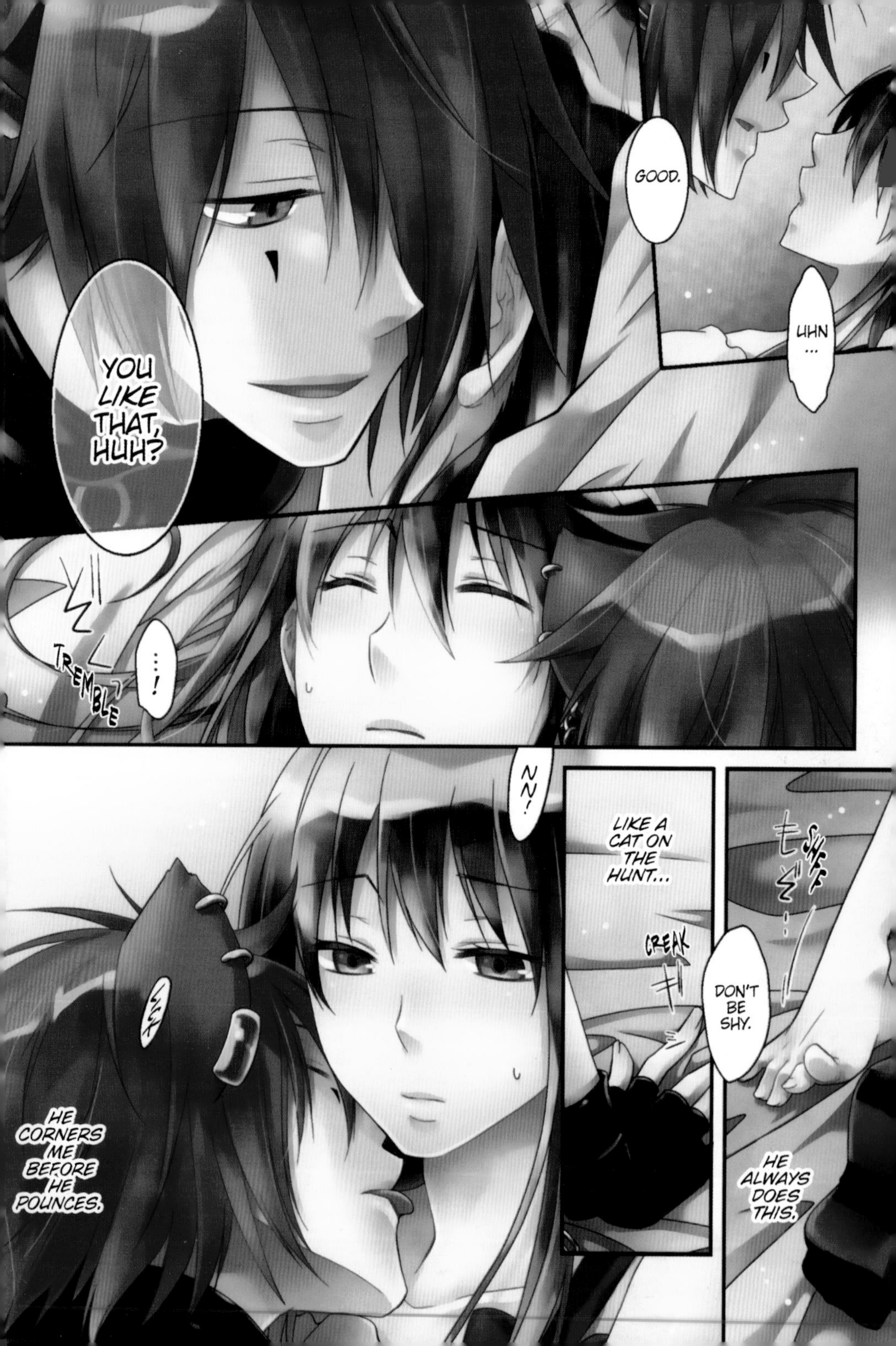
GOOD.
UHN...
YOU LIKE THAT, HUH?
TREMBLE
...!
SHFF
DON'T BE SHY.
HE ALWAYS DOES THIS.
LIKE A CAT ON THE HUNT...
CREAK
NN!
LICK
HE CORNERS ME BEFORE HE POUNCES.

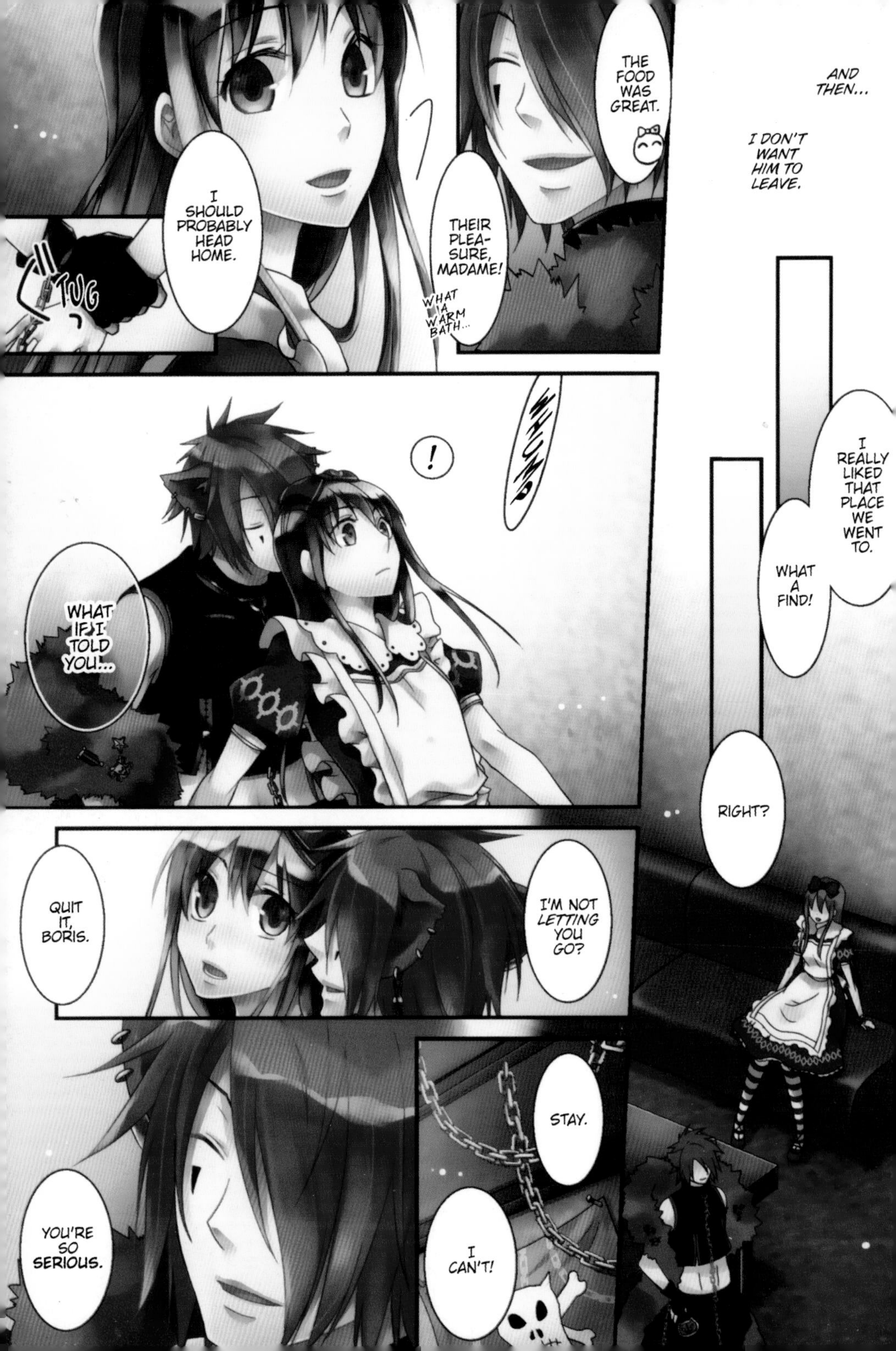
AND THEN...
I DON'T WANT HIM TO LEAVE.
I REALLY LIKED THAT PLACE WE WENT TO.
WHAT A FIND!
RIGHT?
THE FOOD WAS GREAT.
THEIR PLEASURE, MADAME!
WHAT A WARM BATH...
I SHOULD PROBABLY HEAD HOME.
TUG
WHUMP
!
WHAT IF I TOLD YOU...
I'M NOT LETTING YOU GO?
QUIT IT, BORIS.
STAY.
I CAN'T!
YOU'RE SO SERIOUS.

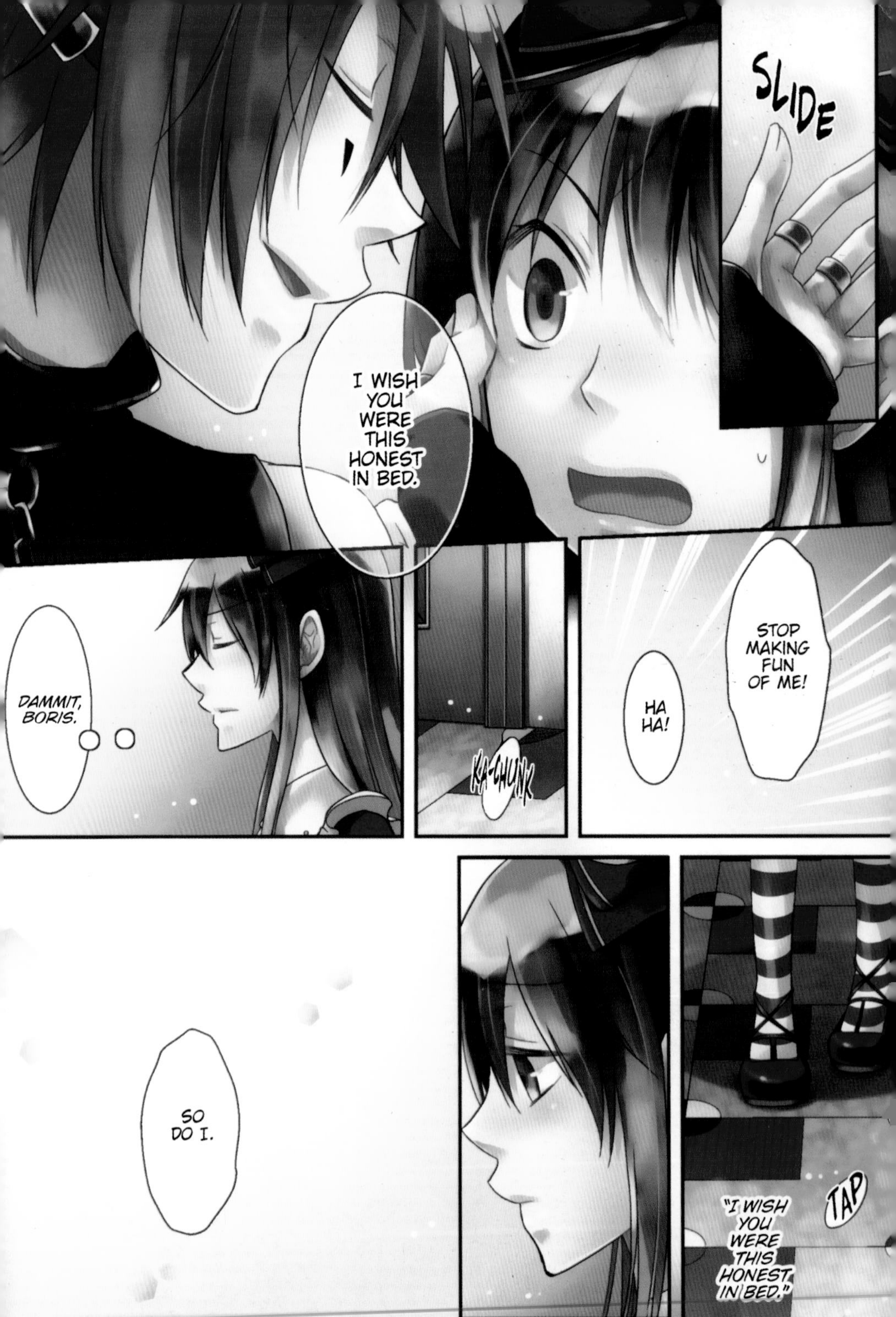
SLIDE
I WISH YOU WERE THIS HONEST IN BED.
STOP MAKING FUN OF ME!
HA HA!
KA-CHUNK
DAMMIT, BORIS.
TAP
"I WISH YOU WERE THIS HONEST IN BED."
SO DO I.

Alice in the Country of Clover
~Cheshire Cat Waltz~ 5

Mamenosuke Fujimaru
藤丸 豆ノ介

Alice IN THE COUNTRY OF Clover
CHESHIRE CAT WALTZ
VOLUME 5

story by **QuinRose**
art by **Mamenosuke Fujimaru**

STAFF CREDITS

translation **Angela Liu**
adaptation **Lianne Sentar**
lettering **Roland Amago**
layout **Bambi Eloriaga-Amago**
cover design **Nicky Lim**
copy editor **Shanti Whitesides**
editor **Adam Arnold**

publisher **Jason DeAngelis**
Seven Seas Entertainment

ALICE IN THE COUNTRY OF CLOVER: CHESHIRE CAT WALTZ VOL. 5
Copyright © Mamenosuke Fujimaru / QuinRose 2010
First published in Japan in 2010 by ICHIJINSHA Inc., Tokyo.
English translation rights arranged with ICHIJINSHA Inc., Tokyo, Japan.

ISBN: 978-1-937867-33-1

Printed in Canada

First Printing: July 2013

10 9 8 7 6 5 4 3 2 1

FOLLOW US ONLINE: **www.gomanga.com**

READING DIRECTIONS

This book reads from *right to left*, Japanese style.
If this is your first time reading manga, you start
reading from the top right panel on each page and
take it from there. If you get lost, just follow the
numbered diagram here. It may seem backwards
at first, but you'll get the hang of it! Have fun!!

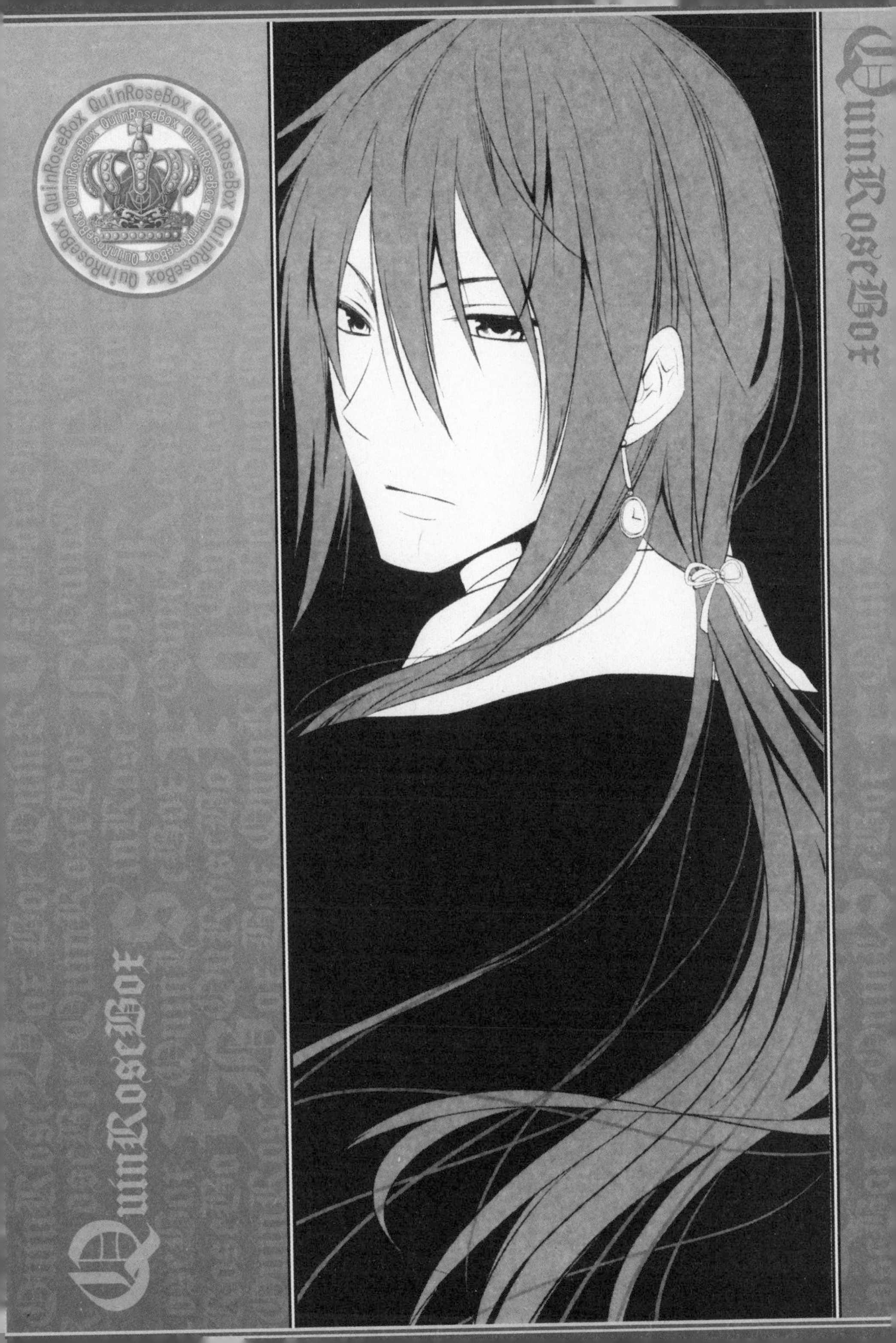
QuinRoseBox

Alice in the Country of Clover
クローバーの国の
アリス
~Wonderful Wonder World~

- STORY -

In *Alice in the Country of Clover*, the game starts with Alice having not fallen in love,
but still deciding to stay in Wonderland.

She's acquainted with all the characters from the previous game, *Alice in the Country of Hearts*.

Since love would now start from a place of friendship rather than passion with a new stranger, she can experi-
ence a different type of romance from that in the previous game. Her dynamic with the characters is different
through this friendship—characters can't always be forceful with her, and in many ways it's more comfortable
to grow intimate. The relationships *between* the Ones With Duties have also become more of a factor.

In this game, the story focuses on the mafia. Alice attends the suited meetings (forcefully) and gets involved in
various gunfights (forcefully), among other things.

Land fluctuations, sea creatures in the forest, and whispering doors—it's a game more fantastic and more
eerie than the first.

Will our everywoman Alice be able to have a romantic relationship in a world devoid of common sense?

Alice in the Country of Clover Character Information

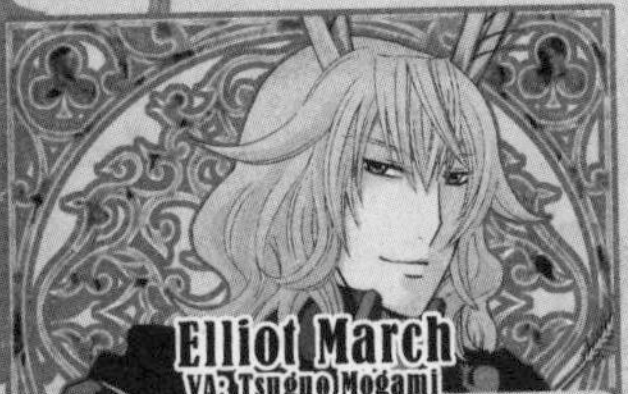

Elliot March
VA: Tsuguo Mogami

Blood's right-hand man has a criminal past… and a temperamental present. But he's not as bad as he used to be, so that's something. Joining Blood has been good(?) for him.

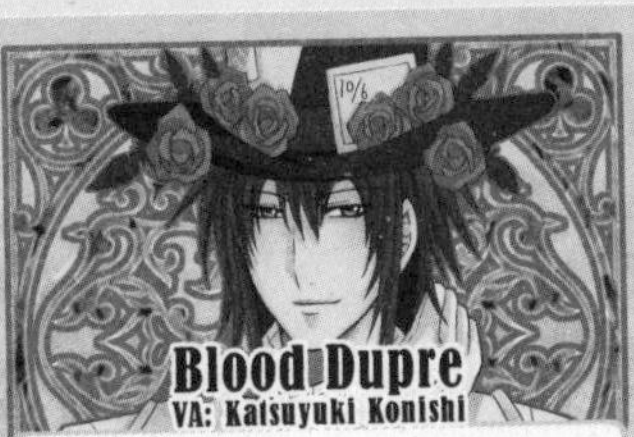

Blood Dupre
VA: Katsuyuki Konishi

The head of the mafia Hatter Family, Blood is a cunning yet moody puppet-master. Alice now has the pleasure of having him for a landlord.

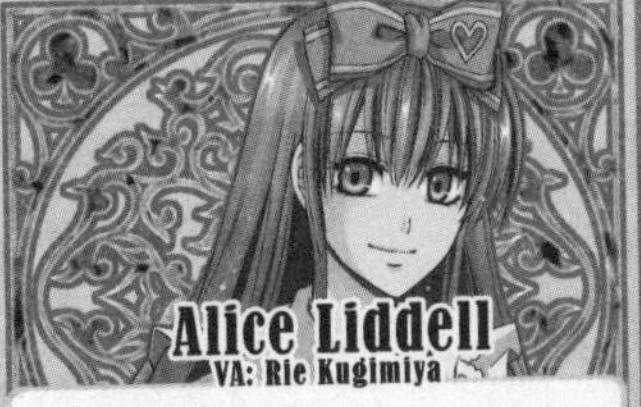

Alice Liddell
VA: Rie Kugimiya

A normal girl with a bit of a chip on her shoulder. Deciding to stay in the Wonderland she was carried to, she's adapted to her strange new lifestyle.

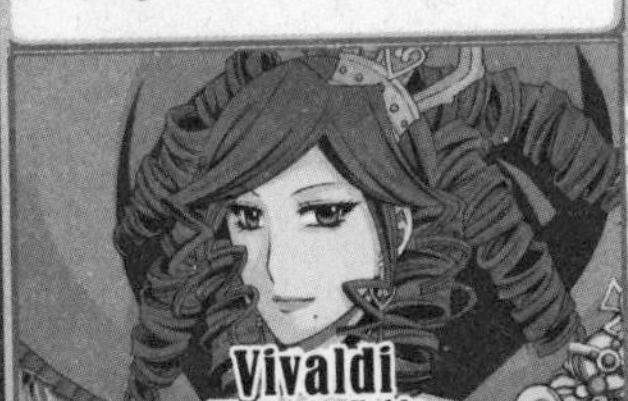

Vivaldi
VA: Yuuko Kaida

The beautiful Queen of Hearts has an unrivaled temper—which is really saying something in Wonderland. Although a picture-perfect Mad Queen, she cares for Alice as if Alice were her little sister...or a very interesting plaything.

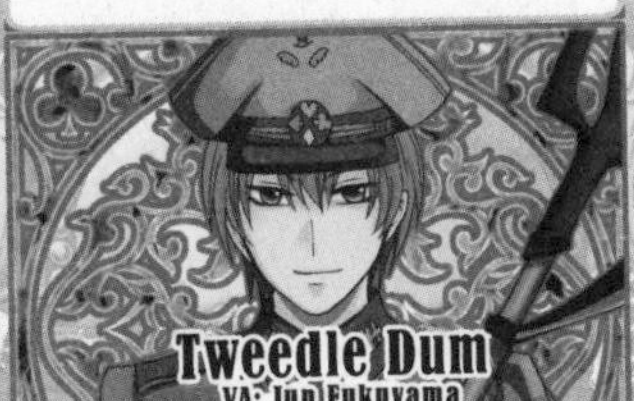

Tweedle Dum
VA: Jun Fukuyama

The second "Bloody Twin" is equally cute and equally scary. In *Clover,* Dum can also turn into an adult.

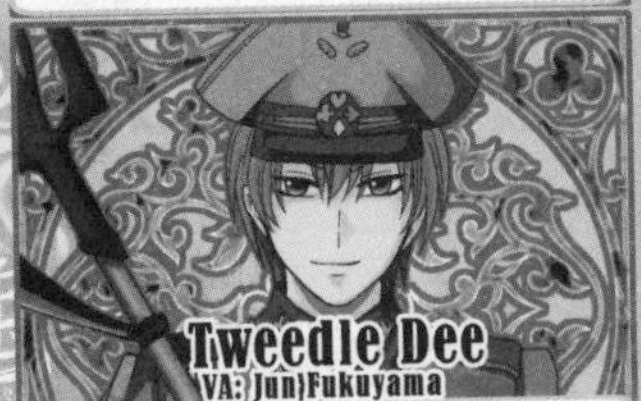

Tweedle Dee
VA: Jun Fukuyama

One of the "Bloody Twin" gatekeepers of the Hatter territory, Dee can be cute when he's not being terrifying. In *Clover,* he sometimes turns into an adult.

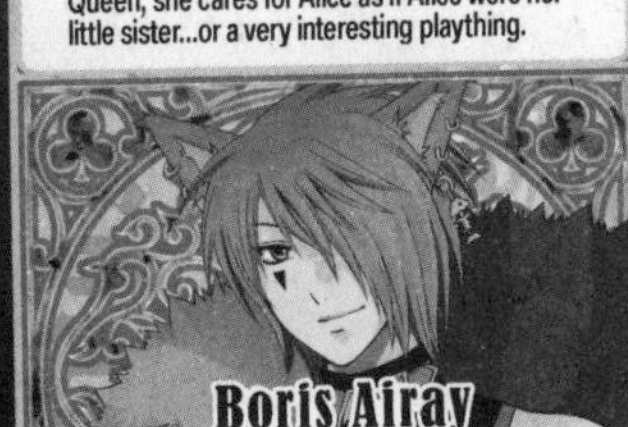

Boris Airay
VA: Noriaki Sugiyama

This riddle-loving cat has a signature smirk—and in *Clover,* a new toy. One of his favorite pastimes is giving the Sleepy Mouse a hard time.

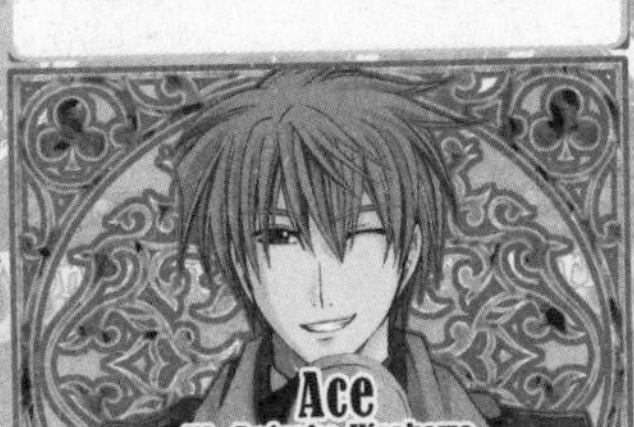

Ace
VA: Daisuke Hirakawa

The unlucky knight of Hearts was a former subordinate of Vivaldi and is perpetually lost. Even though he's depressed to be separated from his friend and boss Julius, he stays positive and tries to overcome it with a smile. He seems like a classic nice guy... or is he?

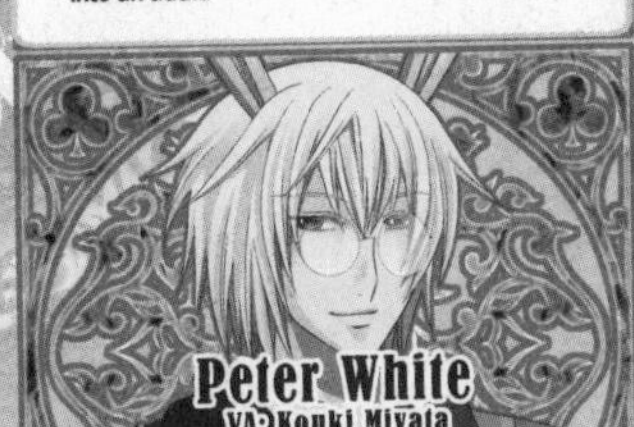

Peter White
VA: Kouki Miyata

The Prime Minister of Heart Castle—who has rabbit ears growing out of his head—invited (kidnapped) Alice to Wonderland. He loves Alice and hates everything else. His cruel, irrational actions are disturbing, but he acts like a completely different person (rabbit?) when in the throes of his love for Alice.

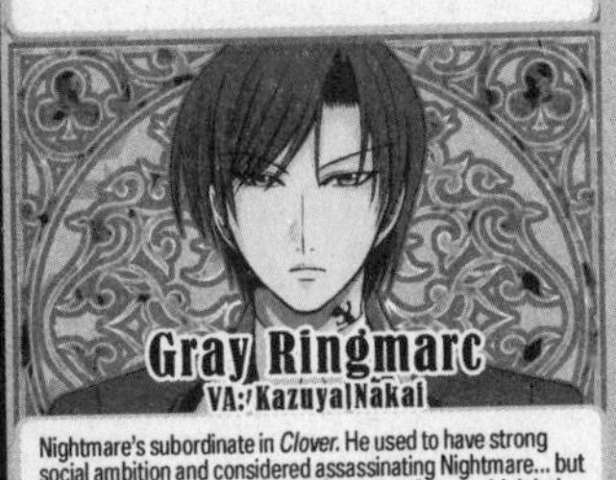

Gray Ringmarc
VA: Kazuya Nakai

Nightmare's subordinate in *Clover.* He used to have strong social ambition and considered assassinating Nightmare... but since Nightmare was such a useless boss, Gray couldn't help but feel sorry for him and ended up a dedicated assistant. He's a sound thinker with a strong work ethic. He's also highly skilled with his blades, rivaling even Ace.

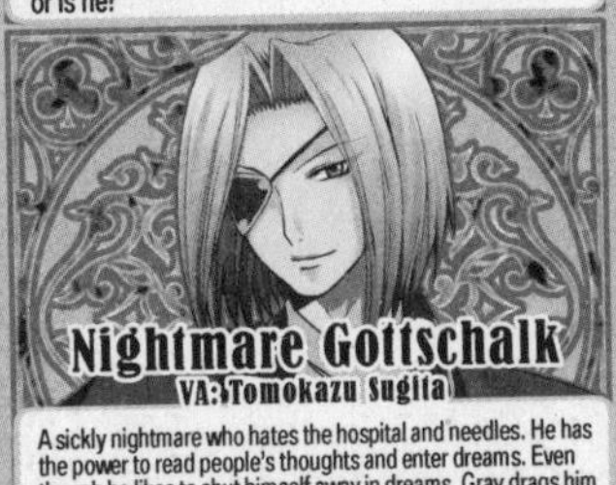

Nightmare Gottschalk
VA: Tomokazu Sugita

A sickly nightmare who hates the hospital and needles. He has the power to read people's thoughts and enter dreams. Even though he likes to shut himself away in dreams, Gray drags him out to sulk from time to time. He technically holds a high position and has many subordinates, but since he can't even take care of his own health, he leaves most things to Gray.

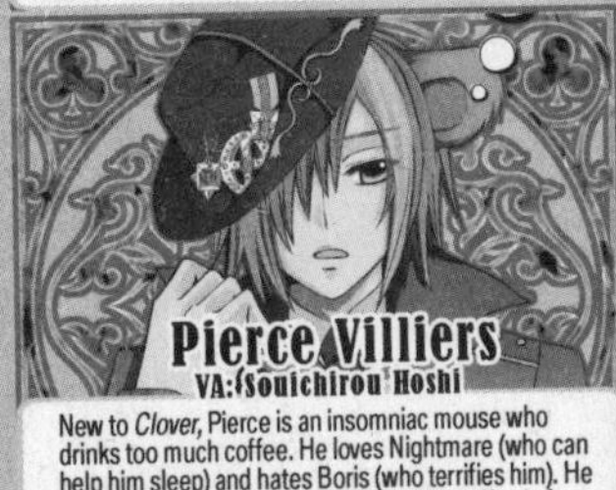

Pierce Villiers
VA: Souichirou Hoshi

New to *Clover,* Pierce is an insomniac mouse who drinks too much coffee. He loves Nightmare (who can help him sleep) and hates Boris (who terrifies him). He dislikes Blood and Vivaldi for discarding coffee in favor of tea. He likes Elliot and Peter well enough, since rabbits aren't natural predators of mice.

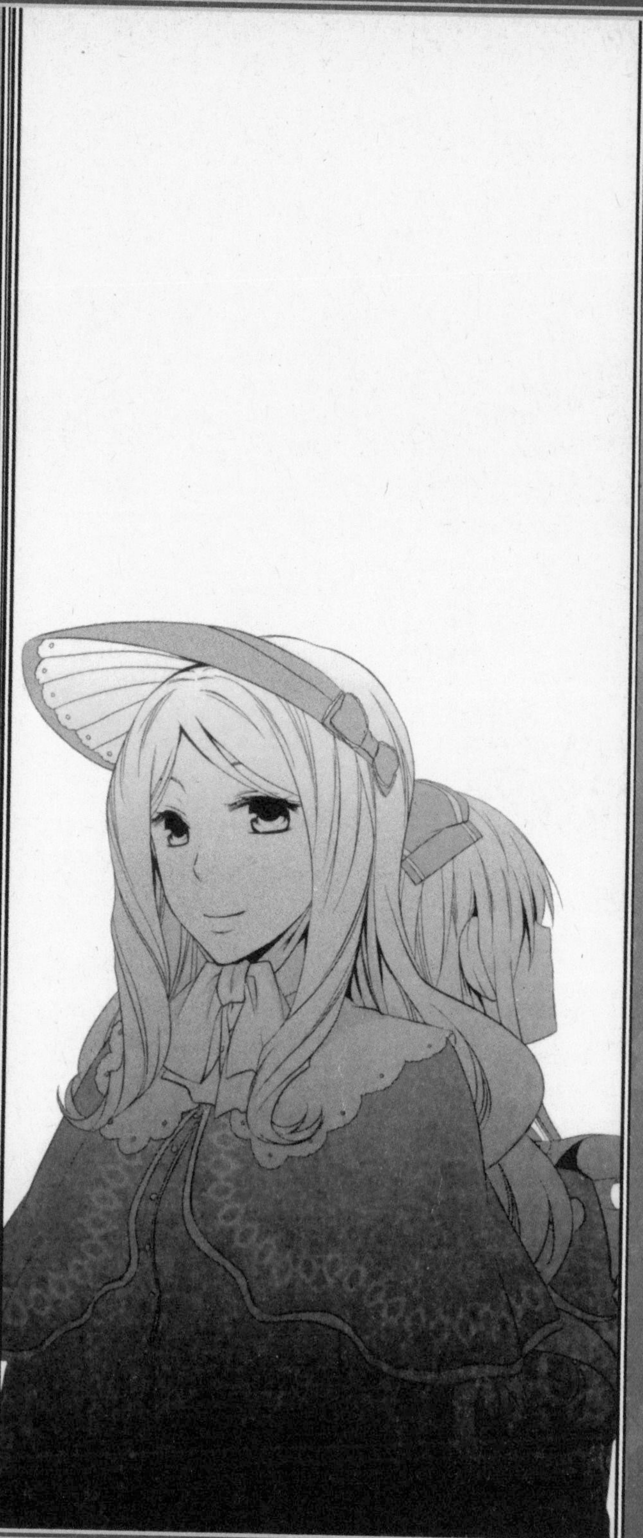

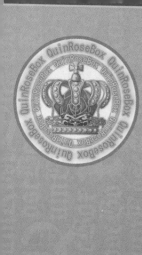

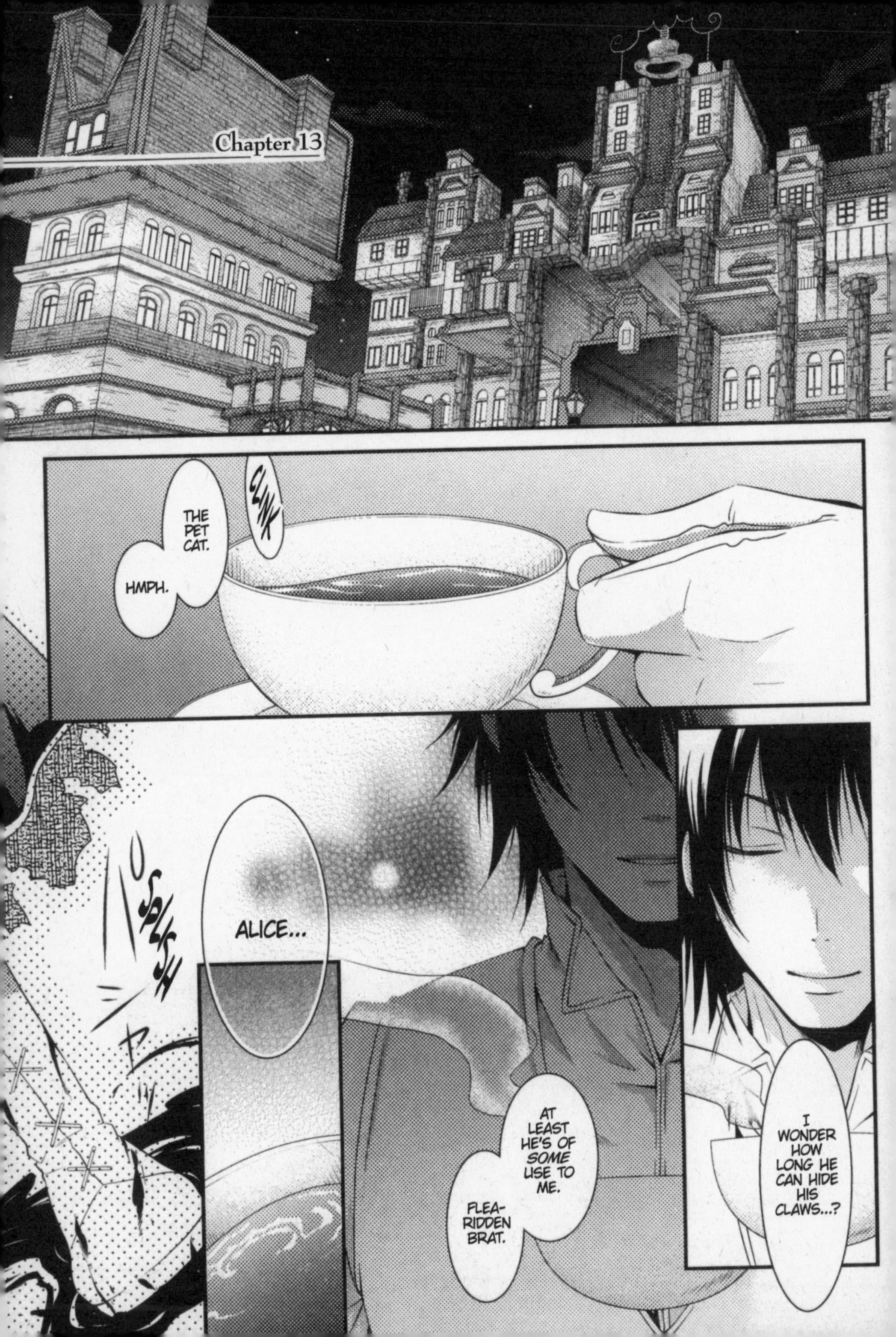
Chapter 13
CLINK
THE PET CAT.
HMPH.
I WONDER HOW LONG HE CAN HIDE HIS CLAWS...?
ALICE...
AT LEAST HE'S OF SOME USE TO ME.
FLEA-RIDDEN BRAT.
SPLISH

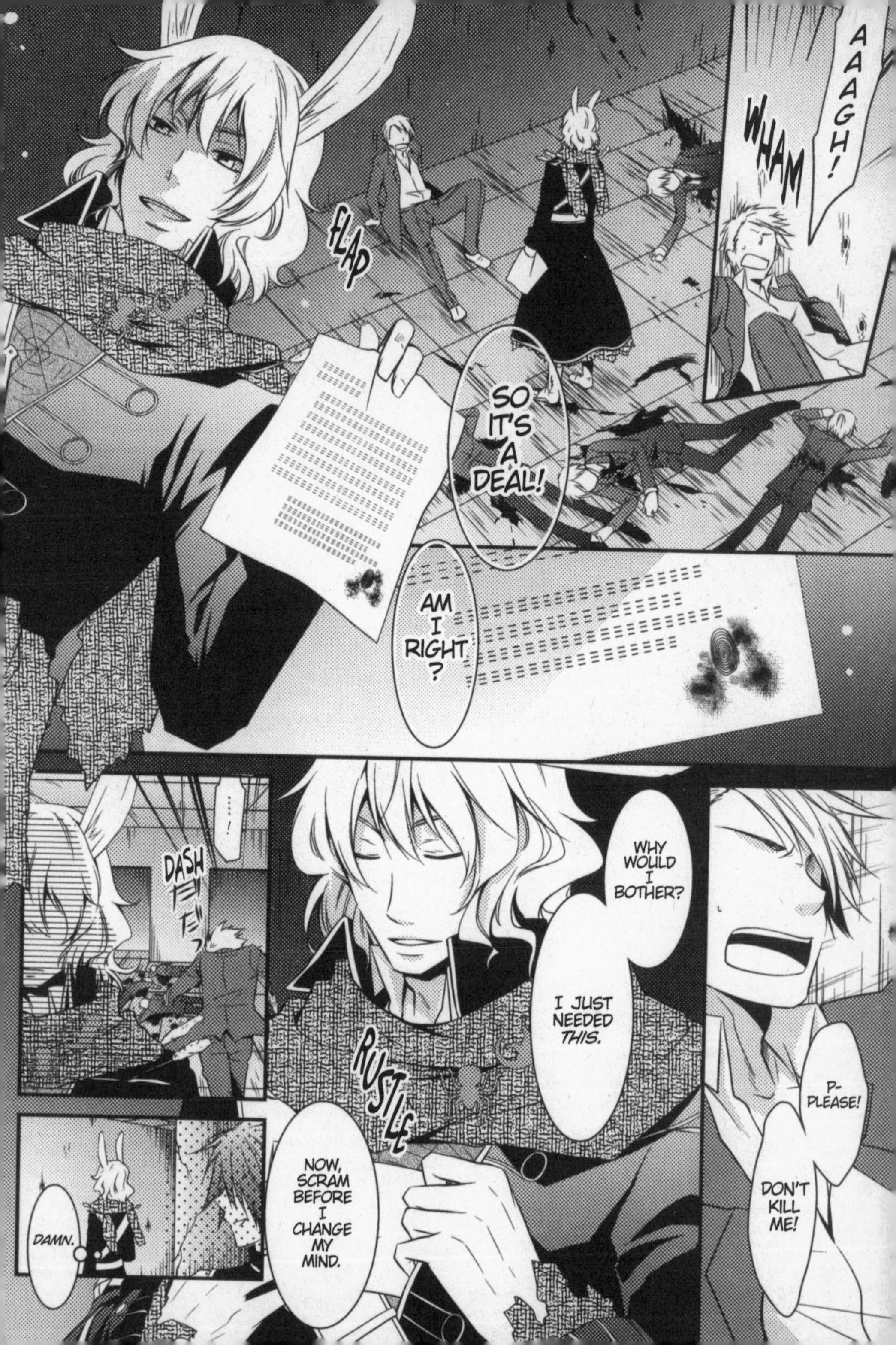
AAAGH!
WHAM
FLAP
SO IT'S A DEAL!
AM I RIGHT?
P-PLEASE!
DON'T KILL ME!
WHY WOULD I BOTHER?
I JUST NEEDED THIS.
RUSTLE
NOW, SCRAM BEFORE I CHANGE MY MIND.
...!
DASH
DAMN.

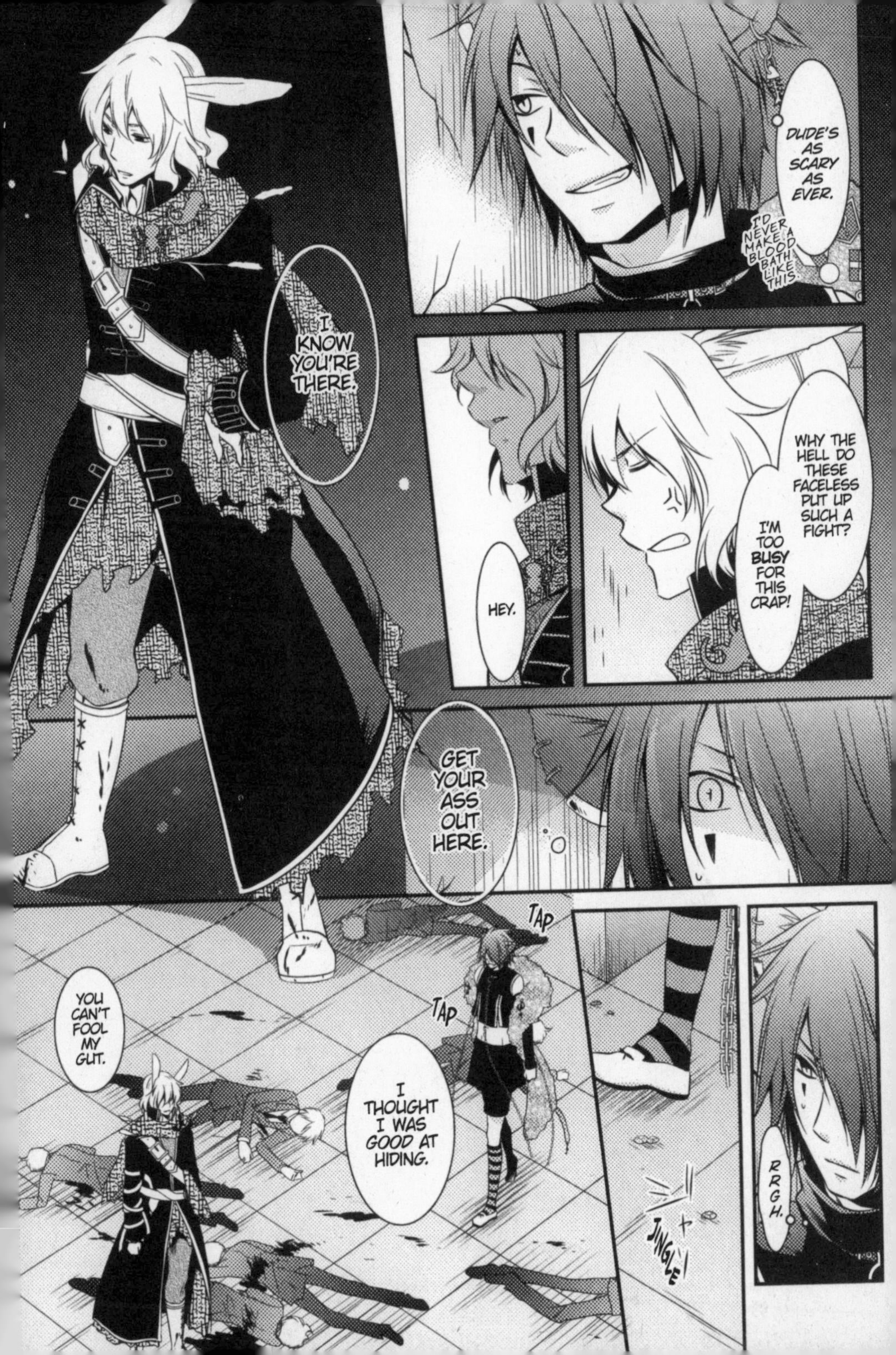

DUDE'S AS SCARY AS EVER.
I'D NEVER MAKE A BLOOD BATH LIKE THIS.
WHY THE HELL DO THESE FACELESS PUT UP SUCH A FIGHT?
I'M TOO BUSY FOR THIS CRAP!
HEY.
GET YOUR ASS OUT HERE.
I KNOW YOU'RE THERE.
RRGH.
JINGLE
TAP
TAP
I THOUGHT I WAS GOOD AT HIDING.
YOU CAN'T FOOL MY GUT.

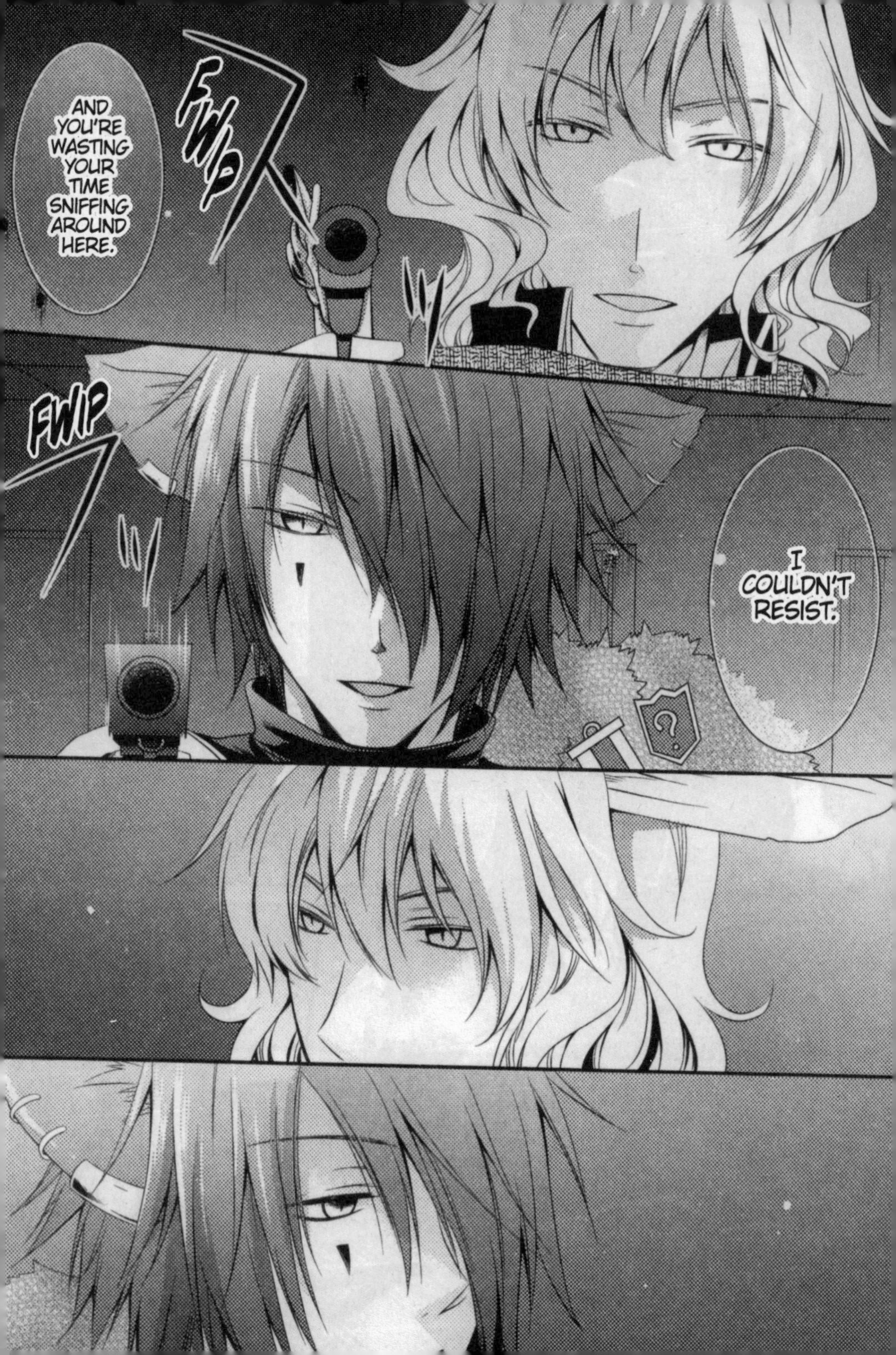

FWIP
AND YOU'RE WASTING YOUR TIME SNIFFING AROUND HERE.
I COULDN'T RESIST.
FWIP

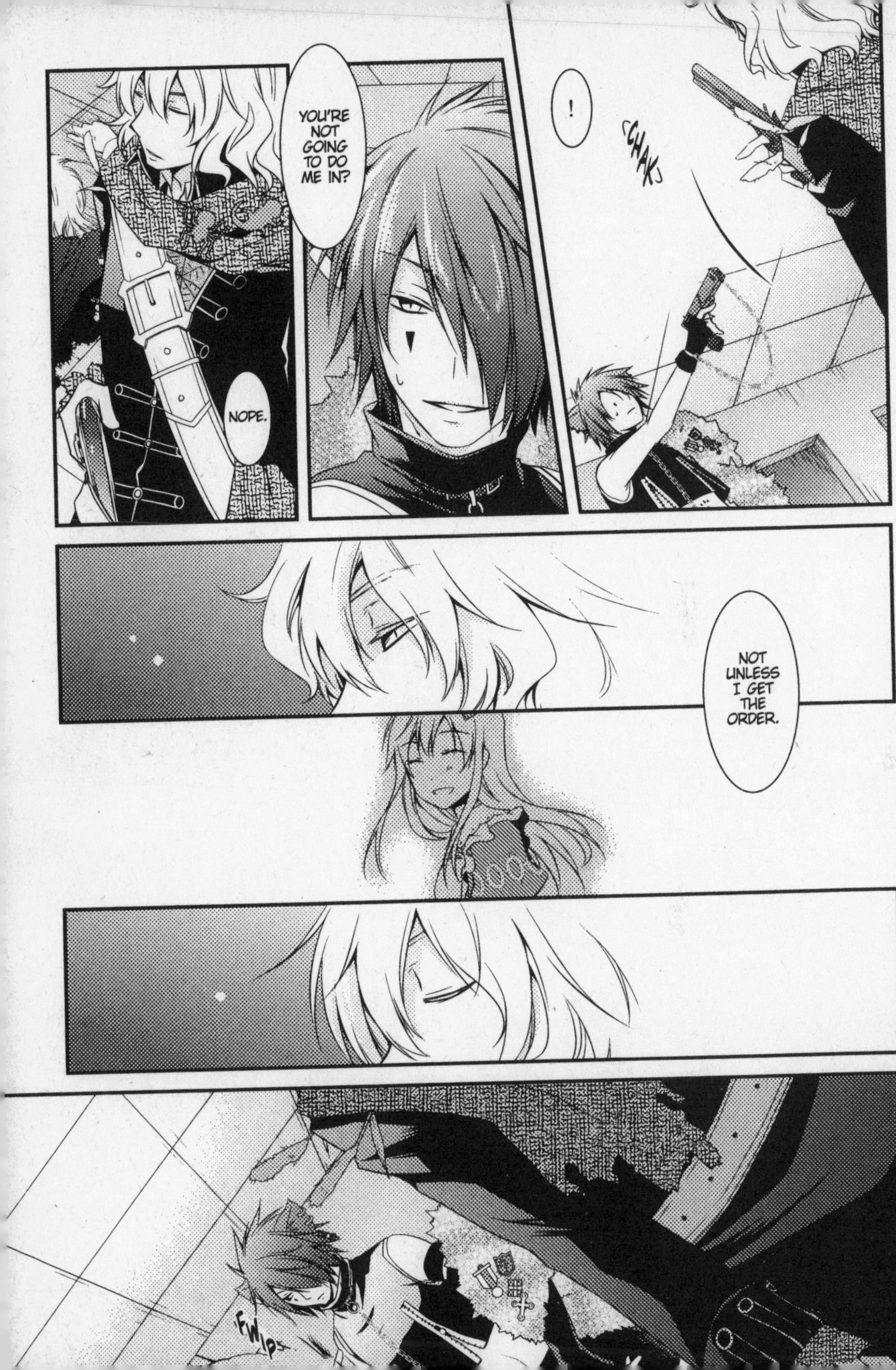
!
CHAK
YOU'RE NOT GOING TO DO ME IN?
NOPE.
NOT UNLESS I GET THE ORDER.
FWIP

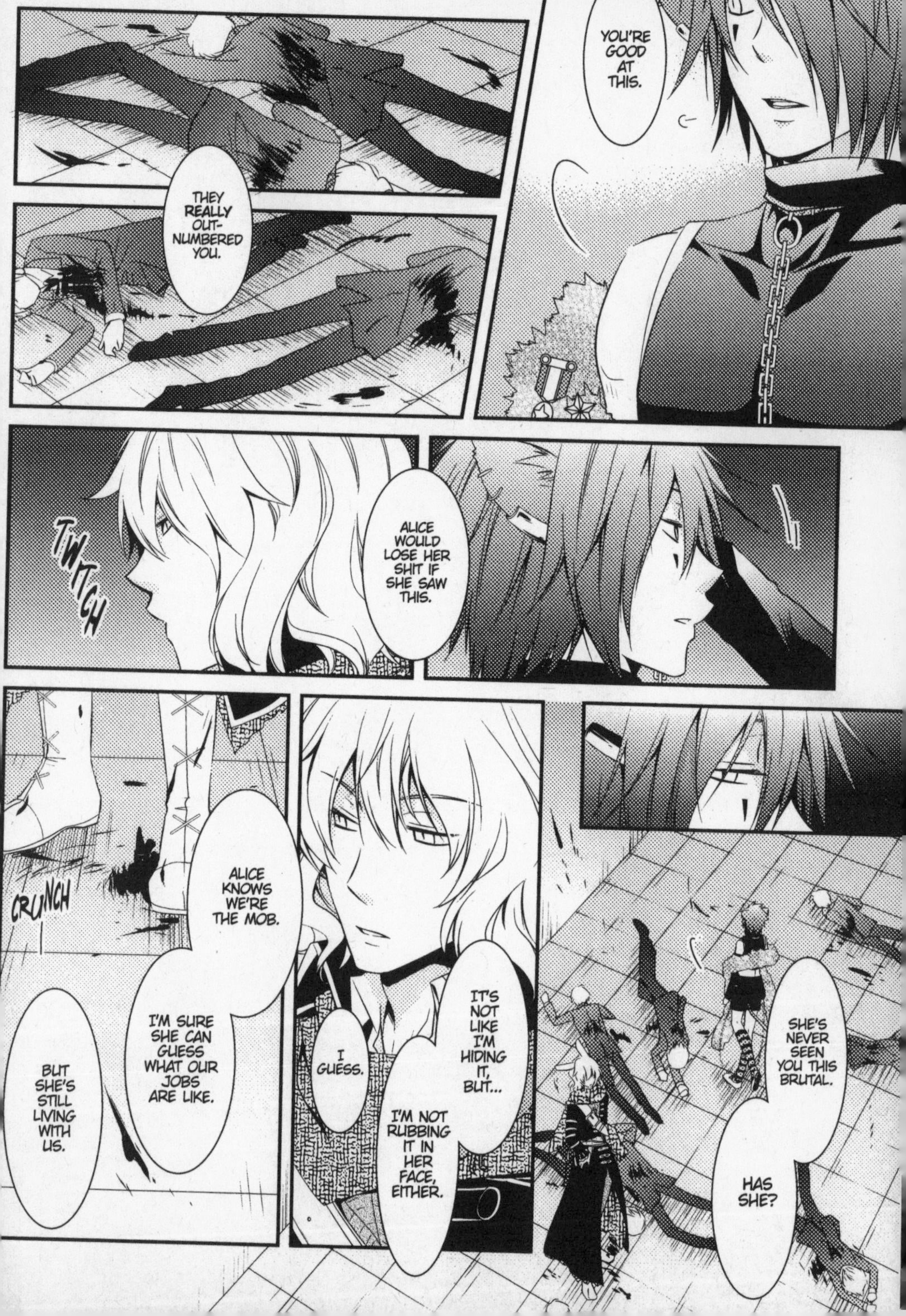
YOU'RE GOOD AT THIS.
THEY REALLY OUT-NUMBERED YOU.
ALICE WOULD LOSE HER SHIT IF SHE SAW THIS.
TWITCH
SHE'S NEVER SEEN YOU THIS BRUTAL.
HAS SHE?
ALICE KNOWS WE'RE THE MOB.
I'M SURE SHE CAN GUESS WHAT OUR JOBS ARE LIKE.
BUT SHE'S STILL LIVING WITH US.
I GUESS.
IT'S NOT LIKE I'M HIDING IT, BUT...
I'M NOT RUBBING IT IN HER FACE, EITHER.
CRUNCH

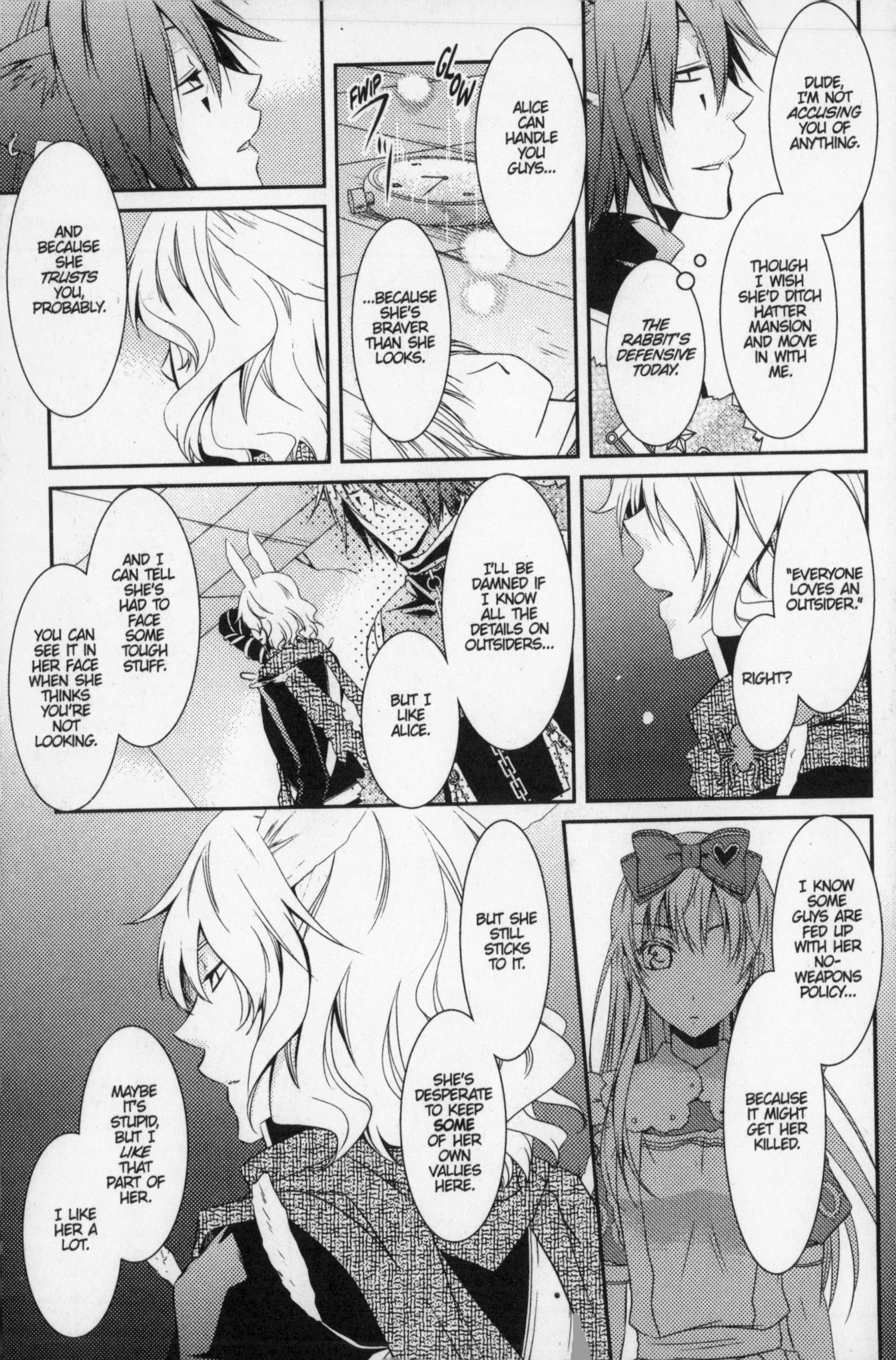
DUDE, I'M NOT ACCUSING YOU OF ANYTHING.
THOUGH I WISH SHE'D DITCH HATTER MANSION AND MOVE IN WITH ME.
THE RABBIT'S DEFENSIVE TODAY.
GLOW
FWIP
ALICE CAN HANDLE YOU GUYS...
...BECAUSE SHE'S BRAVER THAN SHE LOOKS.
AND BECAUSE SHE TRUSTS YOU, PROBABLY.
"EVERYONE LOVES AN OUTSIDER."
RIGHT?
I'LL BE DAMNED IF I KNOW ALL THE DETAILS ON OUTSIDERS...
BUT I LIKE ALICE.
AND I CAN TELL SHE'S HAD TO FACE SOME TOUGH STUFF.
YOU CAN SEE IT IN HER FACE WHEN SHE THINKS YOU'RE NOT LOOKING.
I KNOW SOME GUYS ARE FED UP WITH HER NO-WEAPONS POLICY...
BECAUSE IT MIGHT GET HER KILLED.
BUT SHE STILL STICKS TO IT.
SHE'S DESPERATE TO KEEP SOME OF HER OWN VALUES HERE.
MAYBE IT'S STUPID, BUT I LIKE THAT PART OF HER.
I LIKE HER A LOT.

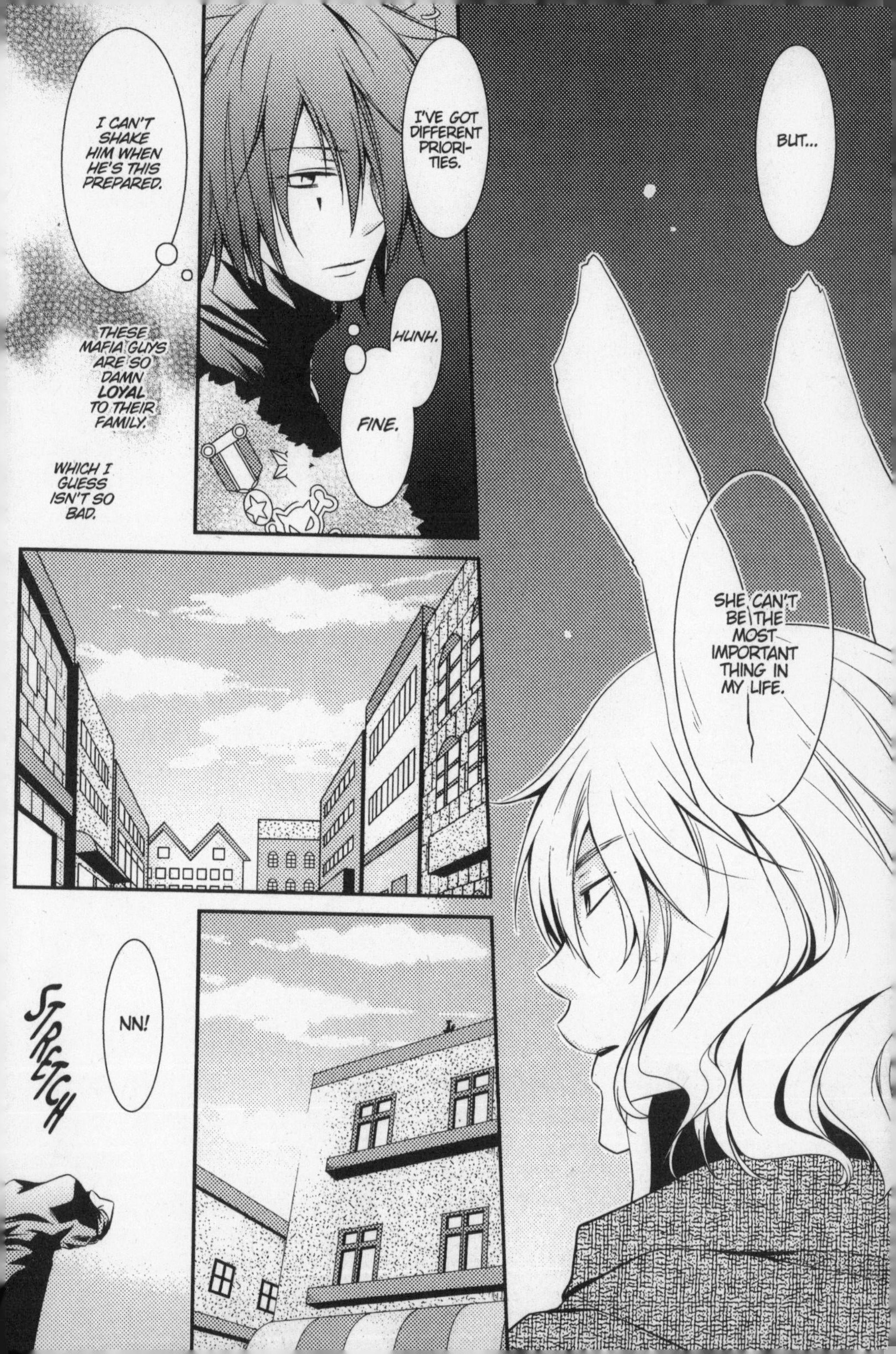
BUT...
SHE CAN'T BE THE MOST IMPORTANT THING IN MY LIFE.
I'VE GOT DIFFERENT PRIORI-TIES.
HUNH.
FINE.
I CAN'T SHAKE HIM WHEN HE'S THIS PREPARED.
THESE MAFIA GUYS ARE SO DAMN LOYAL TO THEIR FAMILY.
WHICH I GUESS ISN'T SO BAD.
NN!
STRETCH

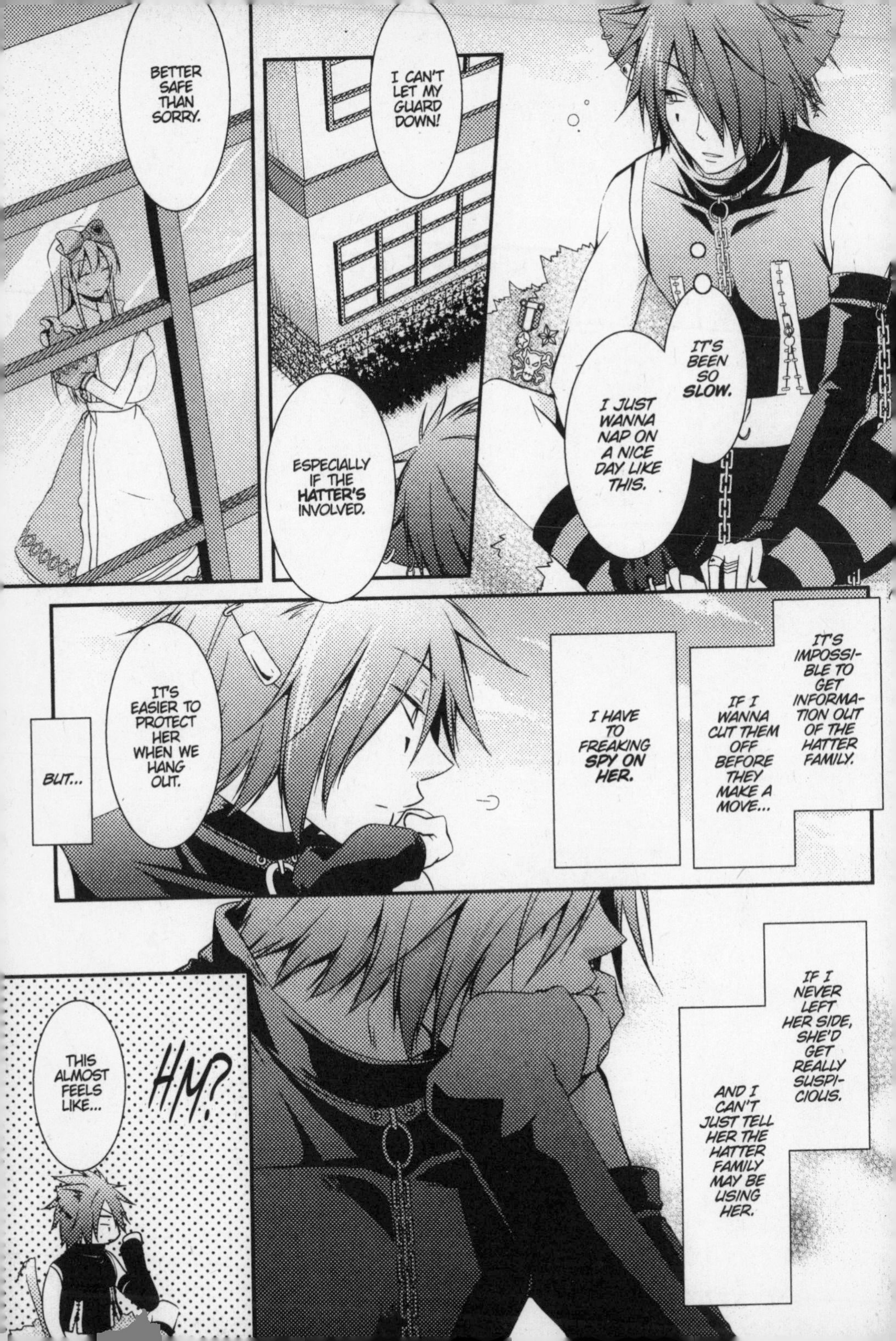
IT'S BEEN SO SLOW.
I JUST WANNA NAP ON A NICE DAY LIKE THIS.
I CAN'T LET MY GUARD DOWN!
ESPECIALLY IF THE HATTER'S INVOLVED.
BETTER SAFE THAN SORRY.
IT'S IMPOSSIBLE TO GET INFORMATION OUT OF THE HATTER FAMILY.
IF I WANNA CUT THEM OFF BEFORE THEY MAKE A MOVE...
I HAVE TO FREAKING SPY ON HER.
IT'S EASIER TO PROTECT HER WHEN WE HANG OUT.
BUT...
IF I NEVER LEFT HER SIDE, SHE'D GET REALLY SUSPICIOUS.
AND I CAN'T JUST TELL HER THE HATTER FAMILY MAY BE USING HER.
HM?
THIS ALMOST FEELS LIKE...

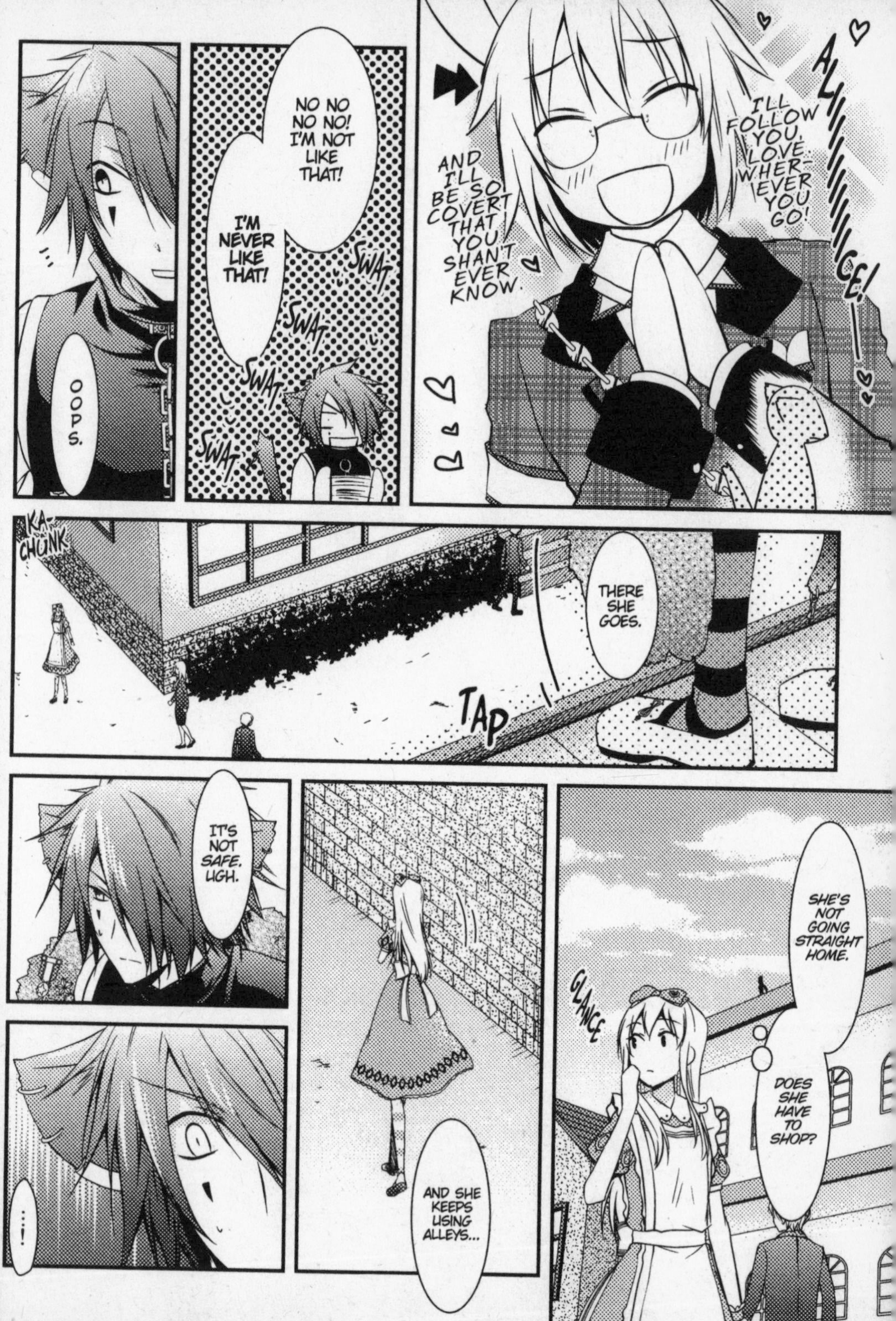
ALIIIIIICE!
I'LL FOLLOW YOU, LOVE, WHEREVER YOU GO!
AND I'LL BE SO COVERT THAT YOU SHAN'T EVER KNOW.
NO NO NO NO! I'M NOT LIKE THAT!
I'M NEVER LIKE THAT!
SWAT
SWAT
SWAT
SWAT
OOPS.
...
KA-CHUNK
THERE SHE GOES.
TAP
SHE'S NOT GOING STRAIGHT HOME.
DOES SHE HAVE TO SHOP?
GLANCE
AND SHE KEEPS USING ALLEYS...
IT'S NOT SAFE. UGH.
...!

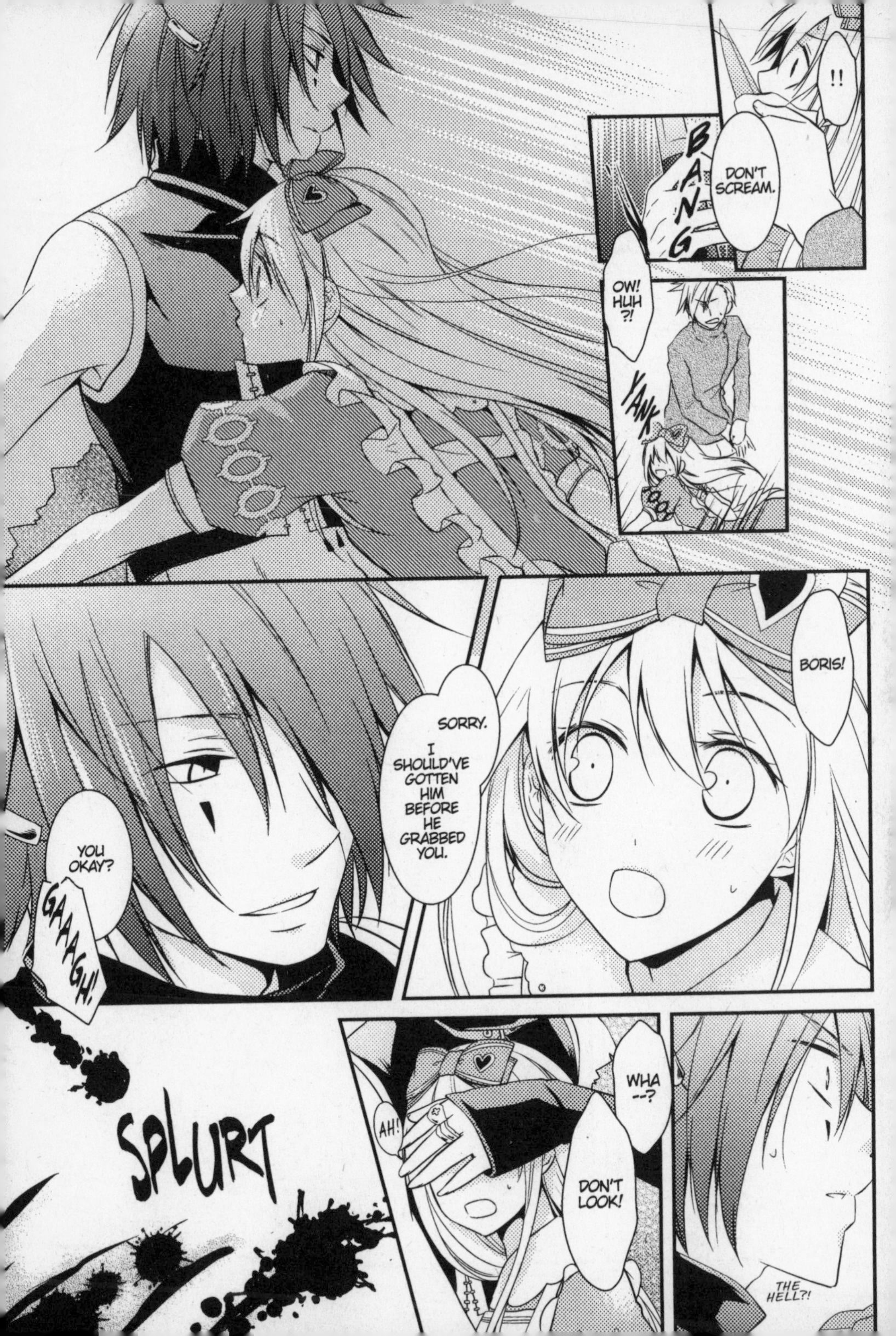
!!
DON'T SCREAM.
BANG
OW! HUH?!
YANK
BORIS!
SORRY.
I SHOULD'VE GOTTEN HIM BEFORE HE GRABBED YOU.
YOU OKAY?
GAAAGH!
THE HELL?!
WHA--?
AH!
DON'T LOOK!
SPLURT

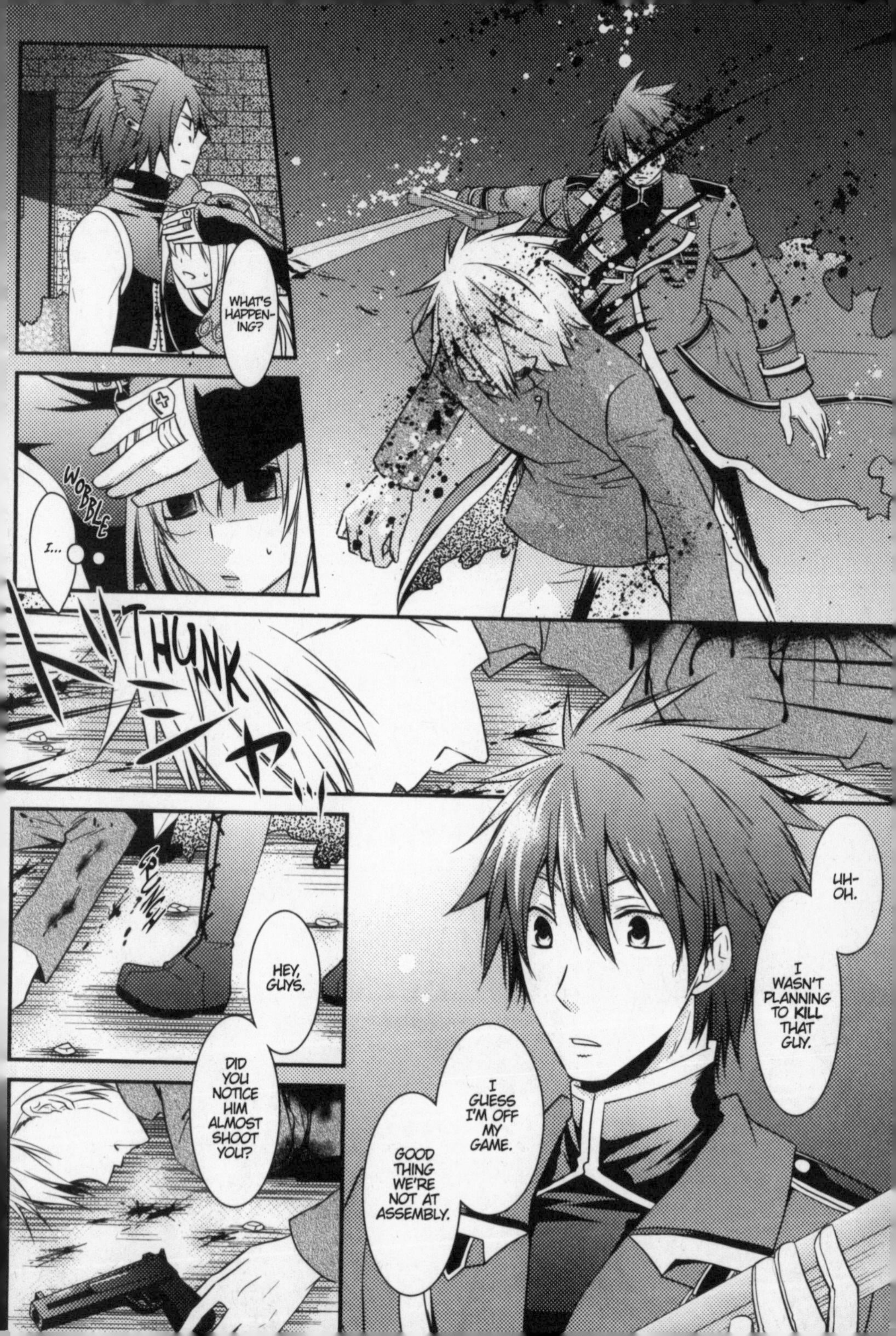
WHAT'S HAPPENING?
WOBBLE
I...
THUNK
UH-OH.
I WASN'T PLANNING TO KILL THAT GUY.
I GUESS I'M OFF MY GAME.
GOOD THING WE'RE NOT AT ASSEMBLY.
CRUNCH
HEY, GUYS.
DID YOU NOTICE HIM ALMOST SHOOT YOU?

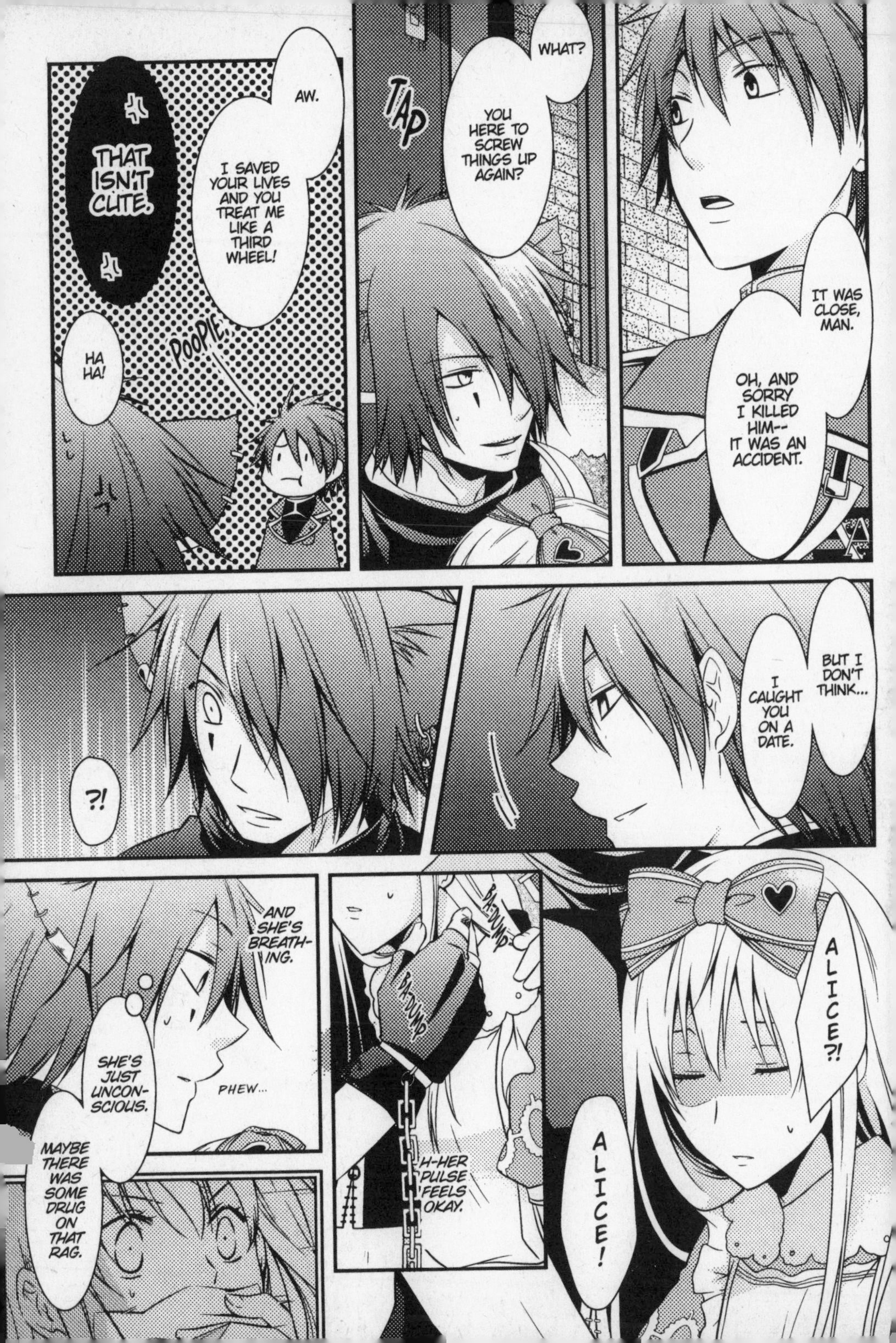
IT WAS CLOSE, MAN.
OH, AND SORRY I KILLED HIM-- IT WAS AN ACCIDENT.
WHAT?
YOU HERE TO SCREW THINGS UP AGAIN?
TAP
AW.
I SAVED YOUR LIVES AND YOU TREAT ME LIKE A THIRD WHEEL!
THAT ISN'T CUTE.
POOPIE.
HA HA!
BUT I DON'T THINK...
I CAUGHT YOU ON A DATE.
?!
ALICE?!
ALICE!
BA-DUMP
BA-DUMP
H-HER PULSE FEELS OKAY.
AND SHE'S BREATHING.
SHE'S JUST UNCONSCIOUS.
PHEW...
MAYBE THERE WAS SOME DRUG ON THAT RAG.

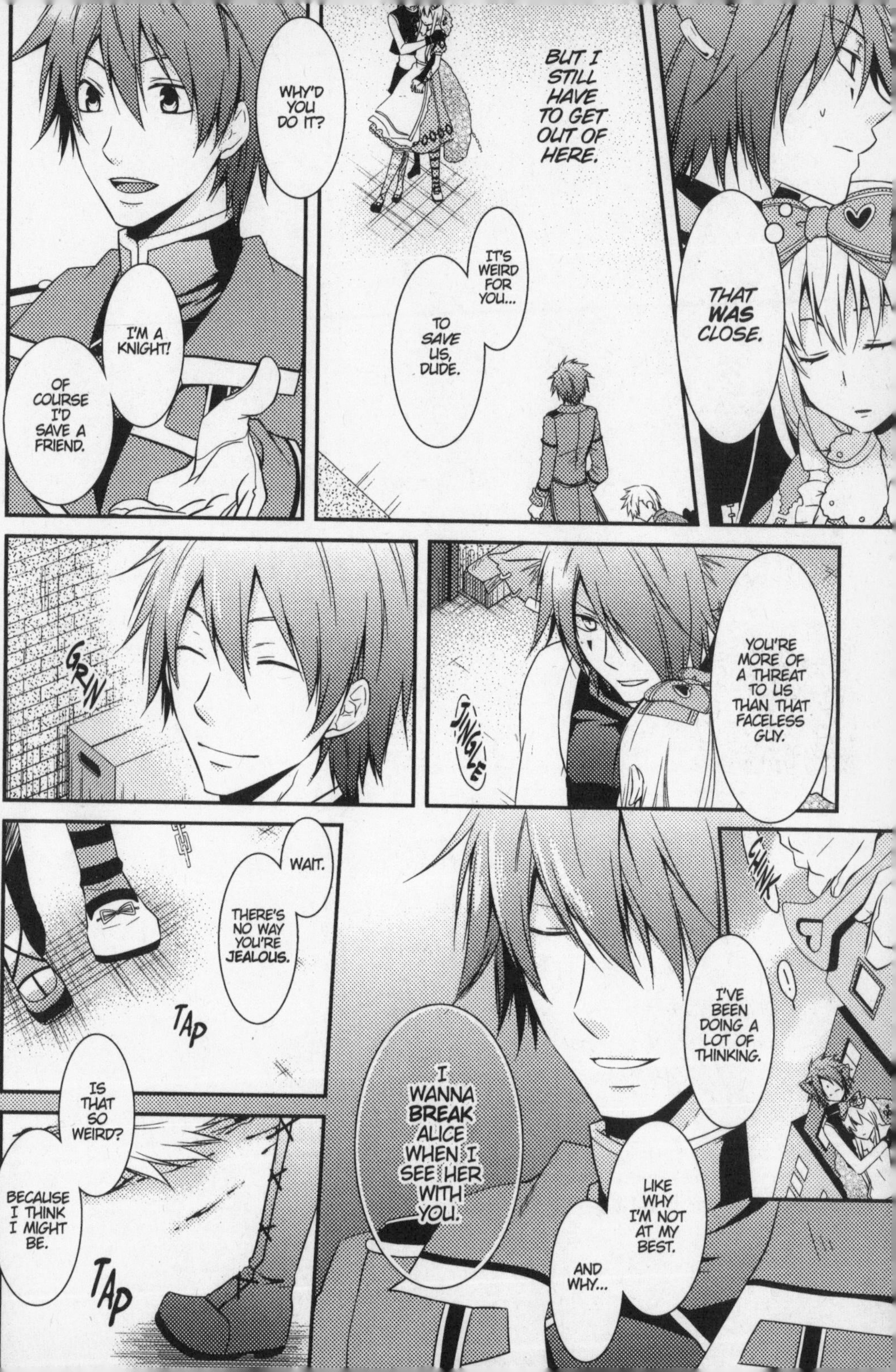
THAT WAS CLOSE.
BUT I STILL HAVE TO GET OUT OF HERE.
IT'S WEIRD FOR YOU...
TO SAVE US, DUDE.
WHY'D YOU DO IT?
I'M A KNIGHT!
OF COURSE I'D SAVE A FRIEND.
JINGLE
YOU'RE MORE OF A THREAT TO US THAN THAT FACELESS GUY.
GRIN
CHINK
!
I'VE BEEN DOING A LOT OF THINKING.
LIKE WHY I'M NOT AT MY BEST.
AND WHY...
I WANNA BREAK ALICE WHEN I SEE HER WITH YOU.
WAIT.
THERE'S NO WAY YOU'RE JEALOUS.
TAP
IS THAT SO WEIRD?
BECAUSE I THINK I MIGHT BE.
TAP

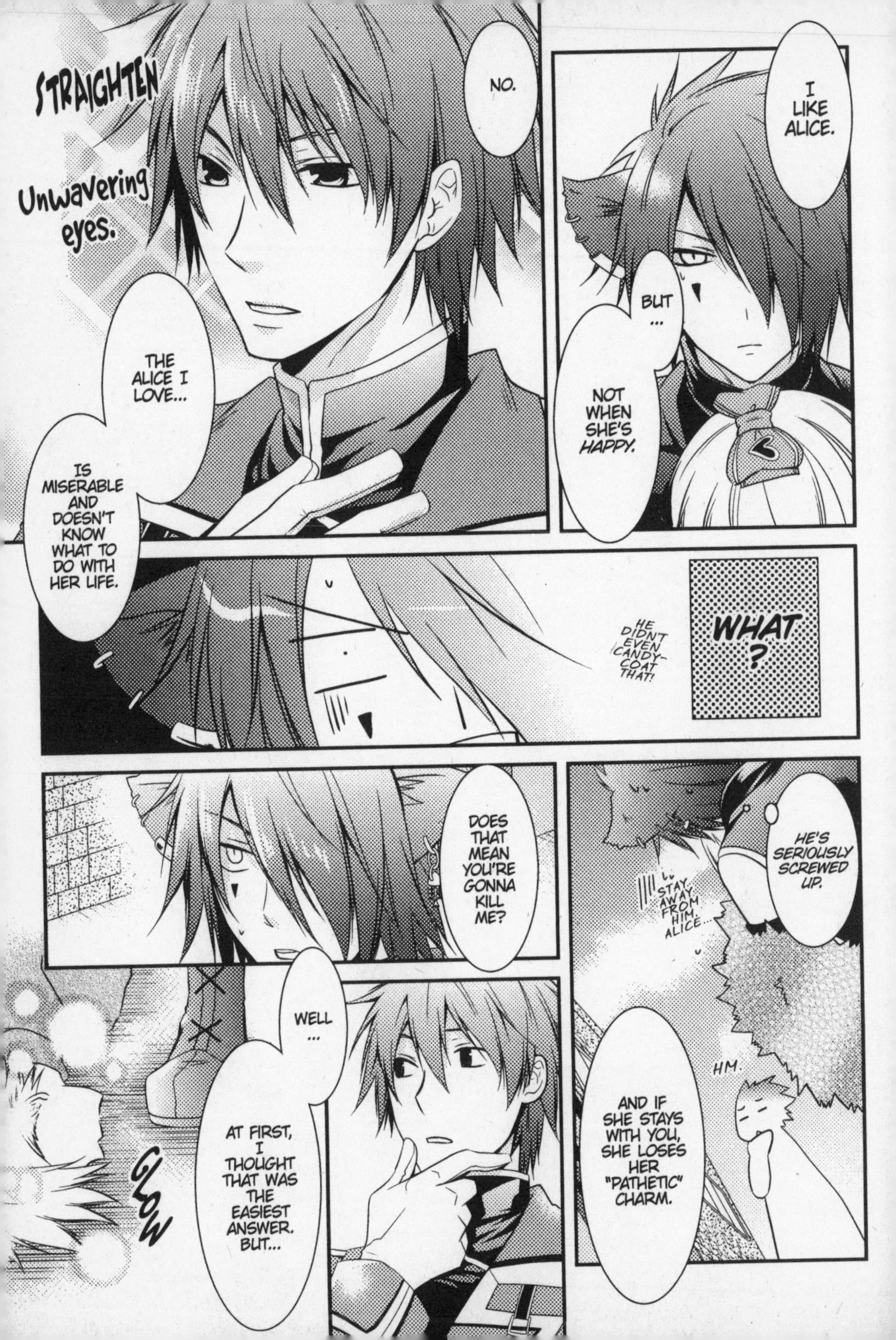
I LIKE ALICE.
BUT...
NOT WHEN SHE'S HAPPY.
NO.
STRAIGHTEN
Unwavering eyes.
THE ALICE I LOVE...
IS MISERABLE AND DOESN'T KNOW WHAT TO DO WITH HER LIFE.
WHAT?
HE DIDN'T EVEN CANDY-COAT THAT!
HE'S SERIOUSLY SCREWED UP.
STAY AWAY FROM HIM, ALICE...
HM.
AND IF SHE STAYS WITH YOU, SHE LOSES HER "PATHETIC" CHARM.
DOES THAT MEAN YOU'RE GONNA KILL ME?
WELL...
AT FIRST, I THOUGHT THAT WAS THE EASIEST ANSWER. BUT...
GLOW

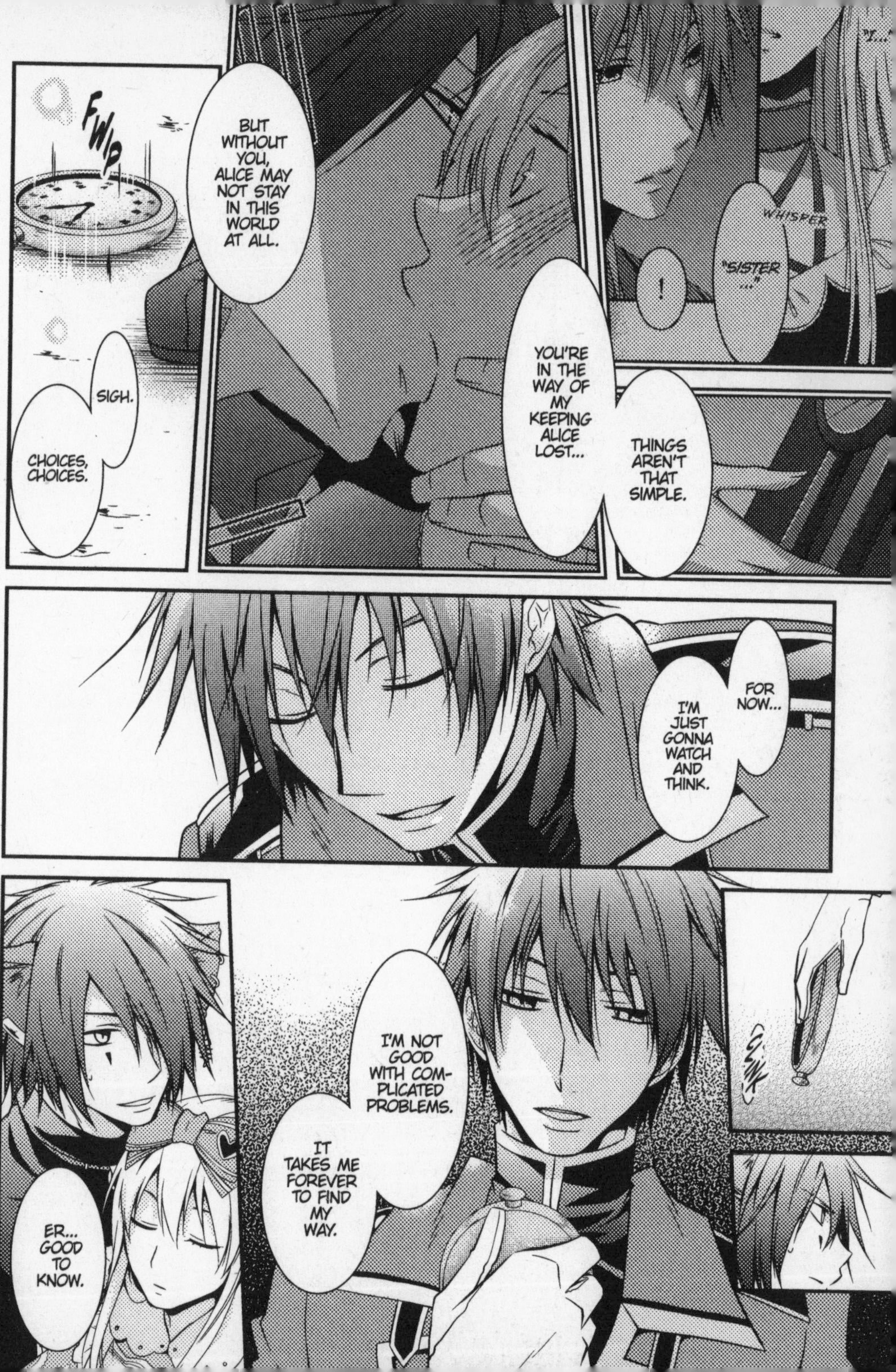
WHISPER
"SISTER..."
!
THINGS AREN'T THAT SIMPLE.
YOU'RE IN THE WAY OF MY KEEPING ALICE LOST...
BUT WITHOUT YOU, ALICE MAY NOT STAY IN THIS WORLD AT ALL.
FWIP
SIGH.
CHOICES, CHOICES.
FOR NOW...
I'M JUST GONNA WATCH AND THINK.
CLINK
I'M NOT GOOD WITH COMPLICATED PROBLEMS.
IT TAKES ME FOREVER TO FIND MY WAY.
ER... GOOD TO KNOW.

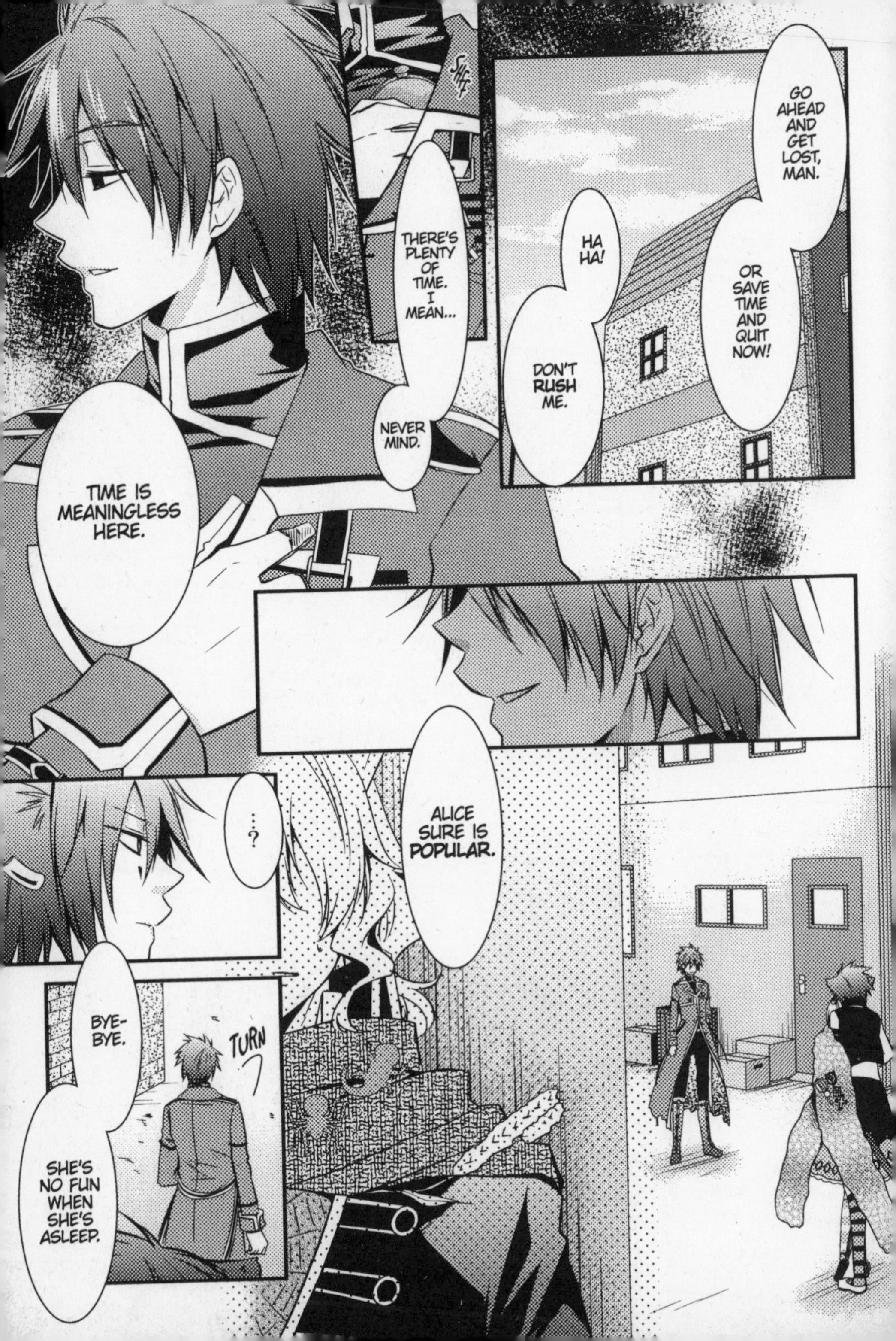
GO AHEAD AND GET LOST, MAN.
OR SAVE TIME AND QUIT NOW!
HA HA!
DON'T RUSH ME.
SHff
THERE'S PLENTY OF TIME. I MEAN...
NEVER MIND.
TIME IS MEANINGLESS HERE.
ALICE SURE IS POPULAR.
...?
BYE-BYE.
TURN
SHE'S NO FUN WHEN SHE'S ASLEEP.

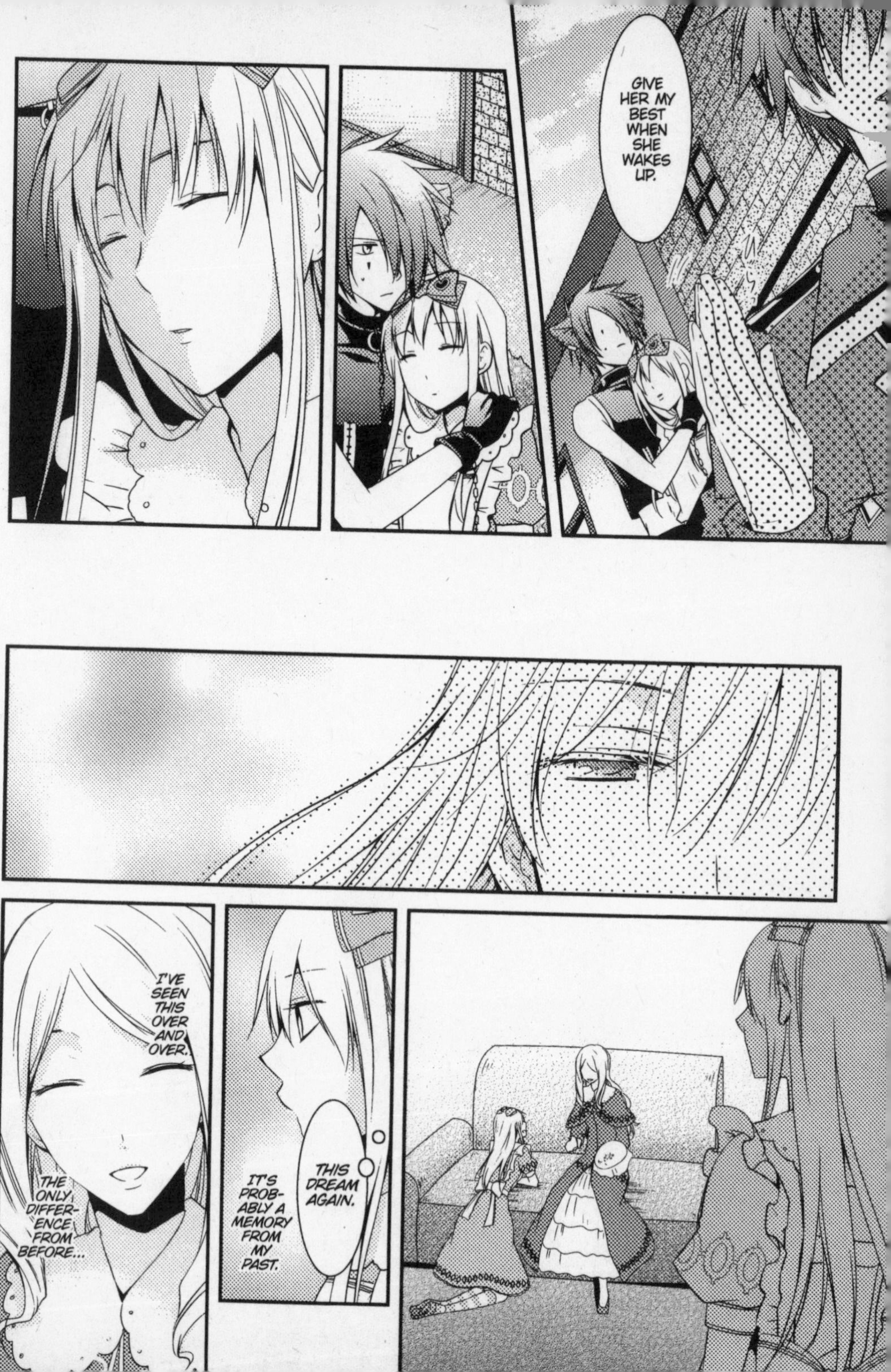
GIVE HER MY BEST WHEN SHE WAKES UP.
THIS DREAM AGAIN.
IT'S PROBABLY A MEMORY FROM MY PAST.
I'VE SEEN THIS OVER AND OVER.
THE ONLY DIFFERENCE FROM BEFORE...

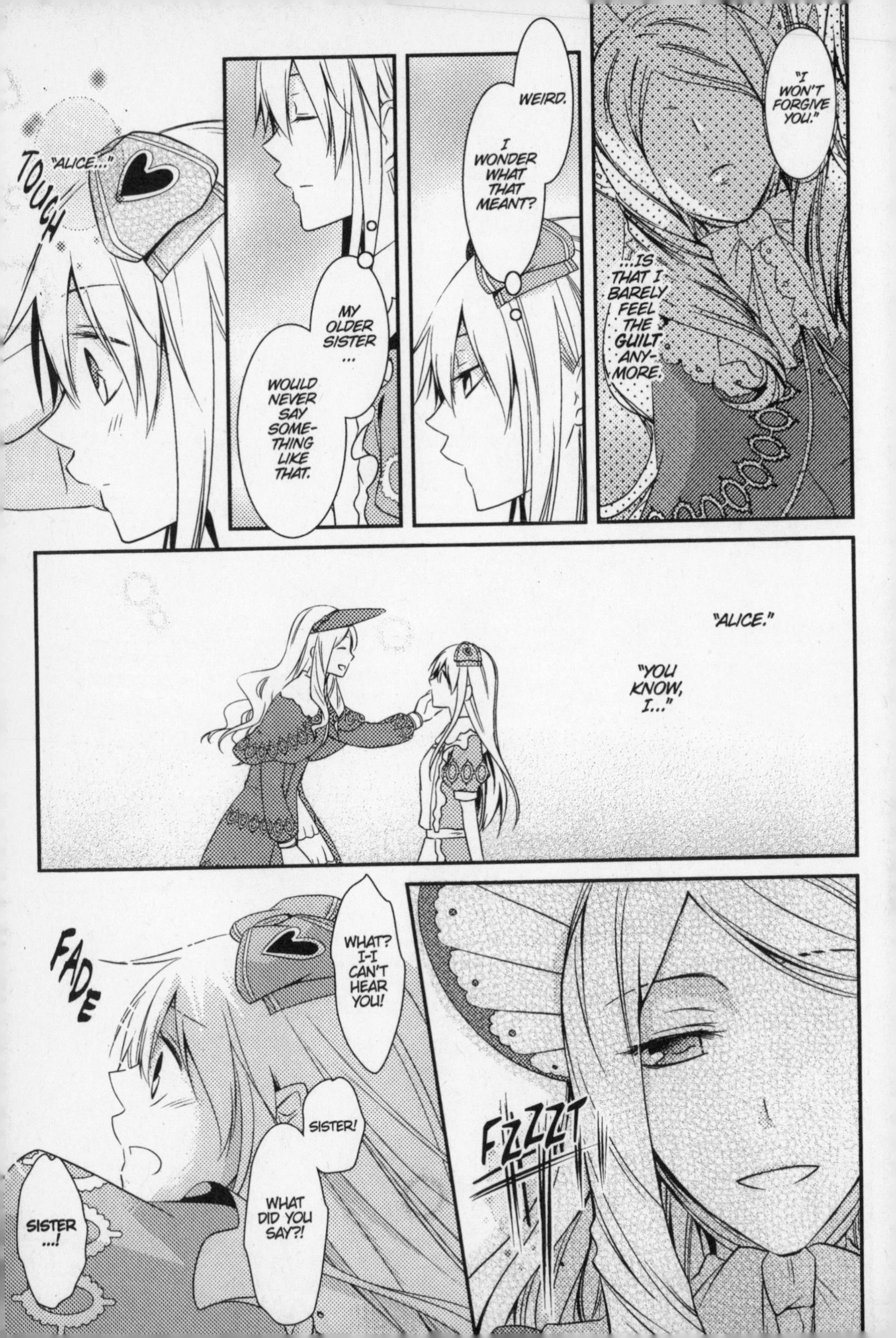
"I WON'T FORGIVE YOU."
...IS THAT I BARELY FEEL THE GUILT ANYMORE.
WEIRD.
I WONDER WHAT THAT MEANT?
MY OLDER SISTER ...
WOULD NEVER SAY SOMETHING LIKE THAT.
TOUCH
"ALICE..."
"ALICE."
"YOU KNOW, I..."
FZZZT
WHAT? I-I CAN'T HEAR YOU!
FADE
SISTER!
WHAT DID YOU SAY?!
SISTER ...!

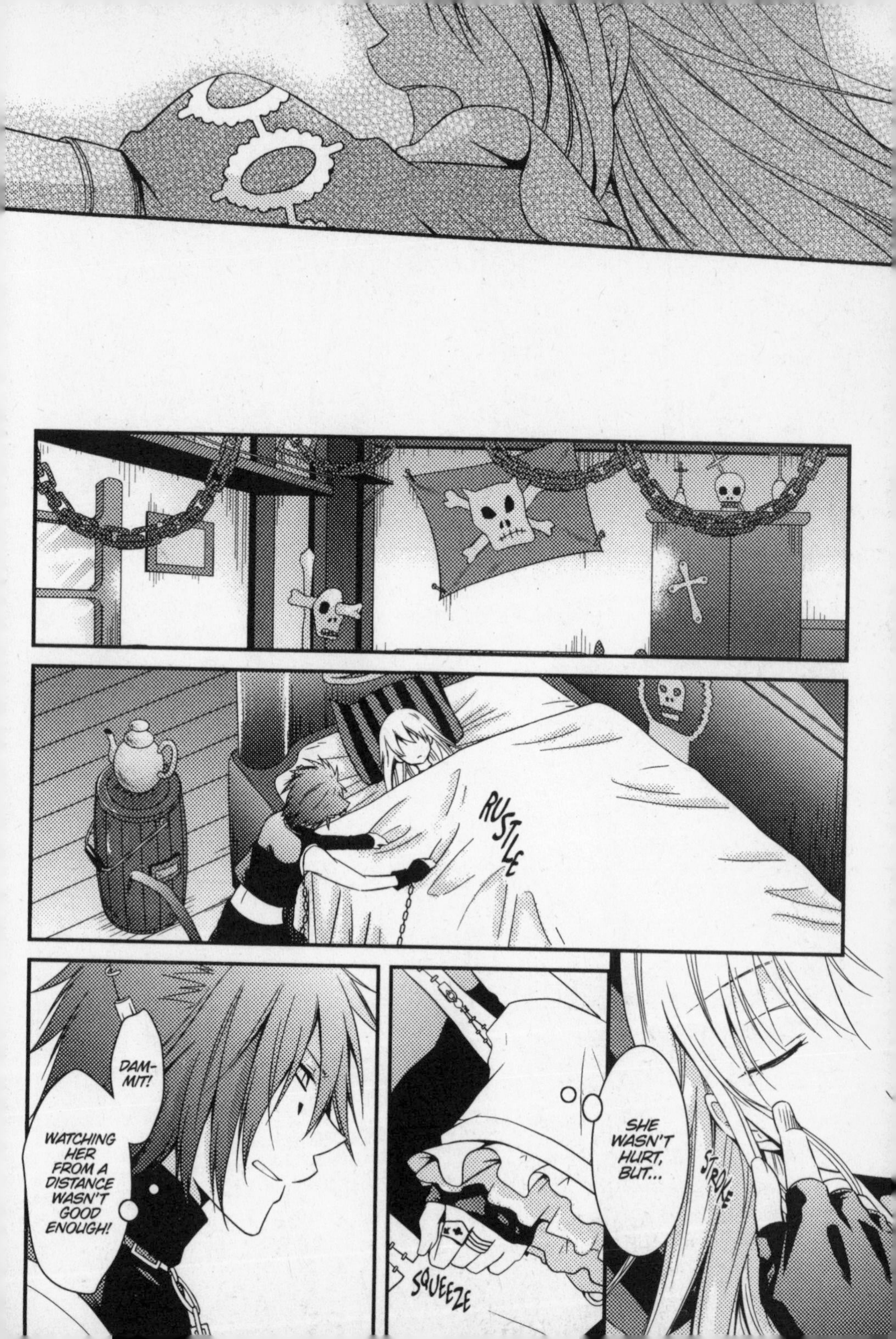
RUSTLE
STROKE
SHE WASN'T HURT, BUT...
SQUEEZE
DAM-MIT!
WATCHING HER FROM A DISTANCE WASN'T GOOD ENOUGH!

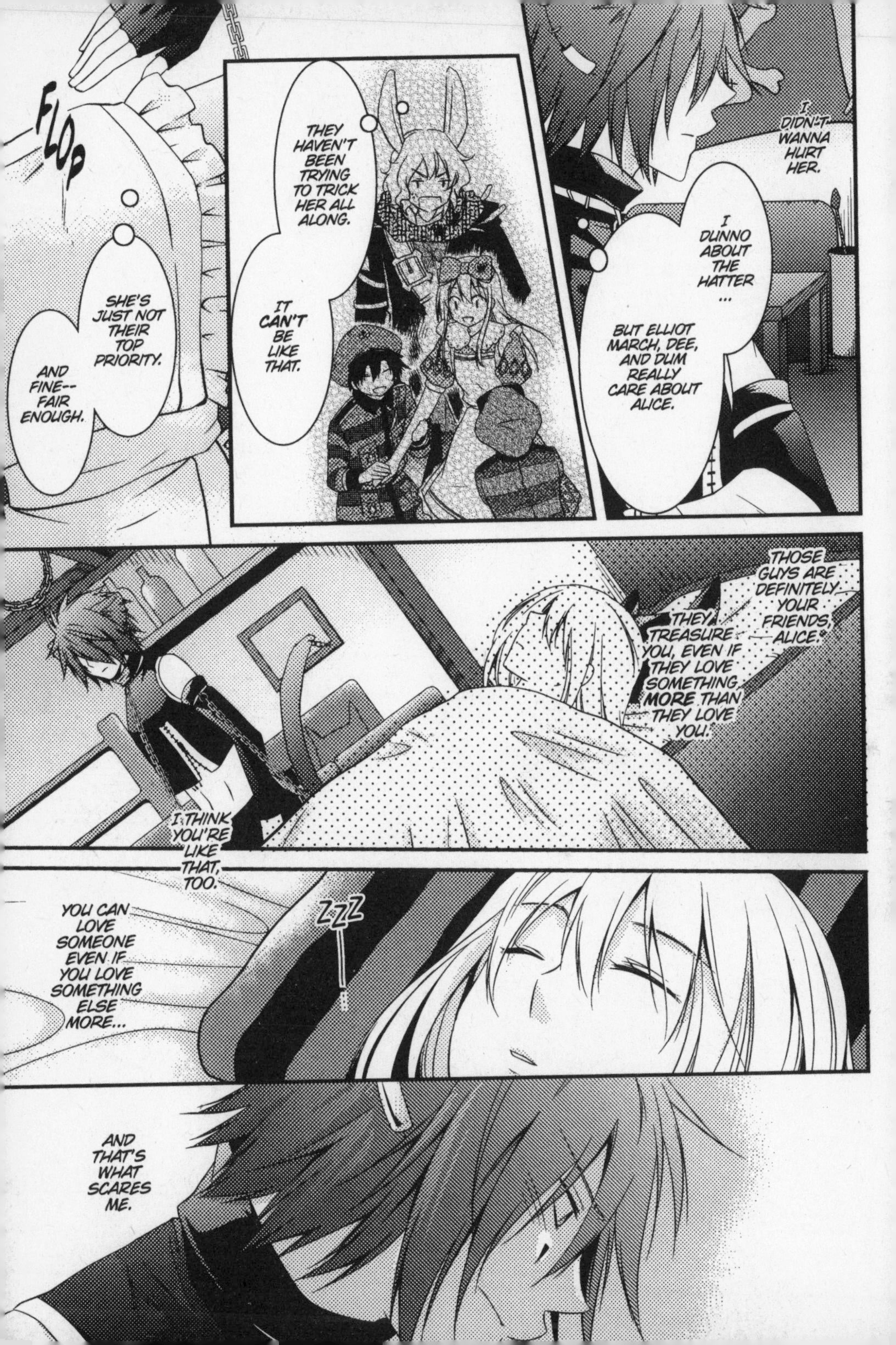
I DIDN'T WANNA HURT HER.
I DUNNO ABOUT THE HATTER...
BUT ELLIOT MARCH, DEE, AND DUM REALLY CARE ABOUT ALICE.
THEY HAVEN'T BEEN TRYING TO TRICK HER ALL ALONG.
IT CAN'T BE LIKE THAT.
FLOP
SHE'S JUST NOT THEIR TOP PRIORITY.
AND FINE-- FAIR ENOUGH.
THOSE GUYS ARE DEFINITELY YOUR FRIENDS, ALICE.
THEY TREASURE YOU, EVEN IF THEY LOVE SOMETHING MORE THAN THEY LOVE YOU.
I THINK YOU'RE LIKE THAT, TOO.
ZZZ
YOU CAN LOVE SOMEONE EVEN IF YOU LOVE SOMETHING ELSE MORE...
AND THAT'S WHAT SCARES ME.

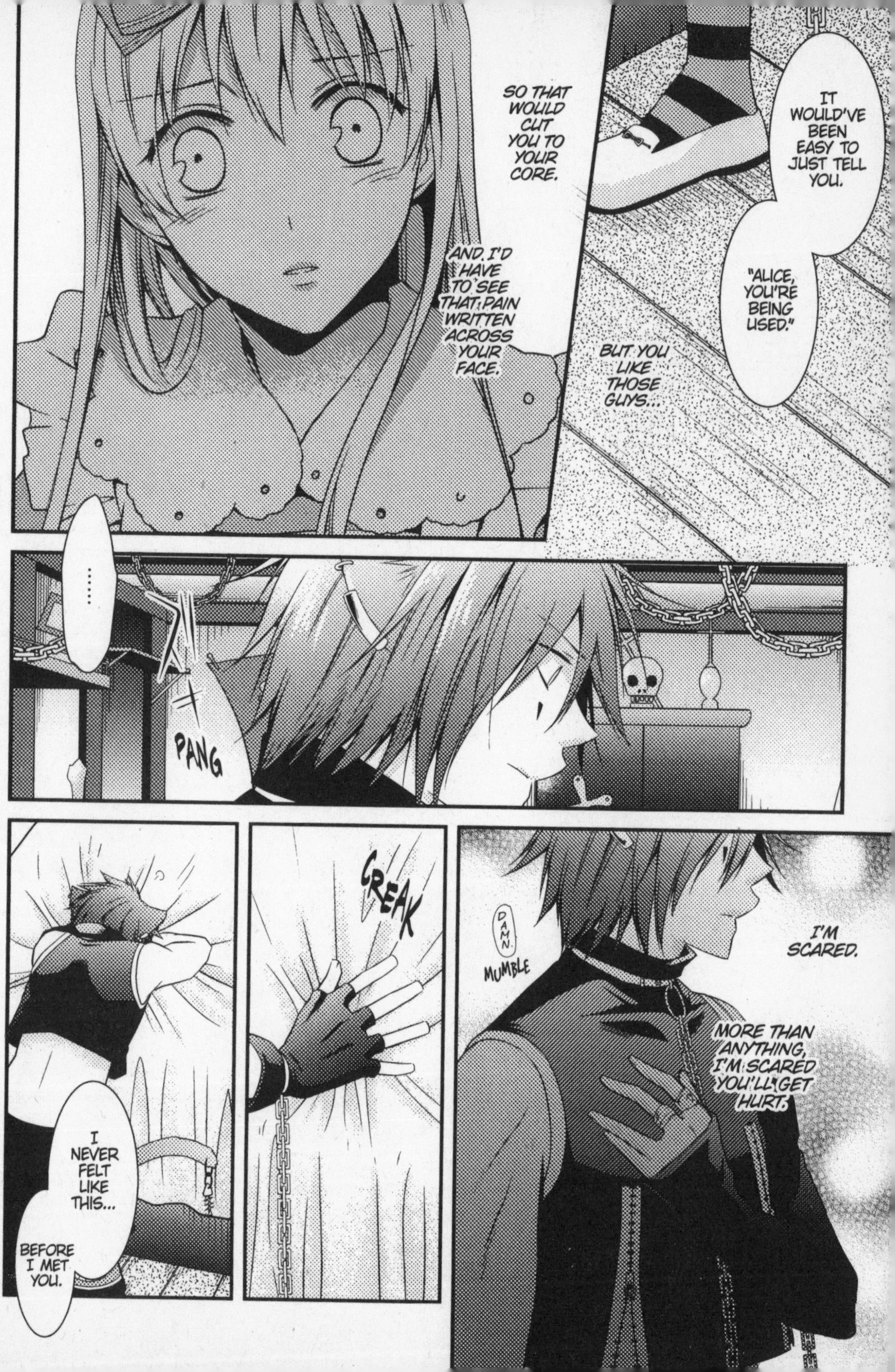
IT WOULD'VE BEEN EASY TO JUST TELL YOU.
"ALICE, YOU'RE BEING USED."
BUT YOU LIKE THOSE GUYS...
SO THAT WOULD CUT YOU TO YOUR CORE.
AND I'D HAVE TO SEE THAT PAIN WRITTEN ACROSS YOUR FACE.
......
PANG
I'M SCARED.
MORE THAN ANYTHING, I'M SCARED YOU'LL GET HURT.
DAMN.
MUMBLE
CREAK
I NEVER FELT LIKE THIS...
BEFORE I MET YOU.

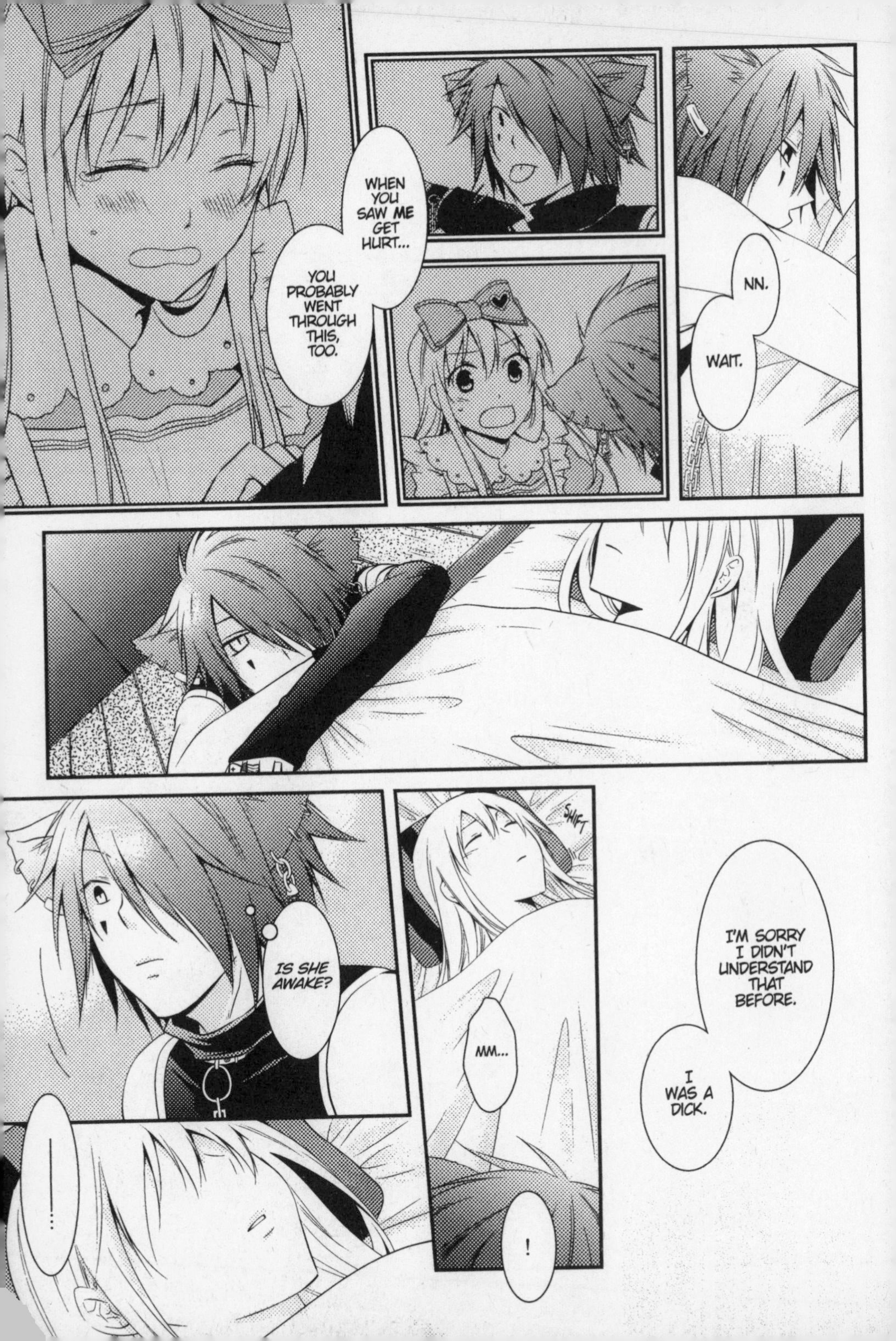
NN.
WAIT.
WHEN YOU SAW ME GET HURT...
YOU PROBABLY WENT THROUGH THIS, TOO.
I'M SORRY I DIDN'T UNDERSTAND THAT BEFORE.
I WAS A DICK.
SHIFT
MM...
!
IS SHE AWAKE?
......

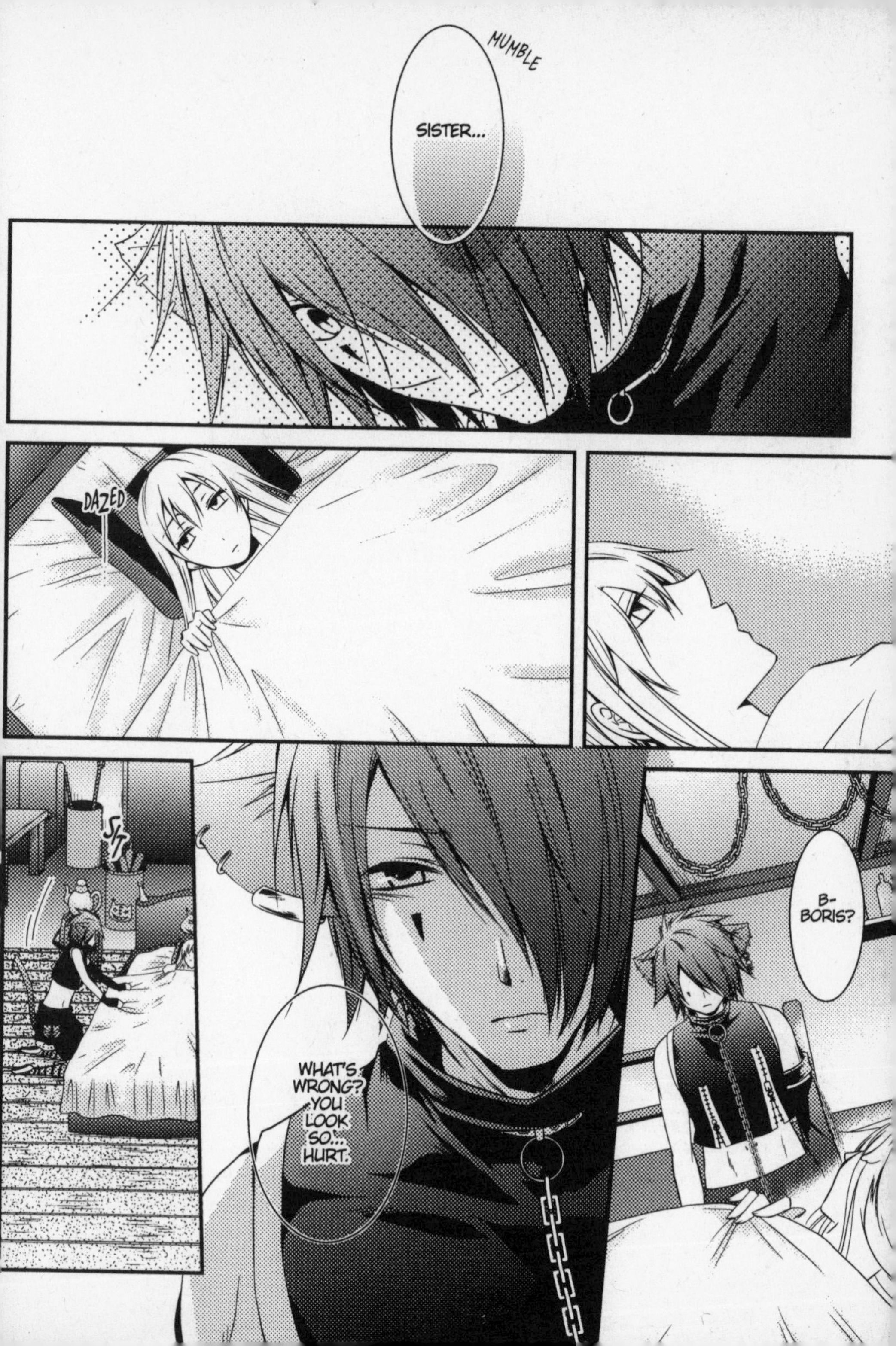
MUMBLE
SISTER...
DAZED
B-BORIS?
WHAT'S WRONG? YOU LOOK SO... HURT.
SIT

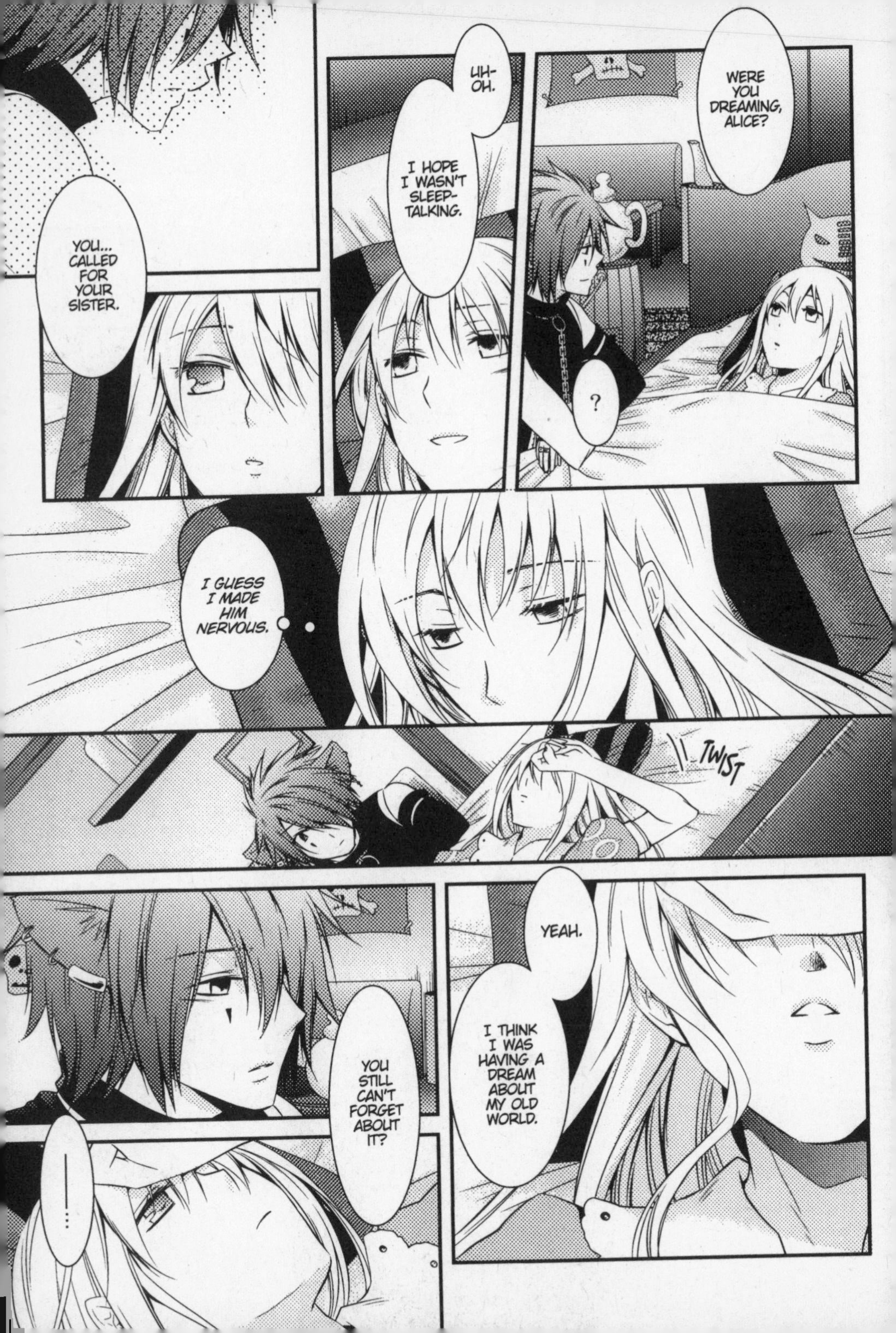
WERE YOU DREAMING, ALICE?
?
UH-OH.
I HOPE I WASN'T SLEEP-TALKING.
YOU... CALLED FOR YOUR SISTER.
I GUESS I MADE HIM NERVOUS.
TWIST
YEAH.
I THINK I WAS HAVING A DREAM ABOUT MY OLD WORLD.
YOU STILL CAN'T FORGET ABOUT IT?
……

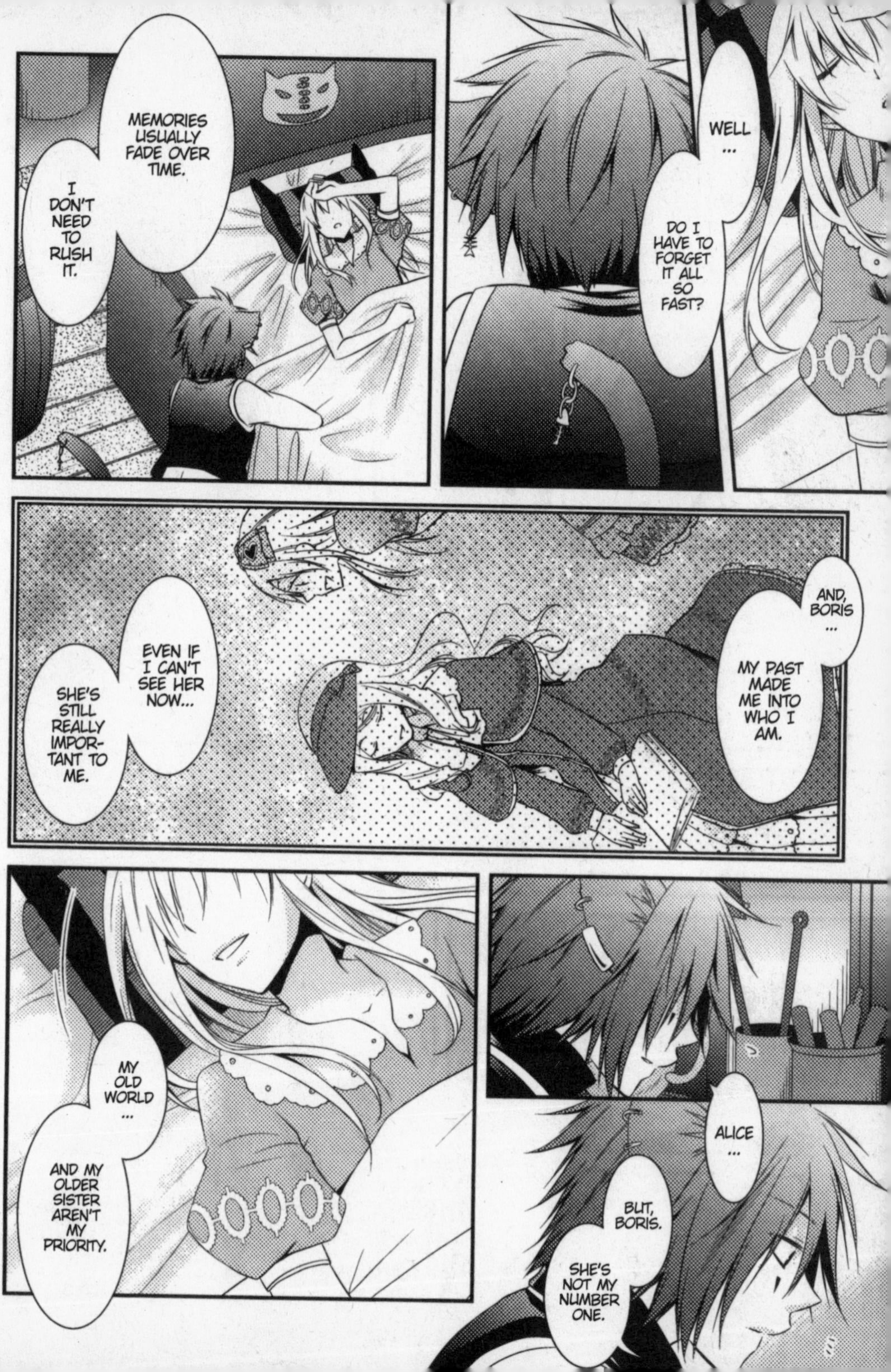
WELL ...
DO I HAVE TO FORGET IT ALL SO FAST?
MEMORIES USUALLY FADE OVER TIME.
I DON'T NEED TO RUSH IT.
AND, BORIS ...
MY PAST MADE ME INTO WHO I AM.
EVEN IF I CAN'T SEE HER NOW...
SHE'S STILL REALLY IMPOR-TANT TO ME.
ALICE ...
BUT, BORIS.
SHE'S NOT MY NUMBER ONE.
MY OLD WORLD ...
AND MY OLDER SISTER AREN'T MY PRIORITY.

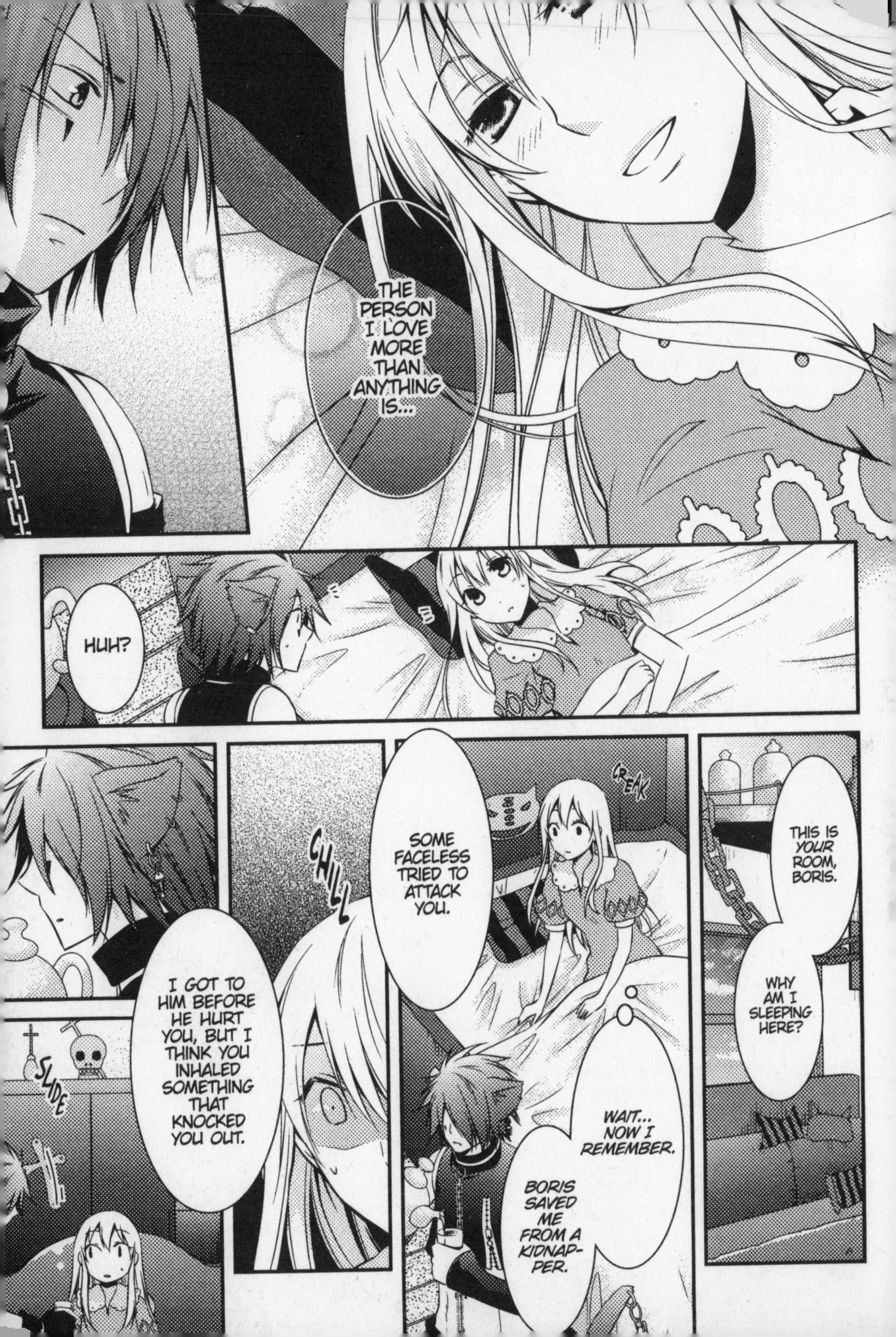
THE PERSON I LOVE MORE THAN ANYTHING IS...
HUH?
THIS IS YOUR ROOM, BORIS.
WHY AM I SLEEPING HERE?
CREAK
WAIT... NOW I REMEMBER.
BORIS SAVED ME FROM A KIDNAP-PER.
SOME FACELESS TRIED TO ATTACK YOU.
CHILL
I GOT TO HIM BEFORE HE HURT YOU, BUT I THINK YOU INHALED SOMETHING THAT KNOCKED YOU OUT.
SLIDE

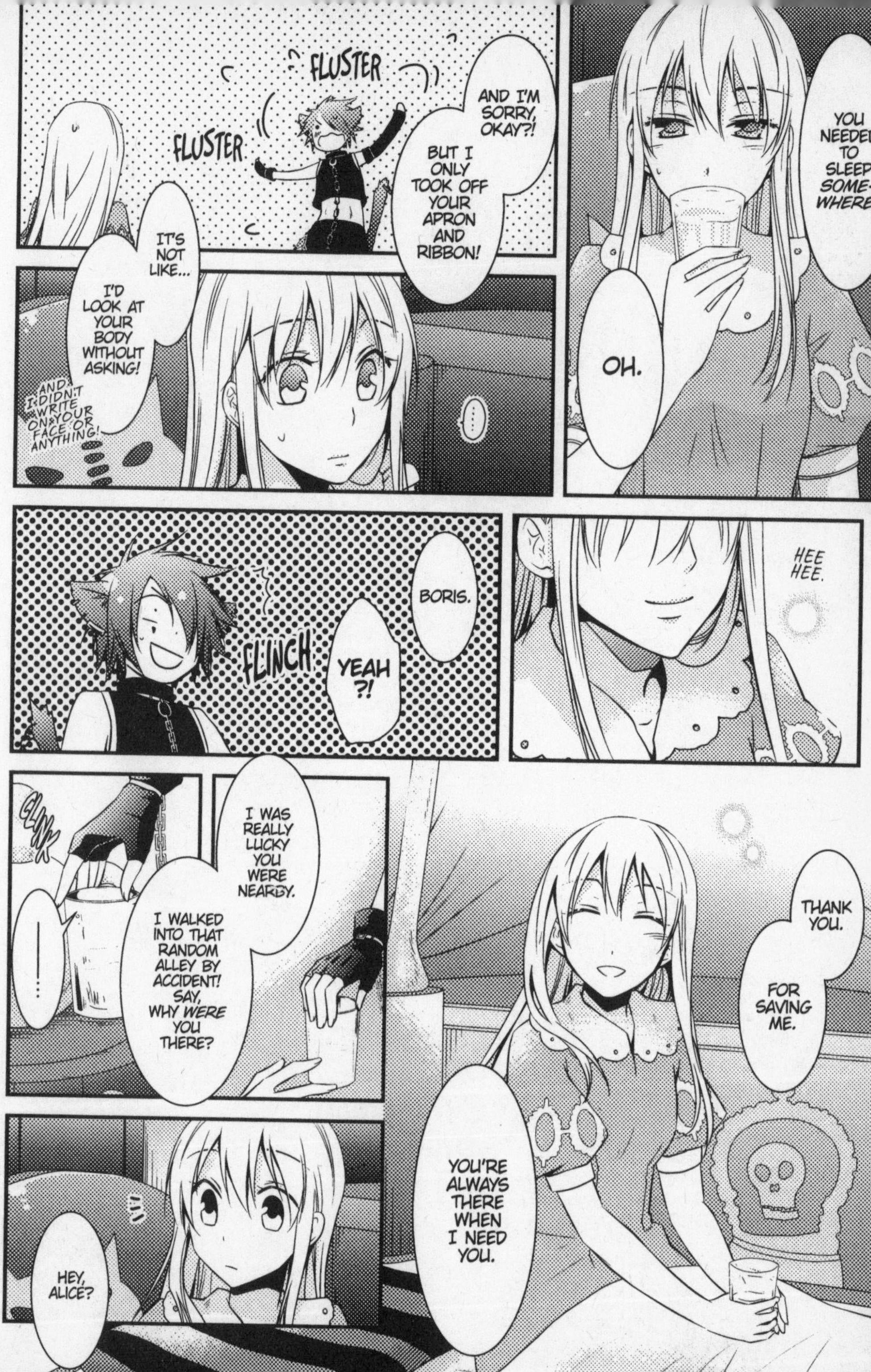
YOU NEEDED TO SLEEP SOMEWHERE.
OH.
FLUSTER
FLUSTER
AND I'M SORRY, OKAY?!
BUT I ONLY TOOK OFF YOUR APRON AND RIBBON!
IT'S NOT LIKE...
I'D LOOK AT YOUR BODY WITHOUT ASKING!
AND I DIDN'T WRITE ON YOUR FACE OR ANYTHING!
...
HEE HEE.
BORIS.
FLINCH
YEAH?!
THANK YOU.
FOR SAVING ME.
YOU'RE ALWAYS THERE WHEN I NEED YOU.
I WAS REALLY LUCKY YOU WERE NEARBY.
I WALKED INTO THAT RANDOM ALLEY BY ACCIDENT! SAY, WHY WERE YOU THERE?
CLINK
...!
HEY, ALICE?

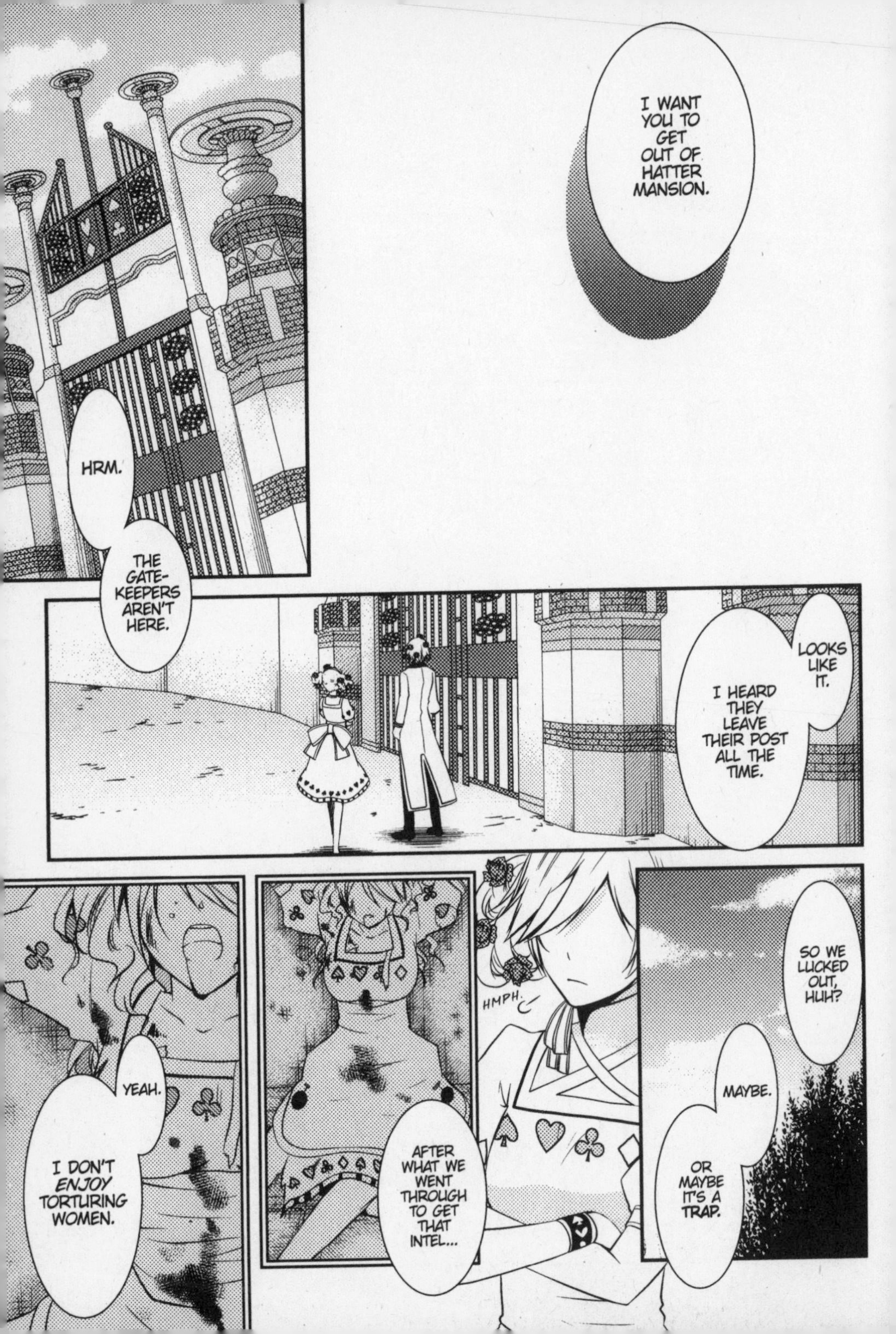
I WANT YOU TO GET OUT OF HATTER MANSION.
HRM.
THE GATE-KEEPERS AREN'T HERE.
LOOKS LIKE IT.
I HEARD THEY LEAVE THEIR POST ALL THE TIME.
SO WE LUCKED OUT, HUH?
MAYBE.
OR MAYBE IT'S A TRAP.
HMPH.
AFTER WHAT WE WENT THROUGH TO GET THAT INTEL...
YEAH.
I DON'T *ENJOY* TORTURING WOMEN.

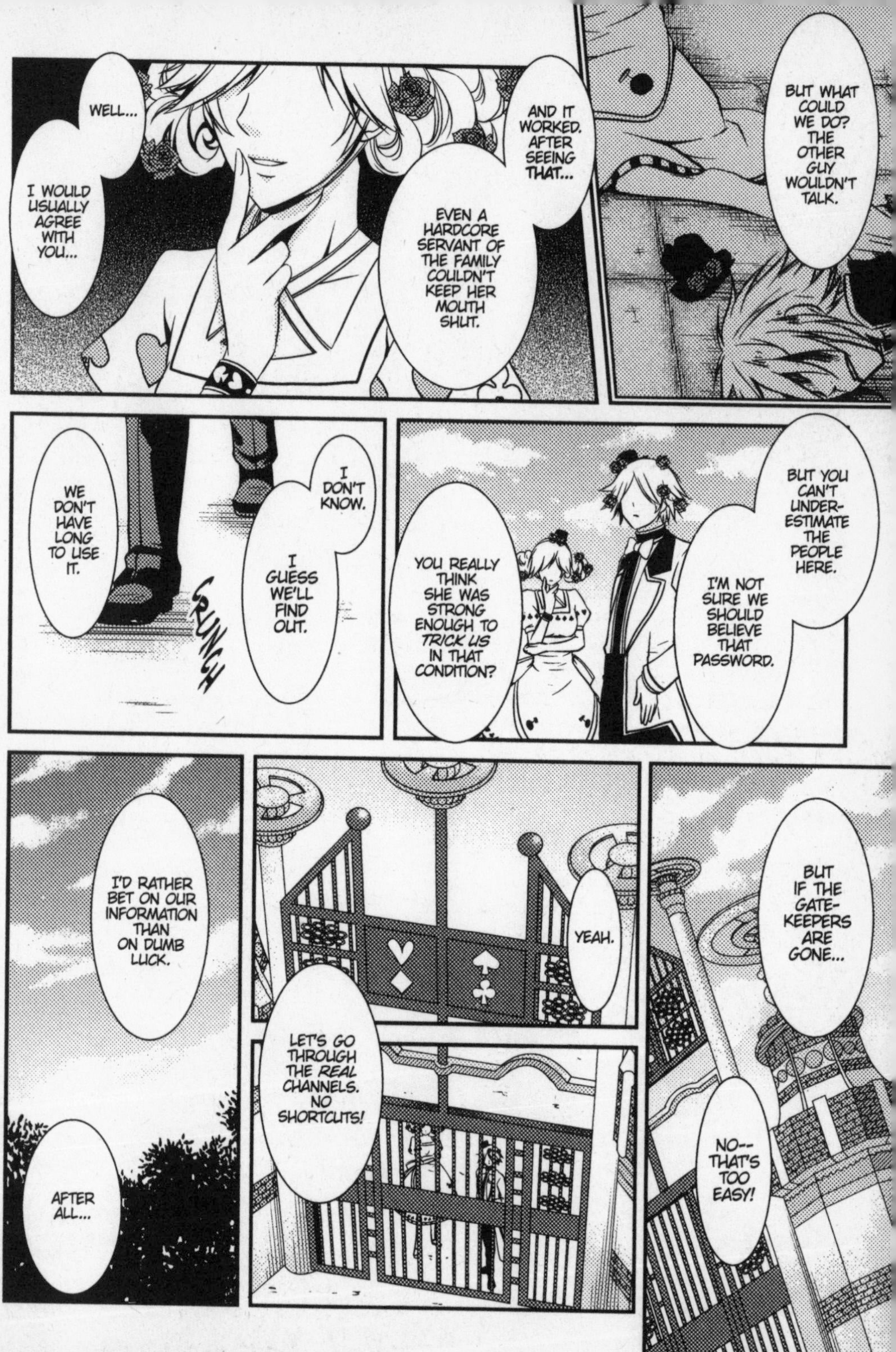
BUT WHAT COULD WE DO? THE OTHER GUY WOULDN'T TALK.
AND IT WORKED. AFTER SEEING THAT...
EVEN A HARDCORE SERVANT OF THE FAMILY COULDN'T KEEP HER MOUTH SHUT.
WELL...
I WOULD USUALLY AGREE WITH YOU...
BUT YOU CAN'T UNDER-ESTIMATE THE PEOPLE HERE.
I'M NOT SURE WE SHOULD BELIEVE THAT PASSWORD.
YOU REALLY THINK SHE WAS STRONG ENOUGH TO *TRICK US* IN THAT CONDITION?
I DON'T KNOW.
I GUESS WE'LL FIND OUT.
WE DON'T HAVE LONG TO USE IT.
CRUNCH
BUT IF THE GATE-KEEPERS ARE GONE...
NO--THAT'S TOO EASY!
YEAH.
LET'S GO THROUGH THE *REAL* CHANNELS. NO SHORTCUTS!
I'D RATHER BET ON OUR INFORMATION THAN ON DUMB LUCK.
AFTER ALL...

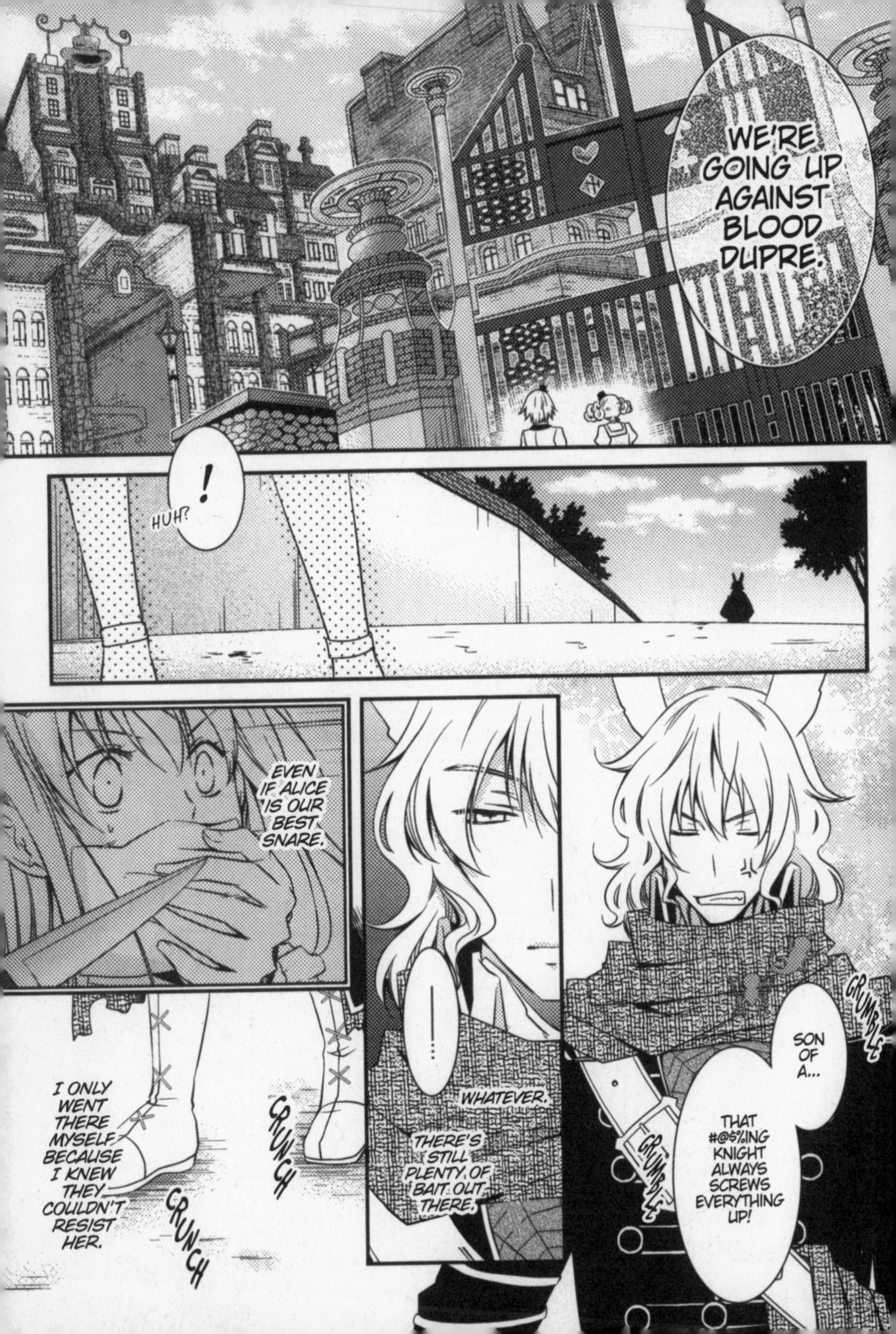
WE'RE GOING UP AGAINST BLOOD DUPRE.
!
HUH?
GRUMBLE
SON OF A...
THAT #@$%ING KNIGHT ALWAYS SCREWS EVERYTHING UP!
GRUMBLE
......
WHATEVER.
THERE'S STILL PLENTY OF BAIT OUT THERE.
EVEN IF ALICE IS OUR BEST SNARE.
I ONLY WENT THERE MYSELF BECAUSE I KNEW THEY COULDN'T RESIST HER.
CRUNCH
CRUNCH

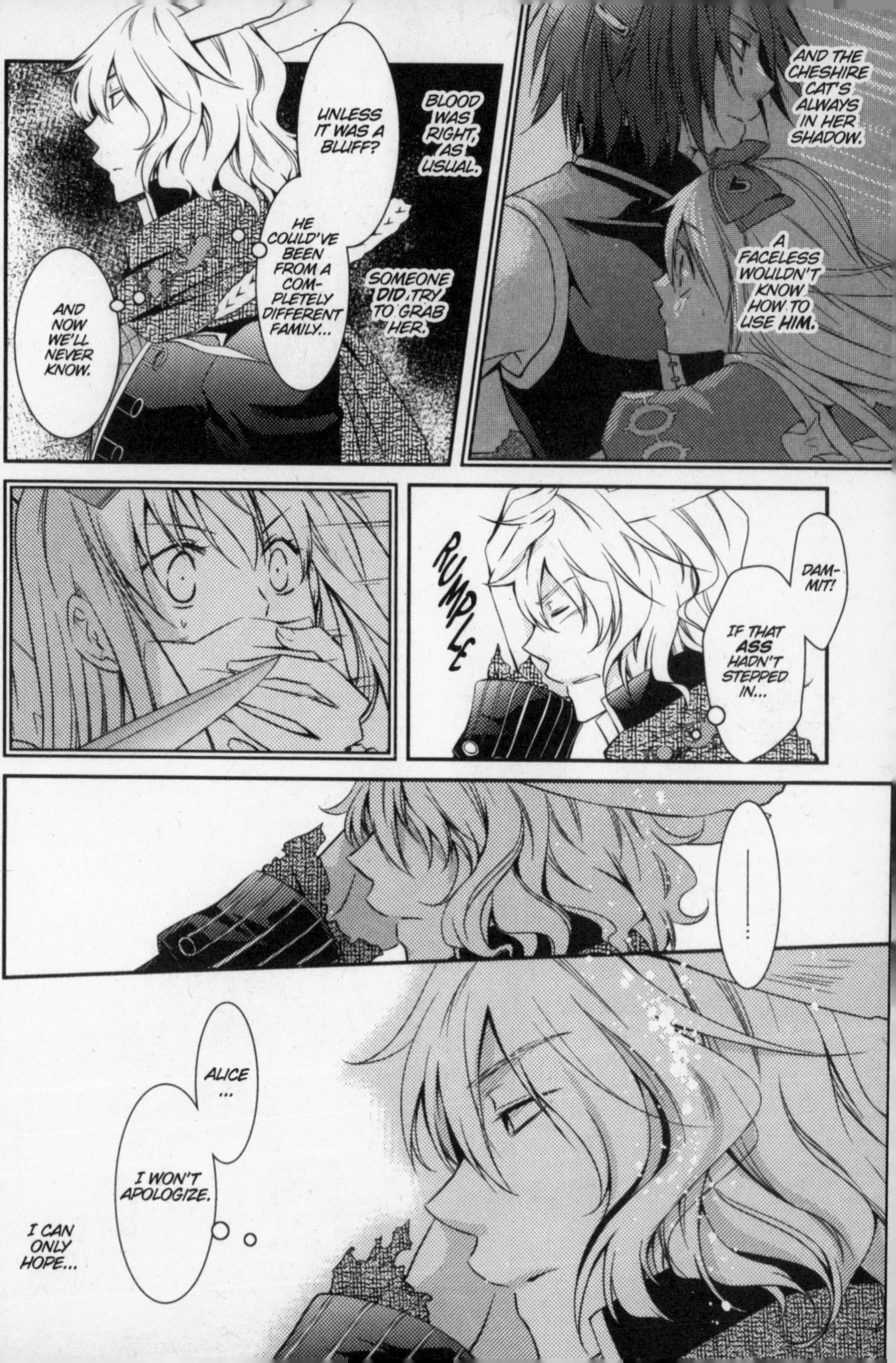
AND THE CHESHIRE CAT'S ALWAYS IN HER SHADOW.
A FACELESS WOULDN'T KNOW HOW TO USE HIM.
BLOOD WAS RIGHT, AS USUAL.
SOMEONE DID TRY TO GRAB HER.
UNLESS IT WAS A BLUFF?
HE COULD'VE BEEN FROM A COM-PLETELY DIFFERENT FAMILY...
AND NOW WE'LL NEVER KNOW.
RUMPLE
DAM-MIT!
IF THAT ASS HADN'T STEPPED IN...
......
ALICE...
I WON'T APOLOGIZE.
I CAN ONLY HOPE...

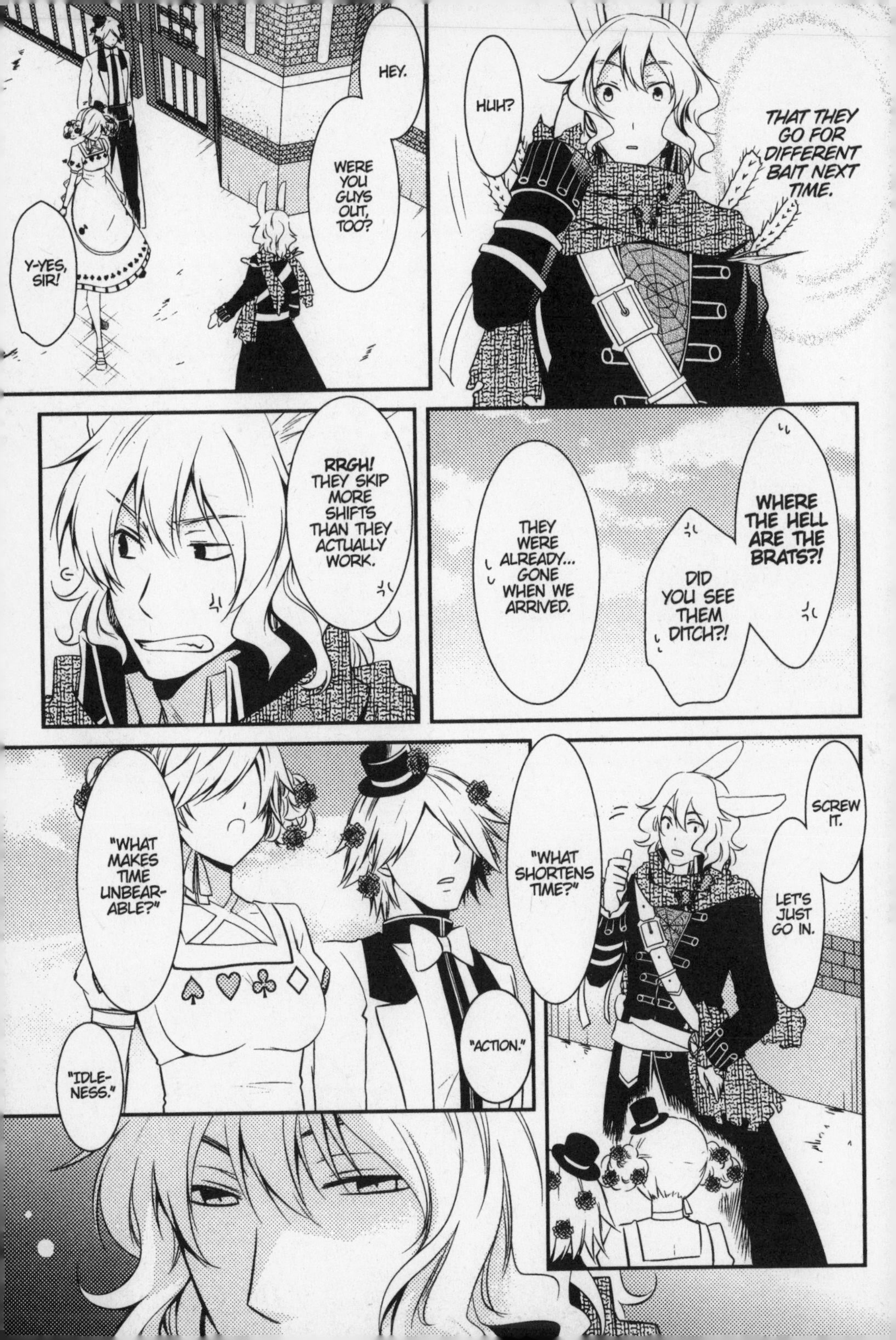
THAT THEY GO FOR DIFFERENT BAIT NEXT TIME.
HUH?
HEY.
WERE YOU GUYS OUT, TOO?
Y-YES, SIR!
WHERE THE HELL ARE THE BRATS?!
DID YOU SEE THEM DITCH?!
THEY WERE ALREADY... GONE WHEN WE ARRIVED.
RRGH! THEY SKIP MORE SHIFTS THAN THEY ACTUALLY WORK.
SCREW IT.
LET'S JUST GO IN.
"WHAT SHORTENS TIME?"
"WHAT MAKES TIME UNBEARABLE?"
"ACTION."
"IDLENESS."

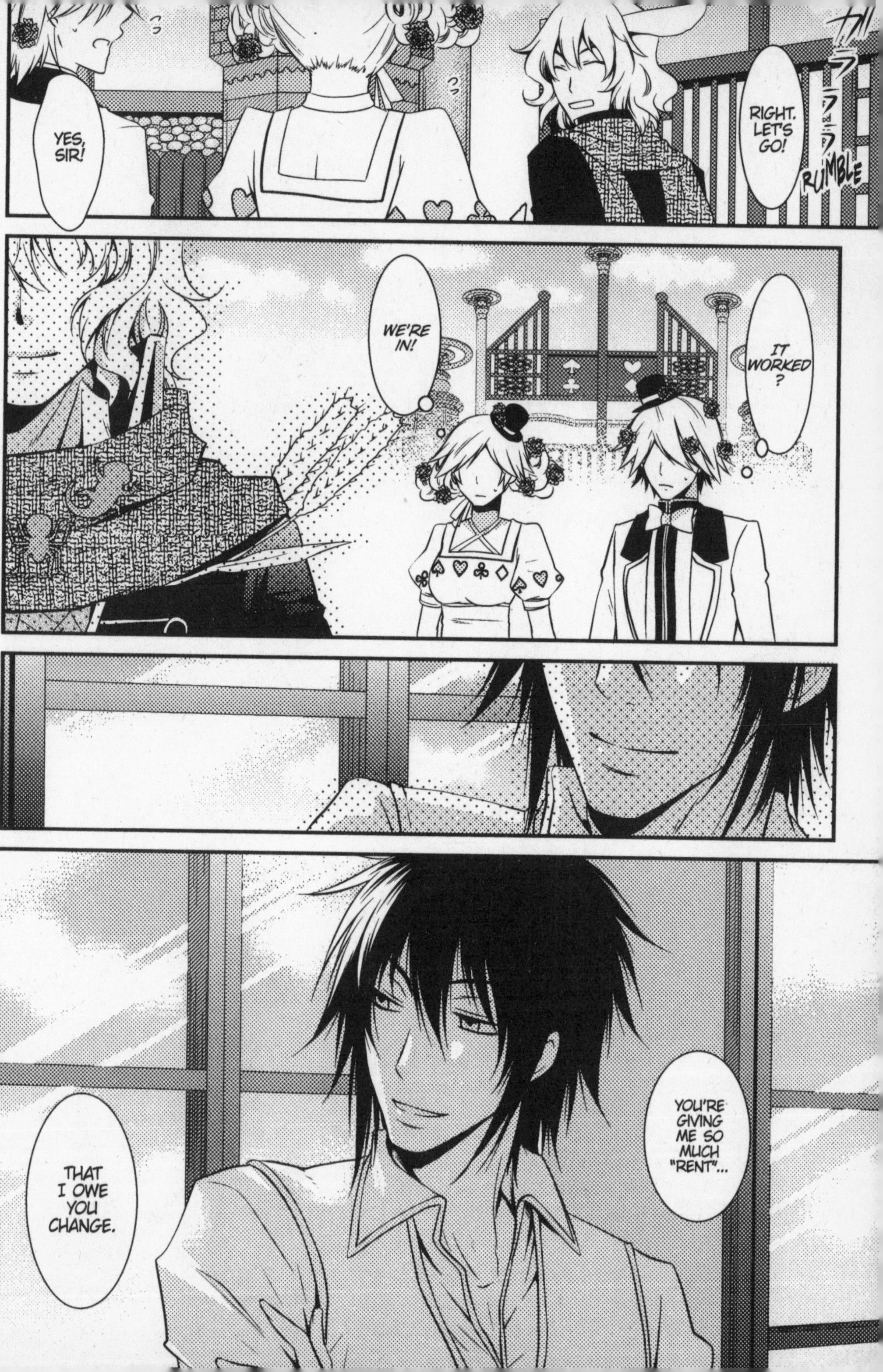
RIGHT. LET'S GO!
RUMBLE
YES, SIR!
IT WORKED?
WE'RE IN!
YOU'RE GIVING ME SO MUCH "RENT"...
THAT I OWE YOU CHANGE.

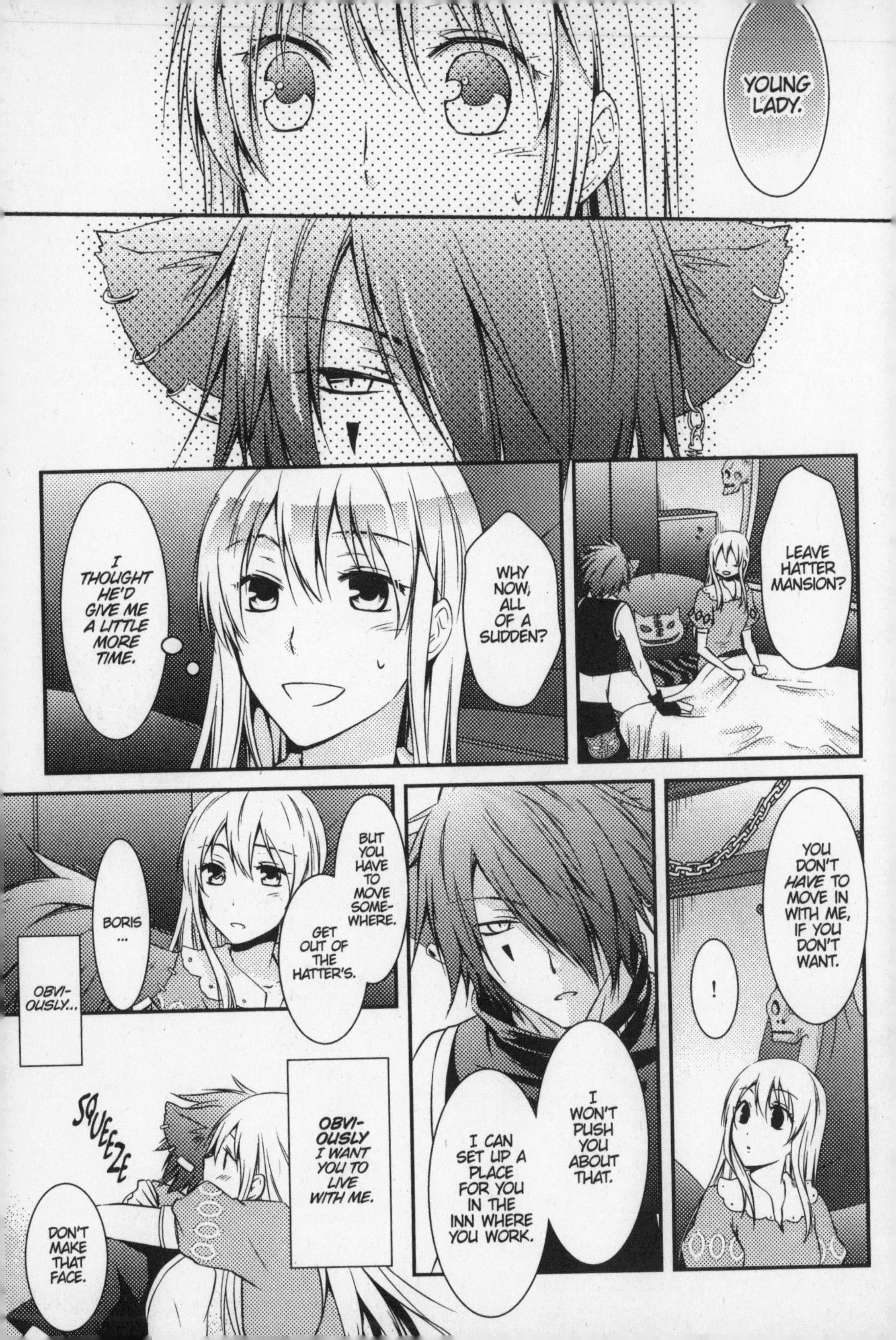
YOUNG LADY.
LEAVE HATTER MANSION?
WHY NOW, ALL OF A SUDDEN?
I THOUGHT HE'D GIVE ME A LITTLE MORE TIME.
YOU DON'T *HAVE* TO MOVE IN WITH ME, IF YOU DON'T WANT.
!
I WON'T PUSH YOU ABOUT THAT.
I CAN SET UP A PLACE FOR YOU IN THE INN WHERE YOU WORK.
BUT YOU HAVE TO MOVE SOMEWHERE.
GET OUT OF THE HATTER'S.
BORIS ...
OBVIOUSLY...
OBVIOUSLY I WANT YOU TO LIVE WITH ME.
SQUEEZE
DON'T MAKE THAT FACE.

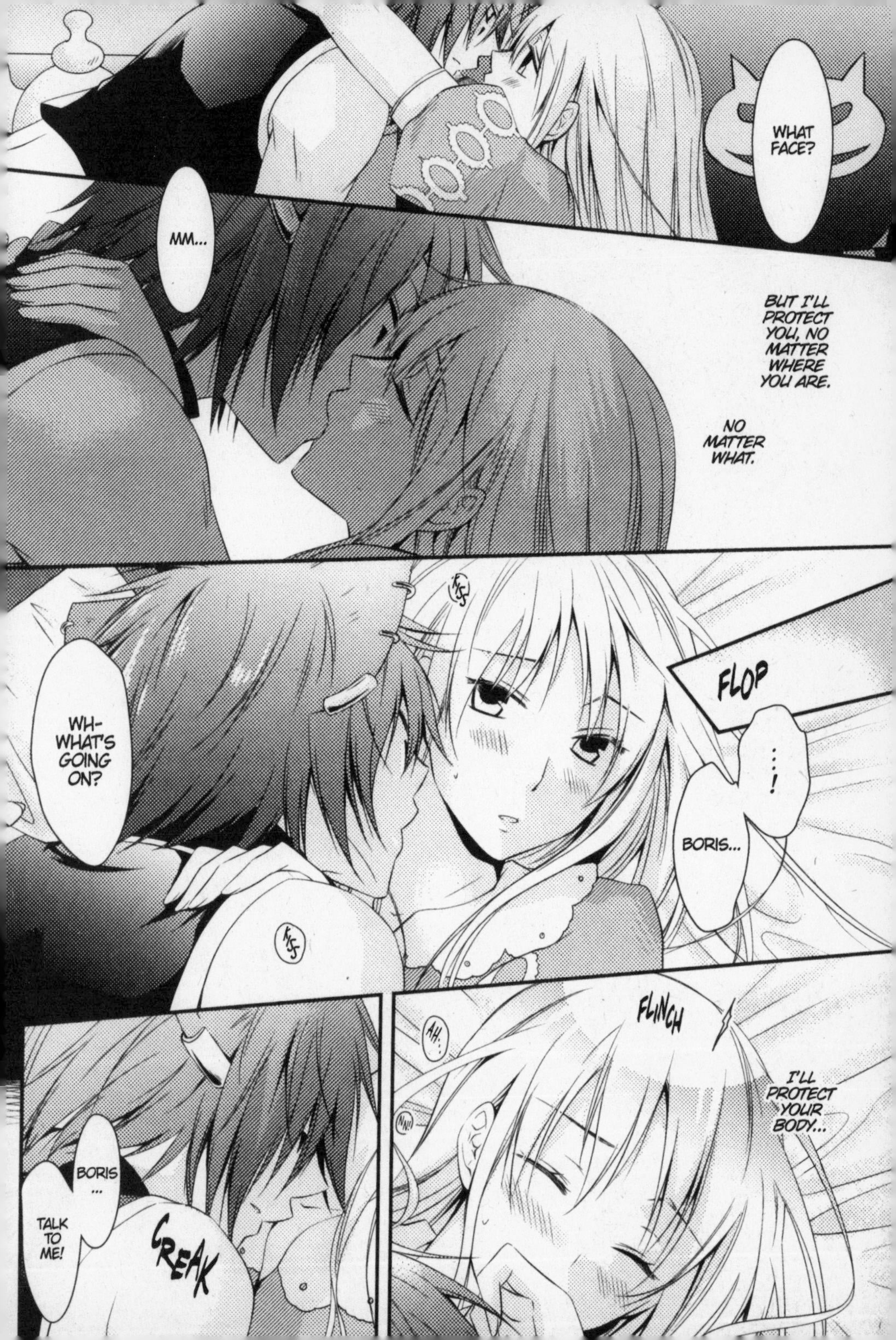
WHAT FACE?
BUT I'LL PROTECT YOU, NO MATTER WHERE YOU ARE.
NO MATTER WHAT.
MM...
FLOP
...!
BORIS...
KISS
WH-WHAT'S GOING ON?
KISS
FLINCH
I'LL PROTECT YOUR BODY...
AH...
NN!
BORIS...
TALK TO ME!
CREAK

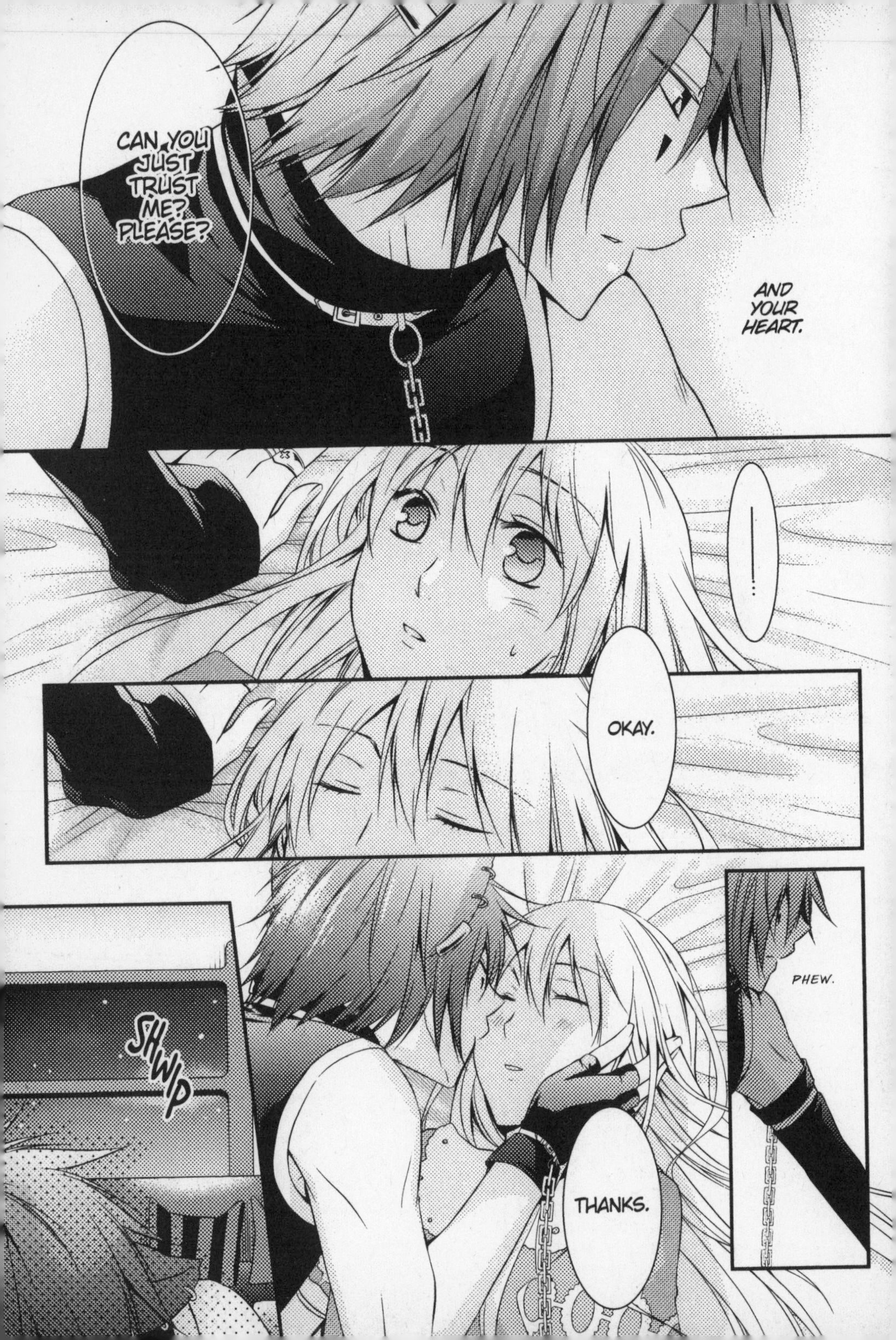
AND YOUR HEART.
CAN YOU JUST TRUST ME? PLEASE?
!
OKAY.
PHEW.
SHWIP
THANKS.

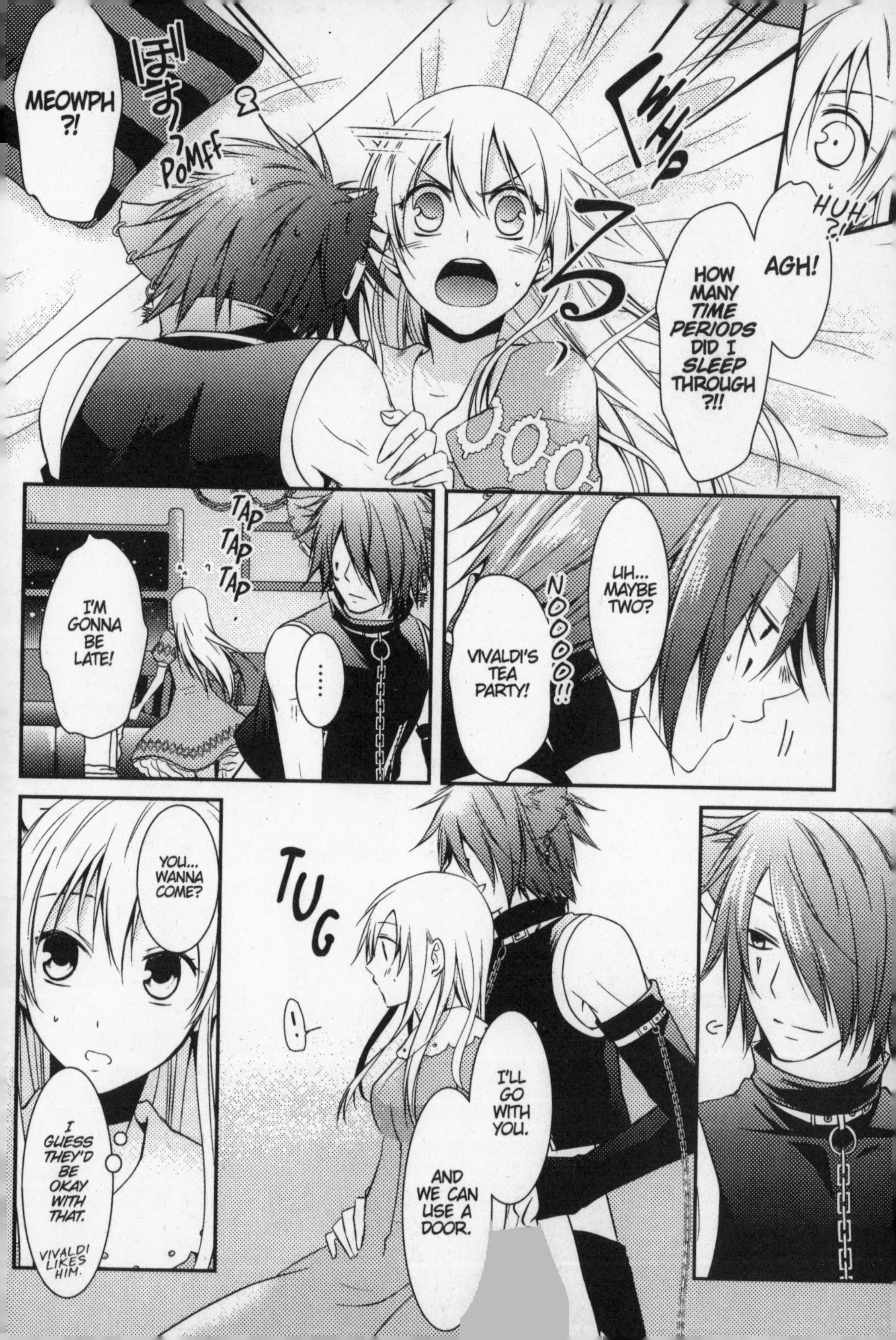
HUH ?!
AGH!
HOW MANY TIME PERIODS DID I SLEEP THROUGH ?!!
WHIP
ぽすっ
POMFF
MEOWPH ?!
UH... MAYBE TWO?
NOOOOOO!!
VIVALDI'S TEA PARTY!
TAP TAP TAP
I'M GONNA BE LATE!
......
TUG
!
I'LL GO WITH YOU.
AND WE CAN USE A DOOR.
YOU... WANNA COME?
I GUESS THEY'D BE OKAY WITH THAT.
VIVALDI LIKES HIM.

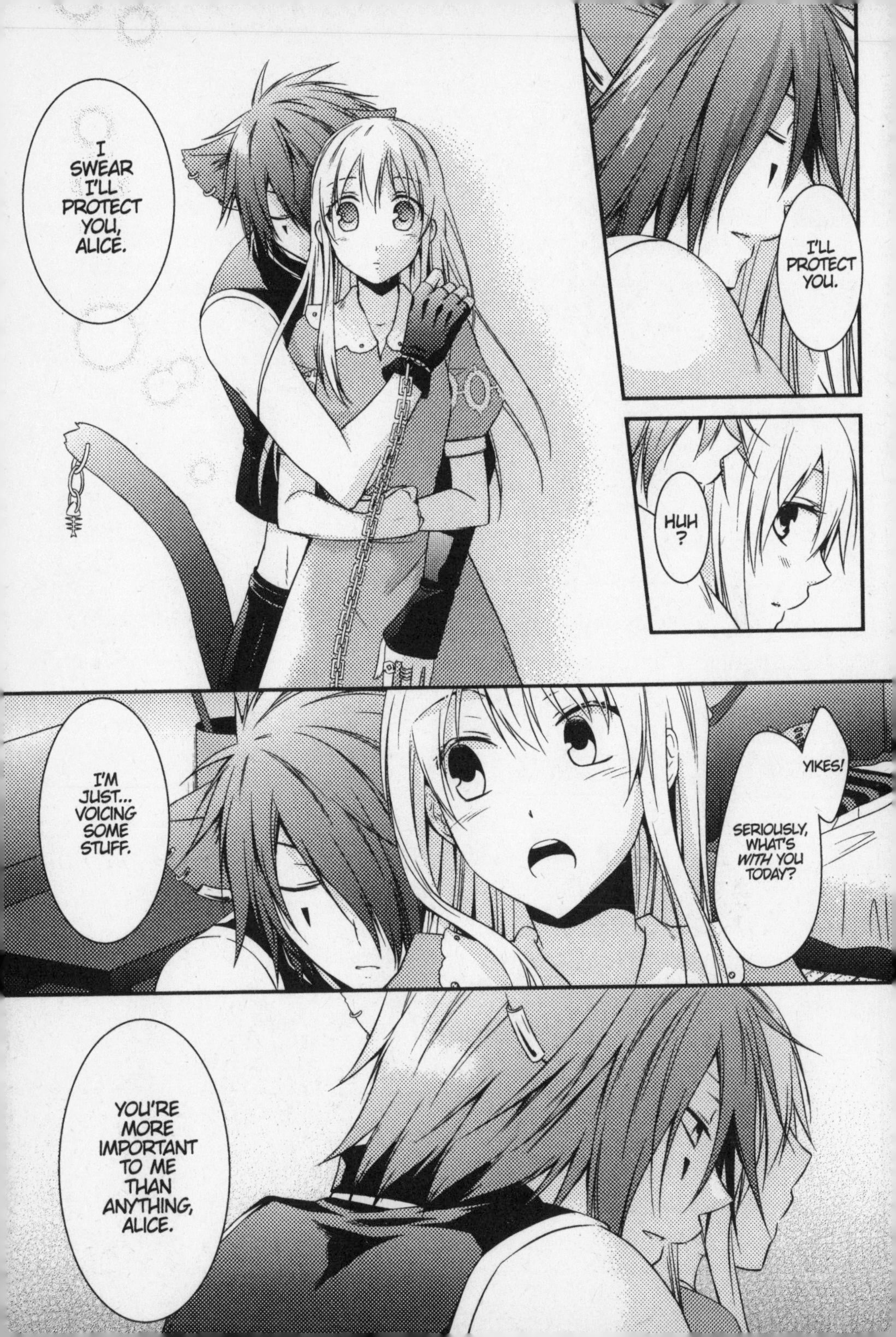
I'LL PROTECT YOU.
HUH?
I SWEAR I'LL PROTECT YOU, ALICE.
YIKES!
SERIOUSLY, WHAT'S *WITH* YOU TODAY?
I'M JUST... VOICING SOME STUFF.
YOU'RE MORE IMPORTANT TO ME THAN ANYTHING, ALICE.

MORE IMPOR-TANT...

THAN ANY-THING?

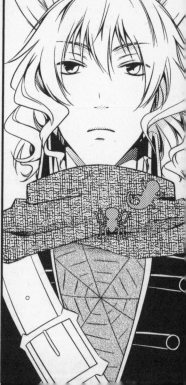

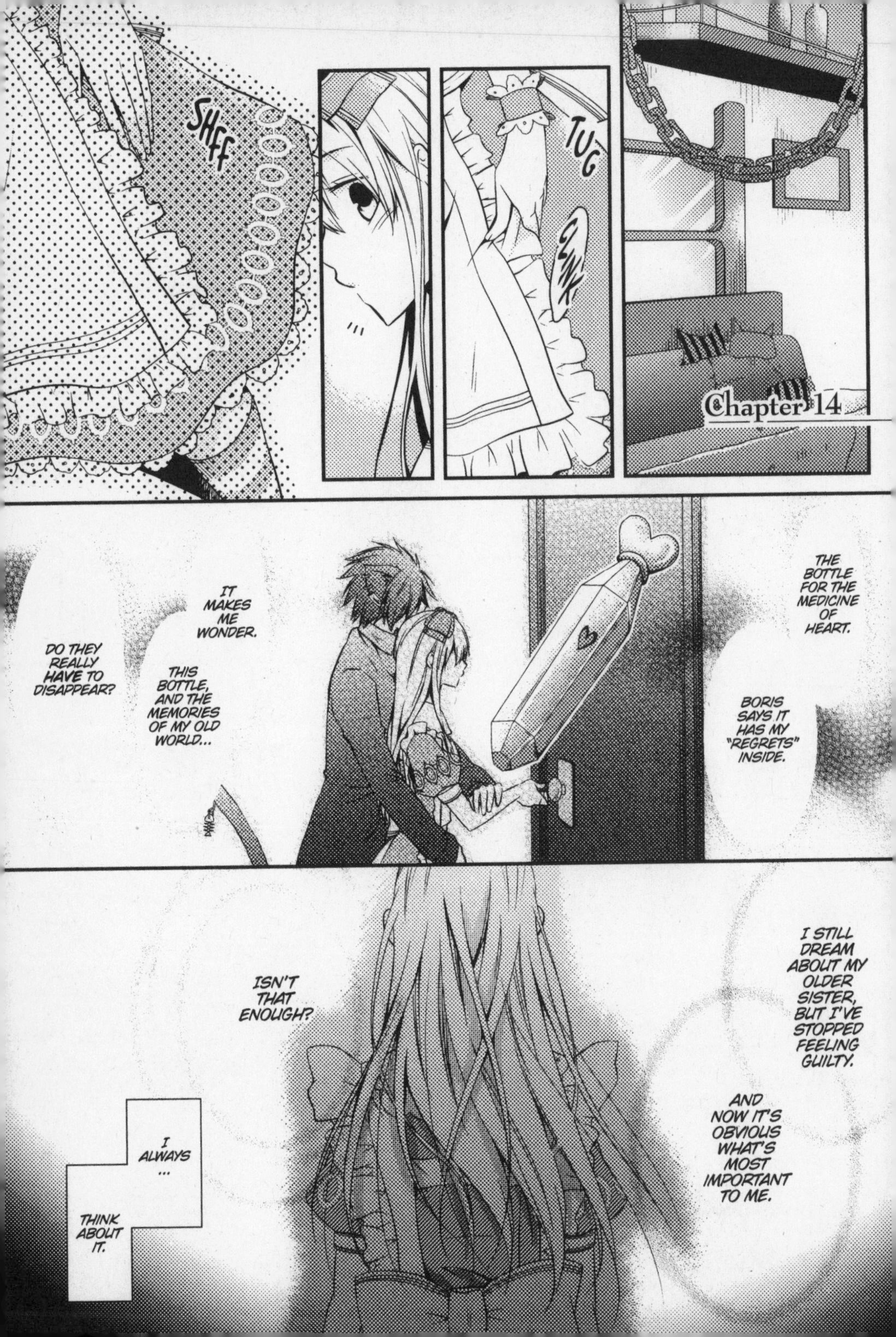
Chapter 14
TUG
CLINK
SHFF
THE BOTTLE FOR THE MEDICINE OF HEART.
BORIS SAYS IT HAS MY "REGRETS" INSIDE.
IT MAKES ME WONDER.
THIS BOTTLE, AND THE MEMORIES OF MY OLD WORLD...
DO THEY REALLY HAVE TO DISAPPEAR?
I STILL DREAM ABOUT MY OLDER SISTER, BUT I'VE STOPPED FEELING GUILTY.
AND NOW IT'S OBVIOUS WHAT'S MOST IMPORTANT TO ME.
ISN'T THAT ENOUGH?
I ALWAYS ...
THINK ABOUT IT.

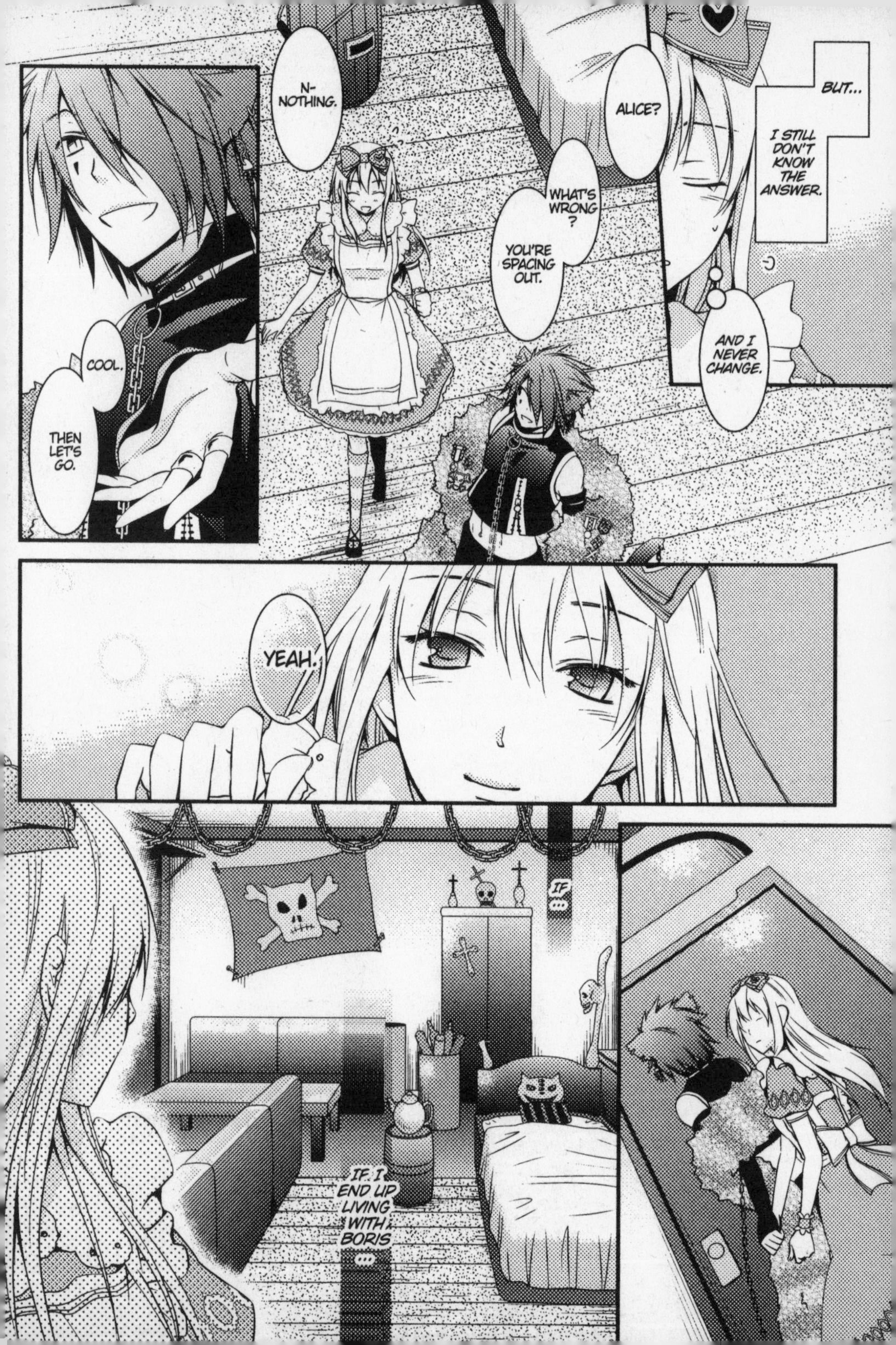
BUT...
I STILL DON'T KNOW THE ANSWER.
AND I NEVER CHANGE.
ALICE?
WHAT'S WRONG?
YOU'RE SPACING OUT.
N-NOTHING.
COOL.
THEN LET'S GO.
YEAH.
IF...
IF I END UP LIVING WITH BORIS...

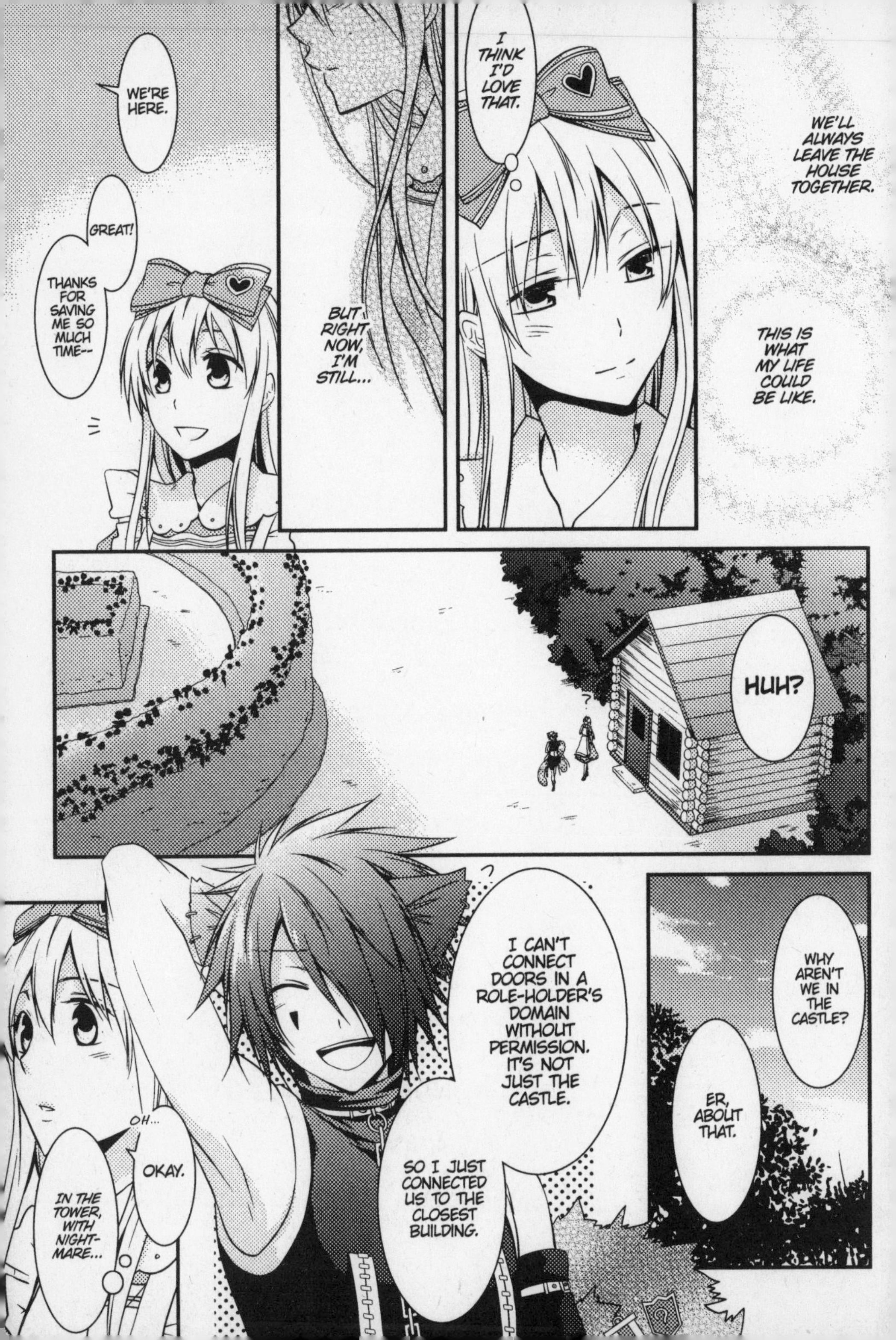
WE'LL ALWAYS LEAVE THE HOUSE TOGETHER.
THIS IS WHAT MY LIFE COULD BE LIKE.
I THINK I'D LOVE THAT.
BUT RIGHT NOW, I'M STILL...
WE'RE HERE.
GREAT!
THANKS FOR SAVING ME SO MUCH TIME--
HUH?
WHY AREN'T WE IN THE CASTLE?
ER, ABOUT THAT.
I CAN'T CONNECT DOORS IN A ROLE-HOLDER'S DOMAIN WITHOUT PERMISSION. IT'S NOT JUST THE CASTLE.
SO I JUST CONNECTED US TO THE CLOSEST BUILDING.
OH...
OKAY.
IN THE TOWER, WITH NIGHT-MARE...

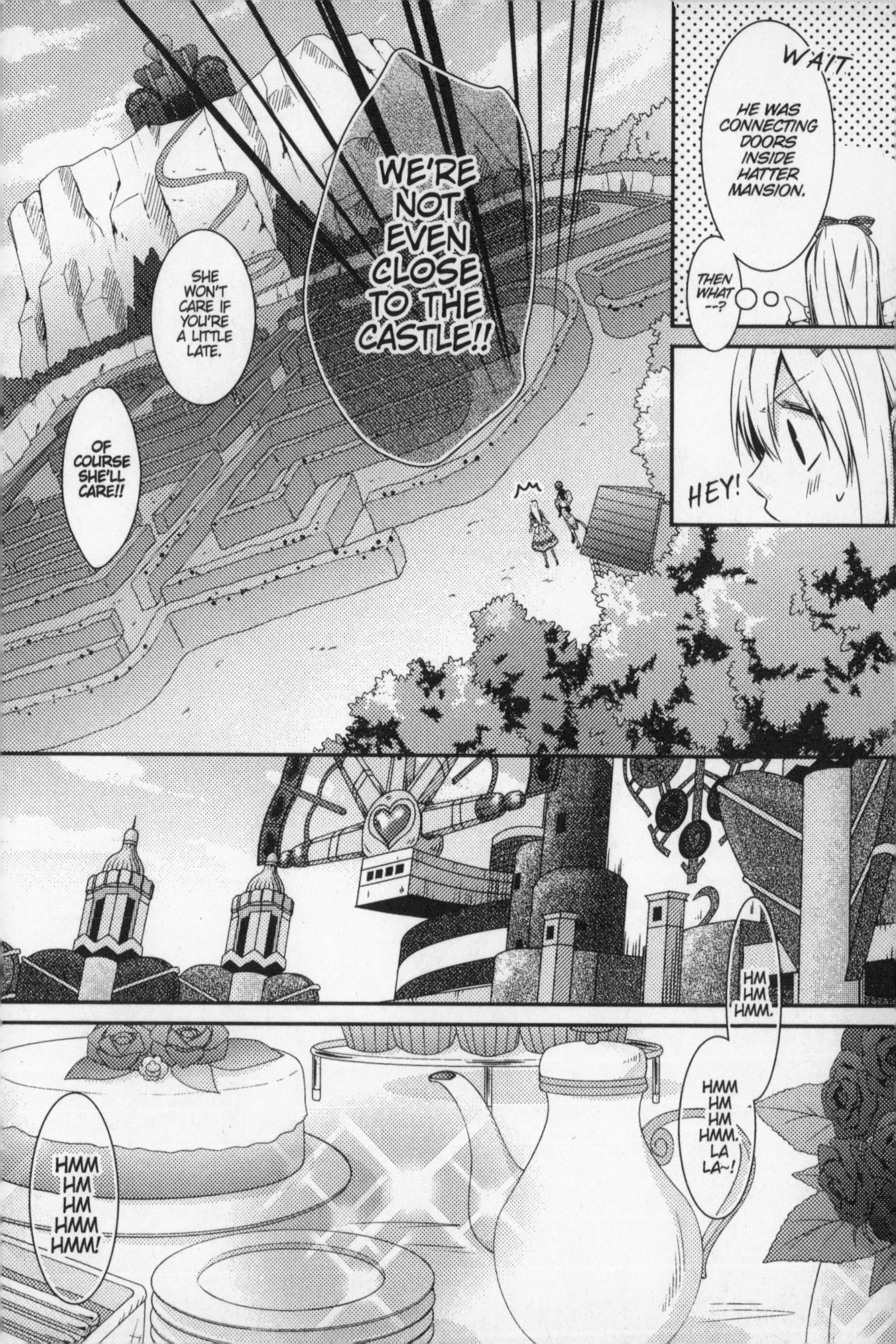
WAIT.
HE WAS CONNECTING DOORS INSIDE HATTER MANSION.
THEN WHAT--?
HEY!
WE'RE NOT EVEN CLOSE TO THE CASTLE!!
SHE WON'T CARE IF YOU'RE A LITTLE LATE.
OF COURSE SHE'LL CARE!!
HM HM HMM.
HMM HM HM HMM. LA LA~!
HMM HM HM HMM HMM!

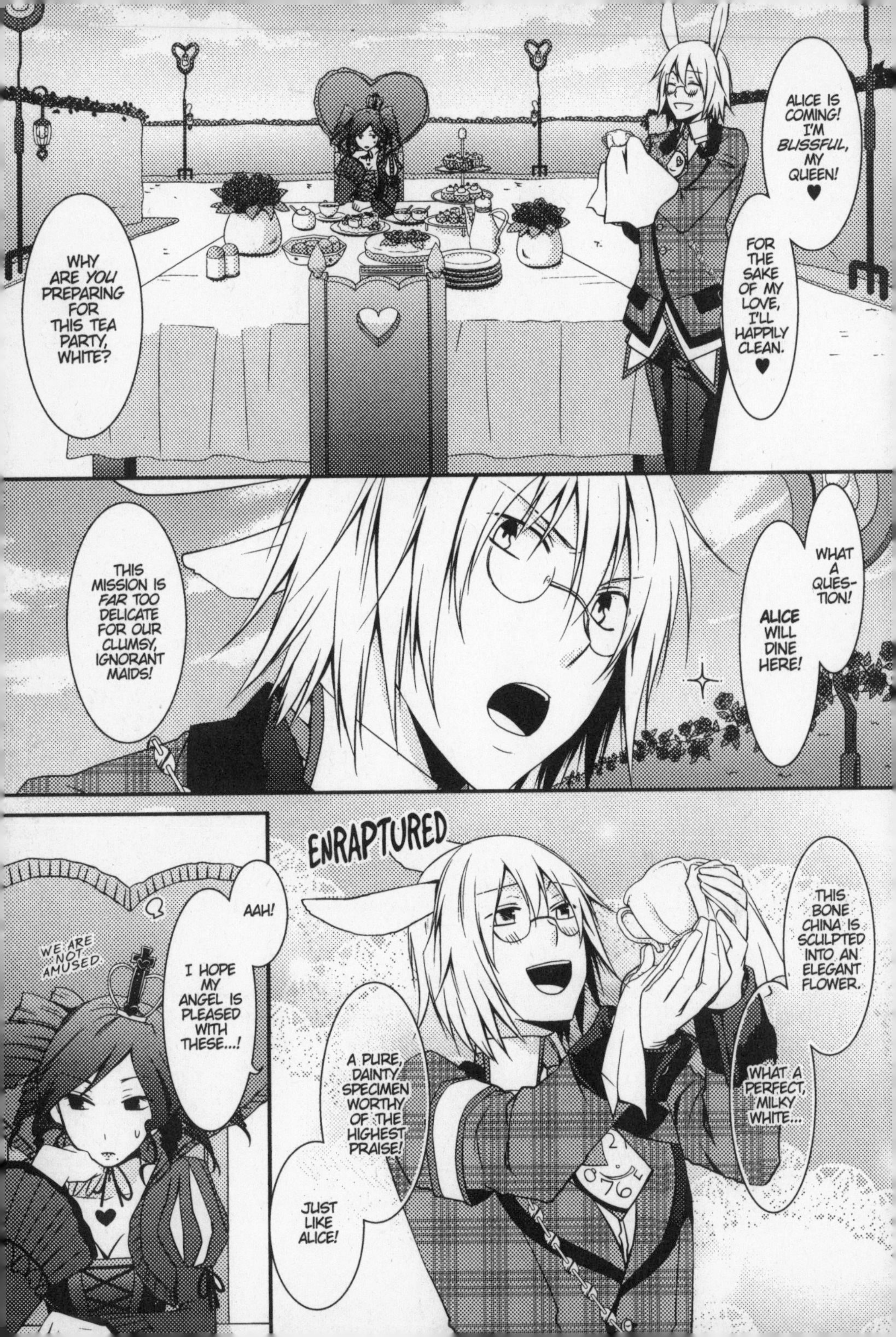
ALICE IS COMING! I'M BLISSFUL, MY QUEEN! ♥
FOR THE SAKE OF MY LOVE, I'LL HAPPILY CLEAN. ♥
WHY ARE YOU PREPARING FOR THIS TEA PARTY, WHITE?
WHAT A QUES-TION!
ALICE WILL DINE HERE!
THIS MISSION IS FAR TOO DELICATE FOR OUR CLUMSY, IGNORANT MAIDS!
ENRAPTURED
THIS BONE CHINA IS SCULPTED INTO AN ELEGANT FLOWER.
WHAT A PERFECT, MILKY WHITE...
A PURE, DAINTY SPECIMEN WORTHY OF THE HIGHEST PRAISE!
JUST LIKE ALICE!
AAH!
I HOPE MY ANGEL IS PLEASED WITH THESE...!
WE ARE NOT AMUSED

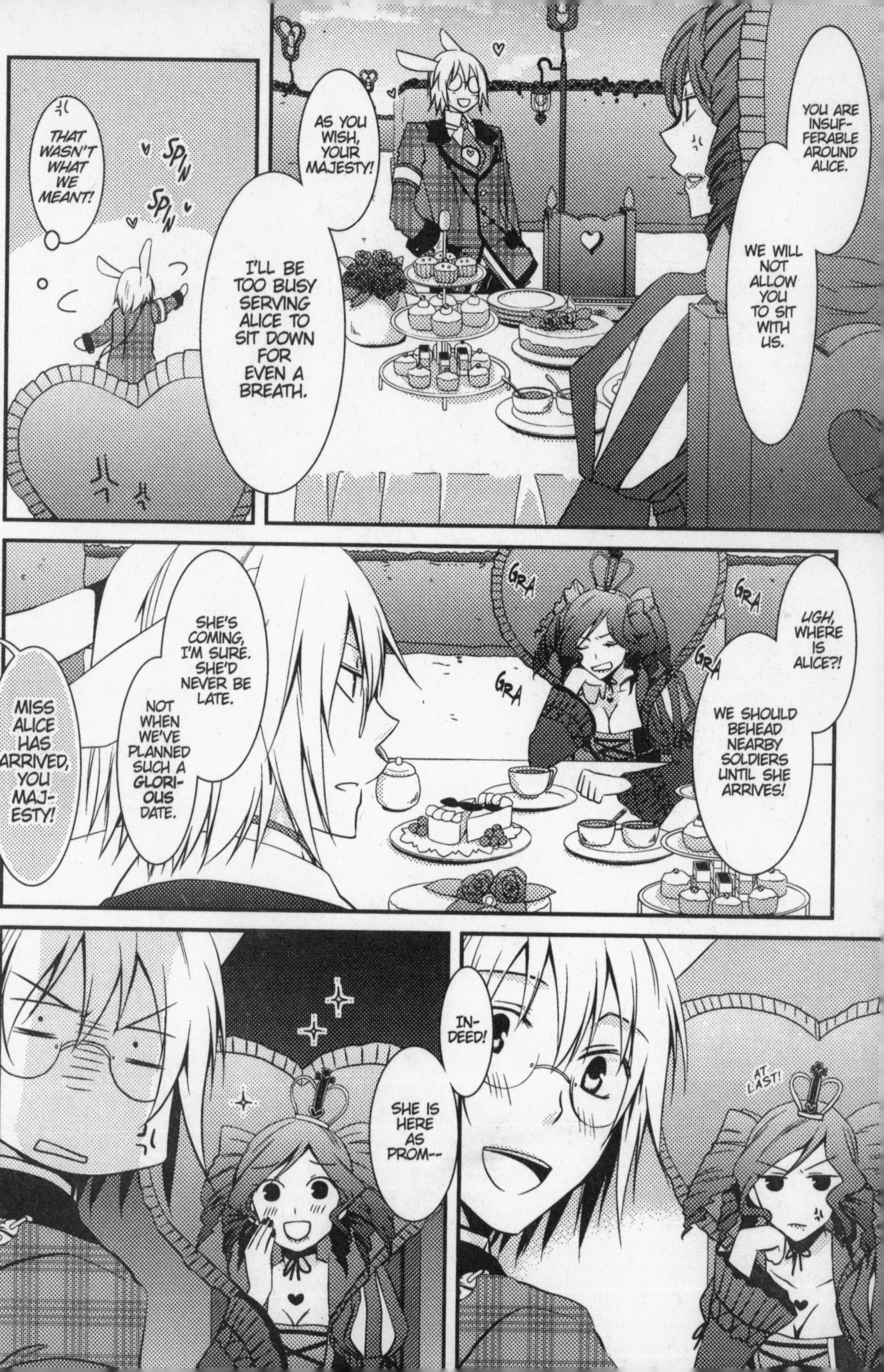
YOU ARE INSUFFERABLE AROUND ALICE.
WE WILL NOT ALLOW YOU TO SIT WITH US.
AS YOU WISH, YOUR MAJESTY!
I'LL BE TOO BUSY SERVING ALICE TO SIT DOWN FOR EVEN A BREATH.
SPIN SPIN
THAT WASN'T WHAT WE MEANT!
UGH, WHERE IS ALICE?!
GRA GRA GRA GRA
WE SHOULD BEHEAD NEARBY SOLDIERS UNTIL SHE ARRIVES!
SHE'S COMING, I'M SURE. SHE'D NEVER BE LATE.
NOT WHEN WE'VE PLANNED SUCH A GLORIOUS DATE.
MISS ALICE HAS ARRIVED, YOU MAJESTY!
AT LAST!
INDEED!
SHE IS HERE AS PROM--

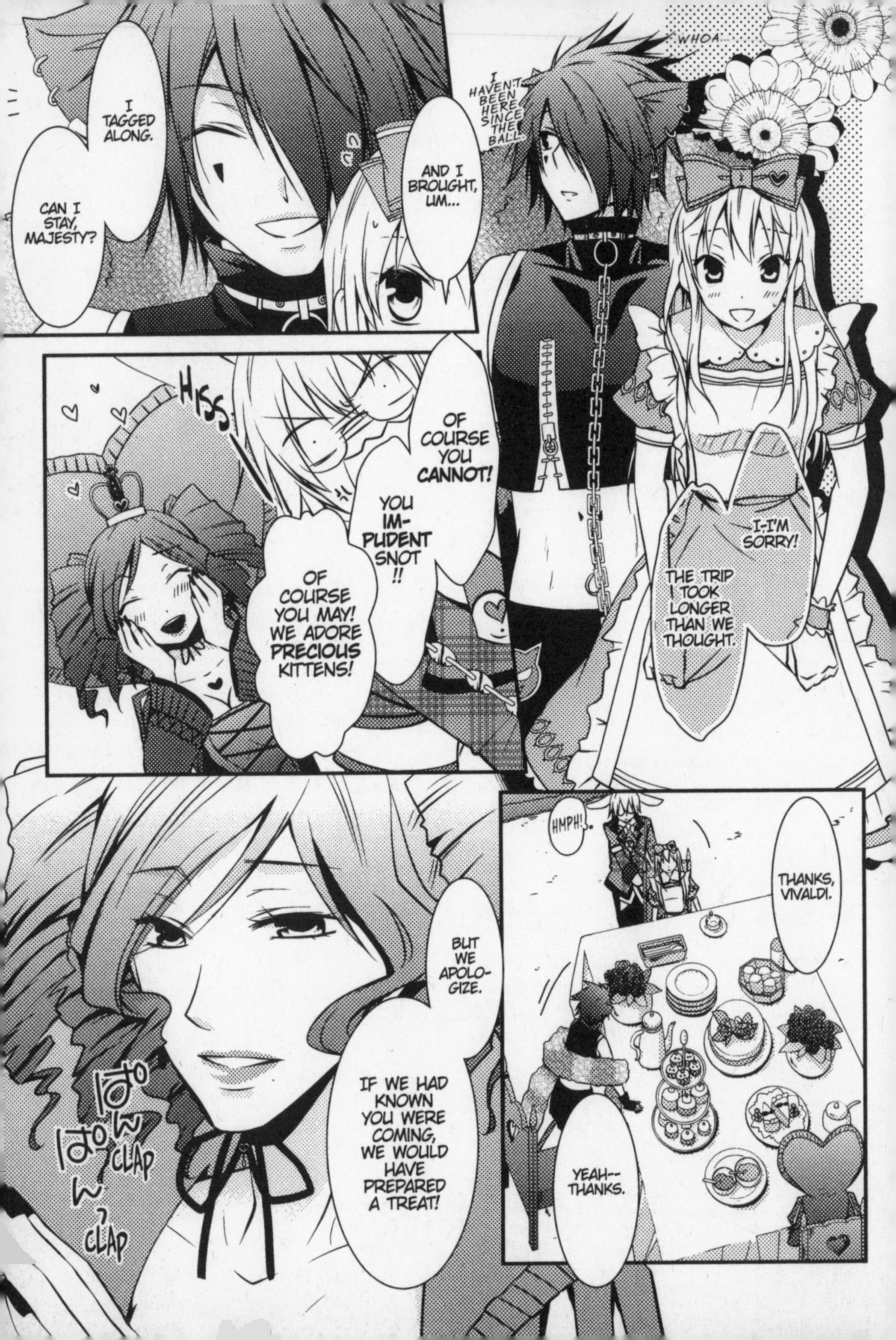
WHOA...
I HAVEN'T BEEN HERE SINCE THE BALL.
I-I'M SORRY!
THE TRIP TOOK LONGER THAN WE THOUGHT.
AND I BROUGHT, UM...
I TAGGED ALONG.
CAN I STAY, MAJESTY?
HISS
OF COURSE YOU CANNOT!
YOU IMPUDENT SNOT!!
OF COURSE YOU MAY! WE ADORE PRECIOUS KITTENS!
HMPH!
THANKS, VIVALDI.
YEAH-- THANKS.
BUT WE APOLOGIZE.
IF WE HAD KNOWN YOU WERE COMING, WE WOULD HAVE PREPARED A TREAT!
ぱん CLAP
ぱん CLAP

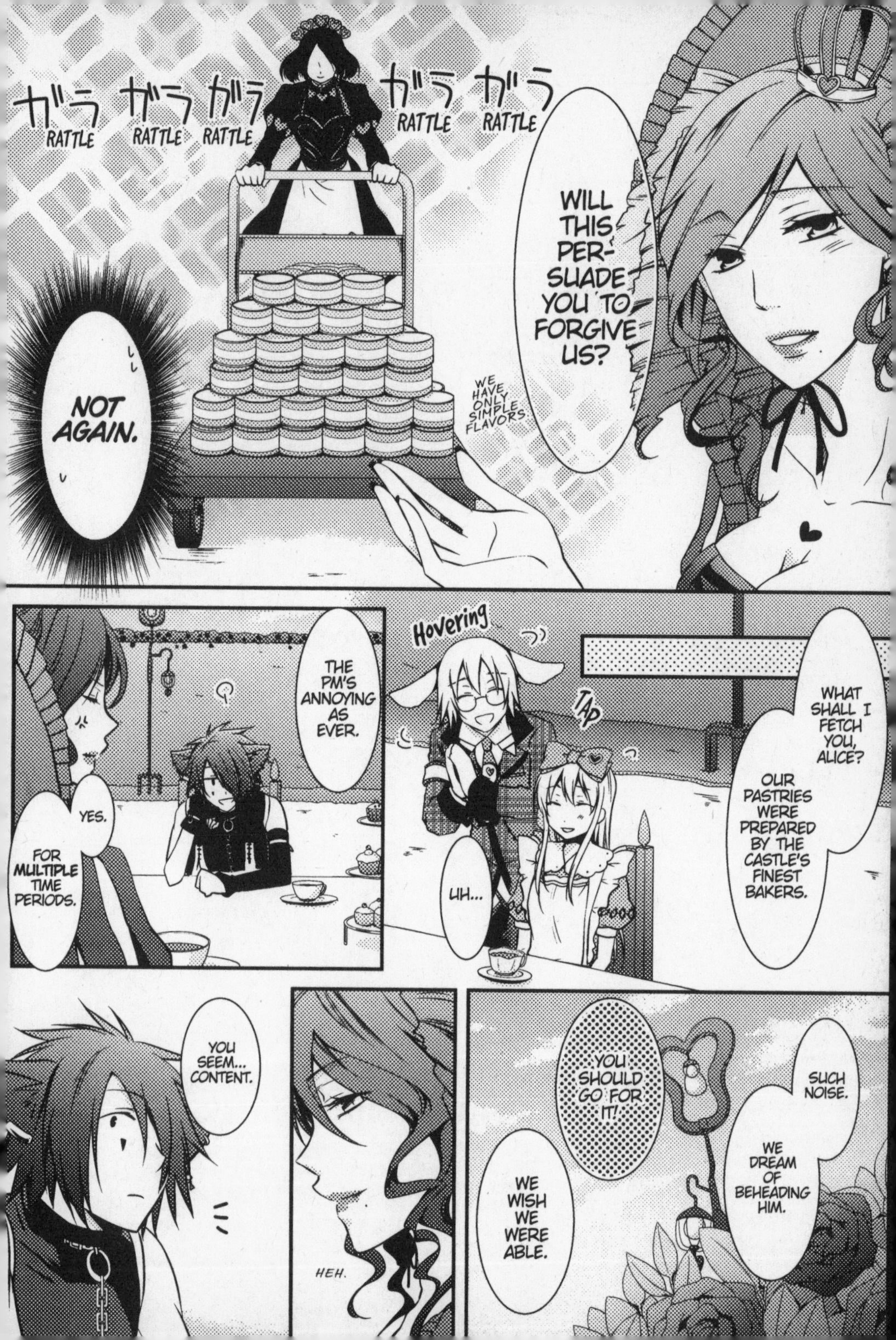
WILL THIS PER-SUADE YOU TO FORGIVE US?
WE HAVE ONLY SIMPLE FLAVORS.
ガラ RATTLE
ガラ RATTLE
ガラ RATTLE
ガラ RATTLE
ガラ RATTLE
NOT AGAIN.
WHAT SHALL I FETCH YOU, ALICE?
OUR PASTRIES WERE PREPARED BY THE CASTLE'S FINEST BAKERS.
Hovering
TAP
UH...
THE PM'S ANNOYING AS EVER.
YES.
FOR MULTIPLE TIME PERIODS.
SUCH NOISE.
WE DREAM OF BEHEADING HIM.
YOU SHOULD GO FOR IT!
WE WISH WE WERE ABLE.
HEH.
YOU SEEM... CONTENT.

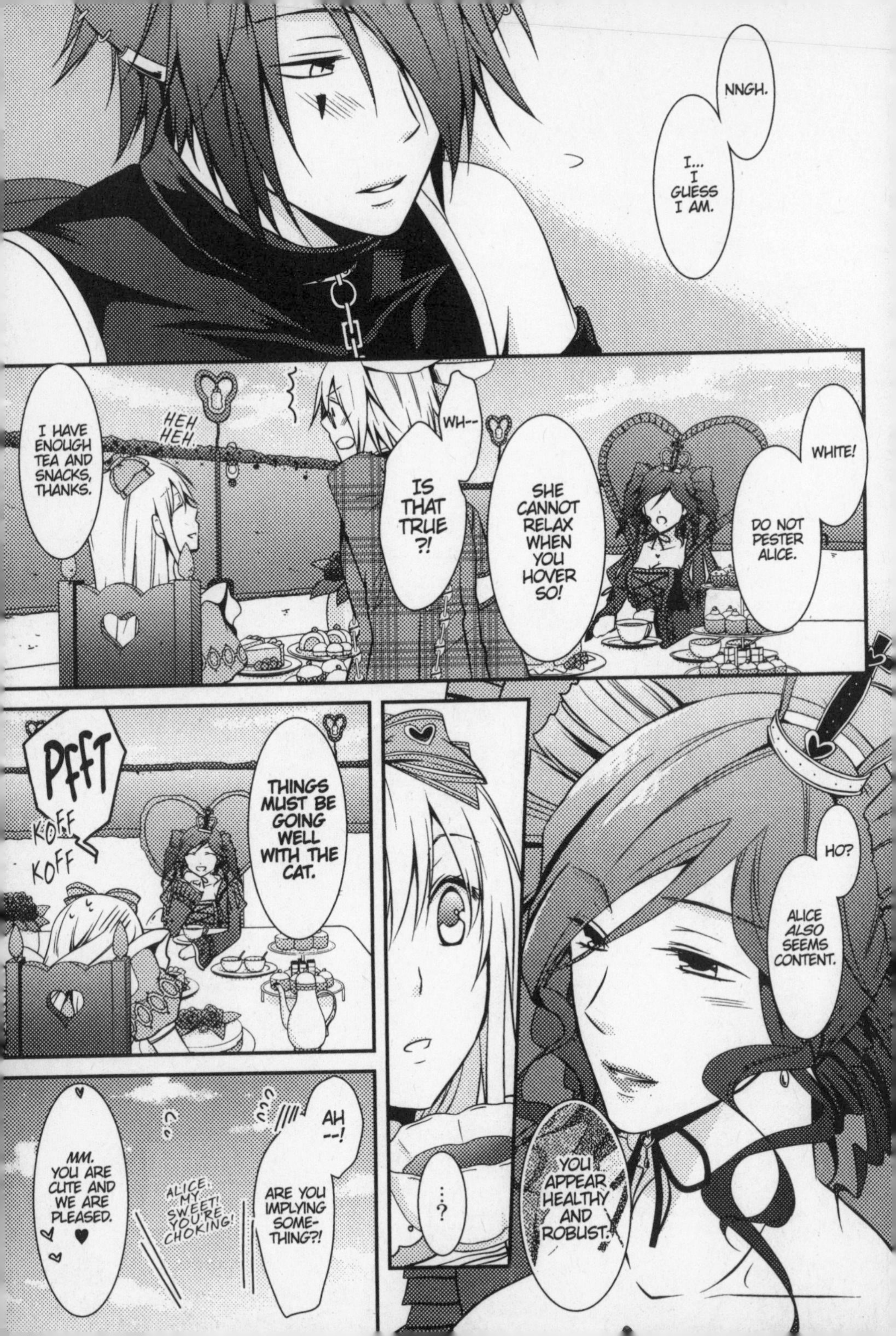
NNGH.
I... I GUESS I AM.
WHITE!
DO NOT PESTER ALICE.
SHE CANNOT RELAX WHEN YOU HOVER SO!
WH--
IS THAT TRUE?!
HEH HEH.
I HAVE ENOUGH TEA AND SNACKS, THANKS.
HO?
ALICE ALSO SEEMS CONTENT.
YOU APPEAR HEALTHY AND ROBUST.
...?
THINGS MUST BE GOING WELL WITH THE CAT.
PFFT
KOFF KOFF
AH--!
ARE YOU IMPLYING SOMETHING?!
ALICE, MY SWEET! YOU'RE CHOKING!
MM. YOU ARE CUTE AND WE ARE PLEASED.

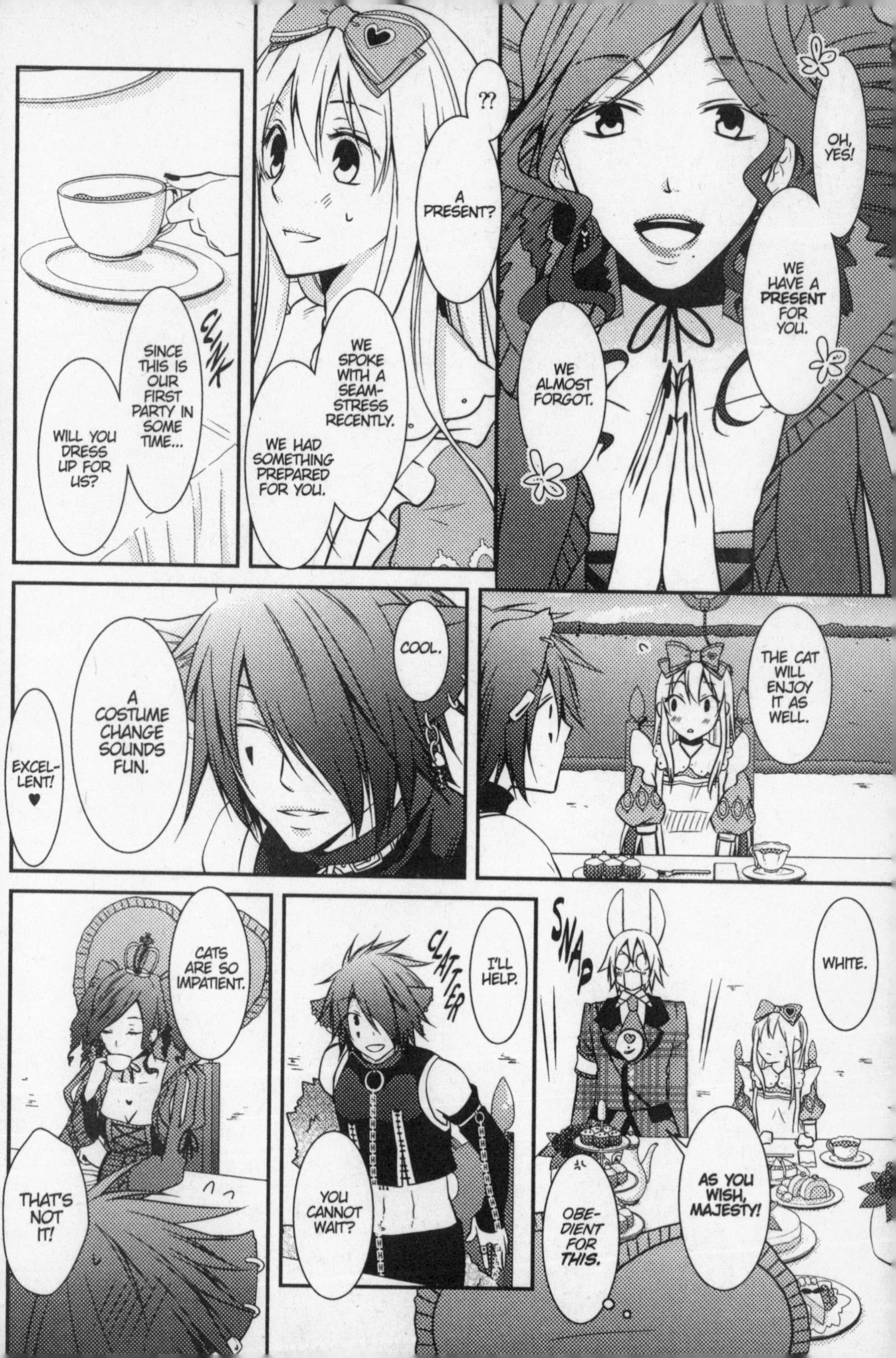
OH, YES!
WE HAVE A PRESENT FOR YOU.
WE ALMOST FORGOT.
??
A PRESENT?
WE SPOKE WITH A SEAM-STRESS RECENTLY.
WE HAD SOMETHING PREPARED FOR YOU.
CLINK
SINCE THIS IS OUR FIRST PARTY IN SOME TIME...
WILL YOU DRESS UP FOR US?
THE CAT WILL ENJOY IT AS WELL.
COOL.
A COSTUME CHANGE SOUNDS FUN.
EXCEL-LENT! ♥
WHITE.
SNAP
AS YOU WISH, MAJESTY!
OBE-DIENT FOR THIS.
CLATTER
I'LL HELP.
YOU CANNOT WAIT?
CATS ARE SO IMPATIENT.
THAT'S NOT IT!

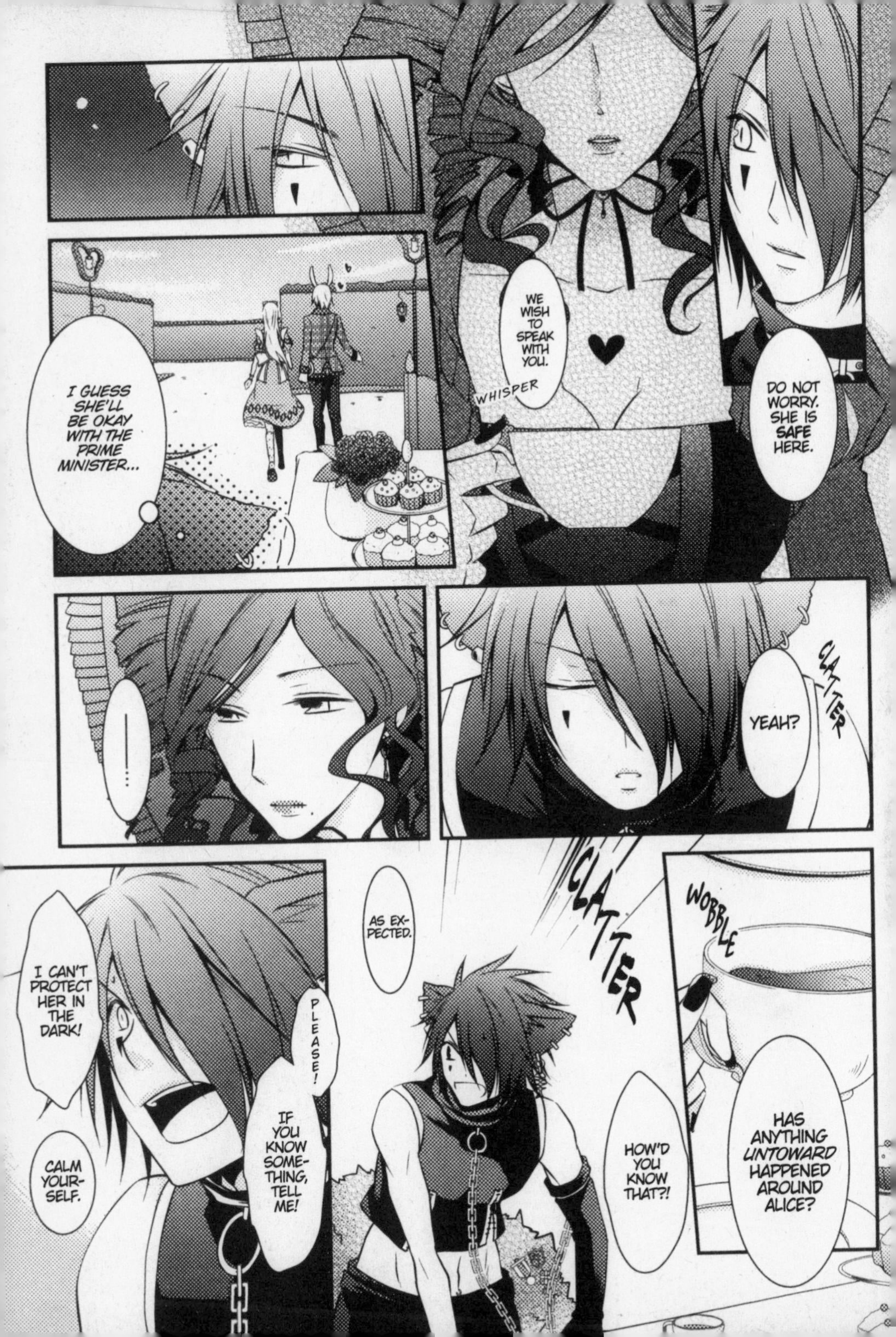
WE WISH TO SPEAK WITH YOU.
WHISPER
DO NOT WORRY. SHE IS SAFE HERE.
I GUESS SHE'LL BE OKAY WITH THE PRIME MINISTER...
CLATTER
YEAH?
......
WOBBLE
HAS ANYTHING *UNTOWARD* HAPPENED AROUND ALICE?
CLATTER
AS EX-PECTED.
HOW'D YOU KNOW THAT?!
PLEASE!
I CAN'T PROTECT HER IN THE DARK!
IF YOU KNOW SOME-THING, TELL ME!
CALM YOUR-SELF.

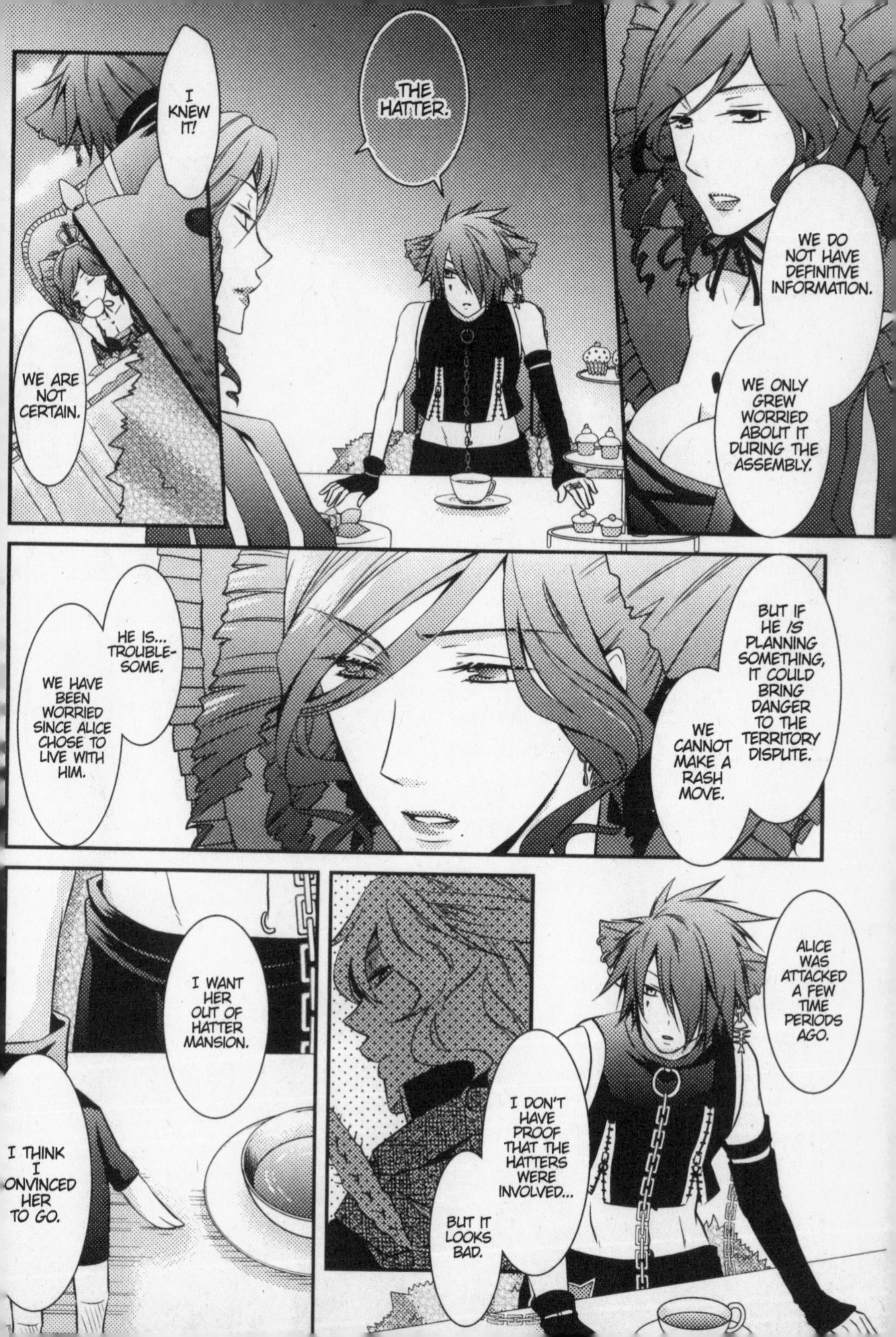

WE DO NOT HAVE DEFINITIVE INFORMATION.
WE ONLY GREW WORRIED ABOUT IT DURING THE ASSEMBLY.
THE HATTER.
I KNEW IT!
WE ARE NOT CERTAIN.
BUT IF HE *IS* PLANNING SOMETHING, IT COULD BRING DANGER TO THE TERRITORY DISPUTE.
WE CANNOT MAKE A RASH MOVE.
HE IS... TROUBLE-SOME.
WE HAVE BEEN WORRIED SINCE ALICE CHOSE TO LIVE WITH HIM.
ALICE WAS ATTACKED A FEW TIME PERIODS AGO.
I DON'T HAVE PROOF THAT THE HATTERS WERE INVOLVED...
BUT IT LOOKS BAD.
I WANT HER OUT OF HATTER MANSION.
I THINK I ONVINCED HER TO GO.

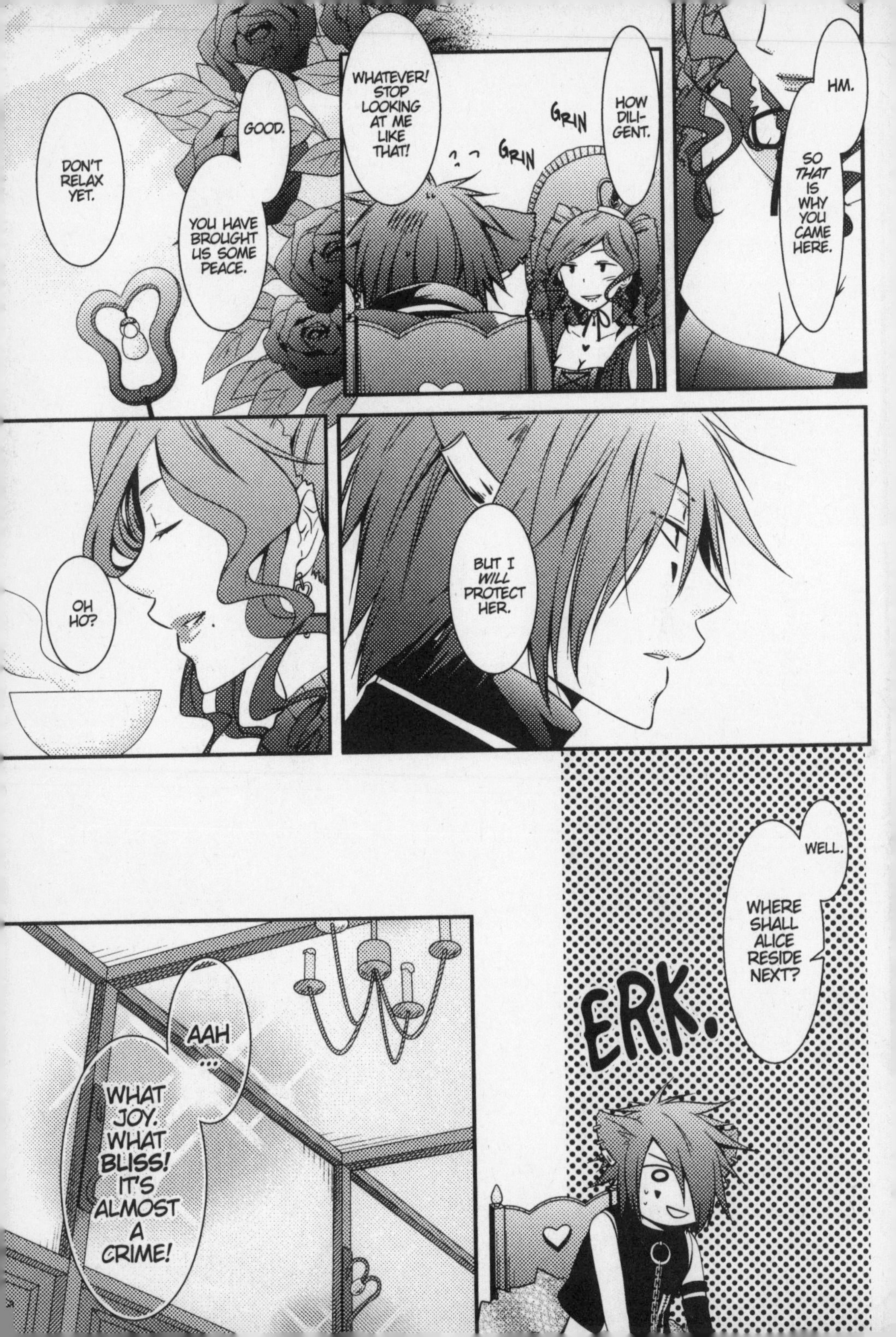
HM.
SO *THAT* IS WHY YOU CAME HERE.
HOW DILI-GENT.
GRIN
GRIN
WHATEVER! STOP LOOKING AT ME LIKE THAT!
GOOD.
YOU HAVE BROUGHT US SOME PEACE.
DON'T RELAX YET.
BUT I *WILL* PROTECT HER.
OH HO?
WELL.
WHERE SHALL ALICE RESIDE NEXT?
ERK.
AAH...
WHAT JOY. WHAT BLISS! IT'S ALMOST A CRIME!

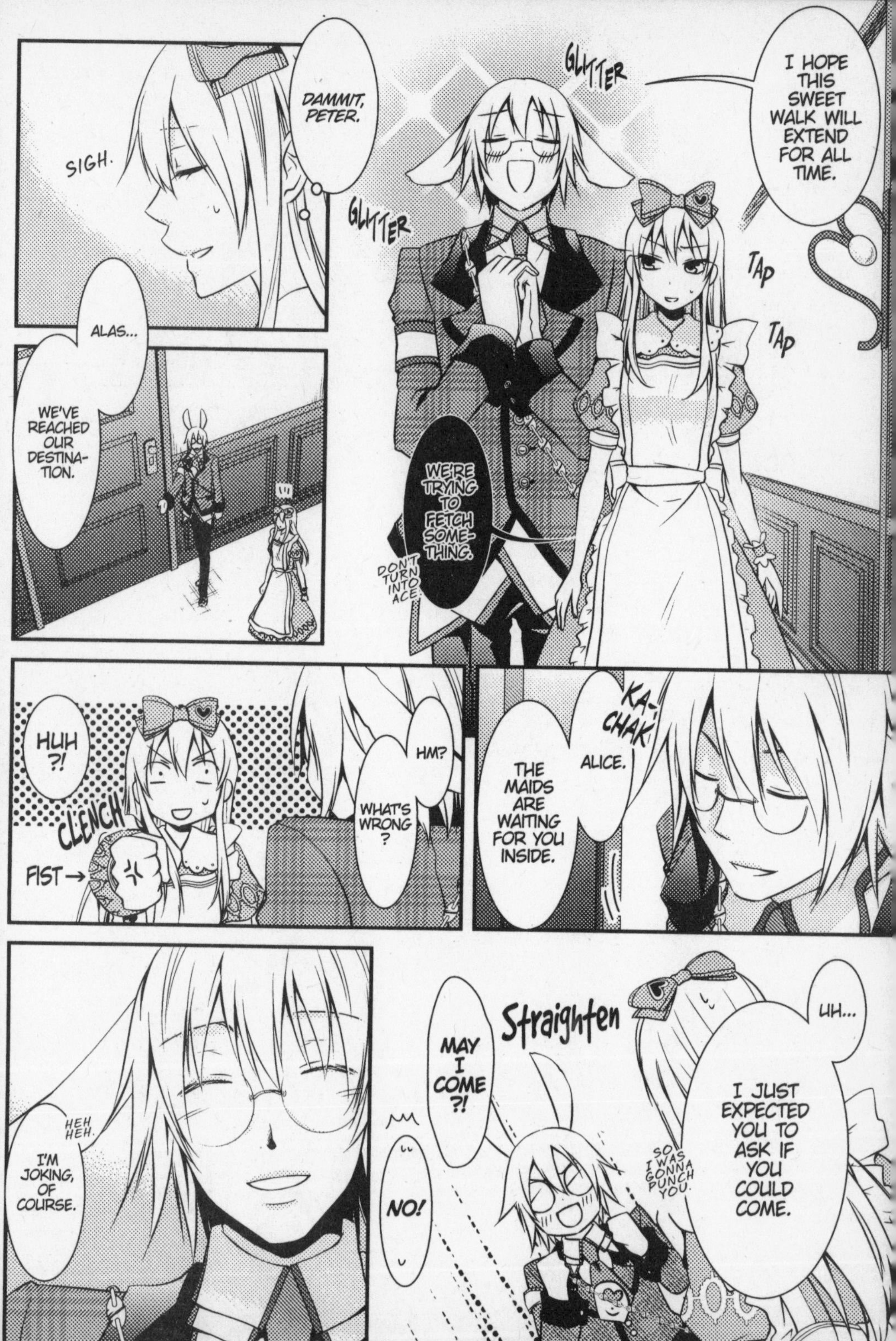

I HOPE THIS SWEET WALK WILL EXTEND FOR ALL TIME.
GLITTER
GLITTER
TAP
TAP
WE'RE TRYING TO FETCH SOME-THING.
DON'T TURN INTO ACE.
DAMMIT, PETER.
SIGH.
ALAS...
WE'VE REACHED OUR DESTINA-TION.
KA-CHAK
ALICE.
THE MAIDS ARE WAITING FOR YOU INSIDE.
HM?
WHAT'S WRONG?
HUH?!
CLENCH
FIST →
UH...
I JUST EXPECTED YOU TO ASK IF YOU COULD COME.
SO I WAS GONNA PUNCH YOU.
Straighten
MAY I COME?!
NO!
HEH HEH.
I'M JOKING, OF COURSE.

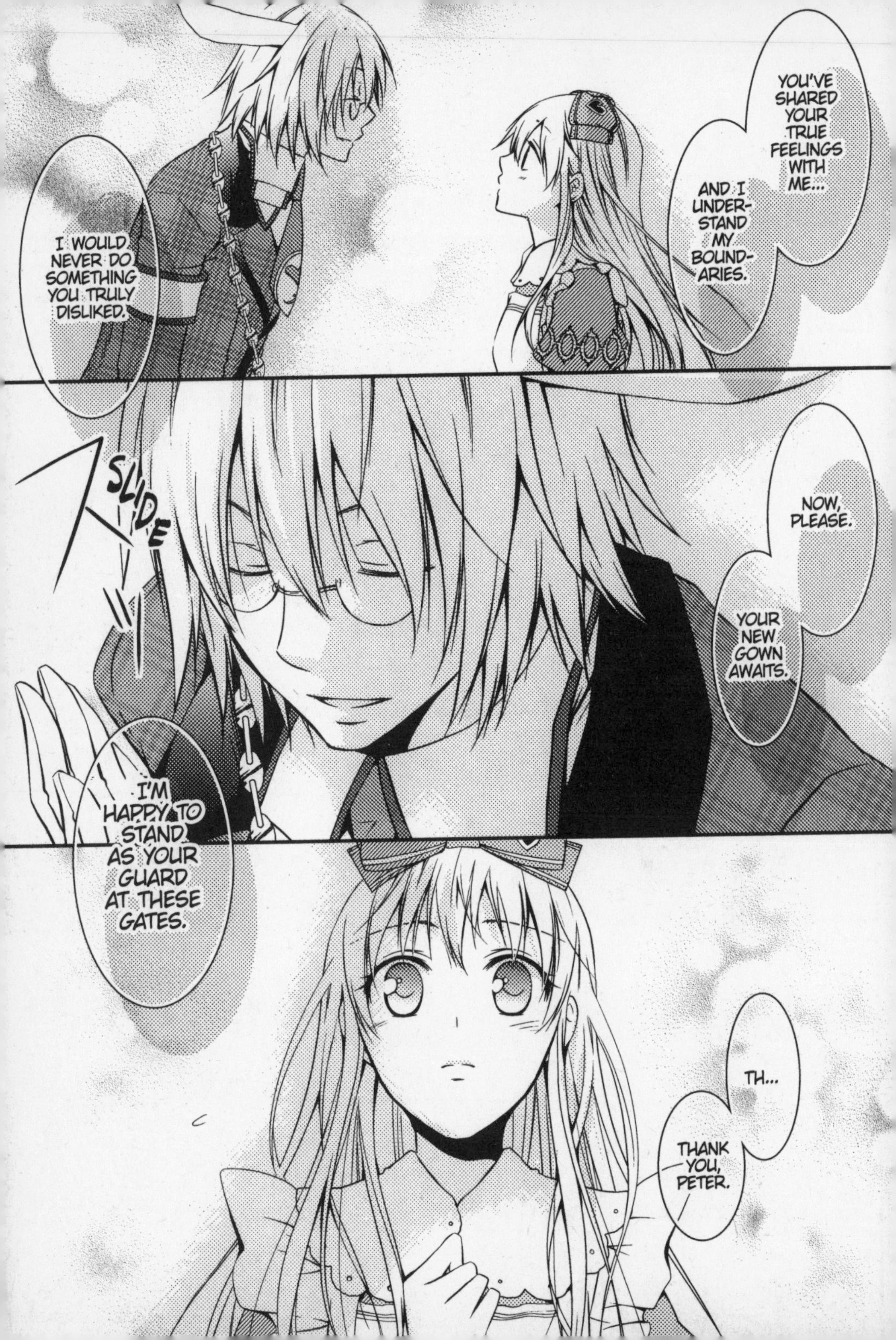
YOU'VE SHARED YOUR TRUE FEELINGS WITH ME...
AND I UNDER-STAND MY BOUND-ARIES.
I WOULD NEVER DO SOMETHING YOU TRULY DISLIKED.
NOW, PLEASE.
YOUR NEW GOWN AWAITS.
SLIDE
I'M HAPPY TO STAND AS YOUR GUARD AT THESE GATES.
TH...
THANK YOU, PETER.

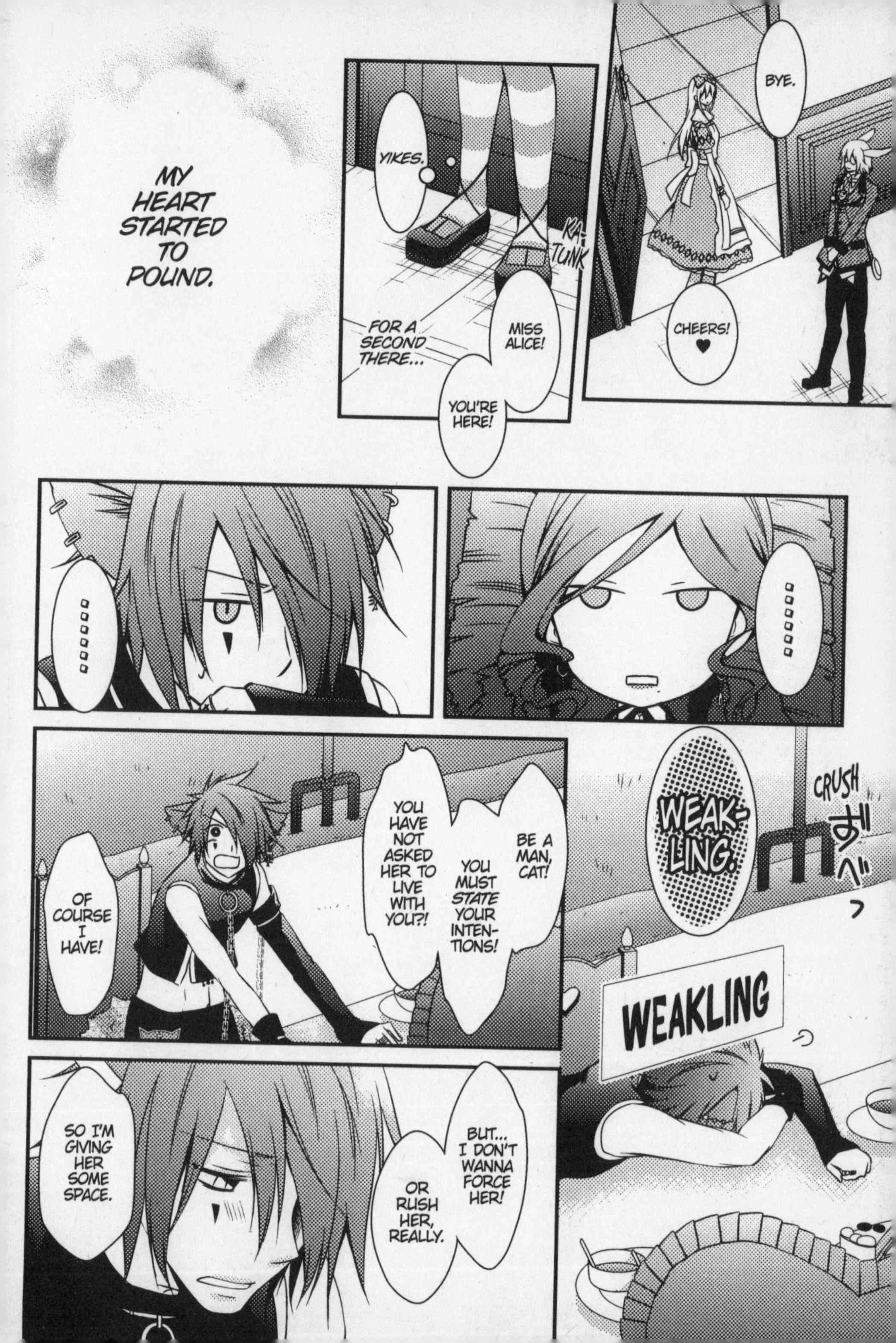
BYE.
CHEERS! ♥
YIKES.
KA-TUNK
MISS ALICE!
YOU'RE HERE!
FOR A SECOND THERE...
MY HEART STARTED TO POUND.
......
......
CRUSH
WEAK-LING.
WEAKLING
BE A MAN, CAT!
YOU MUST STATE YOUR INTENTIONS!
YOU HAVE NOT ASKED HER TO LIVE WITH YOU?!
OF COURSE I HAVE!
BUT... I DON'T WANNA FORCE HER!
OR RUSH HER, REALLY.
SO I'M GIVING HER SOME SPACE.

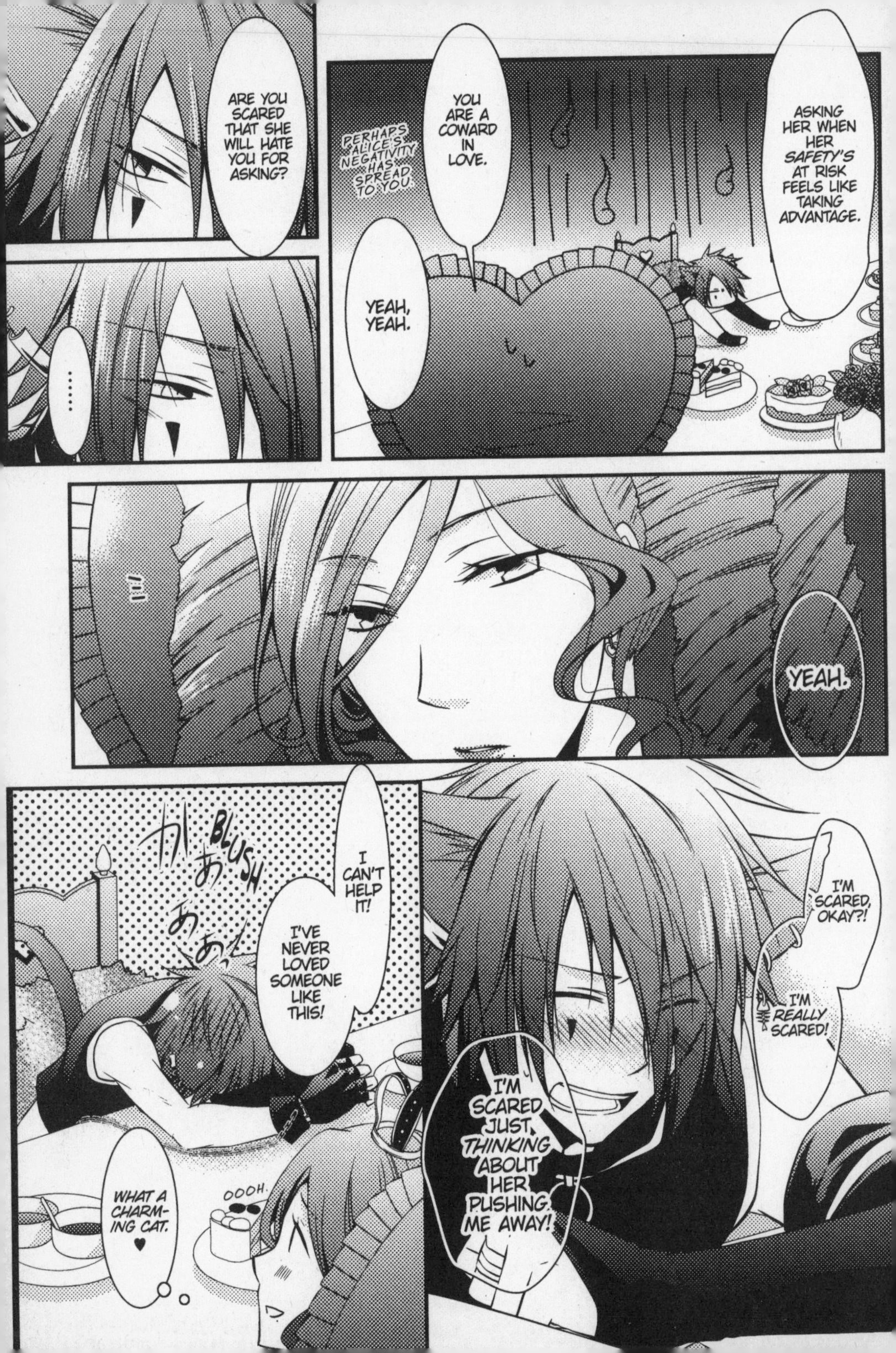
ASKING HER WHEN HER SAFETY'S AT RISK FEELS LIKE TAKING ADVANTAGE.
YOU ARE A COWARD IN LOVE.
PERHAPS ALICE'S NEGATIVITY HAS SPREAD TO YOU.
YEAH, YEAH.
ARE YOU SCARED THAT SHE WILL HATE YOU FOR ASKING?
......
YEAH.
I'M SCARED, OKAY?!
I'M REALLY SCARED!
I'M SCARED JUST THINKING ABOUT HER PUSHING ME AWAY!
I CAN'T HELP IT!
I'VE NEVER LOVED SOMEONE LIKE THIS!
BLUSH
OOOH.
WHAT A CHARMING CAT. ♥

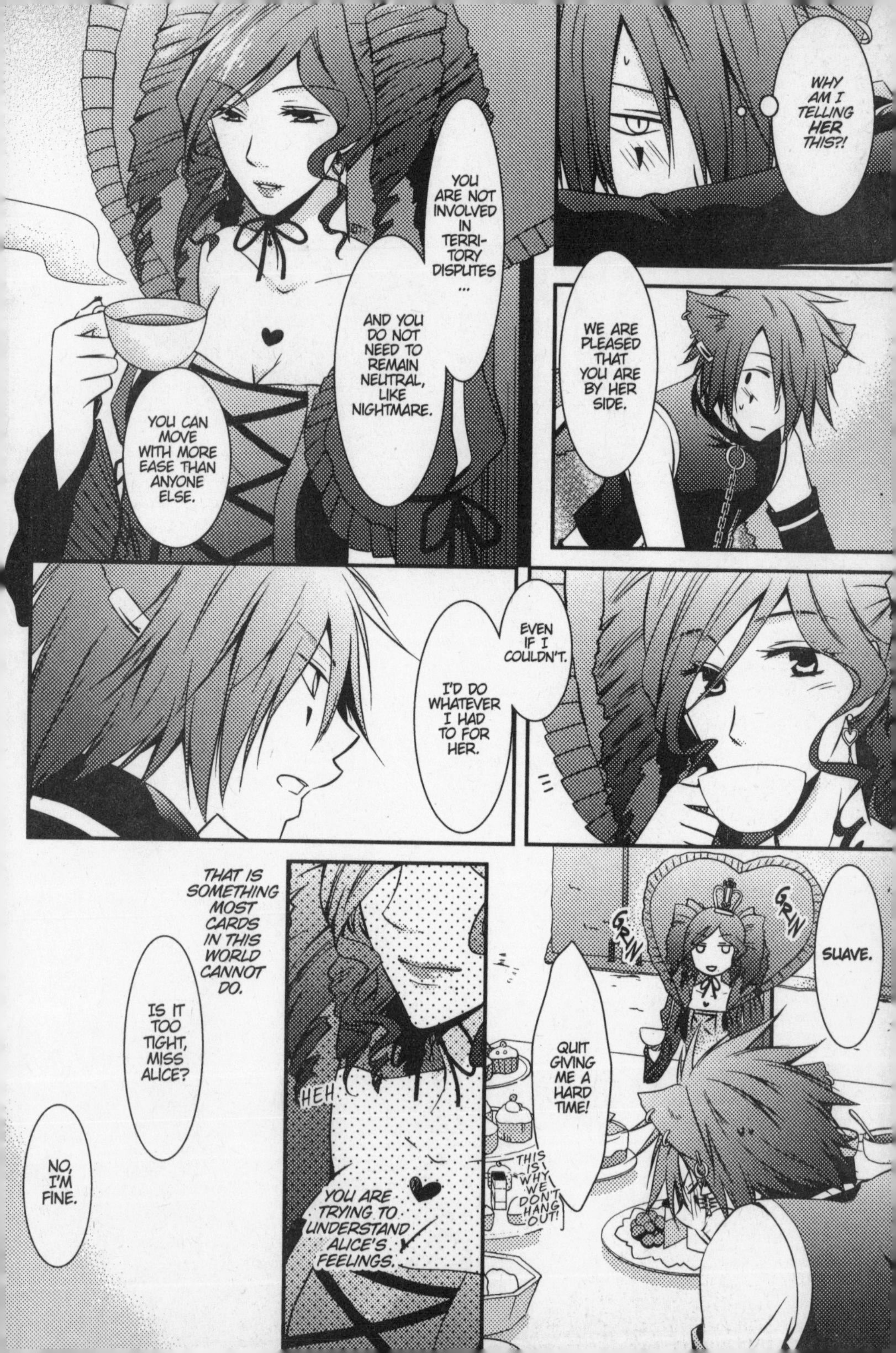
WHY AM I TELLING HER THIS?!
WE ARE PLEASED THAT YOU ARE BY HER SIDE.
YOU ARE NOT INVOLVED IN TERRI-TORY DISPUTES ...
AND YOU DO NOT NEED TO REMAIN NEUTRAL, LIKE NIGHTMARE.
YOU CAN MOVE WITH MORE EASE THAN ANYONE ELSE.
EVEN IF I COULDN'T.
I'D DO WHATEVER I HAD TO FOR HER.
SUAVE.
GRIN
GRIN
QUIT GIVING ME A HARD TIME!
THIS IS WHY WE DON'T HANG OUT!
HEH
YOU ARE TRYING TO UNDERSTAND ALICE'S FEELINGS.
THAT IS SOMETHING MOST CARDS IN THIS WORLD CANNOT DO.
IS IT TOO TIGHT, MISS ALICE?
NO, I'M FINE.

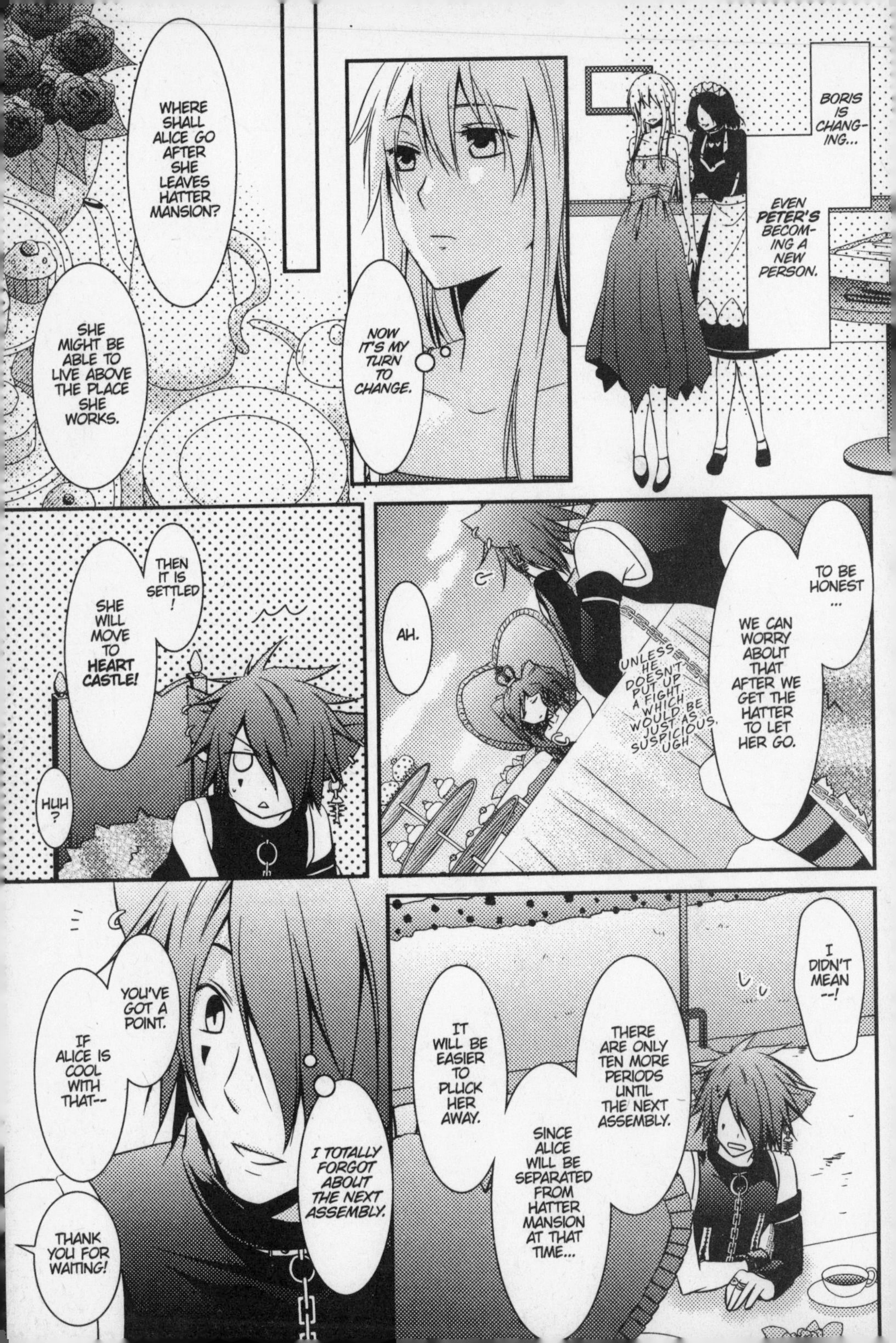
BORIS IS CHANGING...
EVEN PETER'S BECOMING A NEW PERSON.
NOW IT'S MY TURN TO CHANGE.
WHERE SHALL ALICE GO AFTER SHE LEAVES HATTER MANSION?
SHE MIGHT BE ABLE TO LIVE ABOVE THE PLACE SHE WORKS.
TO BE HONEST ...
WE CAN WORRY ABOUT THAT AFTER WE GET THE HATTER TO LET HER GO.
UNLESS HE DOESN'T PUT UP A FIGHT WHICH WOULD BE JUST AS SUSPICIOUS, UGH
AH.
THEN IT IS SETTLED!
SHE WILL MOVE TO HEART CASTLE!
HUH?
I DIDN'T MEAN--!
THERE ARE ONLY TEN MORE PERIODS UNTIL THE NEXT ASSEMBLY.
IT WILL BE EASIER TO PLUCK HER AWAY.
SINCE ALICE WILL BE SEPARATED FROM HATTER MANSION AT THAT TIME...
YOU'VE GOT A POINT.
IF ALICE IS COOL WITH THAT--
I TOTALLY FORGOT ABOUT THE NEXT ASSEMBLY.
THANK YOU FOR WAITING!

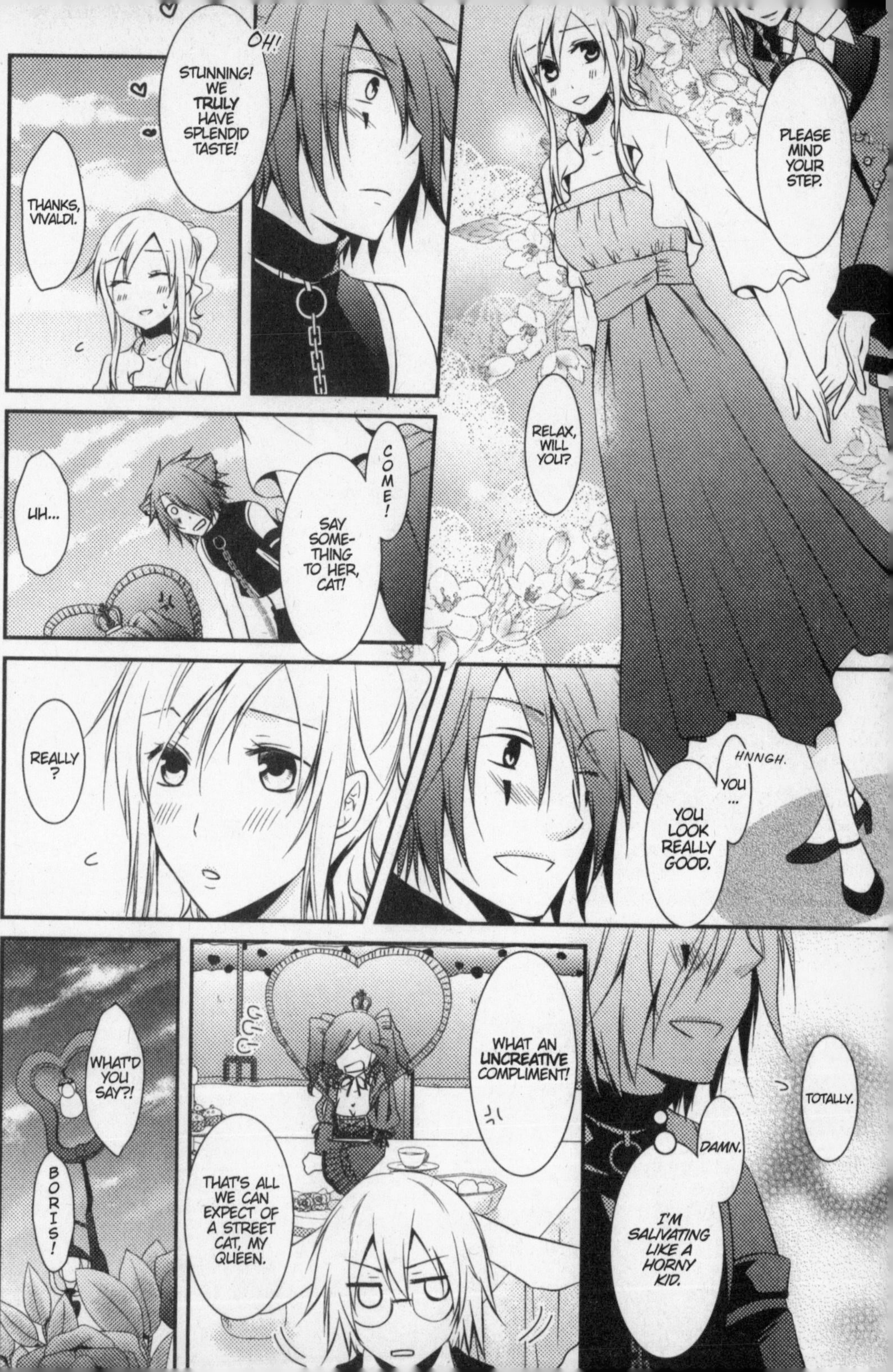
PLEASE MIND YOUR STEP.
RELAX, WILL YOU?
OH!
STUNNING! WE TRULY HAVE SPLENDID TASTE!
THANKS, VIVALDI.
COME!
SAY SOMETHING TO HER, CAT!
UH...
HNNGH.
YOU...
YOU LOOK REALLY GOOD.
REALLY?
TOTALLY.
DAMN.
I'M SALIVATING LIKE A HORNY KID.
WHAT AN UNCREATIVE COMPLIMENT!
THAT'S ALL WE CAN EXPECT OF A STREET CAT, MY QUEEN.
WHAT'D YOU SAY?!
BORIS!

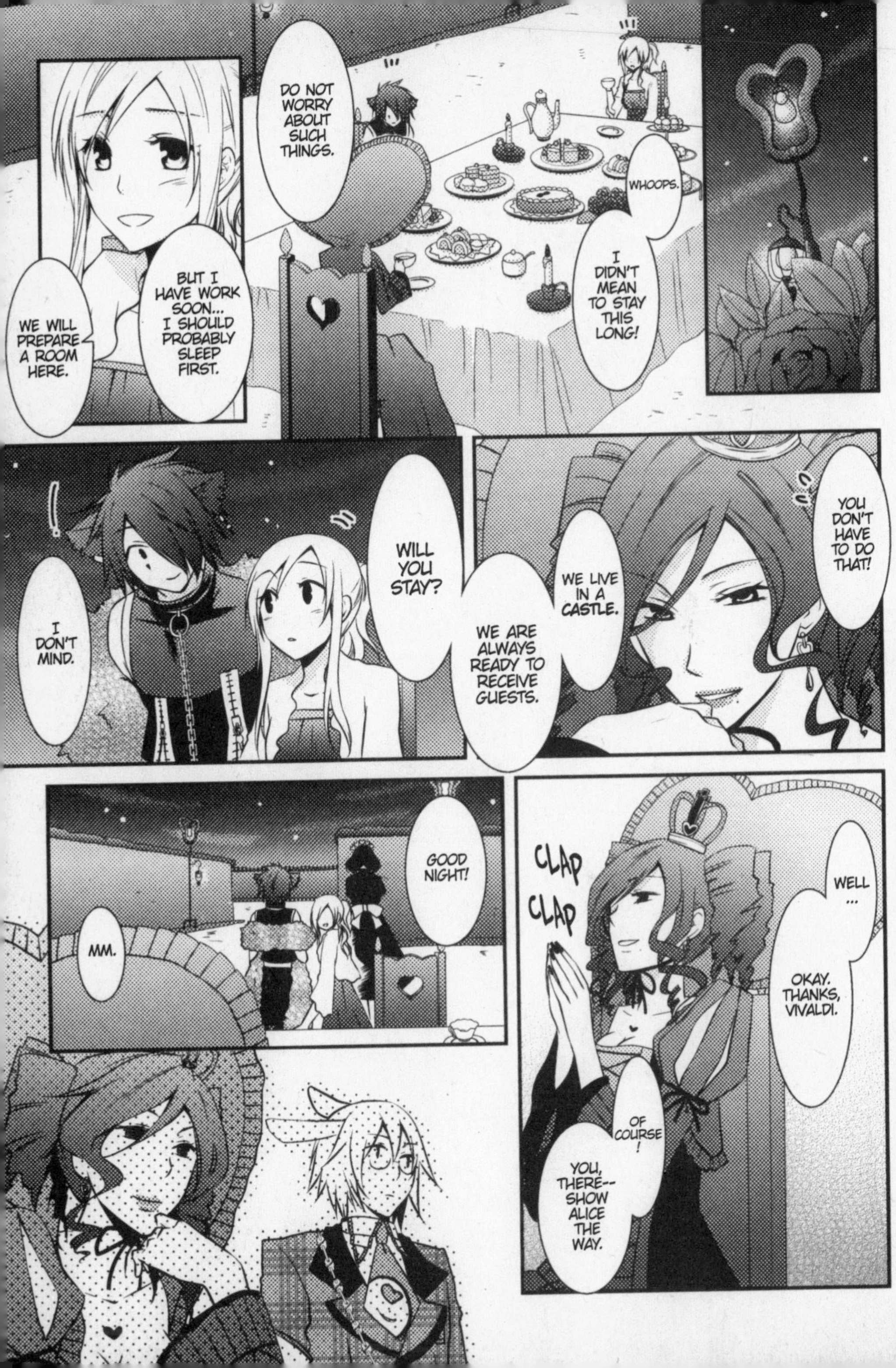
WHOOPS.
I DIDN'T MEAN TO STAY THIS LONG!
DO NOT WORRY ABOUT SUCH THINGS.
BUT I HAVE WORK SOON... I SHOULD PROBABLY SLEEP FIRST.
WE WILL PREPARE A ROOM HERE.
YOU DON'T HAVE TO DO THAT!
WE LIVE IN A CASTLE.
WE ARE ALWAYS READY TO RECEIVE GUESTS.
WILL YOU STAY?
I DON'T MIND.
CLAP
CLAP
WELL...
OKAY. THANKS, VIVALDI.
OF COURSE!
YOU, THERE-- SHOW ALICE THE WAY.
GOOD NIGHT!
MM.

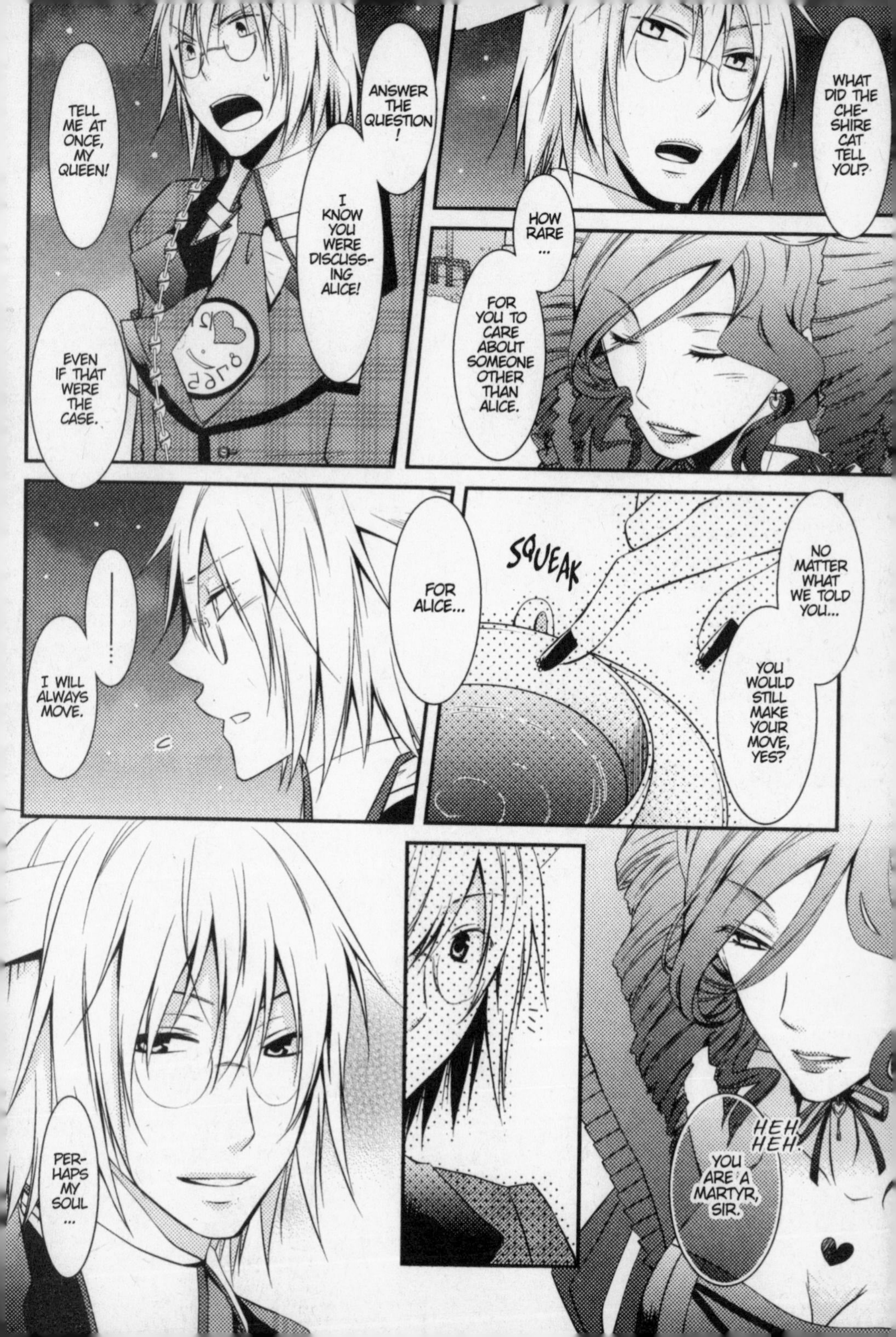
WHAT DID THE CHE-SHIRE CAT TELL YOU?
HOW RARE ...
FOR YOU TO CARE ABOUT SOMEONE OTHER THAN ALICE.
ANSWER THE QUESTION !
TELL ME AT ONCE, MY QUEEN!
I KNOW YOU WERE DISCUSS-ING ALICE!
EVEN IF THAT WERE THE CASE.
SQUEAK
NO MATTER WHAT WE TOLD YOU...
YOU WOULD STILL MAKE YOUR MOVE, YES?
FOR ALICE...
—!......
I WILL ALWAYS MOVE.
HEH HEH
YOU ARE A MARTYR, SIR.
PER-HAPS MY SOUL ...

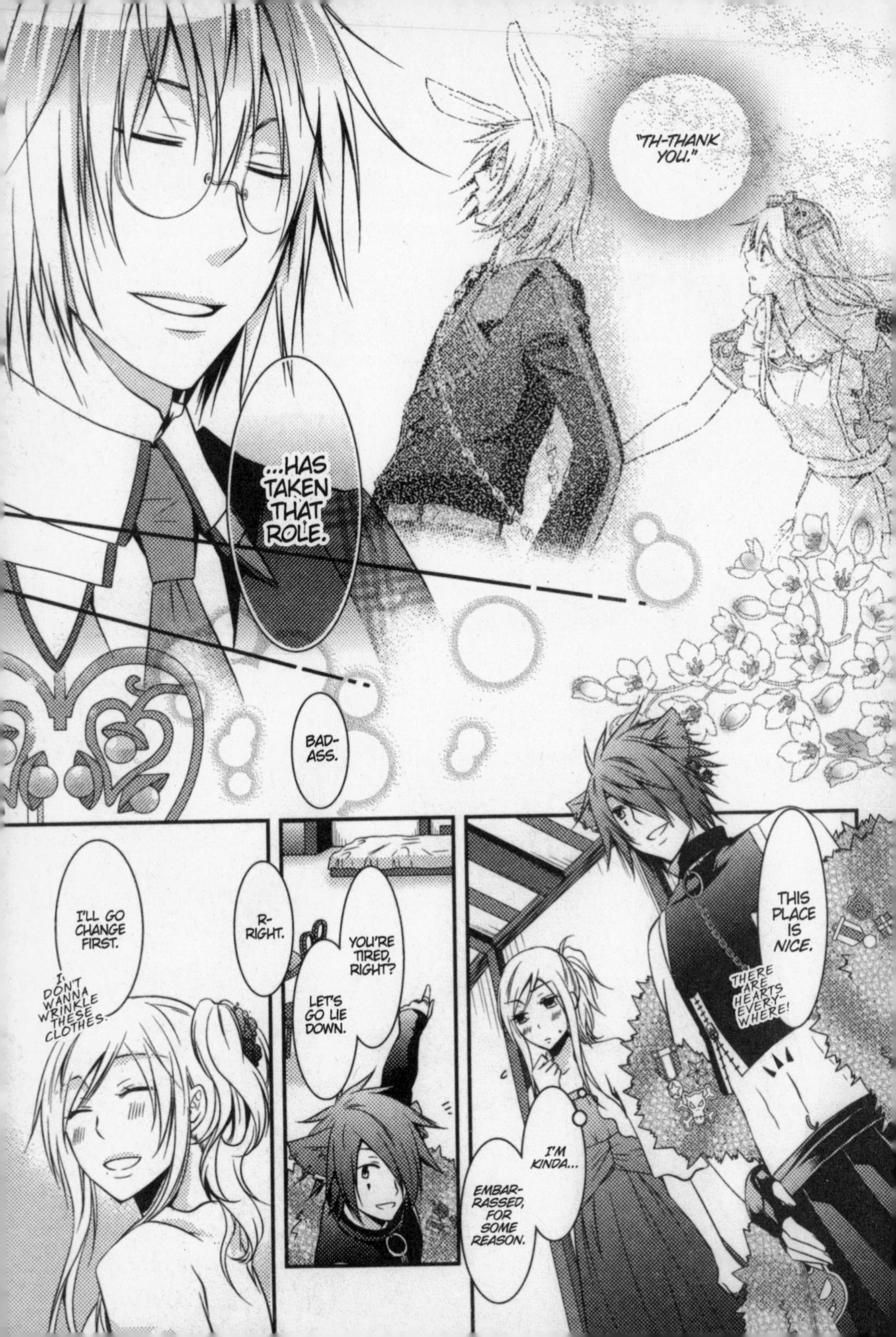
"TH-THANK YOU."
...HAS TAKEN THAT ROLE.
BAD-ASS.
THIS PLACE IS NICE.
THERE ARE HEARTS EVERY-WHERE!
I'M KINDA...
EMBAR-RASSED, FOR SOME REASON.
YOU'RE TIRED, RIGHT?
LET'S GO LIE DOWN.
R-RIGHT.
I'LL GO CHANGE FIRST.
I DON'T WANNA WRINKLE THESE CLOTHES.

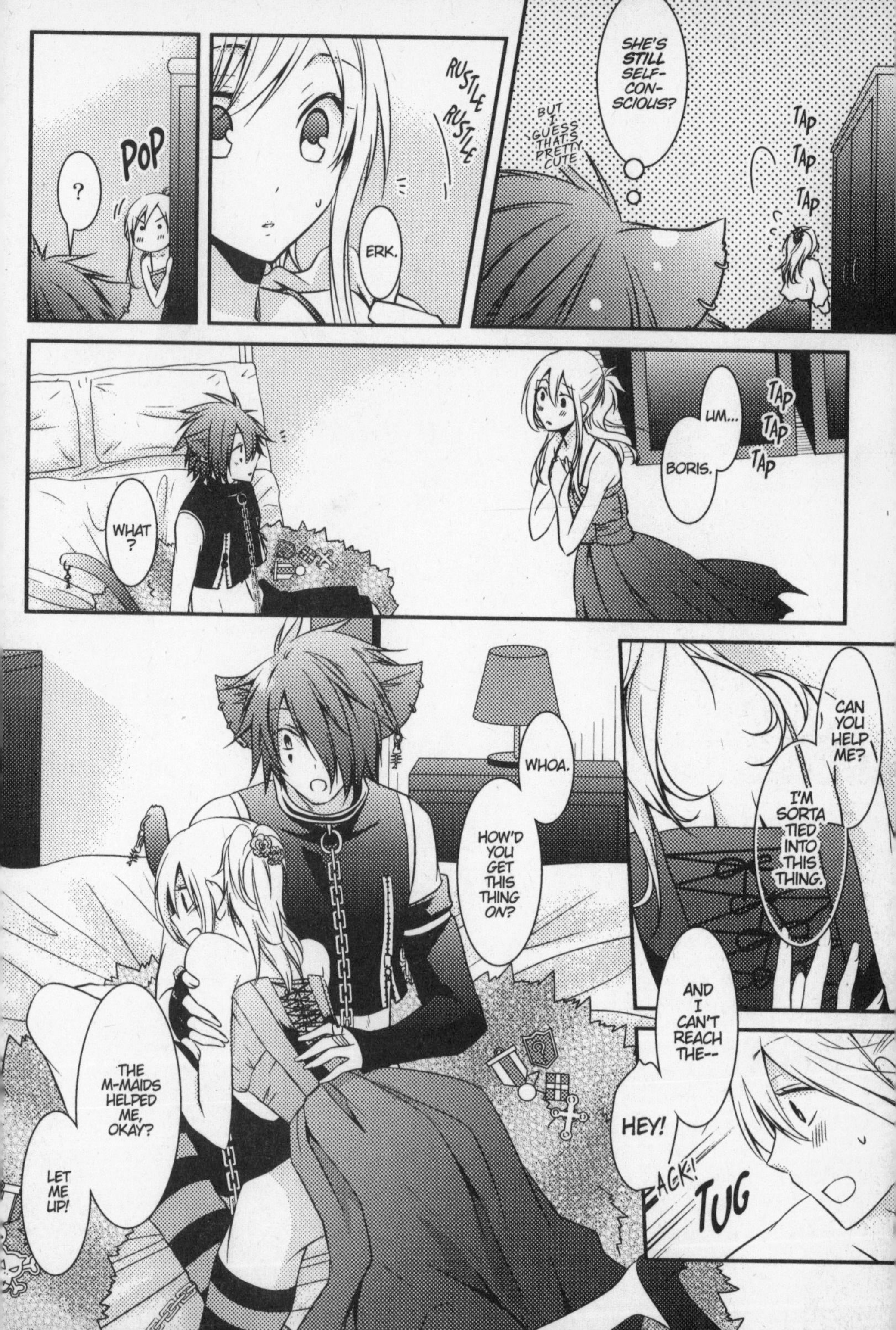
TAP TAP TAP
SHE'S STILL SELF-CONSCIOUS?
BUT I GUESS THAT'S PRETTY CUTE
RUSTLE RUSTLE
ERK.
POP
?
TAP TAP TAP
UM...
BORIS.
WHAT?
CAN YOU HELP ME?
I'M SORTA TIED INTO THIS THING.
AND I CAN'T REACH THE--
HEY!
ACK!
TUG
WHOA.
HOW'D YOU GET THIS THING ON?
THE M-MAIDS HELPED ME, OKAY?
LET ME UP!

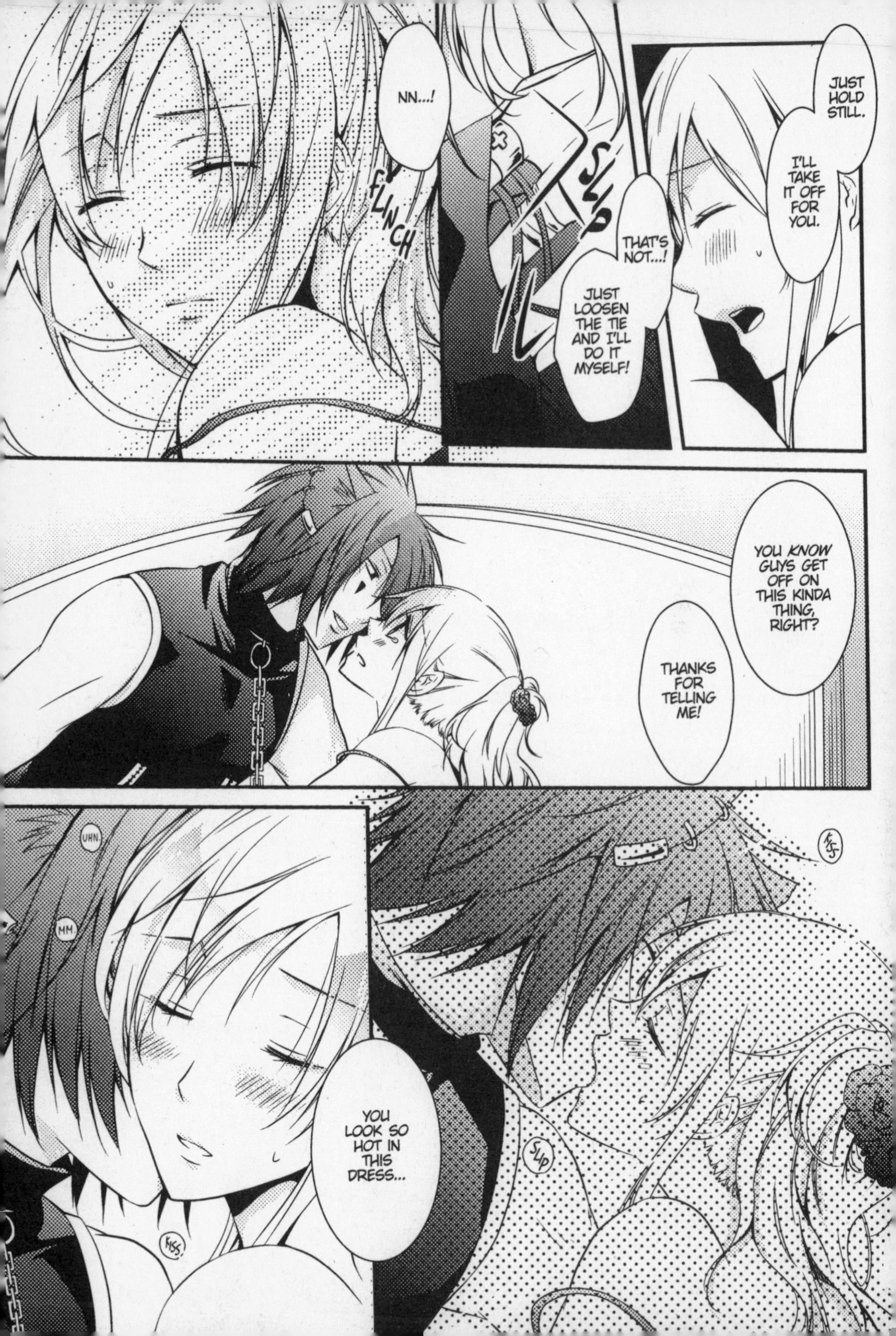
JUST HOLD STILL.
I'LL TAKE IT OFF FOR YOU.
SLIP
THAT'S NOT...!
JUST LOOSEN THE TIE AND I'LL DO IT MYSELF!
NN...!
FLINCH
YOU KNOW GUYS GET OFF ON THIS KINDA THING, RIGHT?
THANKS FOR TELLING ME!
KISS
SLIP
UHN.
MM.
YOU LOOK SO HOT IN THIS DRESS...
KISS

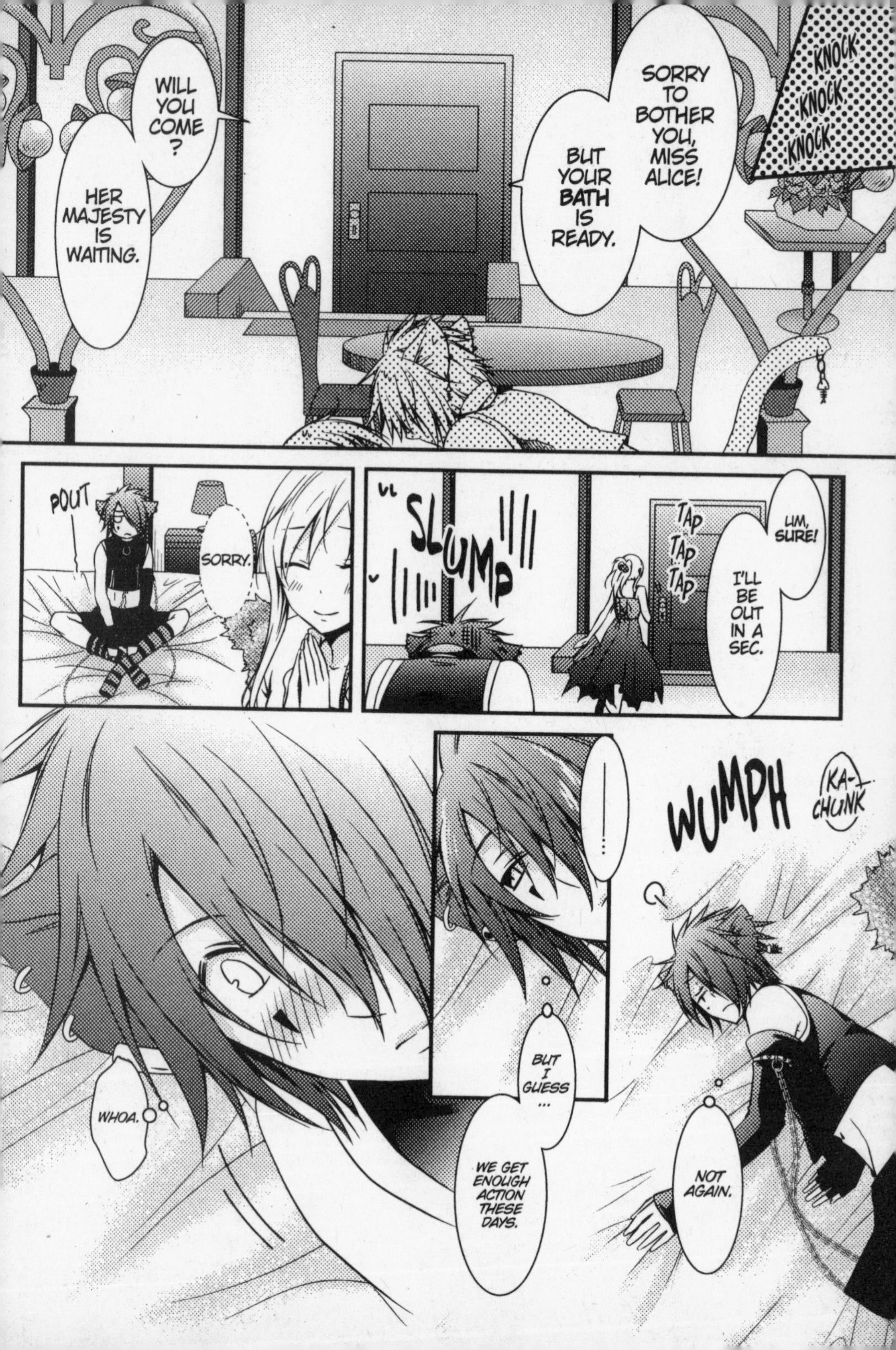
KNOCK KNOCK KNOCK
SORRY TO BOTHER YOU, MISS ALICE!
BUT YOUR BATH IS READY.
WILL YOU COME?
HER MAJESTY IS WAITING.
UM, SURE!
I'LL BE OUT IN A SEC.
TAP TAP TAP
SLUMP
SORRY.
POUT
KA-CHUNK
WUMPH
NOT AGAIN.
...
BUT I GUESS...
WE GET ENOUGH ACTION THESE DAYS.
WHOA.

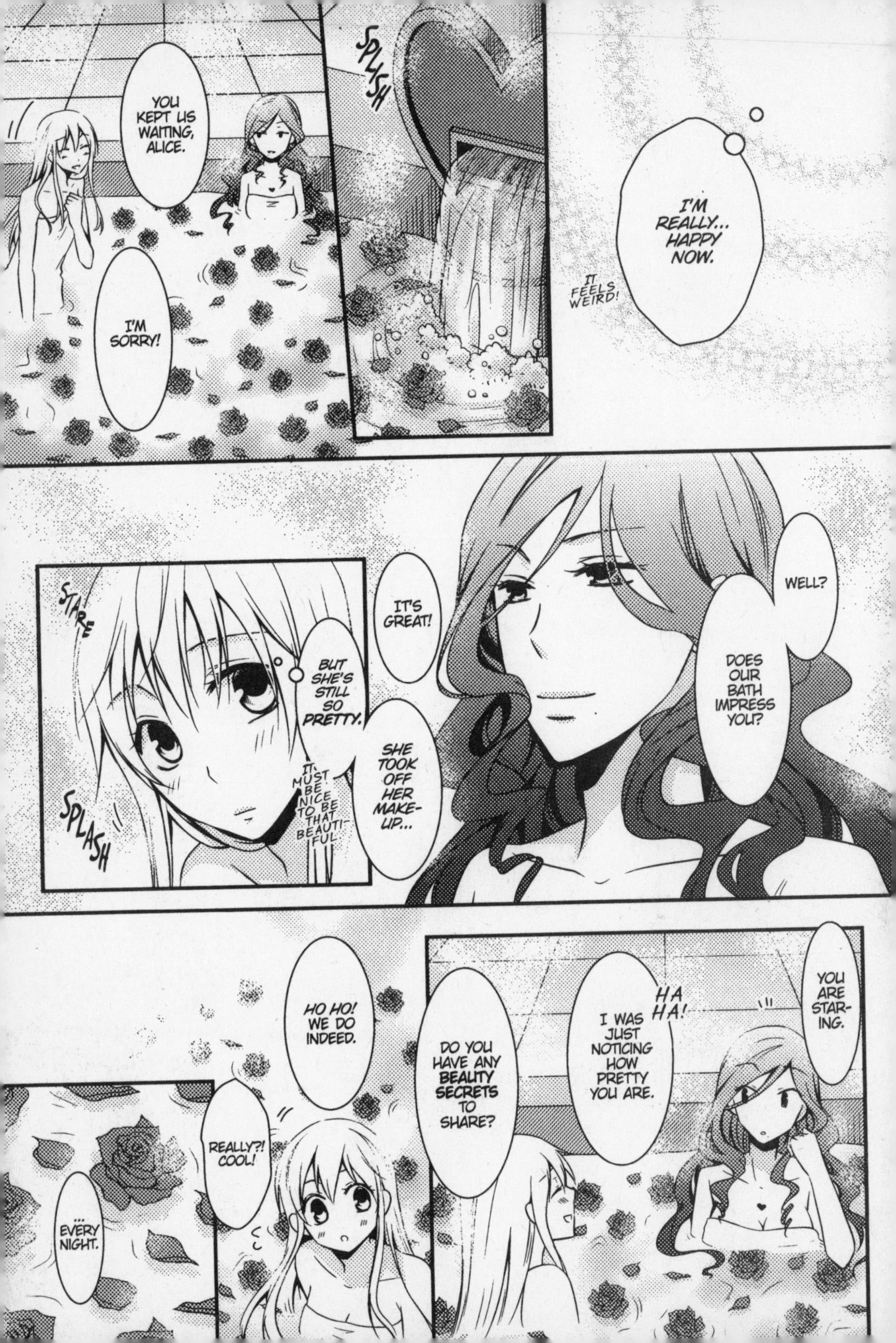
I'M REALLY... HAPPY NOW.
IT FEELS WEIRD!
SPLASH
YOU KEPT US WAITING, ALICE.
I'M SORRY!
WELL?
DOES OUR BATH IMPRESS YOU?
IT'S GREAT!
SHE TOOK OFF HER MAKE-UP...
BUT SHE'S STILL SO PRETTY.
IT MUST BE NICE TO BE THAT BEAUTIFUL
STARE
SPLASH
YOU ARE STARING.
HA HA!
I WAS JUST NOTICING HOW PRETTY YOU ARE.
DO YOU HAVE ANY BEAUTY SECRETS TO SHARE?
HO HO! WE DO INDEED.
REALLY?! COOL!
... EVERY NIGHT.

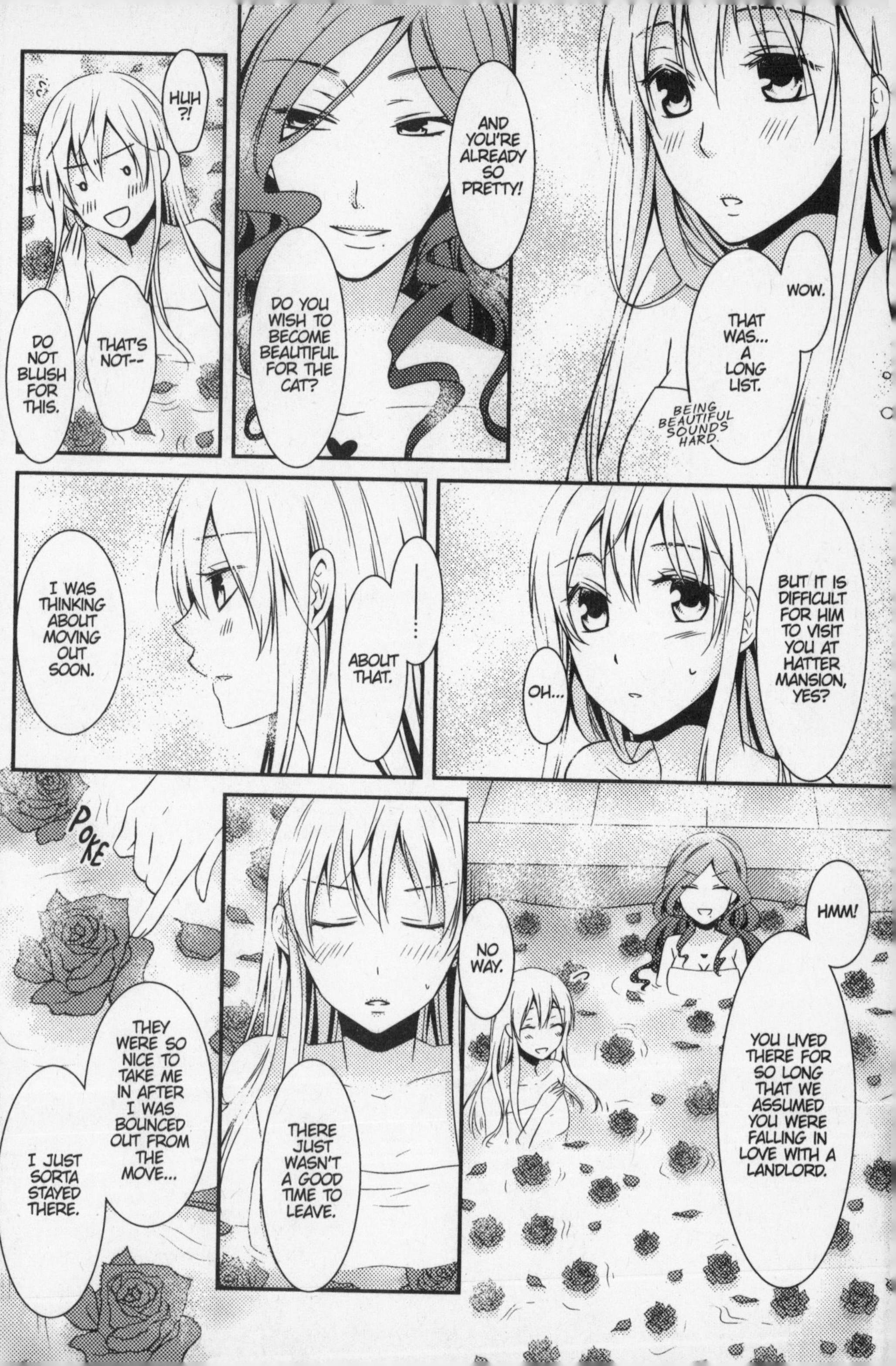
WOW.
THAT WAS... A LONG LIST.
BEING BEAUTIFUL SOUNDS HARD.
AND YOU'RE ALREADY SO PRETTY!
DO YOU WISH TO BECOME BEAUTIFUL FOR THE CAT?
HUH?!
THAT'S NOT--
DO NOT BLUSH FOR THIS.
BUT IT IS DIFFICULT FOR HIM TO VISIT YOU AT HATTER MANSION, YES?
OH...
...!
ABOUT THAT.
I WAS THINKING ABOUT MOVING OUT SOON.
HMM!
YOU LIVED THERE FOR SO LONG THAT WE ASSUMED YOU WERE FALLING IN LOVE WITH A LANDLORD.
NO WAY.
THERE JUST WASN'T A GOOD TIME TO LEAVE.
POKE
THEY WERE SO NICE TO TAKE ME IN AFTER I WAS BOUNCED OUT FROM THE MOVE...
I JUST SORTA STAYED THERE.

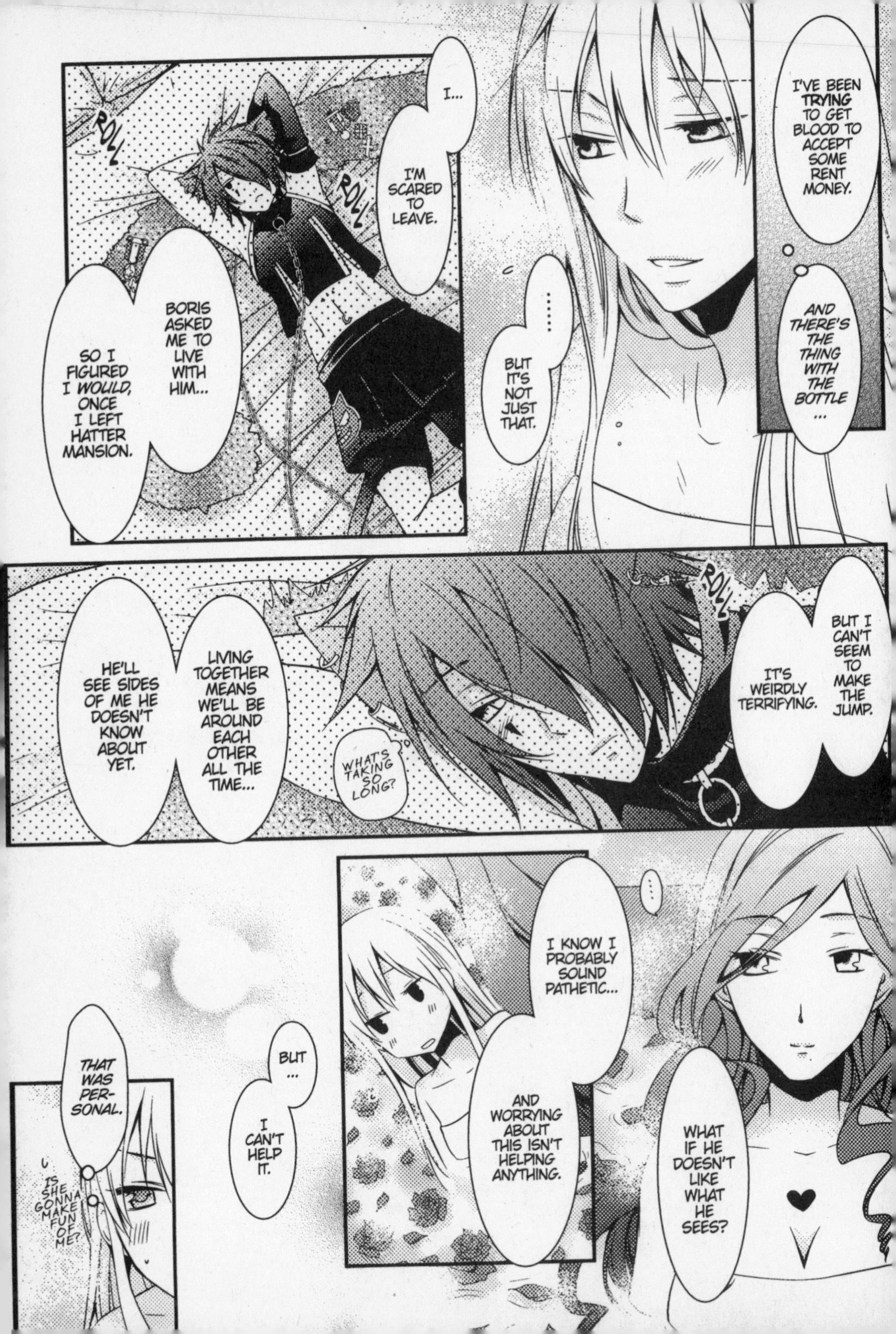
I'VE BEEN TRYING TO GET BLOOD TO ACCEPT SOME RENT MONEY.
AND THERE'S THE THING WITH THE BOTTLE...
......
BUT IT'S NOT JUST THAT.
I...
I'M SCARED TO LEAVE.
ROLL
ROLL
BORIS ASKED ME TO LIVE WITH HIM...
SO I FIGURED I *WOULD*, ONCE I LEFT HATTER MANSION.
ROLL
BUT I CAN'T SEEM TO MAKE THE JUMP.
IT'S WEIRDLY TERRIFYING.
WHAT'S TAKING SO LONG?
LIVING TOGETHER MEANS WE'LL BE AROUND EACH OTHER ALL THE TIME...
HE'LL SEE SIDES OF ME HE DOESN'T KNOW ABOUT YET.
WHAT IF HE DOESN'T LIKE WHAT HE SEES?
...
I KNOW I PROBABLY SOUND PATHETIC...
AND WORRYING ABOUT THIS ISN'T HELPING ANYTHING.
BUT ...
I CAN'T HELP IT.
THAT WAS PER-SONAL.
IS SHE GONNA MAKE FUN OF ME?

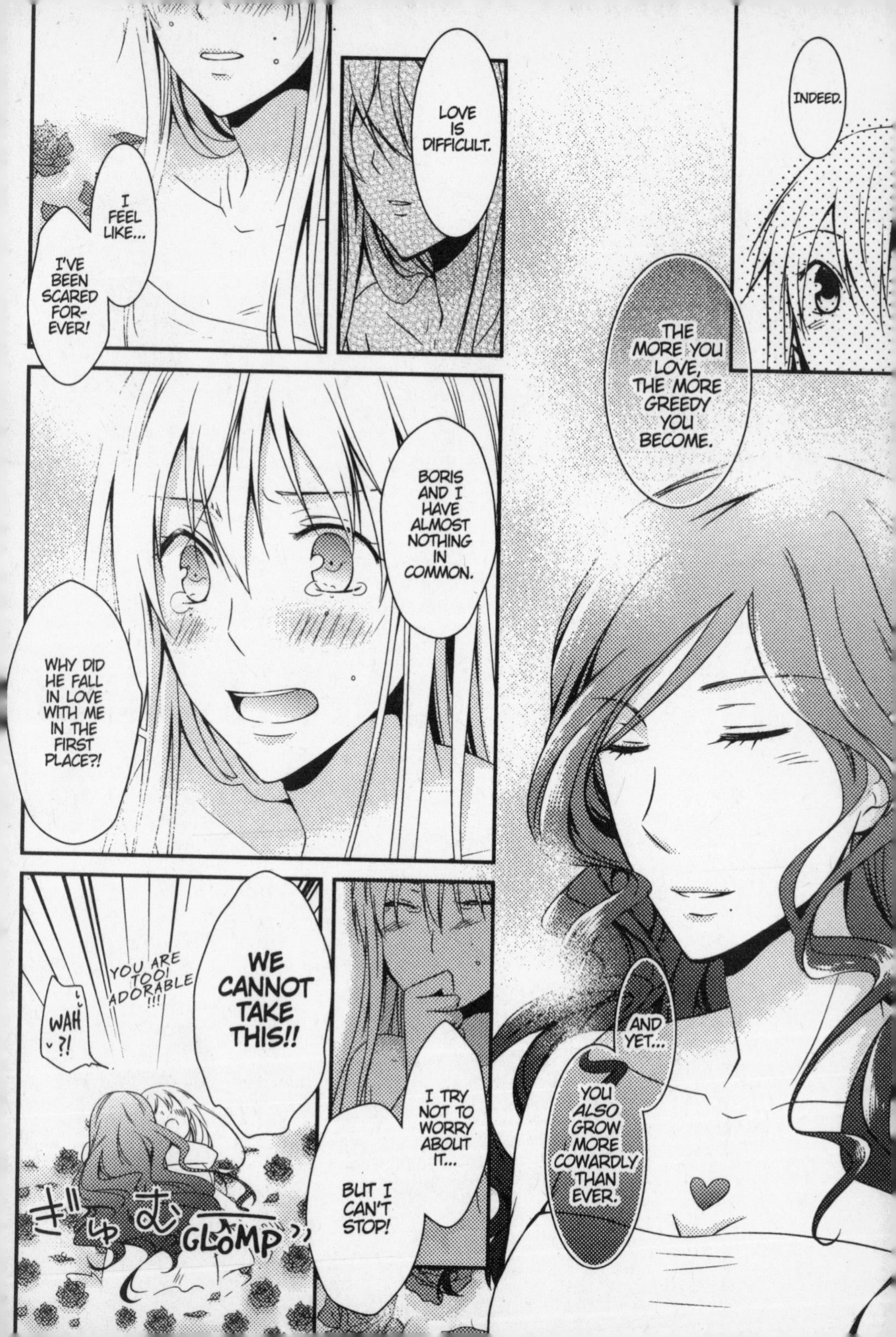
INDEED.
THE MORE YOU LOVE, THE MORE GREEDY YOU BECOME.
AND YET...
YOU ALSO GROW MORE COWARDLY THAN EVER.
LOVE IS DIFFICULT.
I FEEL LIKE...
I'VE BEEN SCARED FOR-EVER!
BORIS AND I HAVE ALMOST NOTHING IN COMMON.
WHY DID HE FALL IN LOVE WITH ME IN THE FIRST PLACE?!
I TRY NOT TO WORRY ABOUT IT...
BUT I CAN'T STOP!
WE CANNOT TAKE THIS!!
YOU ARE TOO! ADORABLE!!!
WAH?!
ぎゅむ
GLOMP

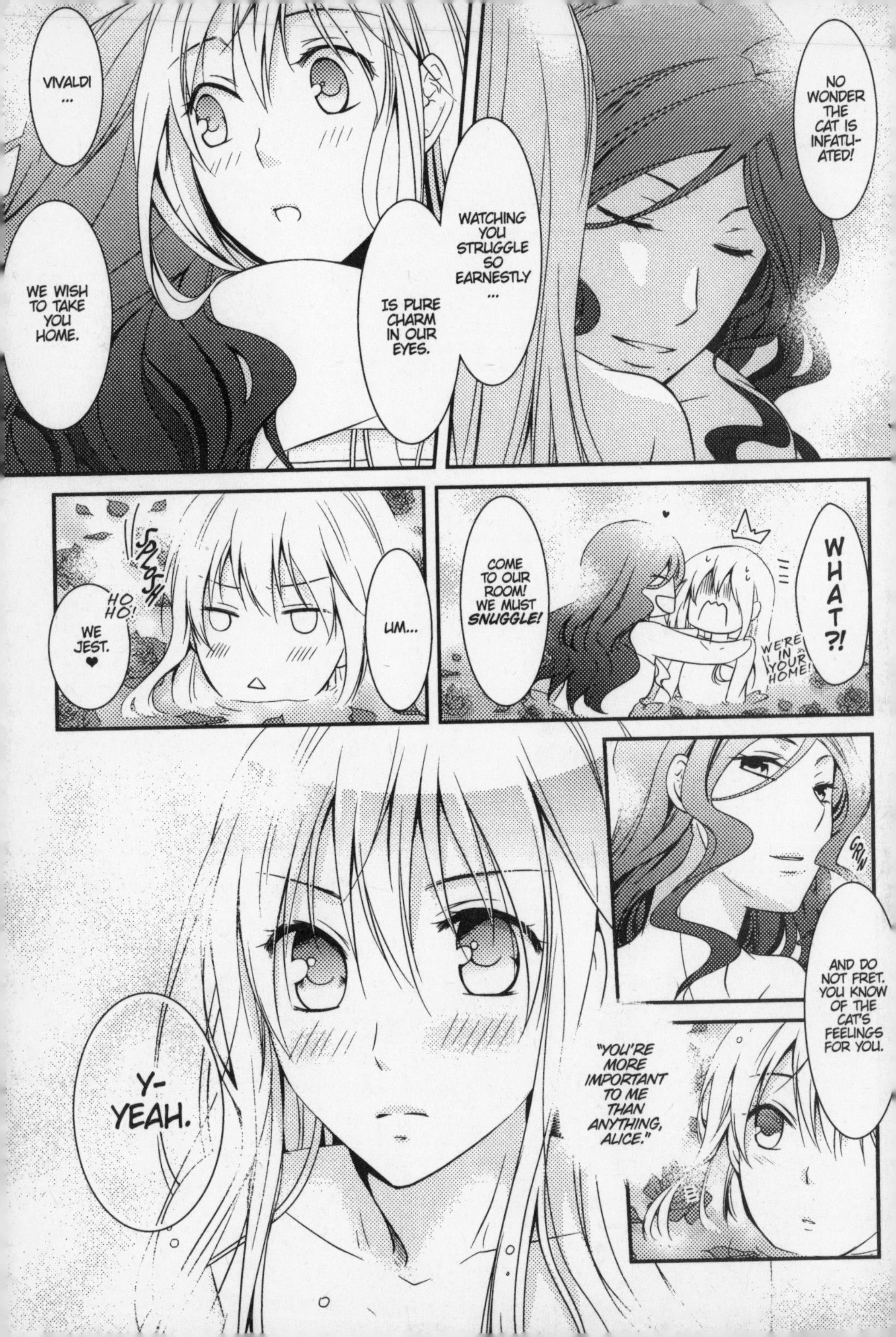
NO WONDER THE CAT IS INFATUATED!
WATCHING YOU STRUGGLE SO EARNESTLY ...
IS PURE CHARM IN OUR EYES.
VIVALDI ...
WE WISH TO TAKE YOU HOME.
WHAT?!
WE'RE IN YOUR HOME!
COME TO OUR ROOM! WE MUST SNUGGLE!
UM...
SPLOSH
HO HO! WE JEST. ♥
GRIN
AND DO NOT FRET. YOU KNOW OF THE CAT'S FEELINGS FOR YOU.
"YOU'RE MORE IMPORTANT TO ME THAN ANYTHING, ALICE."
Y-YEAH.

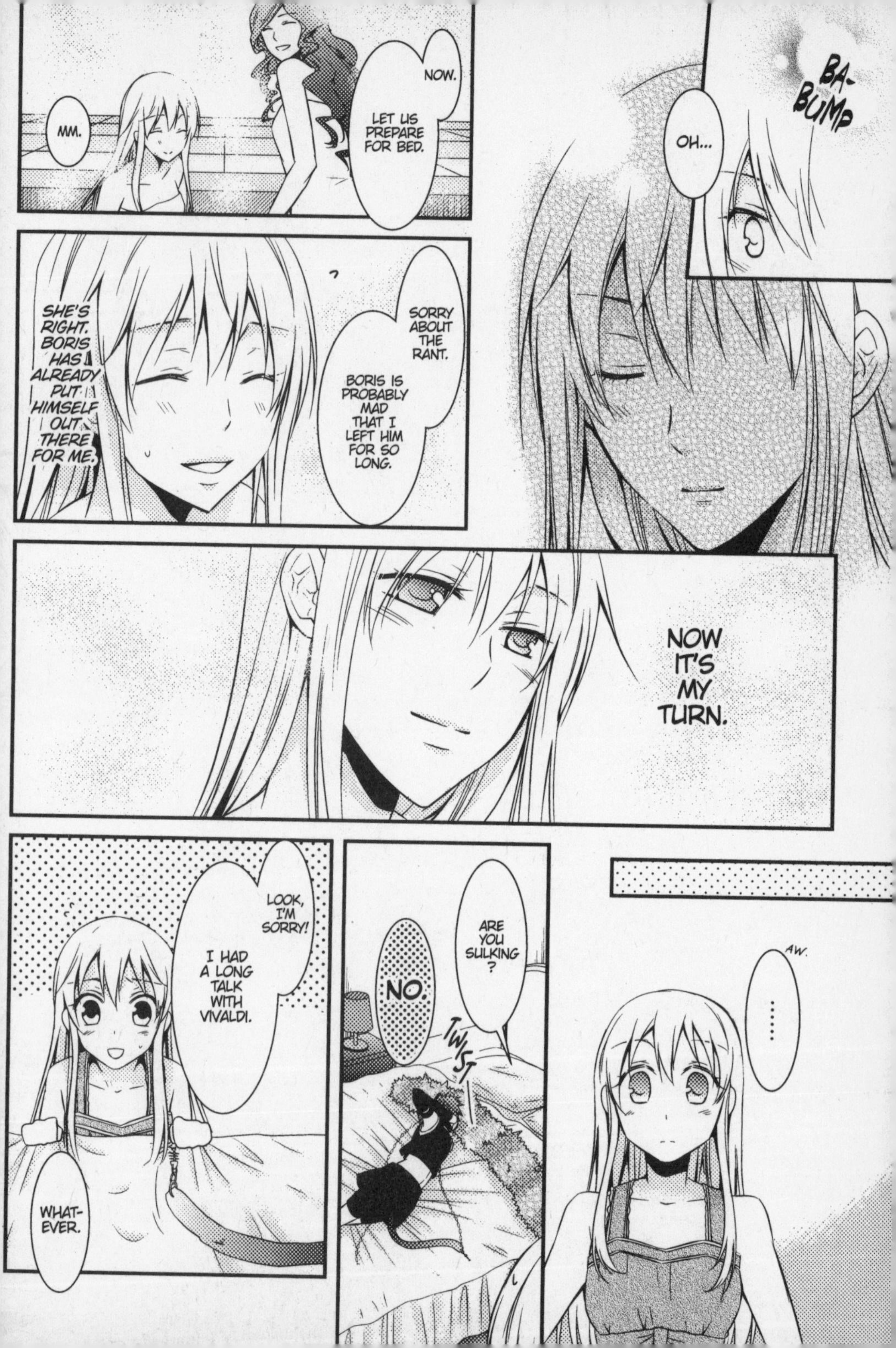
BA-BUMP
OH...
NOW.
LET US PREPARE FOR BED.
MM.
SORRY ABOUT THE RANT.
BORIS IS PROBABLY MAD THAT I LEFT HIM FOR SO LONG.
SHE'S RIGHT. BORIS HAS ALREADY PUT HIMSELF OUT THERE FOR ME.
NOW IT'S MY TURN.
AW.
......
ARE YOU SULKING?
NO.
TWIST
LOOK, I'M SORRY!
I HAD A LONG TALK WITH VIVALDI.
WHAT-EVER.

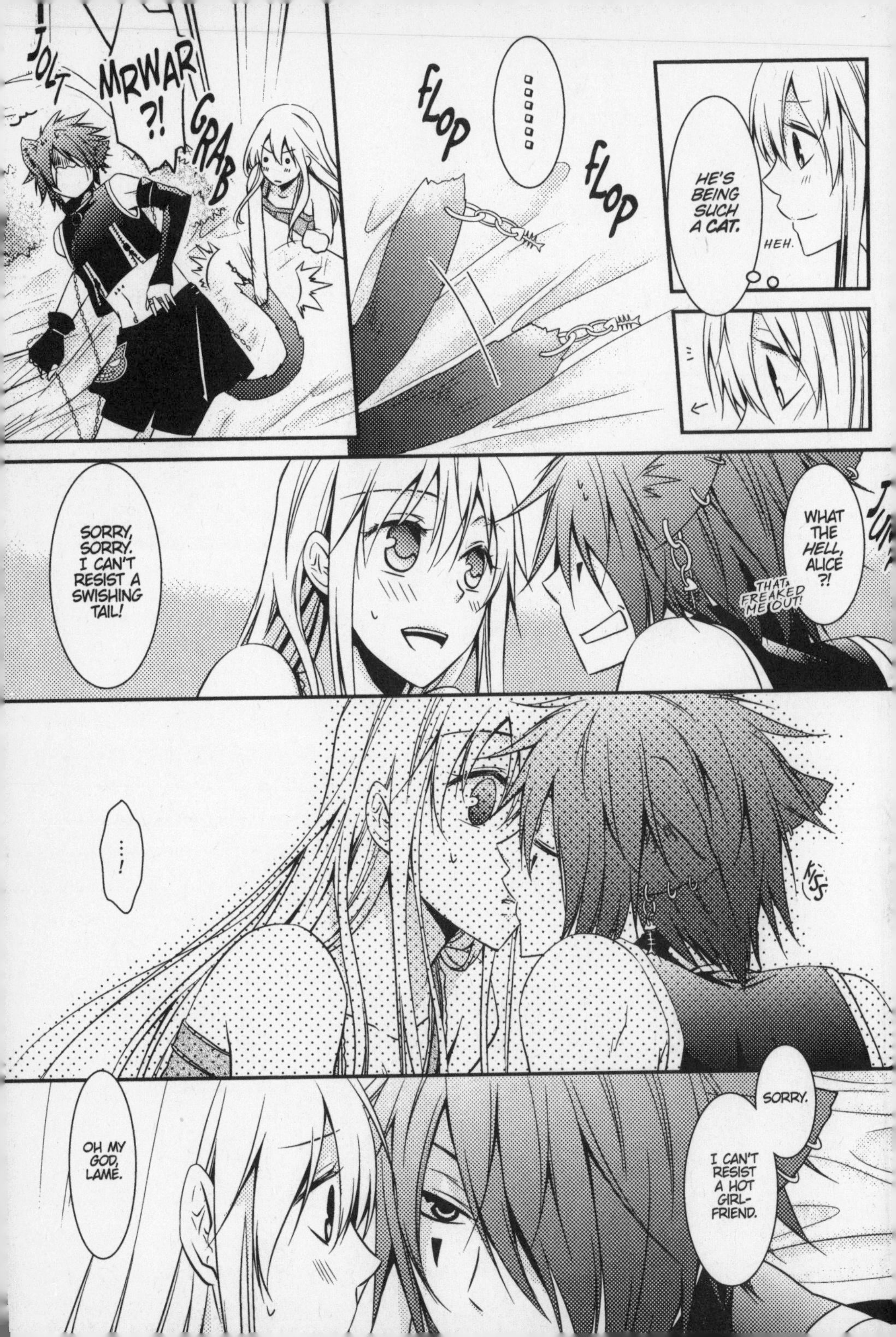
HE'S BEING SUCH A CAT.
HEH.
FLOP
FLOP
......
JOLT
MRWAR ?!
GRAB
WHAT THE HELL, ALICE ?!
THAT FREAKED ME OUT!
SORRY, SORRY. I CAN'T RESIST A SWISHING TAIL!
KISS
...!
SORRY.
I CAN'T RESIST A HOT GIRL-FRIEND.
OH MY GOD, LAME.

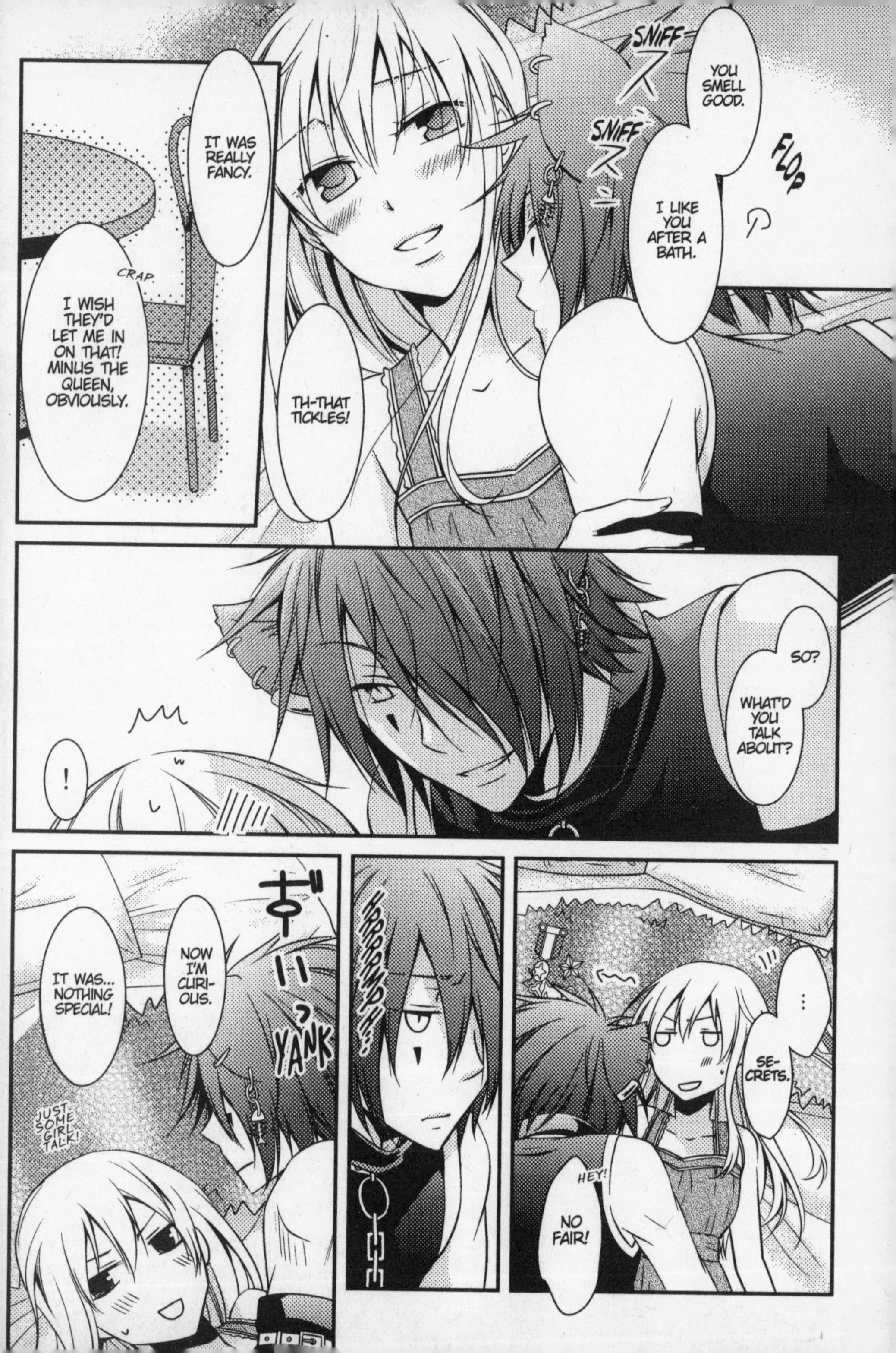
SNIFF
YOU SMELL GOOD.
SNIFF
FLOP
I LIKE YOU AFTER A BATH.
TH-THAT TICKLES!
IT WAS REALLY FANCY.
CRAP
I WISH THEY'D LET ME IN ON THAT! MINUS THE QUEEN, OBVIOUSLY.
SO? WHAT'D YOU TALK ABOUT?
!
...
SE-CRETS.
HEY!
NO FAIR!
HRRRMPH!!
NOW I'M CURI-OUS.
YANK
IT WAS... NOTHING SPECIAL!
JUST SOME GIRL TALK!

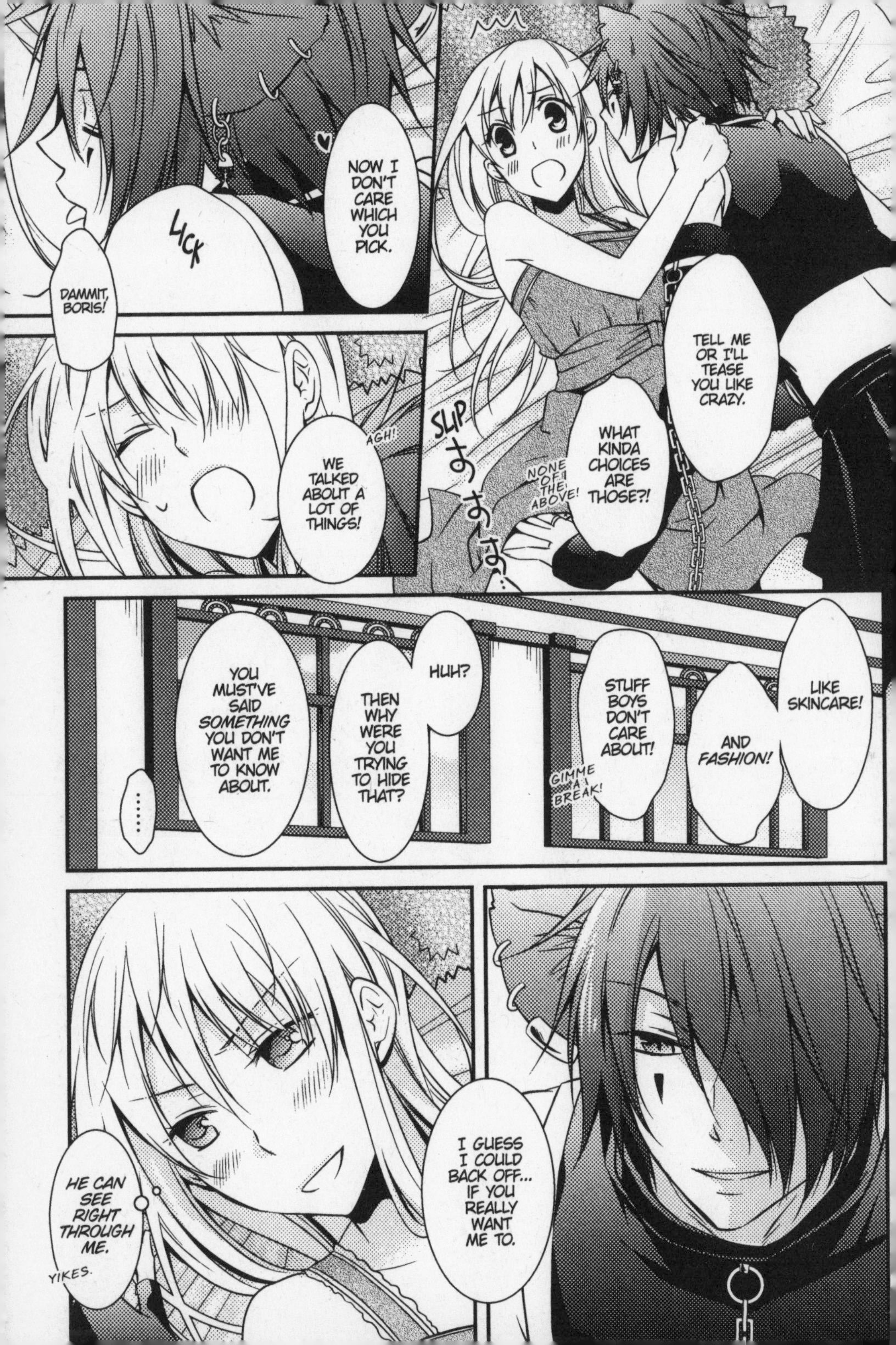
TELL ME OR I'LL TEASE YOU LIKE CRAZY.
WHAT KINDA CHOICES ARE THOSE?!
NONE OF THE ABOVE!
SLIP
すすす…
NOW I DON'T CARE WHICH YOU PICK.
LICK
DAMMIT, BORIS!
AGH!
WE TALKED ABOUT A LOT OF THINGS!
LIKE SKINCARE!
AND FASHION!
STUFF BOYS DON'T CARE ABOUT!
GIMME A BREAK!
HUH?
THEN WHY WERE YOU TRYING TO HIDE THAT?
YOU MUST'VE SAID SOMETHING YOU DON'T WANT ME TO KNOW ABOUT.
......
I GUESS I COULD BACK OFF... IF YOU REALLY WANT ME TO.
HE CAN SEE RIGHT THROUGH ME.
YIKES.

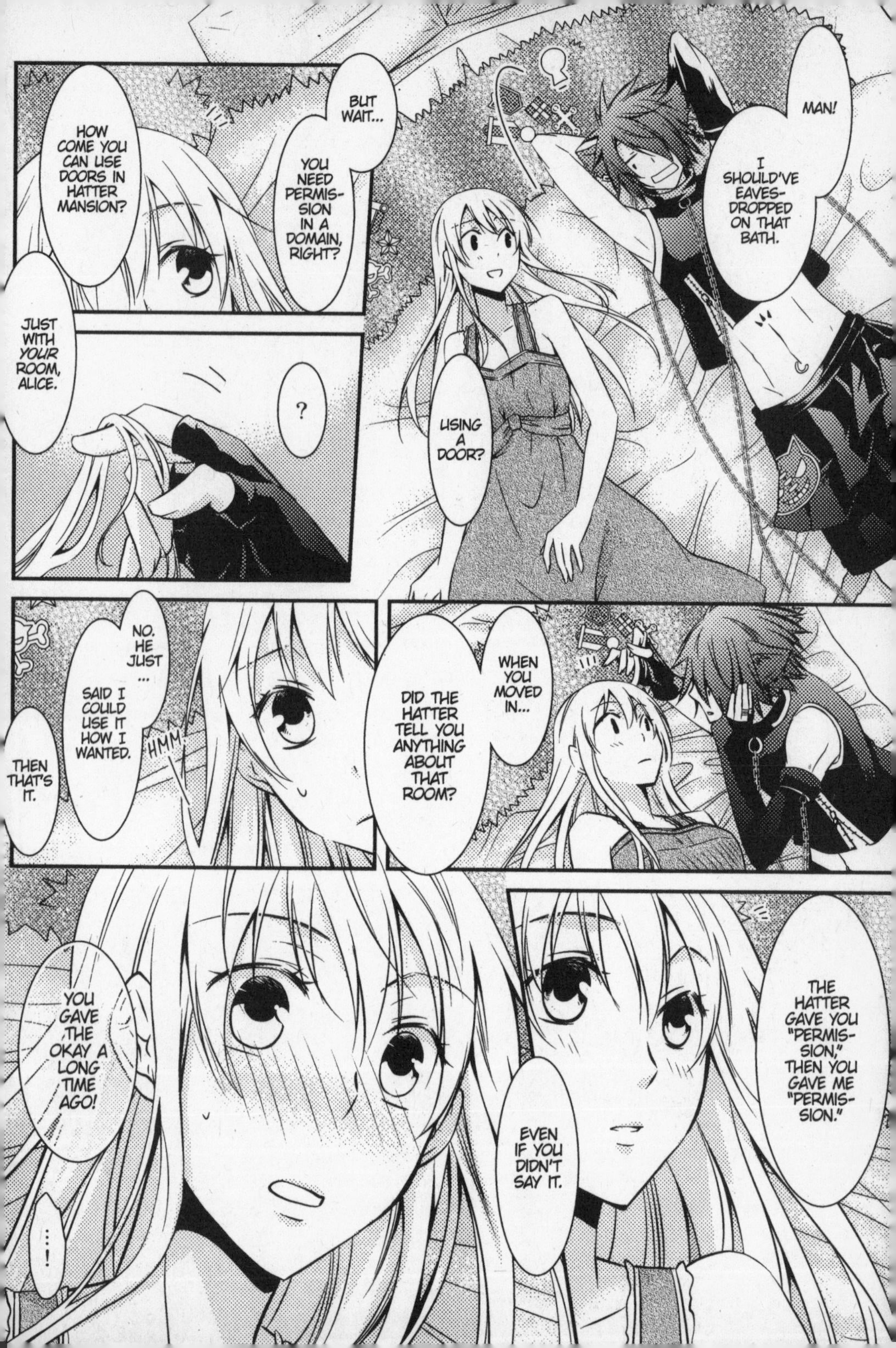
MAN!
I SHOULD'VE EAVES-DROPPED ON THAT BATH.
BUT WAIT...
YOU NEED PERMIS-SION IN A DOMAIN, RIGHT?
USING A DOOR?
HOW COME YOU CAN USE DOORS IN HATTER MANSION?
?
JUST WITH *YOUR* ROOM, ALICE.
WHEN YOU MOVED IN...
DID THE HATTER TELL YOU ANYTHING ABOUT THAT ROOM?
NO. HE JUST ...
SAID I COULD USE IT HOW I WANTED.
HMM
THEN THAT'S IT.
THE HATTER GAVE YOU "PERMIS-SION," THEN YOU GAVE ME "PERMIS-SION."
EVEN IF YOU DIDN'T SAY IT.
YOU GAVE THE OKAY A LONG TIME AGO!
...!

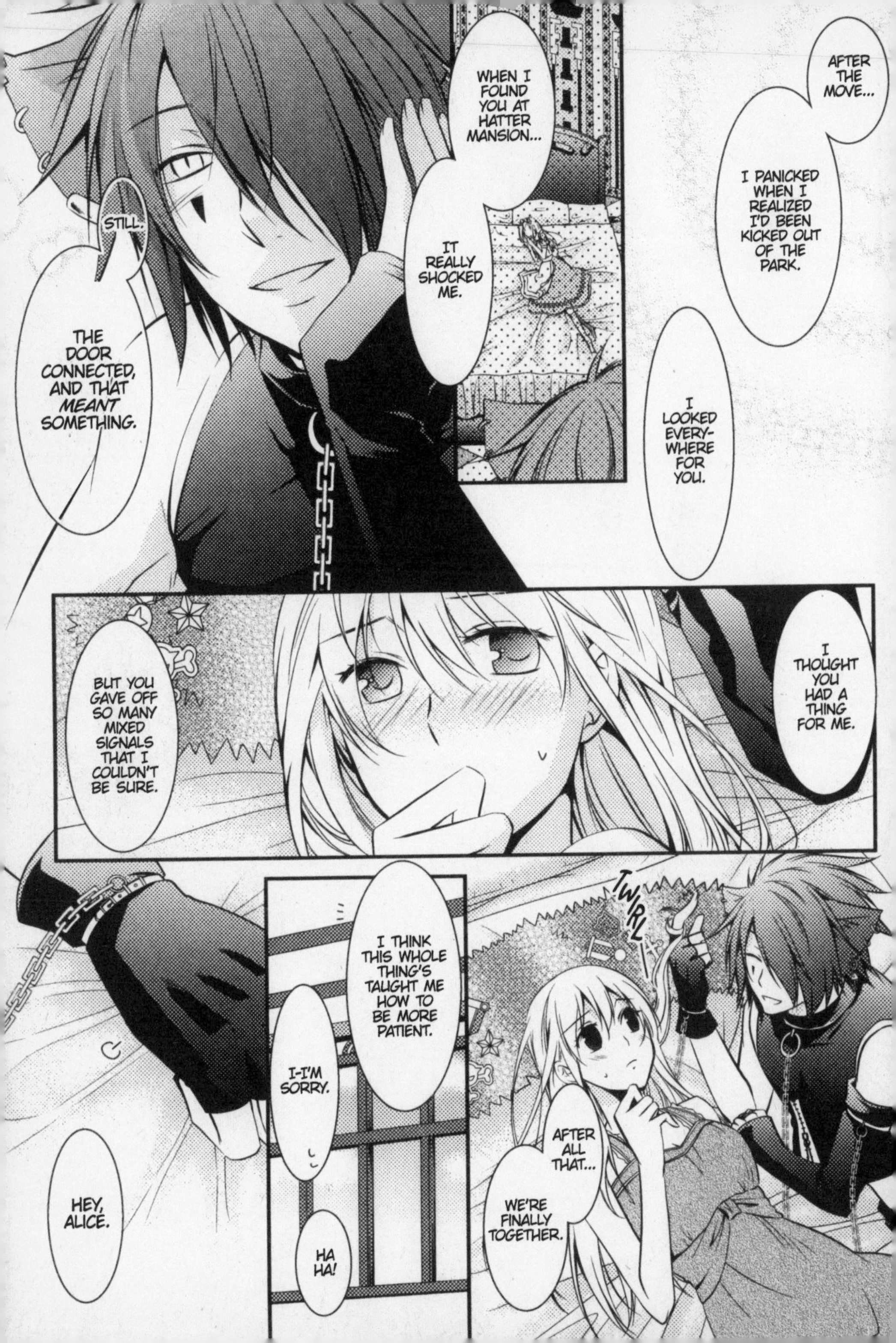
AFTER THE MOVE...
I PANICKED WHEN I REALIZED I'D BEEN KICKED OUT OF THE PARK.
I LOOKED EVERYWHERE FOR YOU.
WHEN I FOUND YOU AT HATTER MANSION...
IT REALLY SHOCKED ME.
STILL.
THE DOOR CONNECTED, AND THAT *MEANT* SOMETHING.
I THOUGHT YOU HAD A THING FOR ME.
BUT YOU GAVE OFF SO MANY MIXED SIGNALS THAT I COULDN'T BE SURE.
TWIRL
AFTER ALL THAT...
WE'RE FINALLY TOGETHER.
I THINK THIS WHOLE THING'S TAUGHT ME HOW TO BE MORE PATIENT.
I-I'M SORRY.
HA HA!
HEY, ALICE.

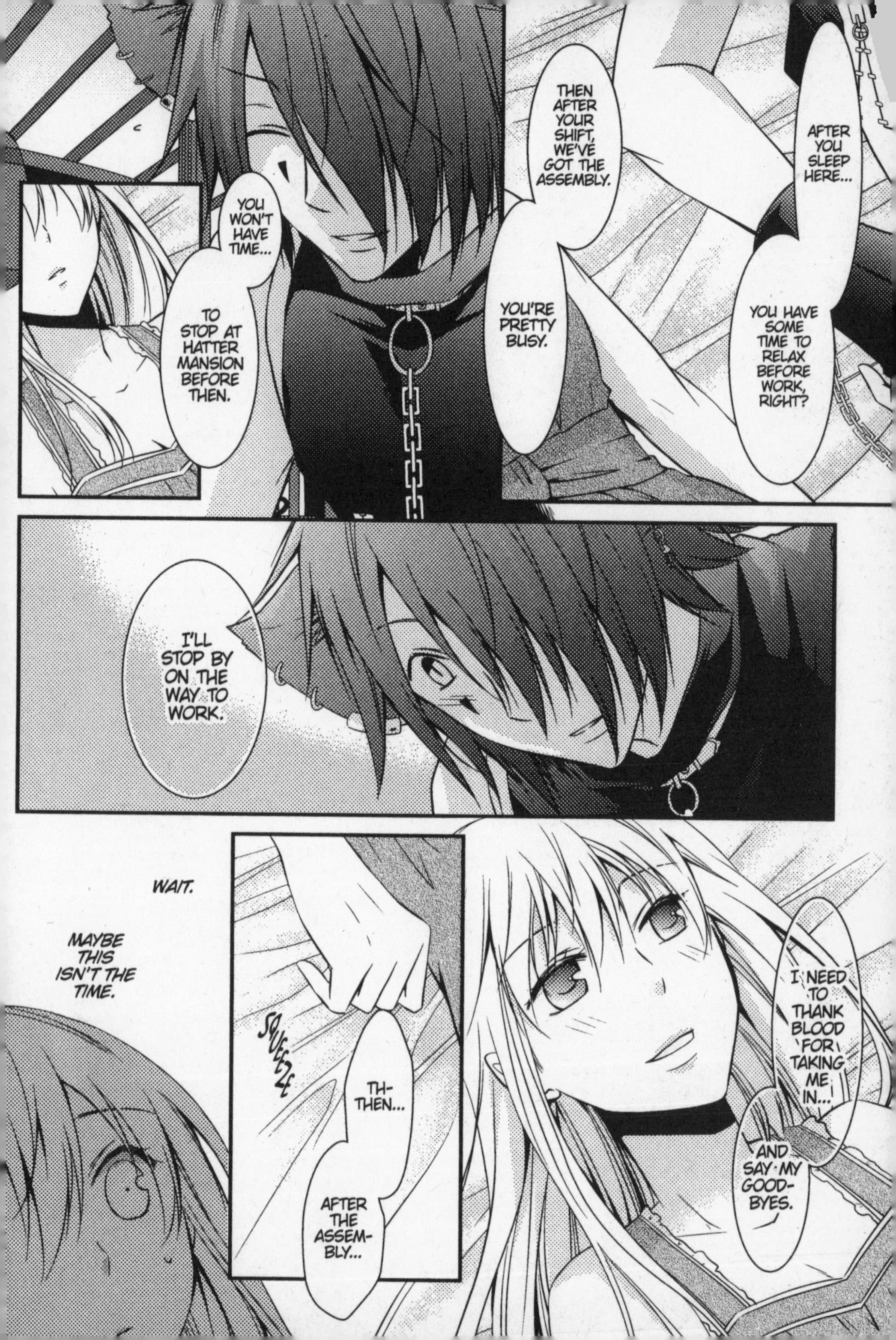
AFTER YOU SLEEP HERE...
YOU HAVE SOME TIME TO RELAX BEFORE WORK, RIGHT?
THEN AFTER YOUR SHIFT, WE'VE GOT THE ASSEMBLY.
YOU'RE PRETTY BUSY.
YOU WON'T HAVE TIME...
TO STOP AT HATTER MANSION BEFORE THEN.
I'LL STOP BY ON THE WAY TO WORK.
I NEED TO THANK BLOOD FOR TAKING ME IN...
AND SAY MY GOOD-BYES.
SQUEEZE
TH-THEN...
AFTER THE ASSEM-BLY...
WAIT.
MAYBE THIS ISN'T THE TIME.

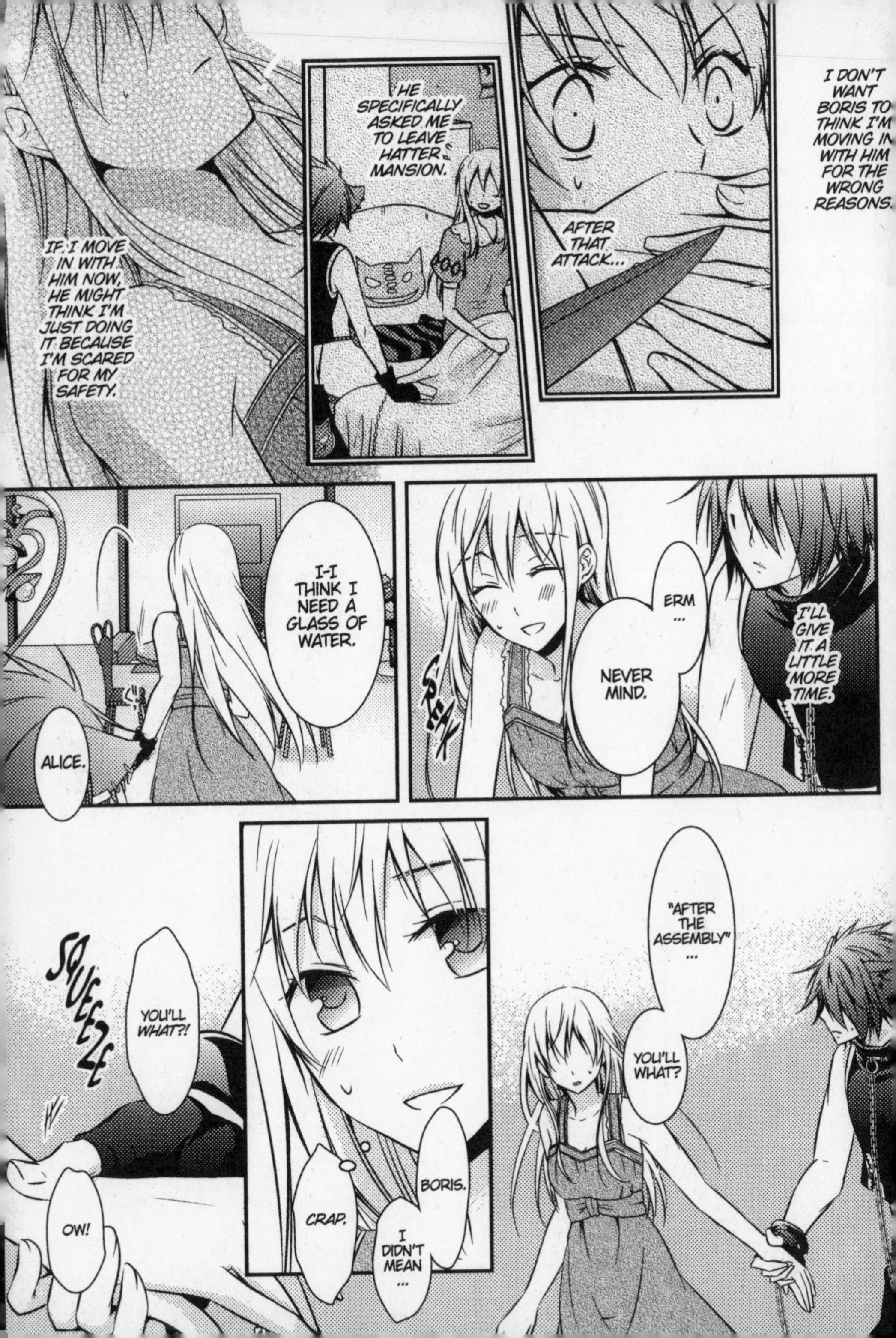
I DON'T WANT BORIS TO THINK I'M MOVING IN WITH HIM FOR THE WRONG REASONS.
AFTER THAT ATTACK...
HE SPECIFICALLY ASKED ME TO LEAVE HATTER MANSION.
IF I MOVE IN WITH HIM NOW, HE MIGHT THINK I'M JUST DOING IT BECAUSE I'M SCARED FOR MY SAFETY.
I'LL GIVE IT A LITTLE MORE TIME.
ERM ...
NEVER MIND.
CREAK
I-I THINK I NEED A GLASS OF WATER.
ALICE.
"AFTER THE ASSEMBLY" ...
YOU'LL WHAT?
BORIS.
I DIDN'T MEAN ...
CRAP.
YOU'LL WHAT?!
SQUEEZE
OW!

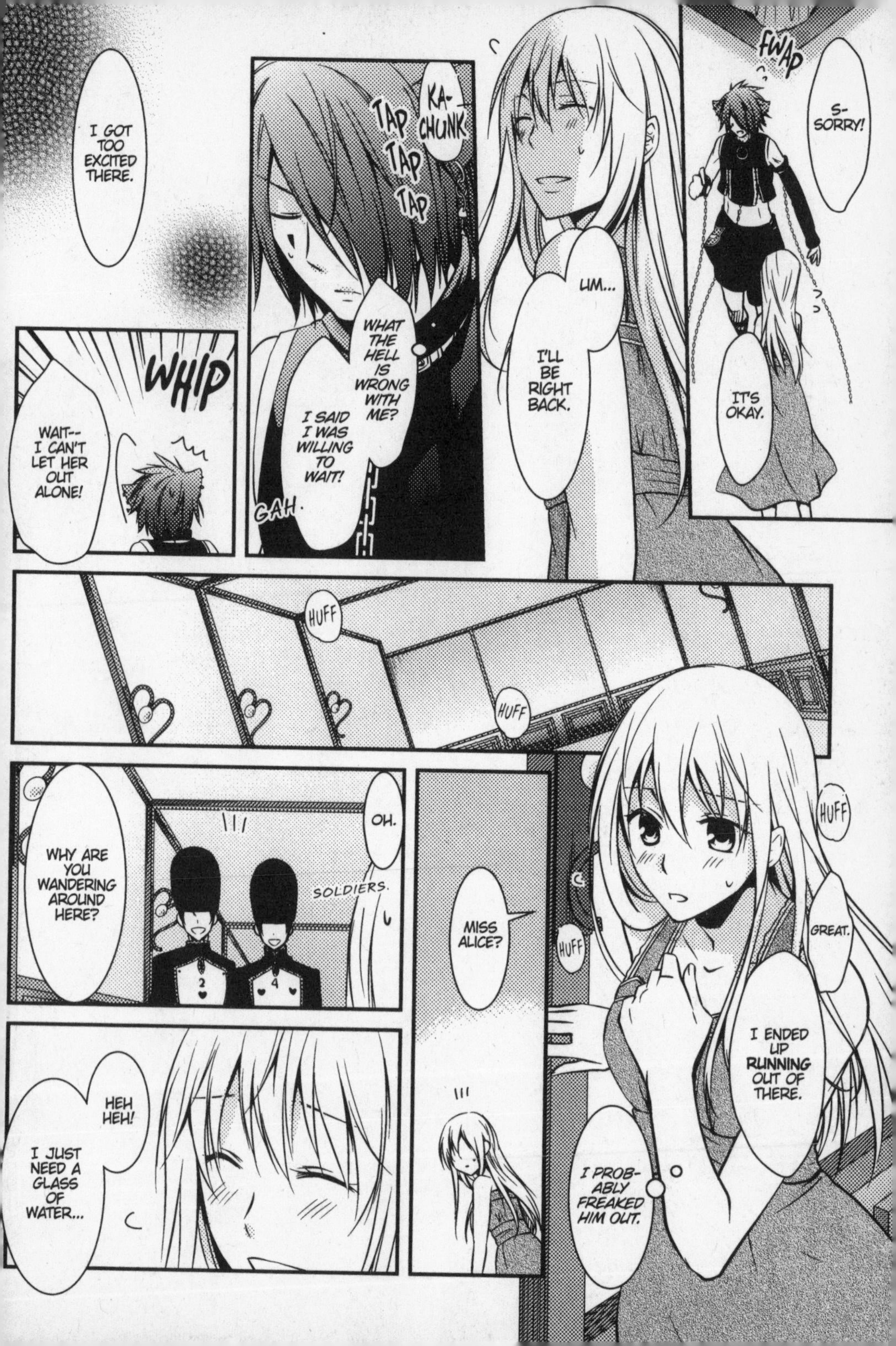
FWAP
S-SORRY!
IT'S OKAY.
UM...
I'LL BE RIGHT BACK.
KA-CHUNK
TAP TAP TAP
WHAT THE HELL IS WRONG WITH ME?
I SAID I WAS WILLING TO WAIT!
GAH.
I GOT TOO EXCITED THERE.
WHIP
WAIT-- I CAN'T LET HER OUT ALONE!
HUFF
HUFF
HUFF
GREAT.
I ENDED UP **RUNNING** OUT OF THERE.
I PROBABLY FREAKED HIM OUT.
HUFF
MISS ALICE?
OH.
SOLDIERS.
WHY ARE YOU WANDERING AROUND HERE?
HEH HEH!
I JUST NEED A GLASS OF WATER...

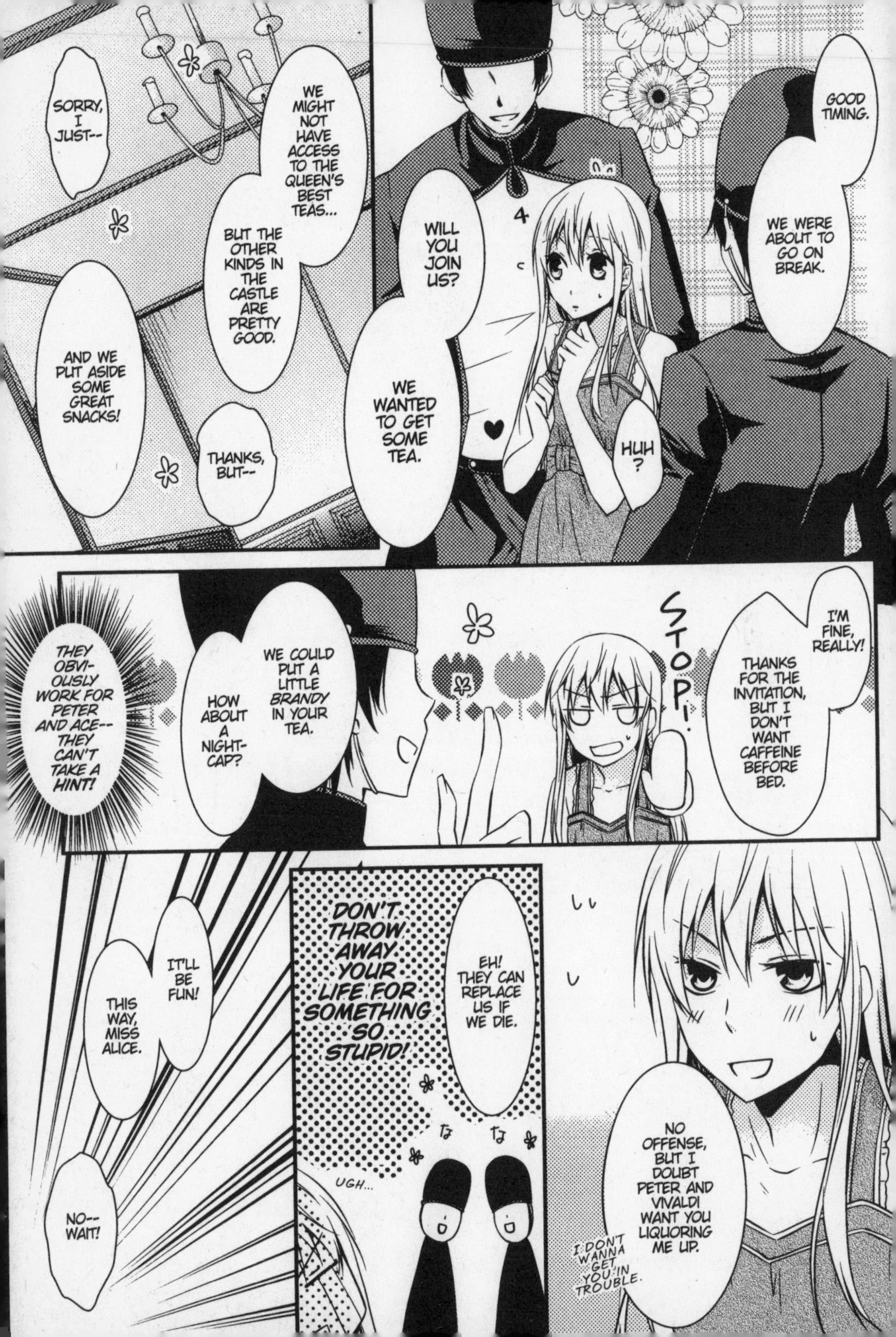
GOOD TIMING.
WE WERE ABOUT TO GO ON BREAK.
HUH?
WILL YOU JOIN US?
WE WANTED TO GET SOME TEA.
WE MIGHT NOT HAVE ACCESS TO THE QUEEN'S BEST TEAS...
BUT THE OTHER KINDS IN THE CASTLE ARE PRETTY GOOD.
SORRY, I JUST--
AND WE PUT ASIDE SOME GREAT SNACKS!
THANKS, BUT--
I'M FINE, REALLY!
STOP!
THANKS FOR THE INVITATION, BUT I DON'T WANT CAFFEINE BEFORE BED.
WE COULD PUT A LITTLE BRANDY IN YOUR TEA.
HOW ABOUT A NIGHT-CAP?
THEY OBVIOUSLY WORK FOR PETER AND ACE-- THEY CAN'T TAKE A HINT!
NO OFFENSE, BUT I DOUBT PETER AND VIVALDI WANT YOU LIQUORING ME UP.
I DON'T WANNA GET YOU IN TROUBLE.
EH! THEY CAN REPLACE US IF WE DIE.
DON'T THROW AWAY YOUR LIFE FOR SOMETHING SO STUPID!
UGH...
IT'LL BE FUN!
THIS WAY, MISS ALICE.
NO-- WAIT!

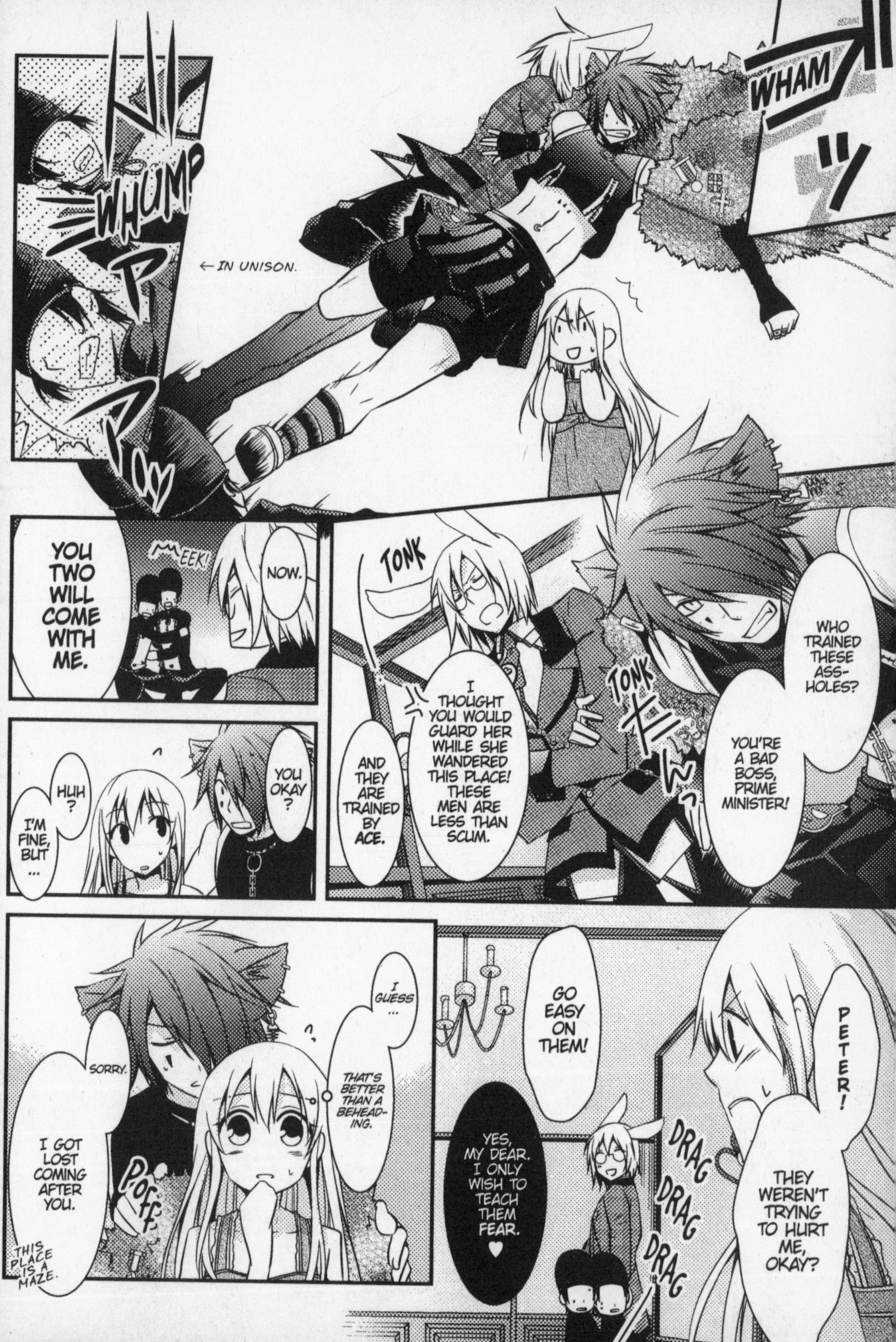
WHAM
WHUMP
← IN UNISON.
WHO TRAINED THESE ASS-HOLES?
YOU'RE A BAD BOSS, PRIME MINISTER!
TONK
I THOUGHT YOU WOULD GUARD HER WHILE SHE WANDERED THIS PLACE! THESE MEN ARE LESS THAN SCUM.
AND THEY ARE TRAINED BY ACE.
TONK
NOW.
EEK!
YOU TWO WILL COME WITH ME.
YOU OKAY?
HUH?
I'M FINE, BUT ...
PETER!
THEY WEREN'T TRYING TO HURT ME, OKAY?
DRAG
DRAG
DRAG
DRAG
GO EASY ON THEM!
YES, MY DEAR. I ONLY WISH TO TEACH THEM FEAR. ♥
I GUESS ...
THAT'S BETTER THAN A BEHEAD-ING.
SORRY.
I GOT LOST COMING AFTER YOU.
Poff
THIS PLACE IS A MAZE.

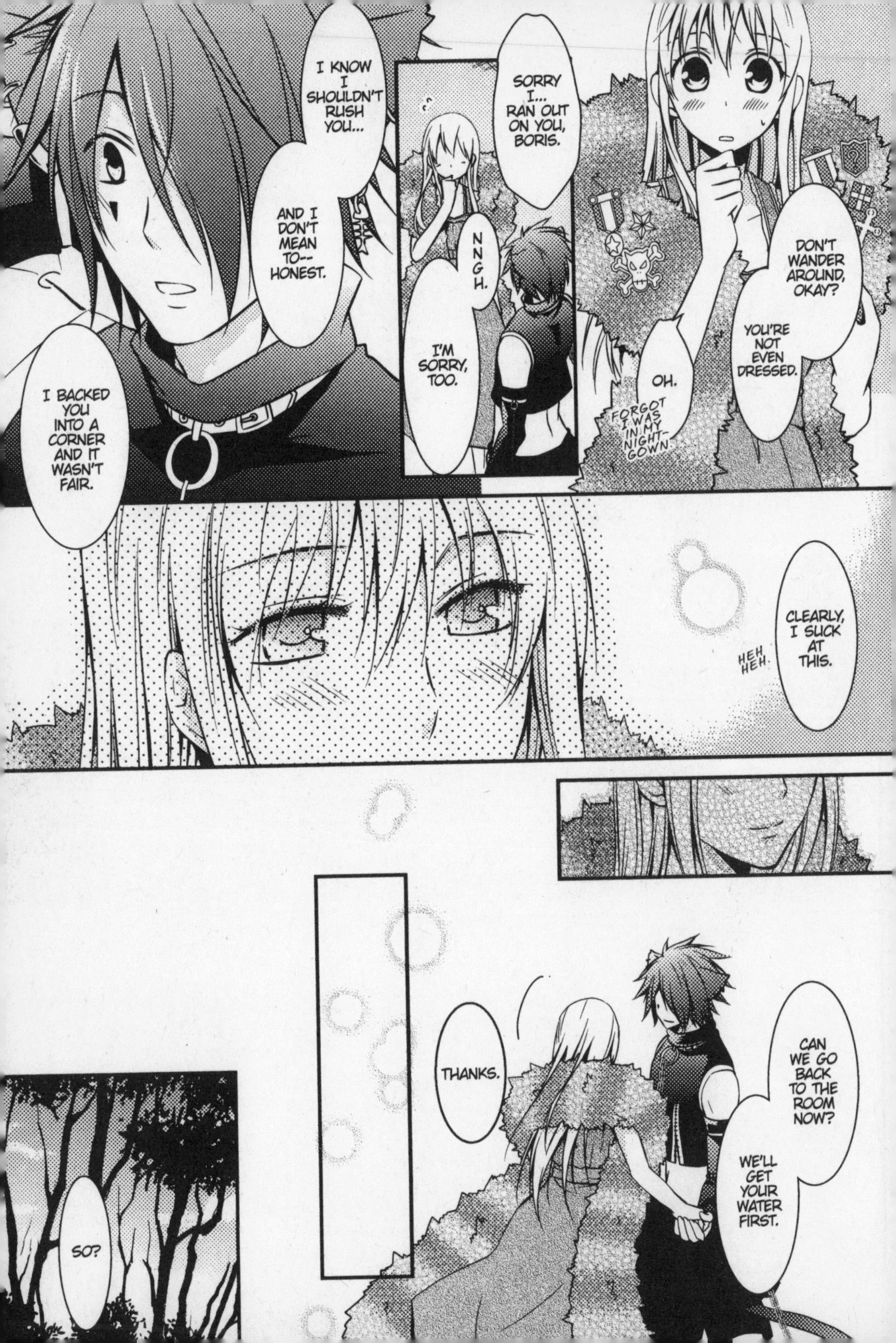
DON'T WANDER AROUND, OKAY?
YOU'RE NOT EVEN DRESSED.
OH.
FORGOT I WAS IN MY NIGHTGOWN.
SORRY I... RAN OUT ON YOU, BORIS.
NNGH.
I'M SORRY, TOO.
I KNOW I SHOULDN'T RUSH YOU...
AND I DON'T MEAN TO-- HONEST.
I BACKED YOU INTO A CORNER AND IT WASN'T FAIR.
CLEARLY, I SUCK AT THIS.
HEH HEH.
CAN WE GO BACK TO THE ROOM NOW?
WE'LL GET YOUR WATER FIRST.
THANKS.
SO?

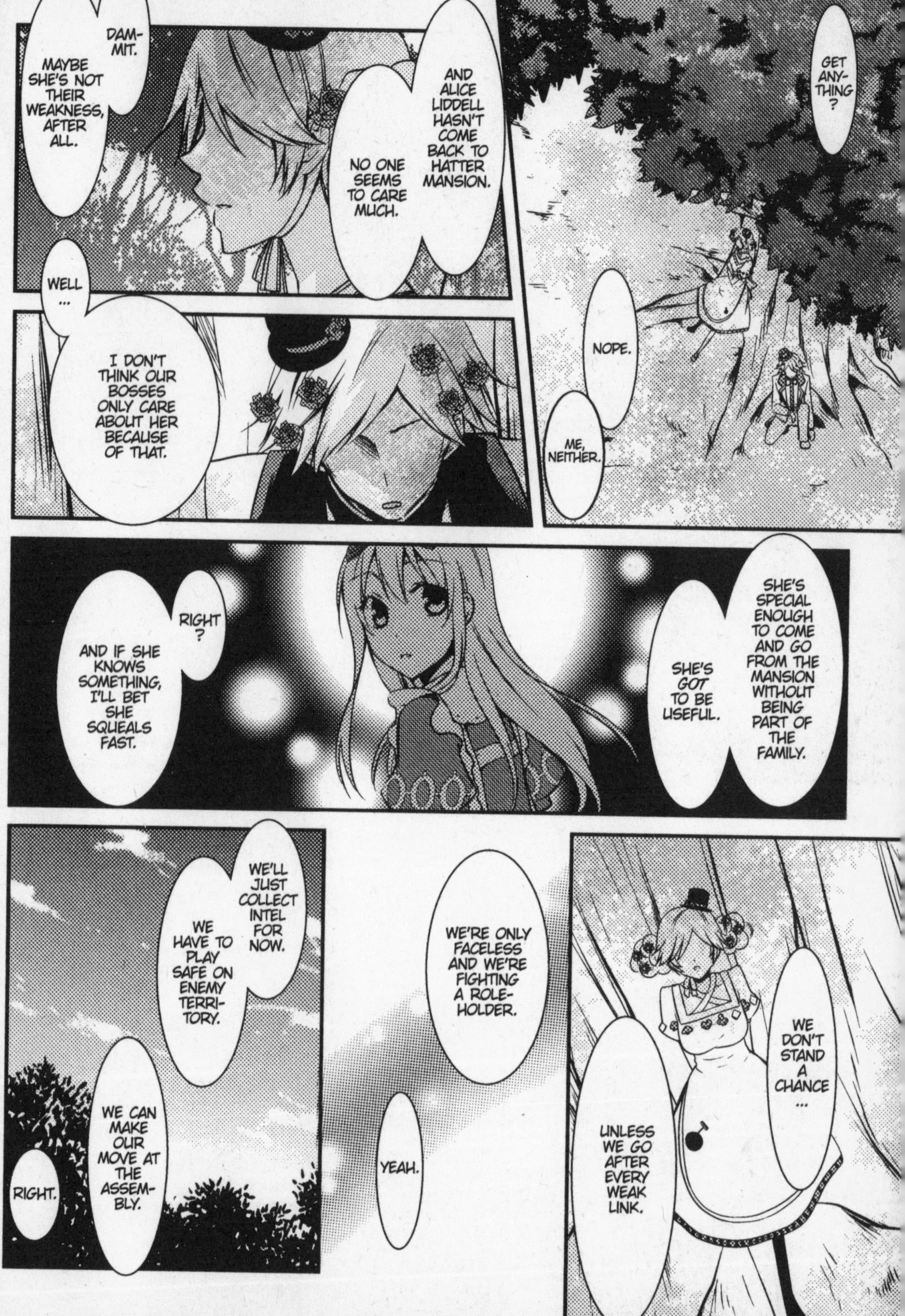
GET ANYTHING?
NOPE.
ME, NEITHER.
AND ALICE LIDDELL HASN'T COME BACK TO HATTER MANSION.
NO ONE SEEMS TO CARE MUCH.
DAMMIT. MAYBE SHE'S NOT THEIR WEAKNESS, AFTER ALL.
WELL...
I DON'T THINK OUR BOSSES ONLY CARE ABOUT HER BECAUSE OF THAT.
SHE'S SPECIAL ENOUGH TO COME AND GO FROM THE MANSION WITHOUT BEING PART OF THE FAMILY.
SHE'S GOT TO BE USEFUL.
RIGHT?
AND IF SHE KNOWS SOMETHING, I'LL BET SHE SQUEALS FAST.
WE DON'T STAND A CHANCE...
UNLESS WE GO AFTER EVERY WEAK LINK.
WE'RE ONLY FACELESS AND WE'RE FIGHTING A ROLE-HOLDER.
YEAH.
WE'LL JUST COLLECT INTEL FOR NOW.
WE HAVE TO PLAY SAFE ON ENEMY TERRITORY.
WE CAN MAKE OUR MOVE AT THE ASSEMBLY.
RIGHT.

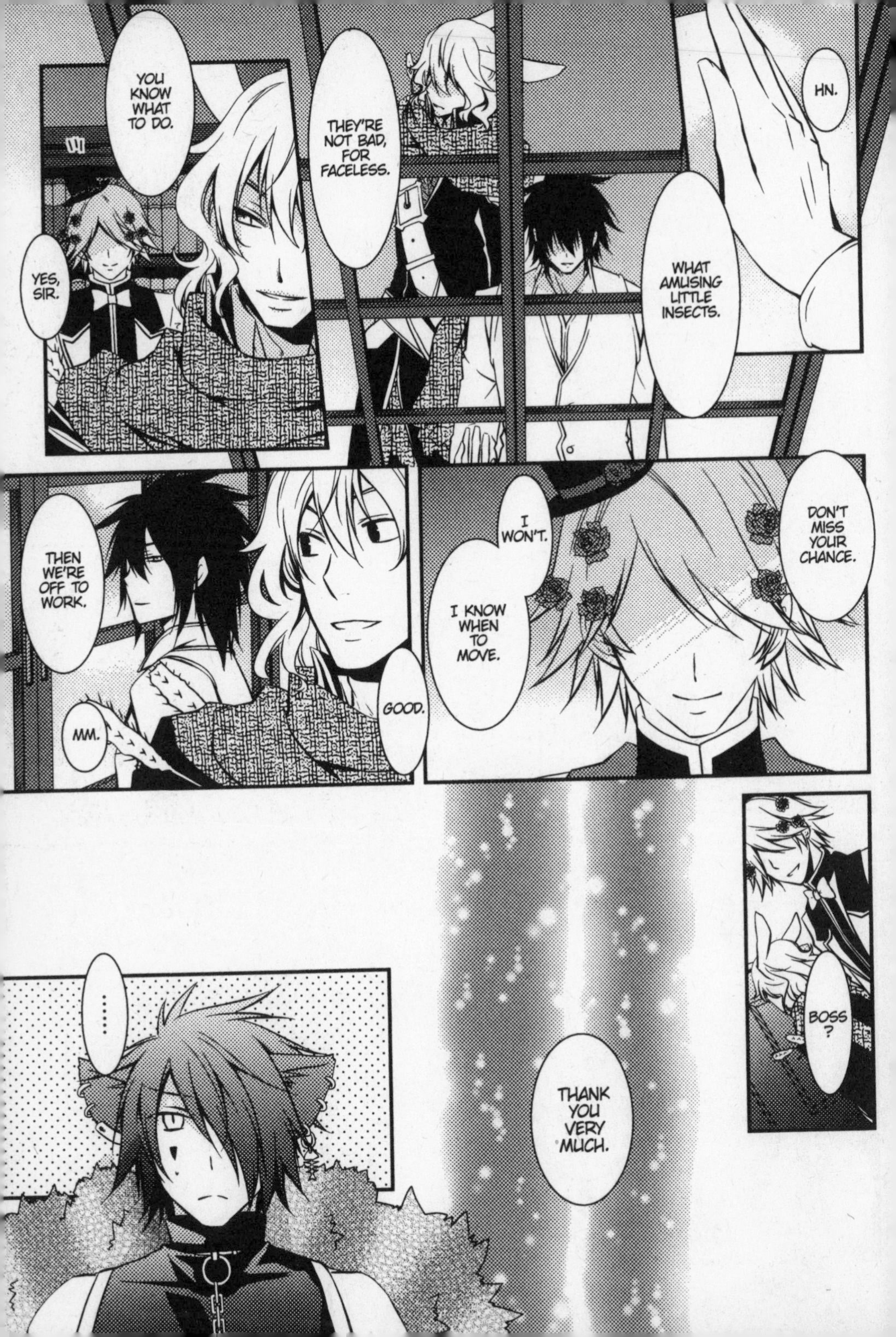
HN.
WHAT AMUSING LITTLE INSECTS.
THEY'RE NOT BAD, FOR FACELESS.
YOU KNOW WHAT TO DO.
YES, SIR.
DON'T MISS YOUR CHANCE.
I WON'T.
I KNOW WHEN TO MOVE.
THEN WE'RE OFF TO WORK.
GOOD.
MM.
BOSS?
THANK YOU VERY MUCH.
......

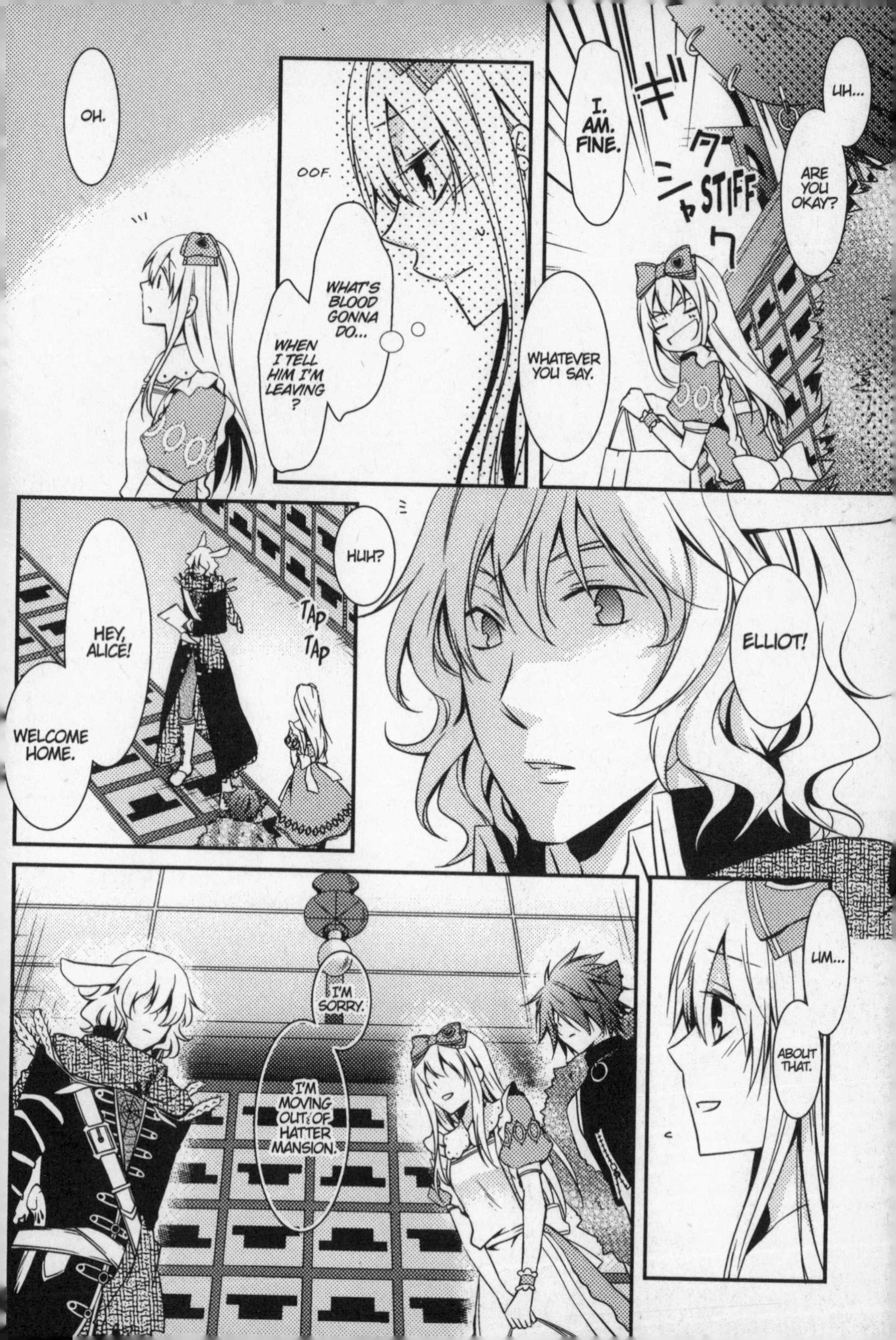
UH...
ARE YOU OKAY?
I. AM. FINE.
ギクシャク
STIFF
WHATEVER YOU SAY.
OOF.
WHAT'S BLOOD GONNA DO...
WHEN I TELL HIM I'M LEAVING?
OH.
ELLIOT!
HUH?
TAP TAP
HEY, ALICE!
WELCOME HOME.
UM...
ABOUT THAT.
I'M SORRY.
I'M MOVING OUT OF HATTER MANSION.

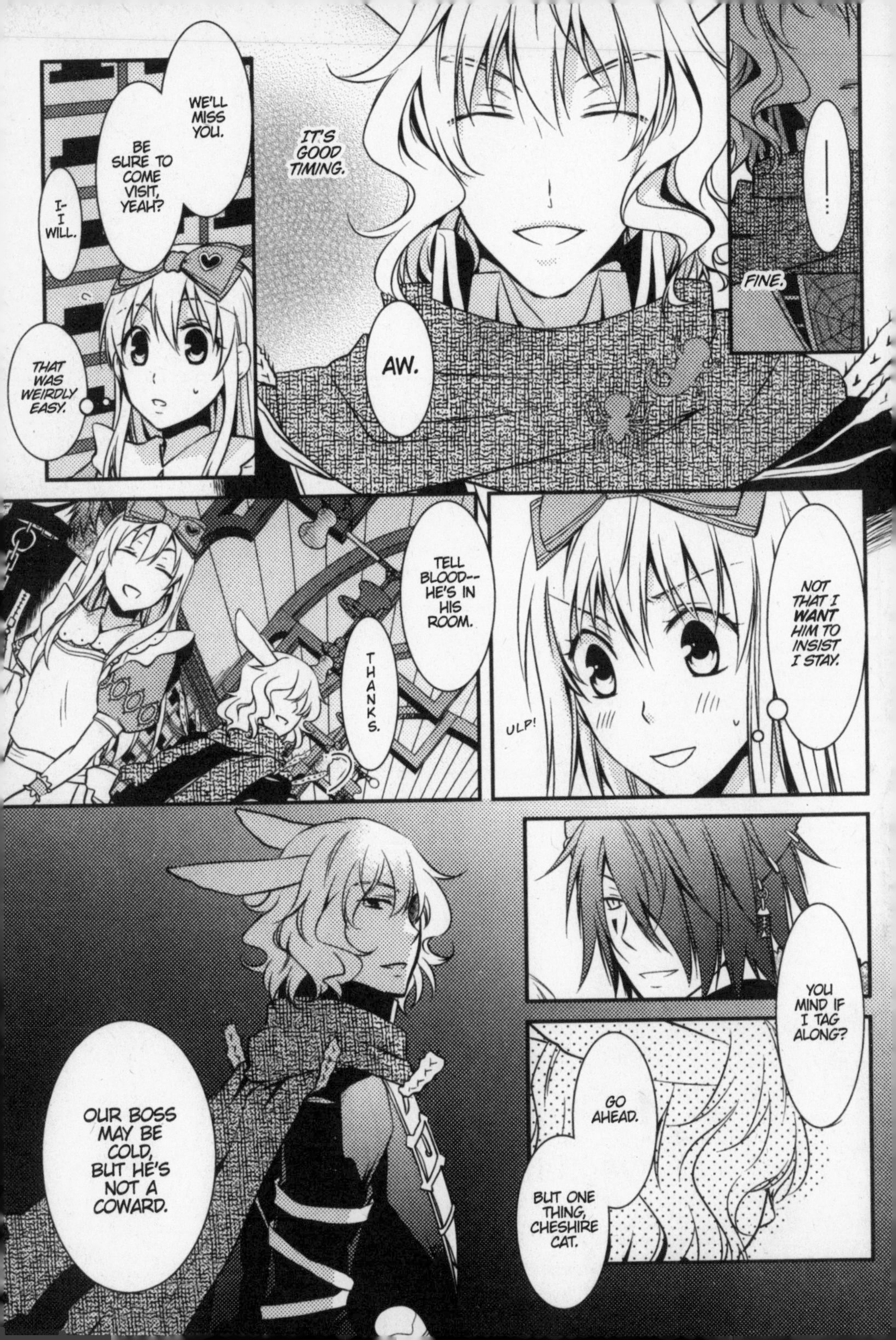
......!
FINE.
IT'S GOOD TIMING.
AW.
WE'LL MISS YOU.
BE SURE TO COME VISIT, YEAH?
I- I WILL.
THAT WAS WEIRDLY EASY.
NOT THAT I WANT HIM TO INSIST I STAY.
ULP!
TELL BLOOD-- HE'S IN HIS ROOM.
THANKS.
YOU MIND IF I TAG ALONG?
GO AHEAD.
BUT ONE THING, CHESHIRE CAT.
OUR BOSS MAY BE COLD, BUT HE'S NOT A COWARD.

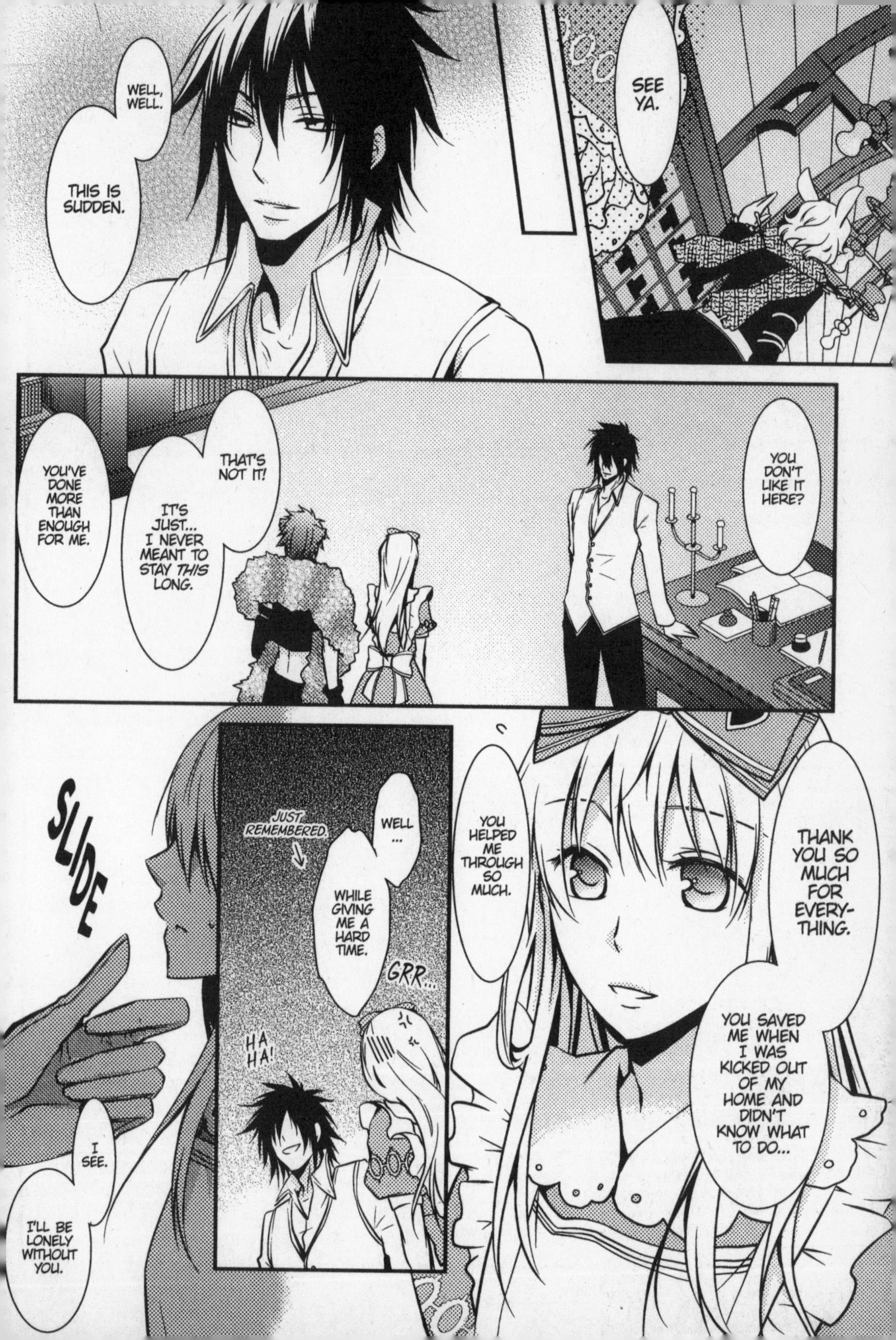
SEE YA.
WELL, WELL.
THIS IS SUDDEN.
YOU DON'T LIKE IT HERE?
THAT'S NOT IT!
IT'S JUST... I NEVER MEANT TO STAY *THIS* LONG.
YOU'VE DONE MORE THAN ENOUGH FOR ME.
THANK YOU SO MUCH FOR EVERY-THING.
YOU HELPED ME THROUGH SO MUCH.
YOU SAVED ME WHEN I WAS KICKED OUT OF MY HOME AND DIDN'T KNOW WHAT TO DO...
WELL ...
JUST REMEMBERED.
WHILE GIVING ME A HARD TIME.
GRR...
HA HA!
SLIDE
I SEE.
I'LL BE LONELY WITHOUT YOU.

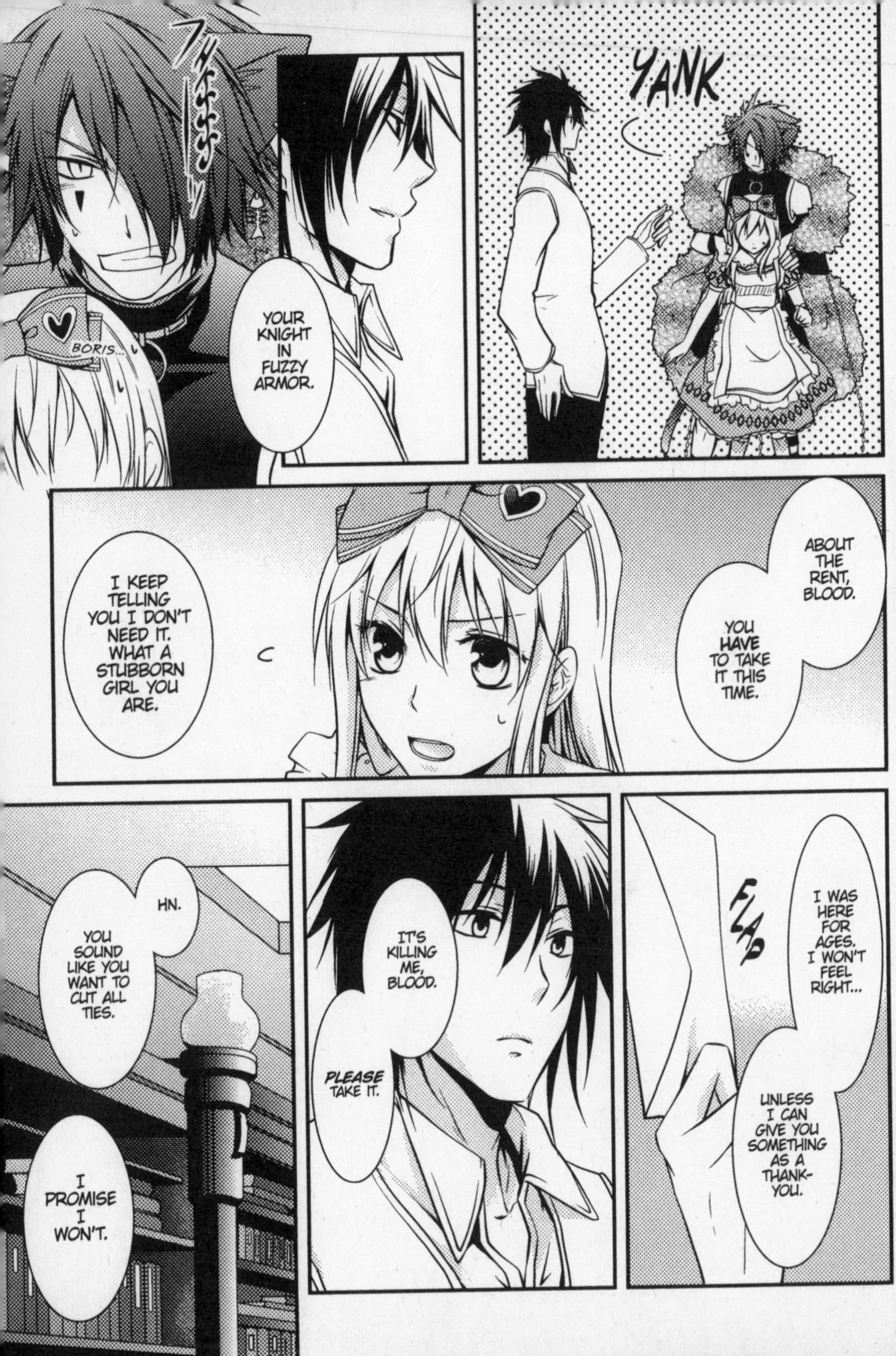
YANK
YOUR KNIGHT IN FUZZY ARMOR.
BORIS...
ABOUT THE RENT, BLOOD.
YOU *HAVE* TO TAKE IT THIS TIME.
I KEEP TELLING YOU I DON'T NEED IT. WHAT A STUBBORN GIRL YOU ARE.
FLAP
I WAS HERE FOR AGES. I WON'T FEEL RIGHT...
UNLESS I CAN GIVE YOU SOMETHING AS A THANK-YOU.
IT'S KILLING ME, BLOOD.
PLEASE TAKE IT.
HN.
YOU SOUND LIKE YOU WANT TO CUT ALL TIES.
I PROMISE I WON'T.

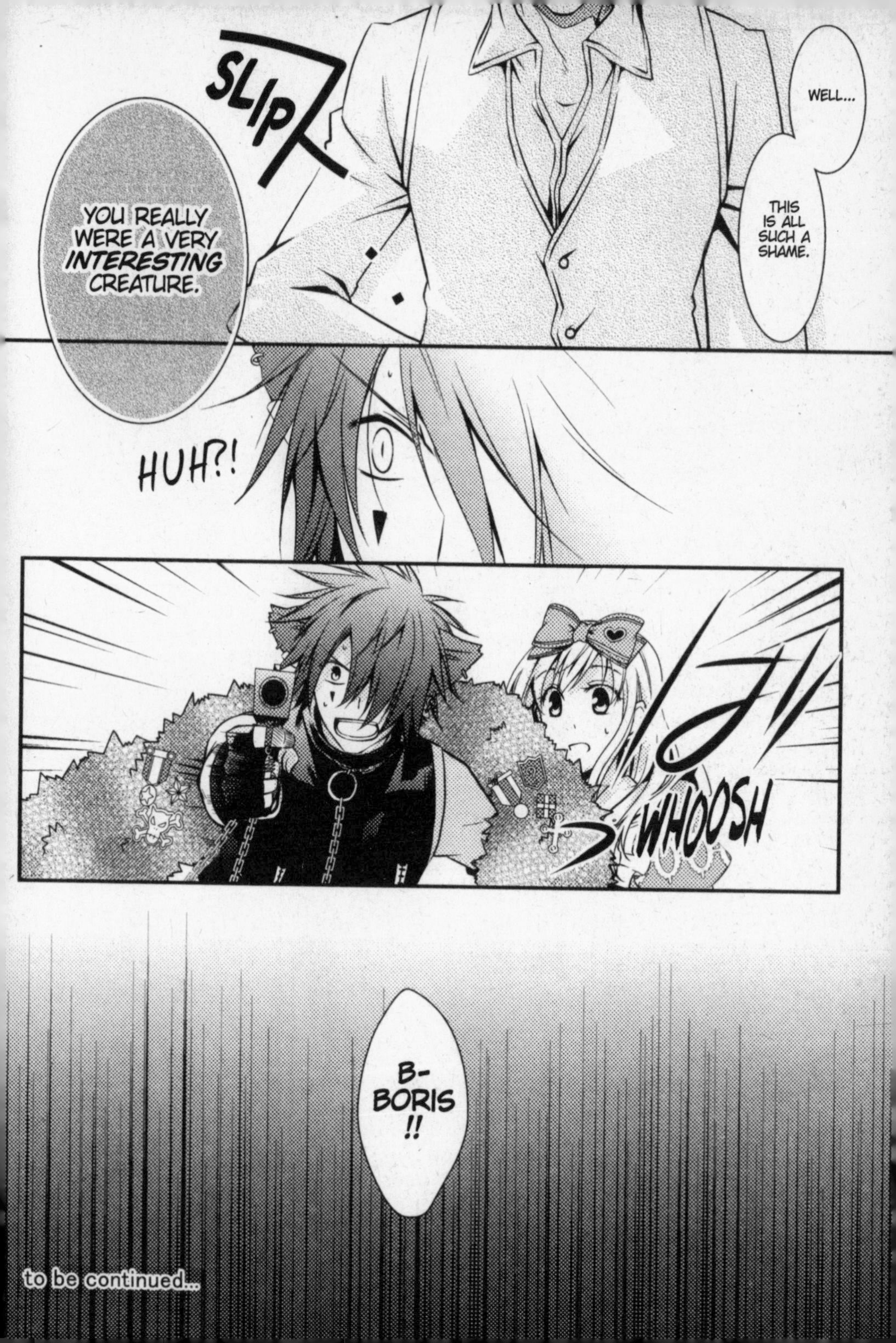
WELL...
THIS IS ALL SUCH A SHAME.
SLIP
YOU REALLY WERE A VERY *INTERESTING* CREATURE.
HUH?!
WHOOSH
B-BORIS!!
to be continued...

The First Step ♥♥
–Part 1–

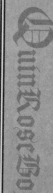

Presenting an all-new side story set in the Country of Hearts!

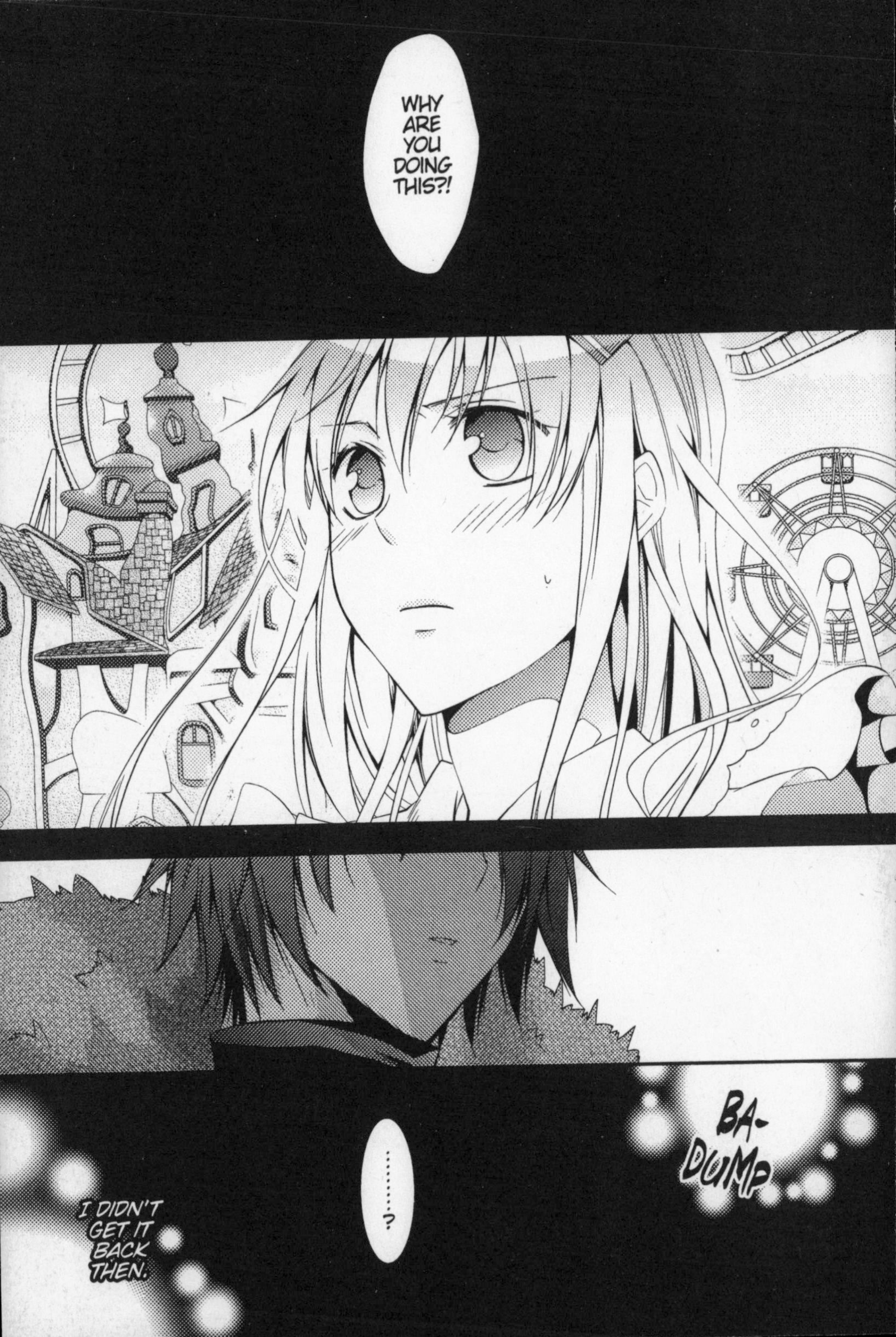
WHY ARE YOU DOING THIS?!
BA-DUMP
......?
I DIDN'T GET IT BACK THEN.

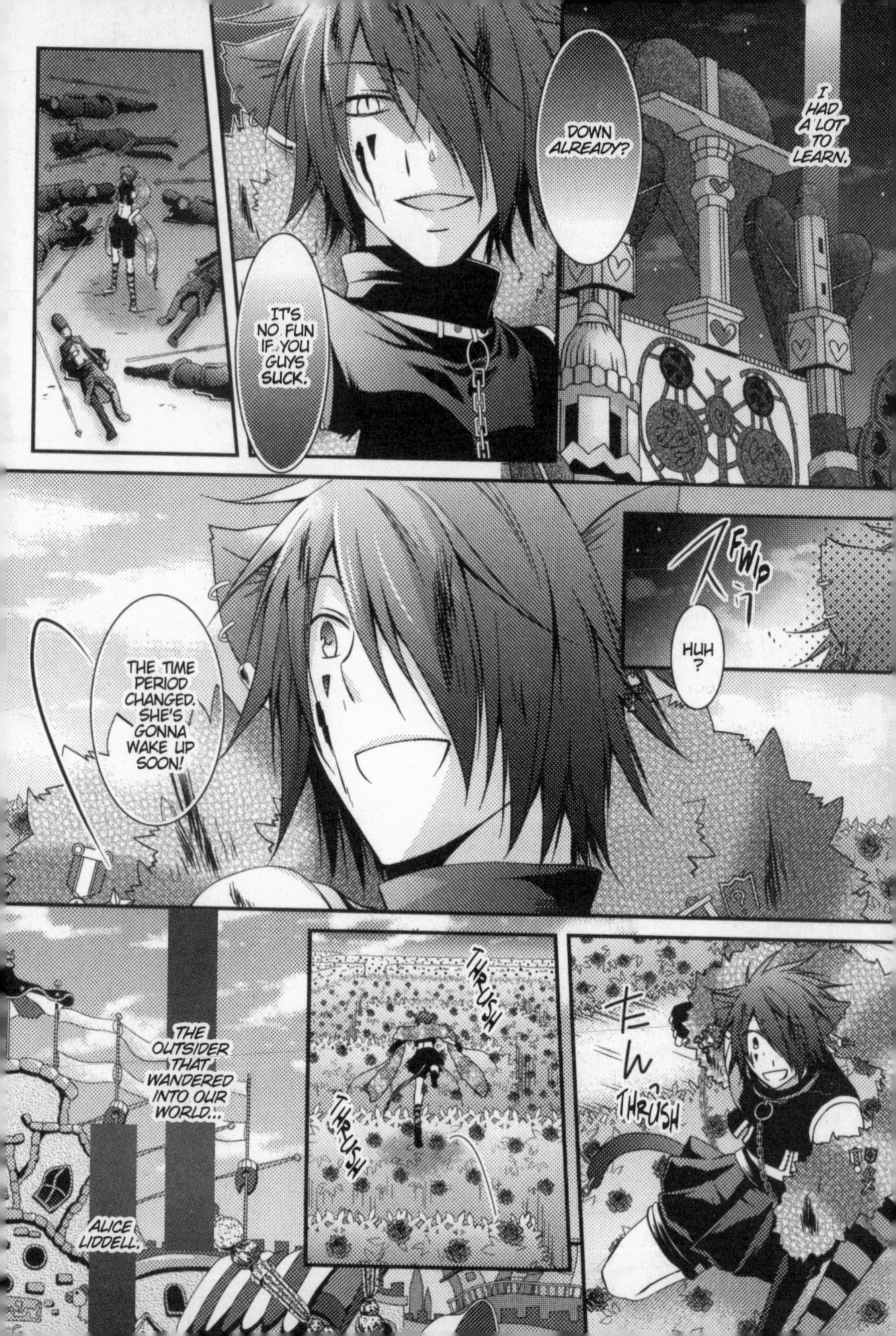
I HAD A LOT TO LEARN.
DOWN ALREADY?
IT'S NO FUN IF YOU GUYS SUCK.
FWIP
HUH?
THE TIME PERIOD CHANGED. SHE'S GONNA WAKE UP SOON!
THRUSH
THRUSH
THRUSH
THE OUTSIDER THAT WANDERED INTO OUR WORLD...
ALICE LIDDELL.

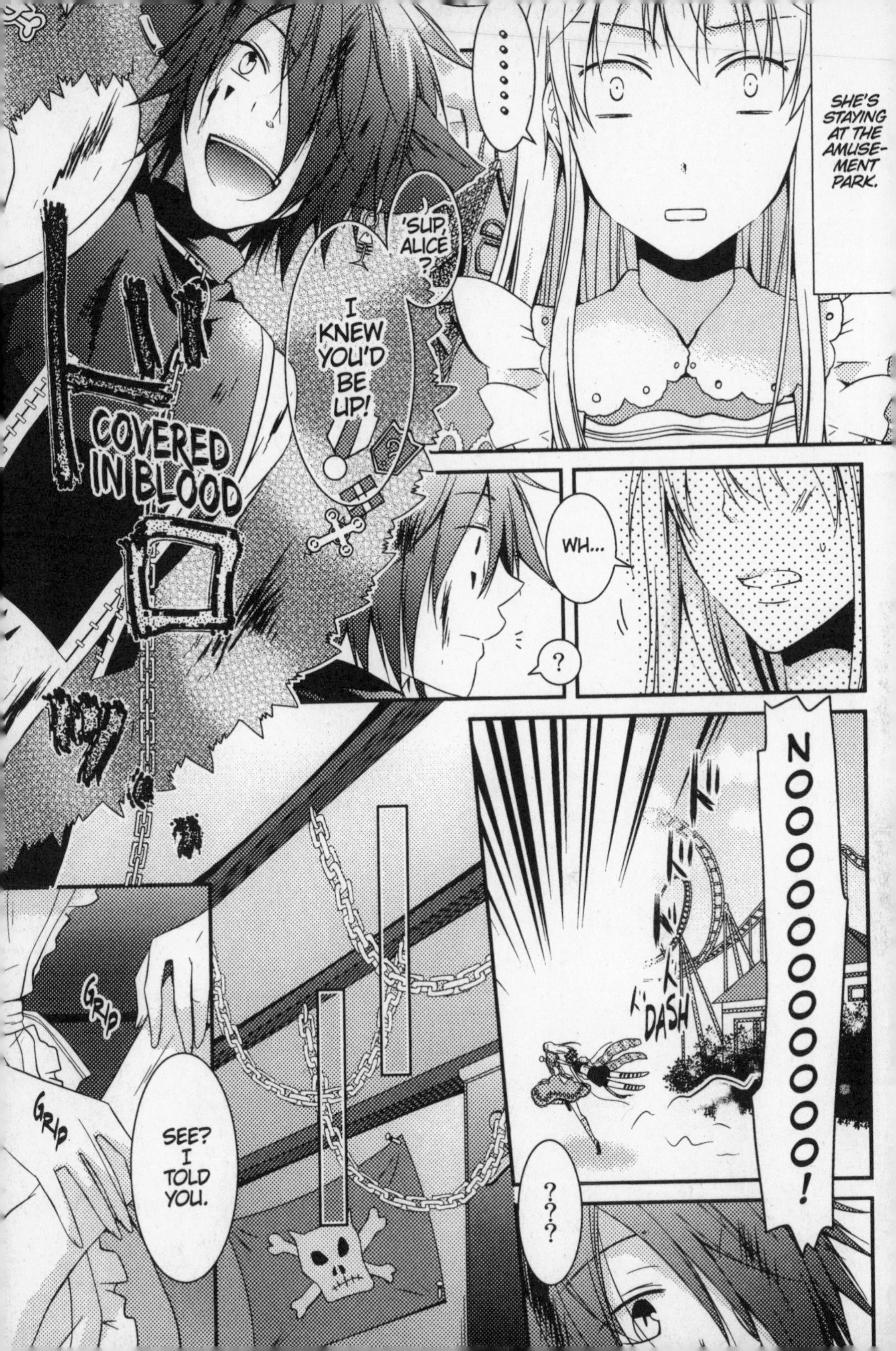
SHE'S STAYING AT THE AMUSEMENT PARK.
......
'SUP, ALICE?
I KNEW YOU'D BE UP!
COVERED IN BLOOD
WH...
?
NOOOOOOOOOOO!
DASH
???
SEE? I TOLD YOU.
GRIP
GRIP

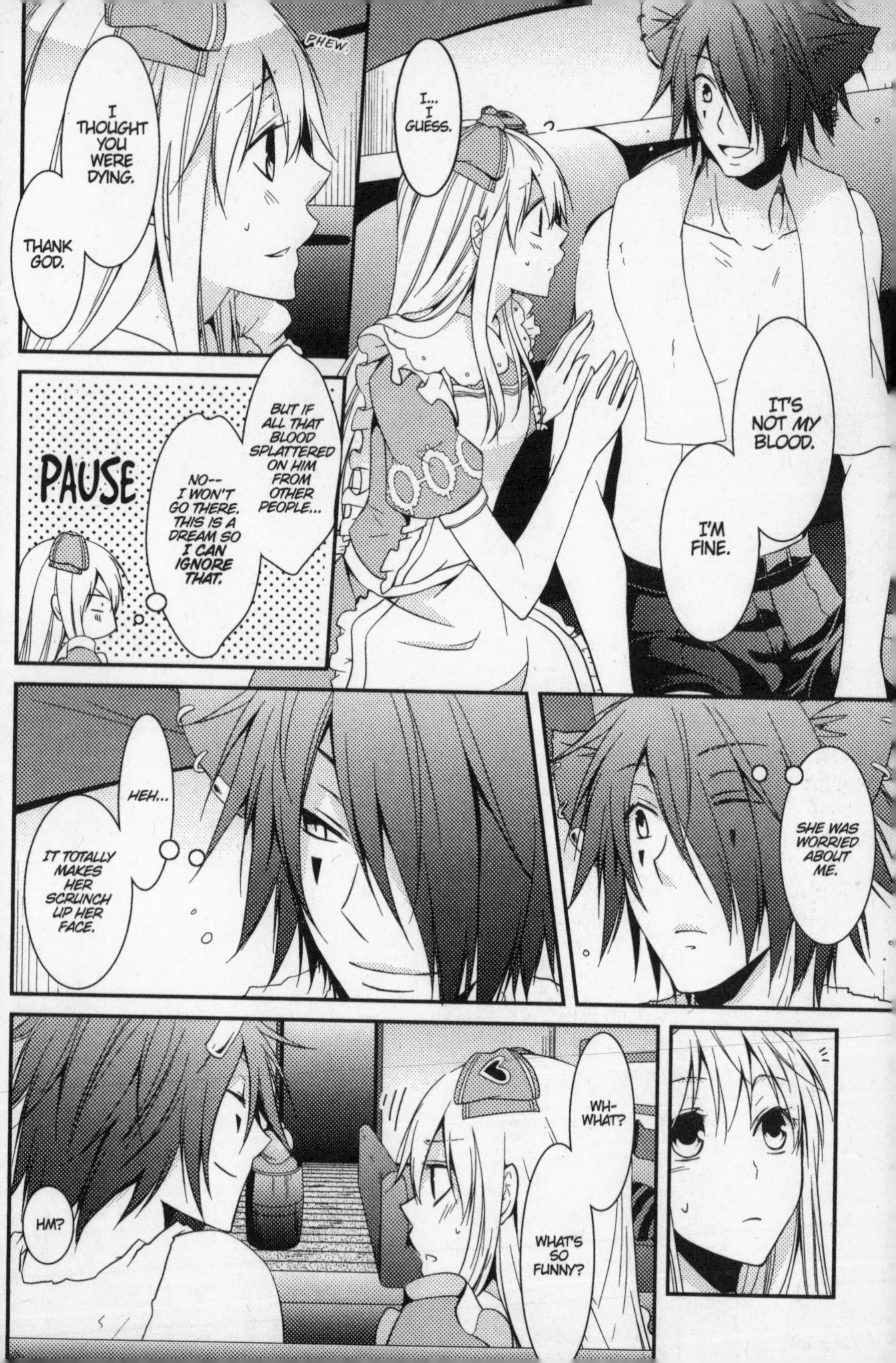
PHEW
I... I GUESS.
IT'S NOT MY BLOOD.
I'M FINE.
I THOUGHT YOU WERE DYING.
THANK GOD.
PAUSE
BUT IF ALL THAT BLOOD SPLATTERED ON HIM FROM OTHER PEOPLE...
NO-- I WON'T GO THERE. THIS IS A DREAM SO I CAN IGNORE THAT.
SHE WAS WORRIED ABOUT ME.
HEH...
IT TOTALLY MAKES HER SCRUNCH UP HER FACE.
WH- WHAT?
WHAT'S SO FUNNY?
HM?

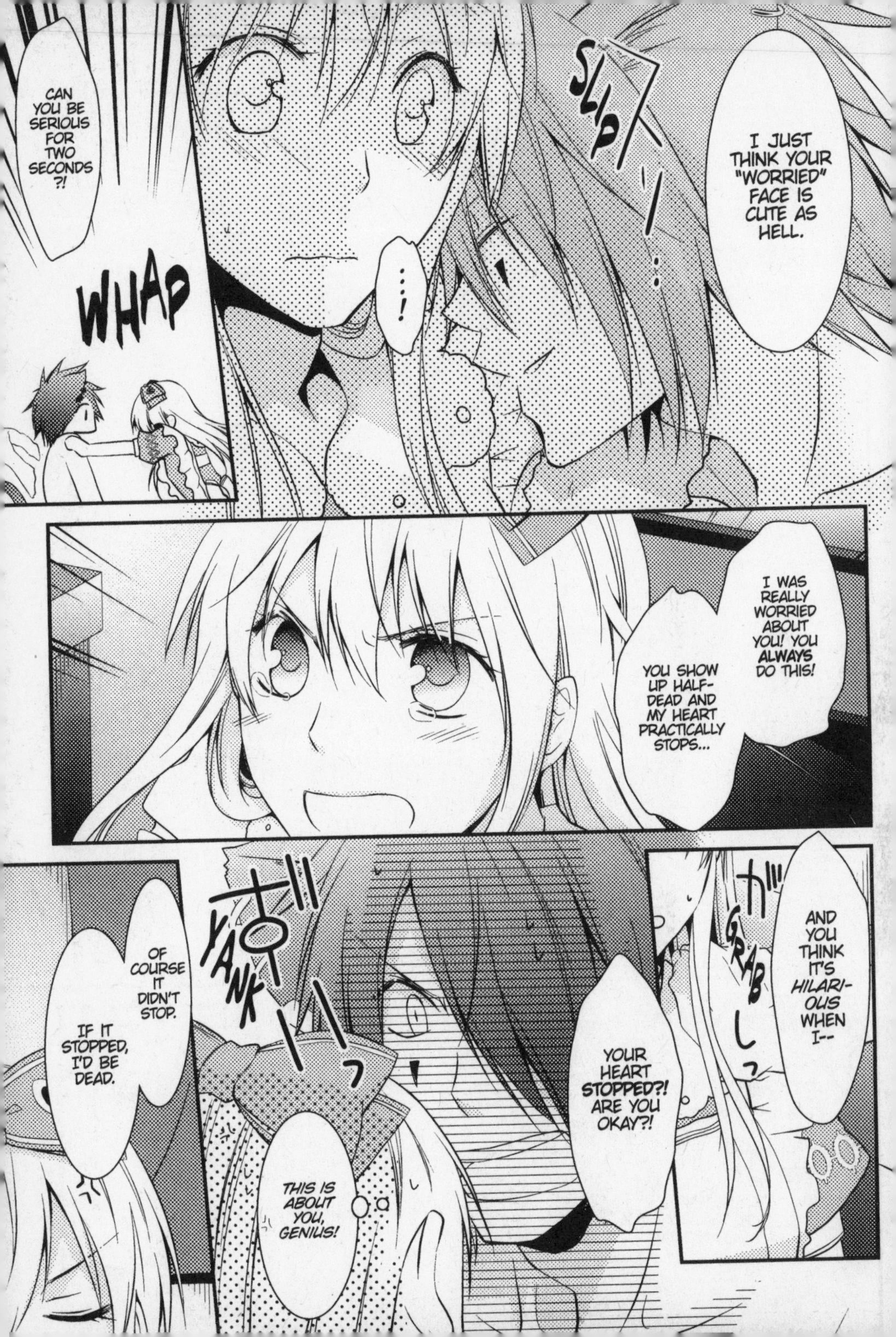

SLIP
I JUST THINK YOUR "WORRIED" FACE IS CUTE AS HELL.
...!
CAN YOU BE SERIOUS FOR TWO SECONDS?!
WHAP
I WAS REALLY WORRIED ABOUT YOU! YOU ALWAYS DO THIS!
YOU SHOW UP HALF-DEAD AND MY HEART PRACTICALLY STOPS...
AND YOU THINK IT'S HILARIOUS WHEN I--
GRAB
YOUR HEART STOPPED?! ARE YOU OKAY?!
YANK
THIS IS ABOUT YOU, GENIUS!
OF COURSE IT DIDN'T STOP.
IF IT STOPPED, I'D BE DEAD.

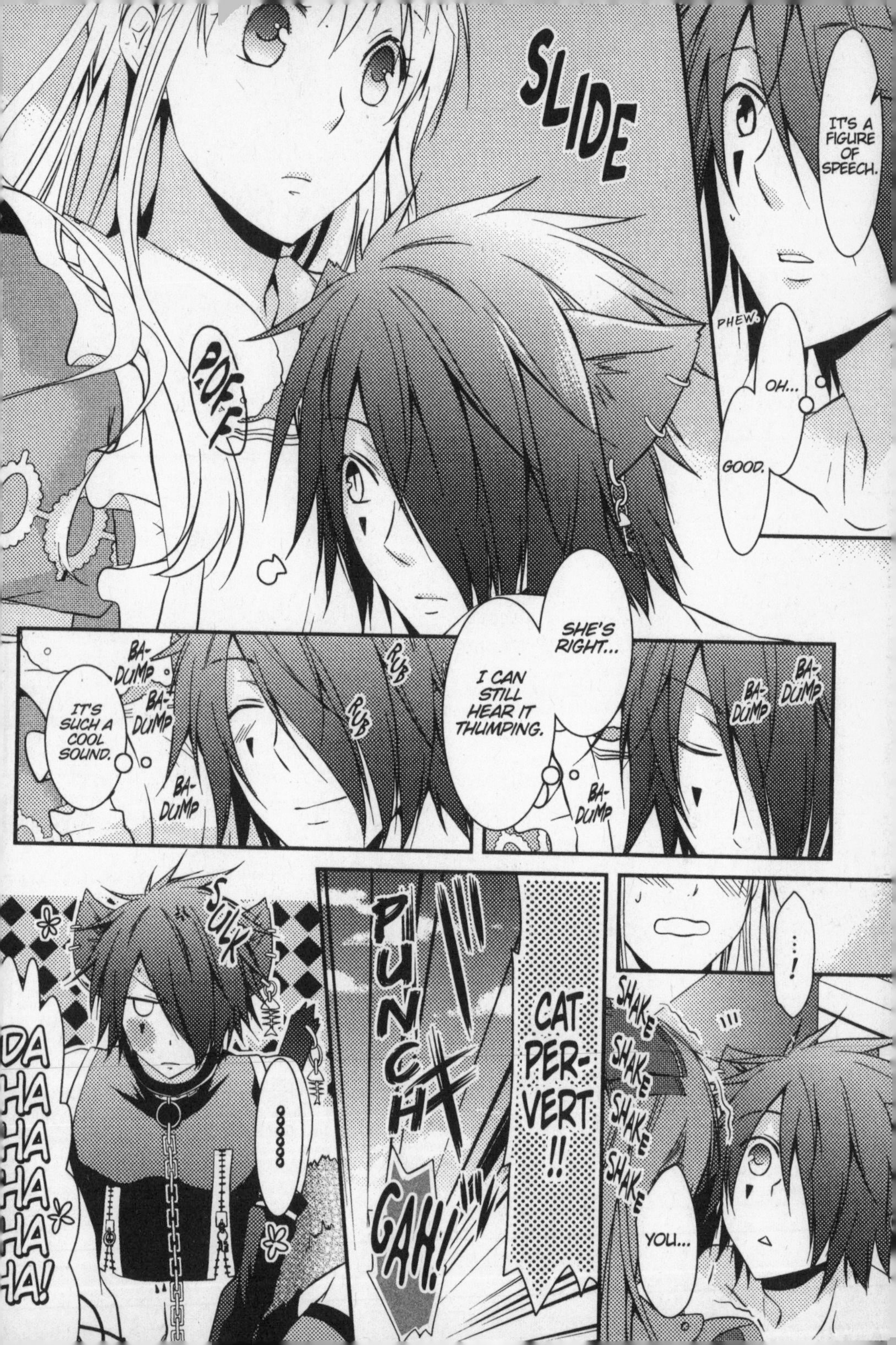
IT'S A FIGURE OF SPEECH.
PHEW.
OH...
GOOD.
SLIDE
POFF
BA-DUMP
BA-DUMP
SHE'S RIGHT...
I CAN STILL HEAR IT THUMPING.
BA-DUMP
RUB
RUB
BA-DUMP
BA-DUMP
IT'S SUCH A COOL SOUND.
BA-DUMP
...!
SHAKE SHAKE SHAKE SHAKE
YOU...
CAT PER-VERT!!
PUNCH
GAH!
SULK
......
DA HA HA HA HA HA HA!

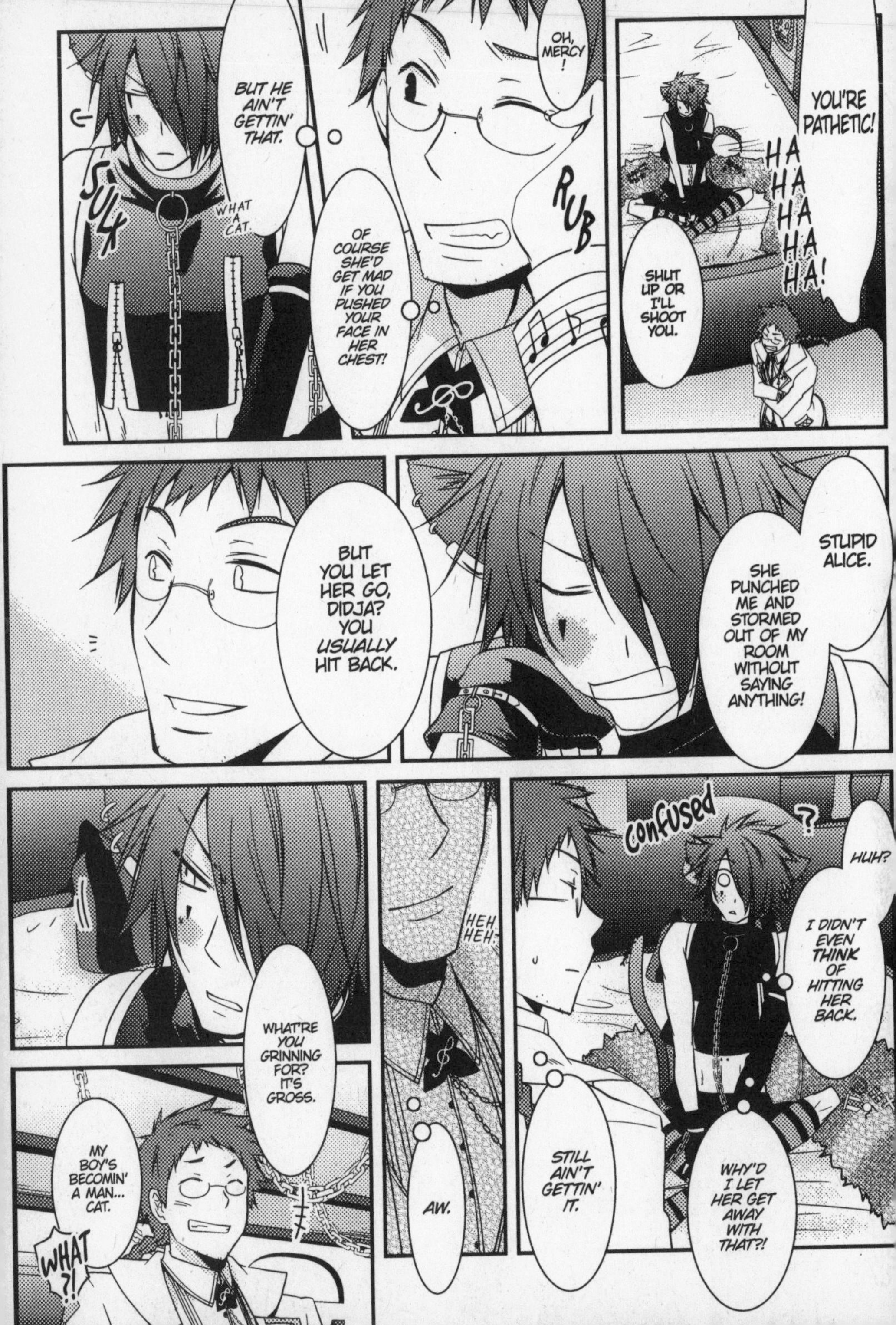
YOU'RE PATHETIC!
HAHAHAHAHA!
SHUT UP OR I'LL SHOOT YOU.
OH, MERCY!
RUB
OF COURSE SHE'D GET MAD IF YOU PUSHED YOUR FACE IN HER CHEST!
BUT HE AIN'T GETTIN' THAT.
SULK
WHAT A CAT.
STUPID ALICE.
SHE PUNCHED ME AND STORMED OUT OF MY ROOM WITHOUT SAYING ANYTHING!
BUT YOU LET HER GO, DIDJA? YOU USUALLY HIT BACK.
HUH?
CONFUSED
?
I DIDN'T EVEN THINK OF HITTING HER BACK.
WHY'D I LET HER GET AWAY WITH THAT?!
HEH HEH
STILL AIN'T GETTIN' IT.
AW.
WHAT'RE YOU GRINNING FOR? IT'S GROSS.
MY BOY'S BECOMIN' A MAN... CAT.
WHAT?!

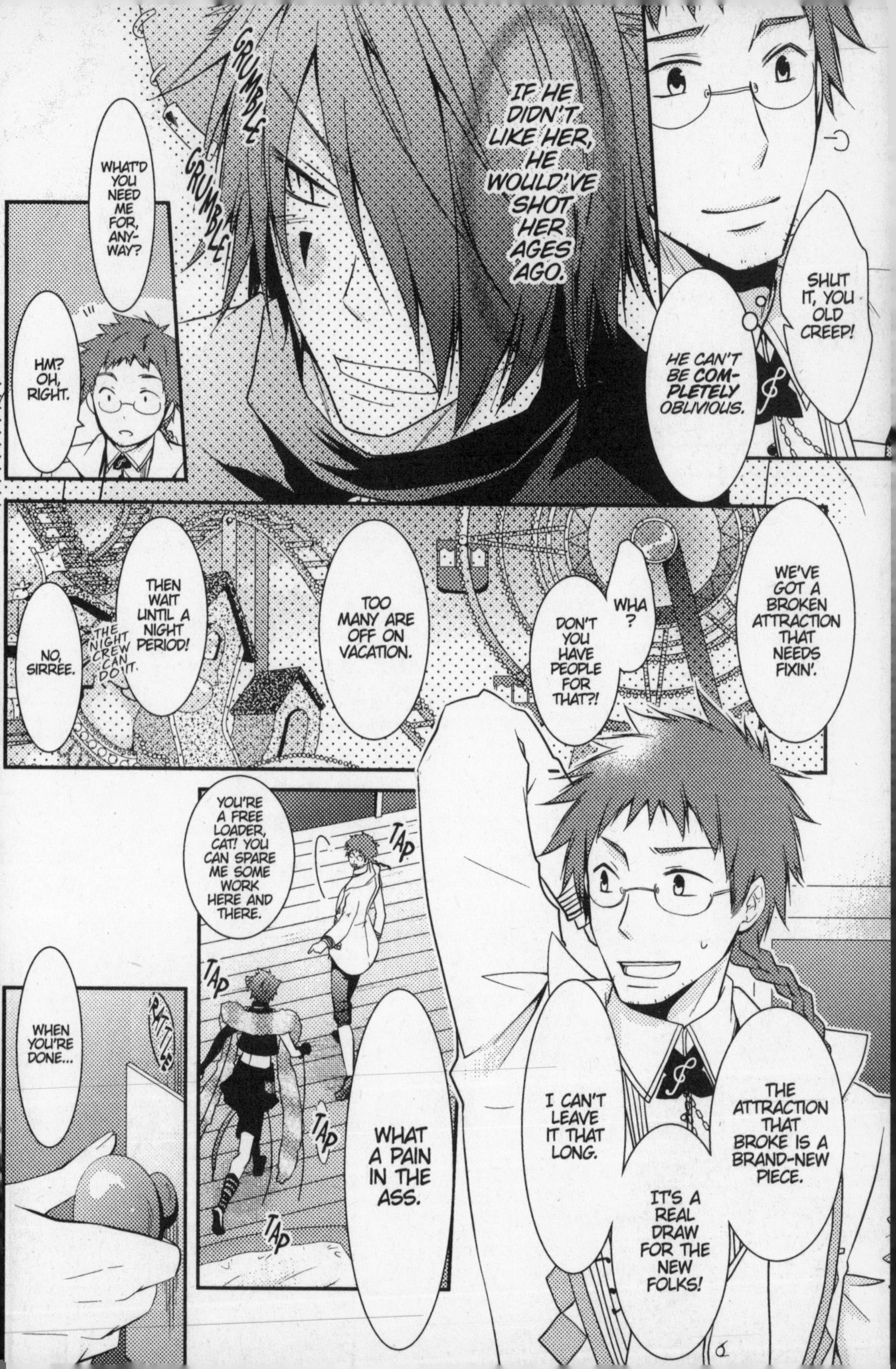
SHUT IT, YOU OLD CREEP!
HE CAN'T BE COMPLETELY OBLIVIOUS.
IF HE DIDN'T LIKE HER, HE WOULD'VE SHOT HER AGES AGO.
GRUMBLE
GRUMBLE
WHAT'D YOU NEED ME FOR, ANYWAY?
HM? OH, RIGHT.
WE'VE GOT A BROKEN ATTRACTION THAT NEEDS FIXIN'.
WHA?
DON'T YOU HAVE PEOPLE FOR THAT?!
TOO MANY ARE OFF ON VACATION.
THEN WAIT UNTIL A NIGHT PERIOD!
THE NIGHT CREW CAN DO IT.
NO, SIRREE.
THE ATTRACTION THAT BROKE IS A BRAND-NEW PIECE.
IT'S A REAL DRAW FOR THE NEW FOLKS!
I CAN'T LEAVE IT THAT LONG.
YOU'RE A FREE LOADER, CAT! YOU CAN SPARE ME SOME WORK HERE AND THERE.
TAP
WHAT A PAIN IN THE ASS.
TAP
TAP
TAP
RATTLE
WHEN YOU'RE DONE...

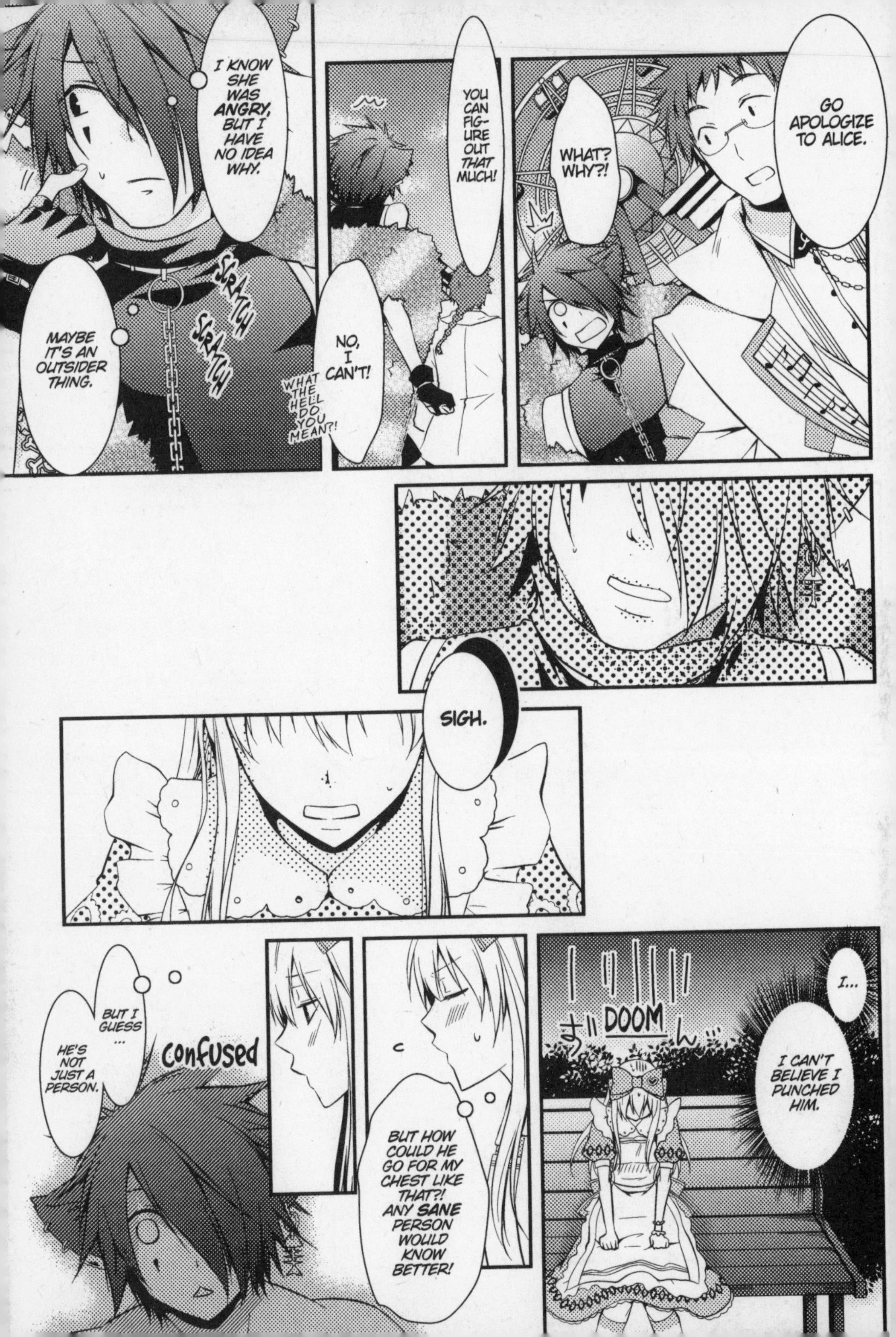
GO APOLOGIZE TO ALICE.
WHAT? WHY?!
YOU CAN FIG-URE OUT THAT MUCH!
NO, I CAN'T!
WHAT THE HELL DO YOU MEAN?!
I KNOW SHE WAS ANGRY, BUT I HAVE NO IDEA WHY.
SCRATCH SCRATCH
MAYBE IT'S AN OUTSIDER THING.
SIGH.
DOOM
I...
I CAN'T BELIEVE I PUNCHED HIM.
BUT HOW COULD HE GO FOR MY CHEST LIKE THAT?! ANY SANE PERSON WOULD KNOW BETTER!
Confused
BUT I GUESS ...
HE'S NOT JUST A PERSON.

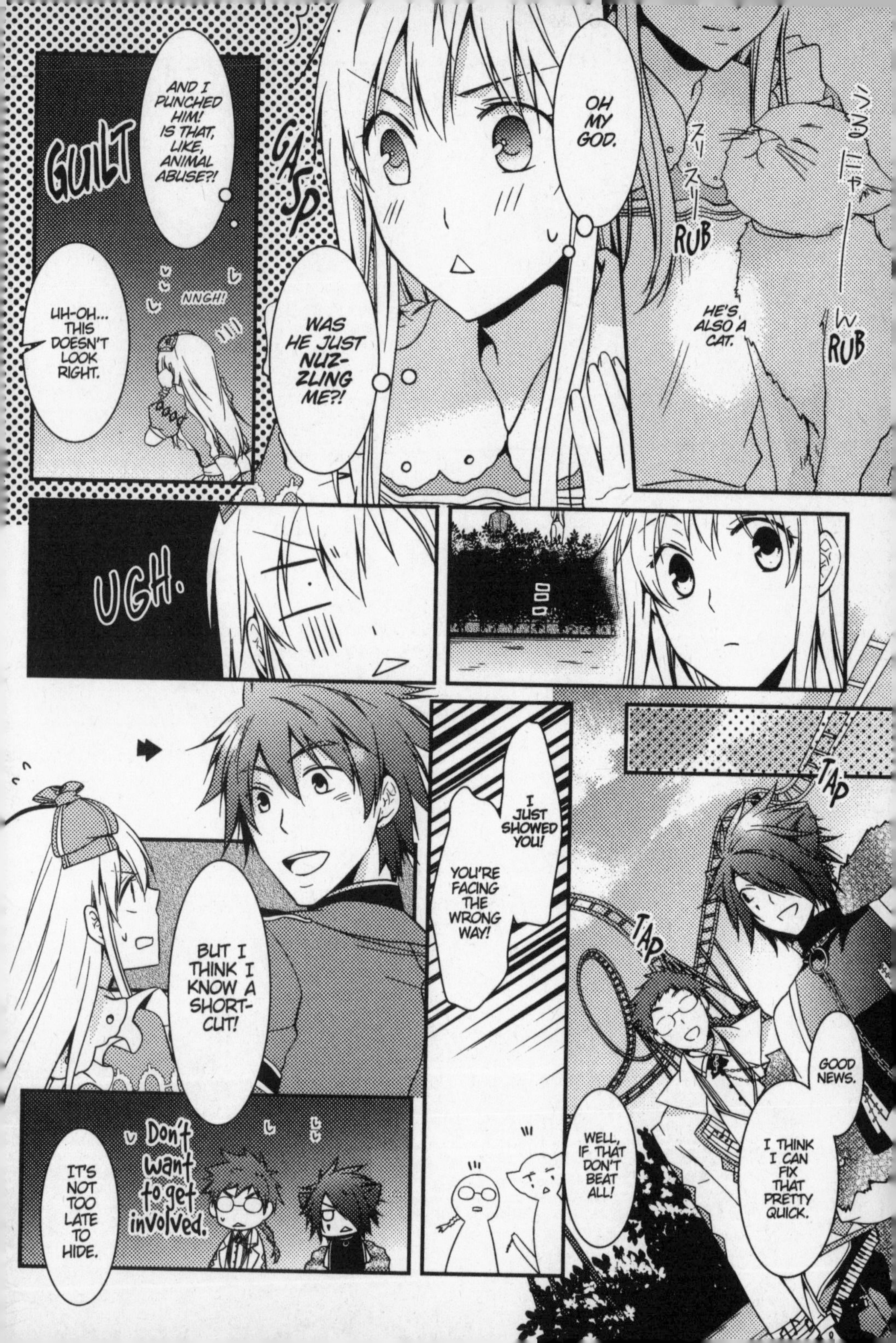
RUB
RUB
HE'S ALSO A CAT.
OH MY GOD.
GASP
WAS HE JUST NUZZLING ME?!
AND I PUNCHED HIM! IS THAT, LIKE, ANIMAL ABUSE?!
GUILT
NNGH!
UH-OH... THIS DOESN'T LOOK RIGHT.
UGH.
TAP
TAP
GOOD NEWS.
I THINK I CAN FIX THAT PRETTY QUICK.
WELL, IF THAT DON'T BEAT ALL!
I JUST SHOWED YOU!
YOU'RE FACING THE WRONG WAY!
BUT I THINK I KNOW A SHORTCUT!
Don't want to get involved.
IT'S NOT TOO LATE TO HIDE.

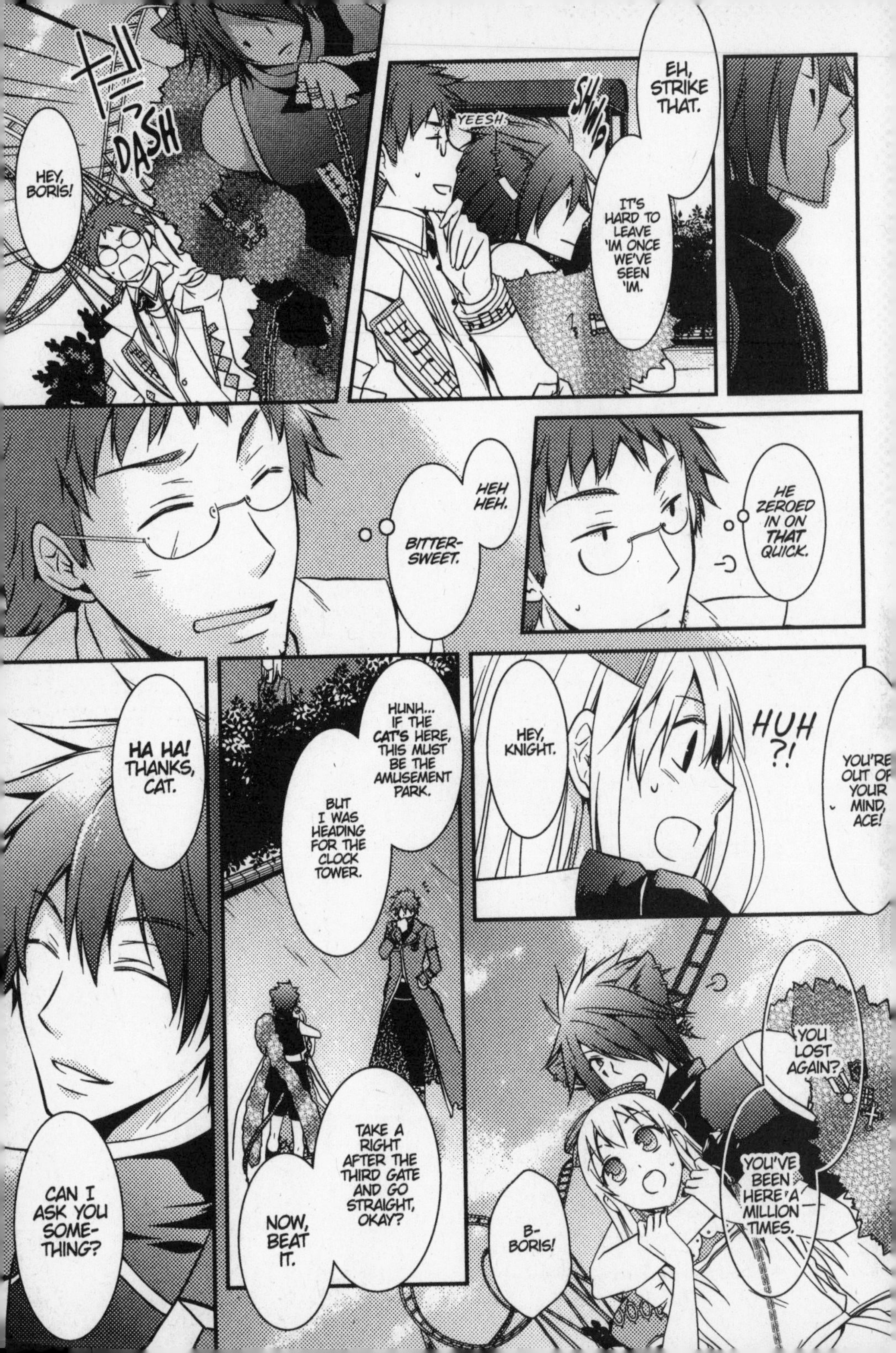
EH, STRIKE THAT.
SHWIP
IT'S HARD TO LEAVE 'IM ONCE WE'VE SEEN 'IM.
YEESH.
DASH
HEY, BORIS!
HE ZEROED IN ON THAT QUICK.
HEH HEH.
BITTER-SWEET.
YOU'RE OUT OF YOUR MIND, ACE!
HUH ?!
HEY, KNIGHT.
YOU LOST AGAIN?
YOU'VE BEEN HERE A MILLION TIMES.
B-BORIS!
HUNH... IF THE CAT'S HERE, THIS MUST BE THE AMUSEMENT PARK.
BUT I WAS HEADING FOR THE CLOCK TOWER.
TAKE A RIGHT AFTER THE THIRD GATE AND GO STRAIGHT, OKAY?
NOW, BEAT IT.
HA HA! THANKS, CAT.
CAN I ASK YOU SOMETHING?

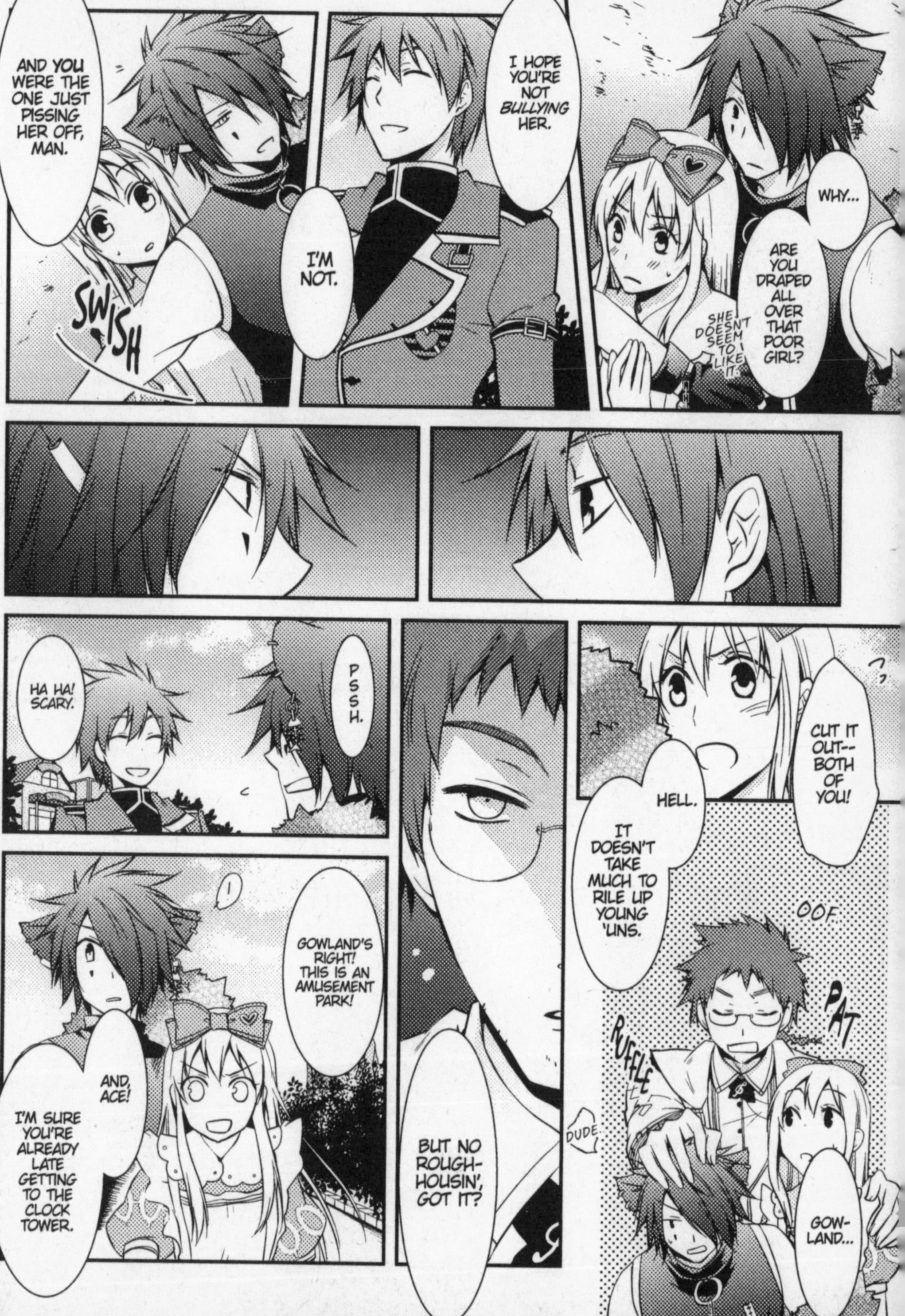
WHY...
ARE YOU DRAPED ALL OVER THAT POOR GIRL?
SHE DOESN'T SEEM TO LIKE IT.
I HOPE YOU'RE NOT *BULLYING* HER.
I'M NOT.
AND YOU WERE THE ONE JUST PISSING HER OFF, MAN.
SWISH
CUT IT OUT-- BOTH OF YOU!
HELL.
IT DOESN'T TAKE MUCH TO RILE UP YOUNG 'UNS.
OOF
PAT
RUFFLE
DUDE...
GOW-LAND...
BUT NO ROUGH-HOUSIN', GOT IT?
PSSH.
HA HA! SCARY.
!
GOWLAND'S RIGHT! THIS IS AN AMUSEMENT PARK!
AND, ACE!
I'M SURE YOU'RE ALREADY LATE GETTING TO THE CLOCK TOWER.

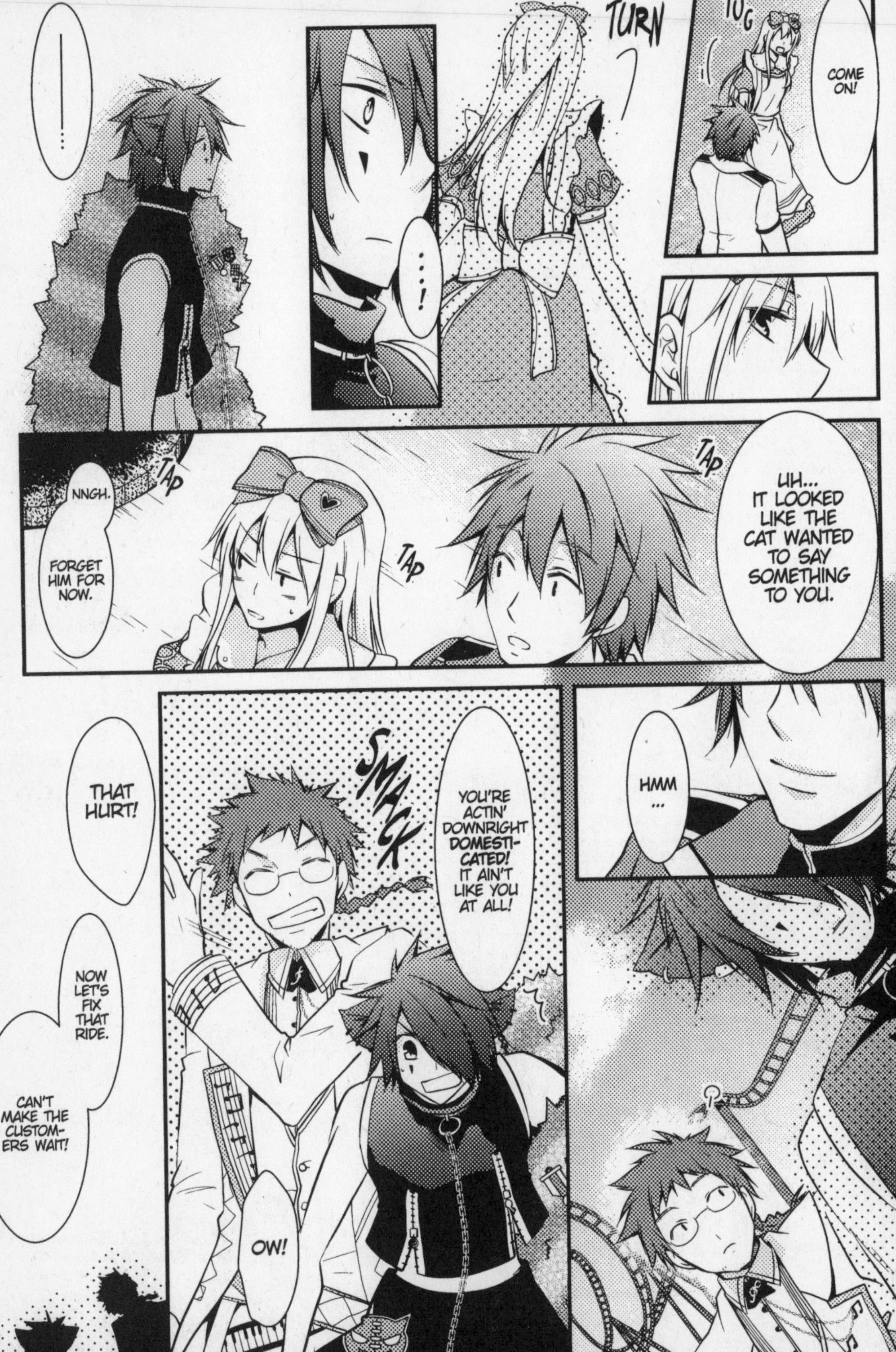
TUG
COME ON!
TURN
...!
!......
UH... IT LOOKED LIKE THE CAT WANTED TO SAY SOMETHING TO YOU.
TAP
TAP
TAP
NNGH.
FORGET HIM FOR NOW.
HMM...
SMACK
YOU'RE ACTIN' DOWNRIGHT DOMESTICATED! IT AIN'T LIKE YOU AT ALL!
THAT HURT!
NOW LET'S FIX THAT RIDE.
OW!
CAN'T MAKE THE CUSTOMERS WAIT!

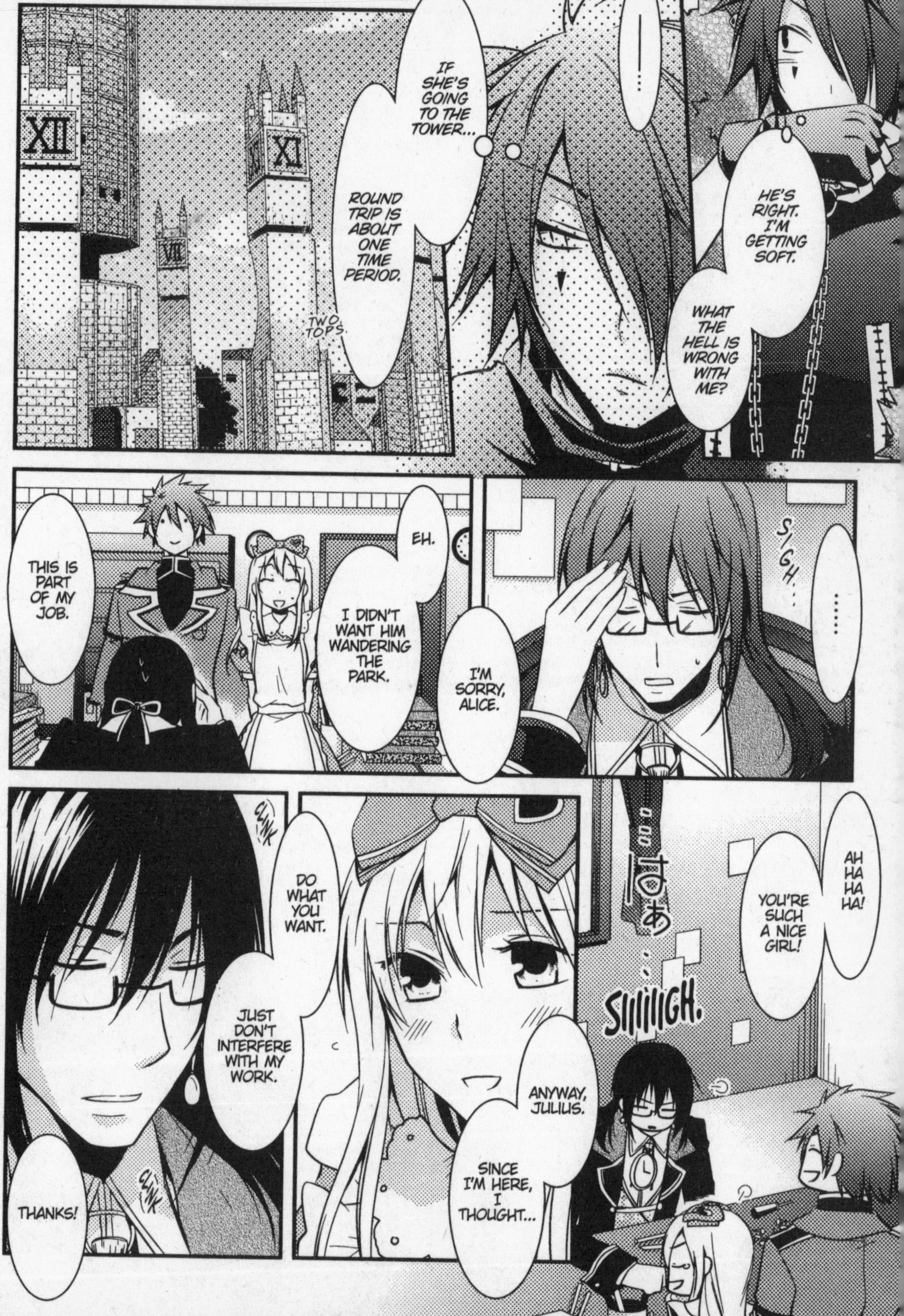
......!
HE'S RIGHT. I'M GETTING SOFT.
WHAT THE HELL IS WRONG WITH ME?
IF SHE'S GOING TO THE TOWER...
ROUND TRIP IS ABOUT ONE TIME PERIOD.
TWO TOPS.
SIGH...
......
I'M SORRY, ALICE.
EH.
I DIDN'T WANT HIM WANDERING THE PARK.
THIS IS PART OF MY JOB.
AH HA HA HA!
YOU'RE SUCH A NICE GIRL!
はぁ...
SIIIIIGH.
ANYWAY, JULIUS.
SINCE I'M HERE, I THOUGHT...
DO WHAT YOU WANT.
JUST DON'T INTERFERE WITH MY WORK.
CLINK
THANKS!
CLINK

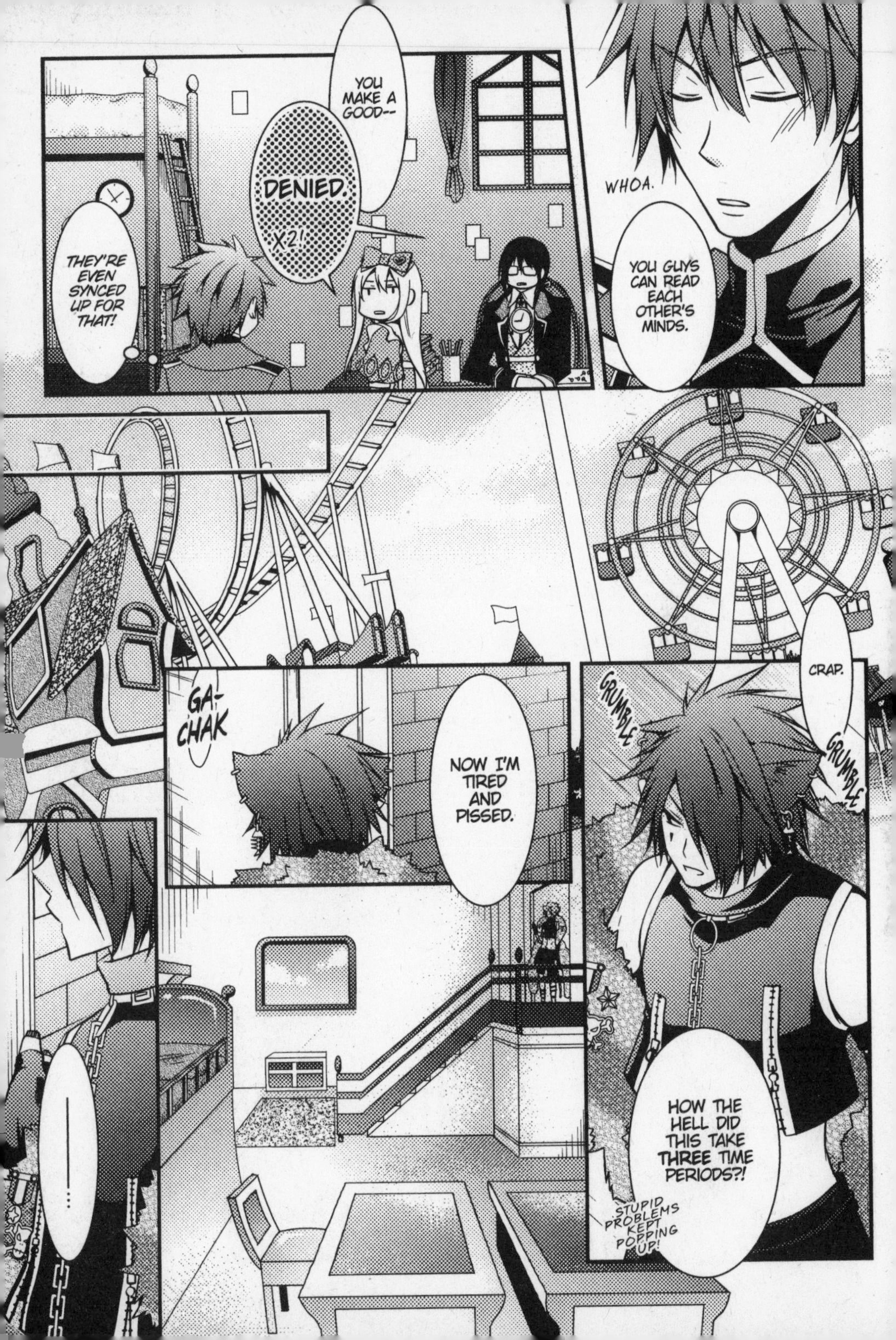
WHOA.
YOU GUYS CAN READ EACH OTHER'S MINDS.
YOU MAKE A GOOD--
DENIED.
X2!
THEY'RE EVEN SYNCED UP FOR THAT!
CRAP.
GRUMBLE
GRUMBLE
HOW THE HELL DID THIS TAKE THREE TIME PERIODS?!
STUPID PROBLEMS KEPT POPPING UP!
GA-CHAK
NOW I'M TIRED AND PISSED.
—...

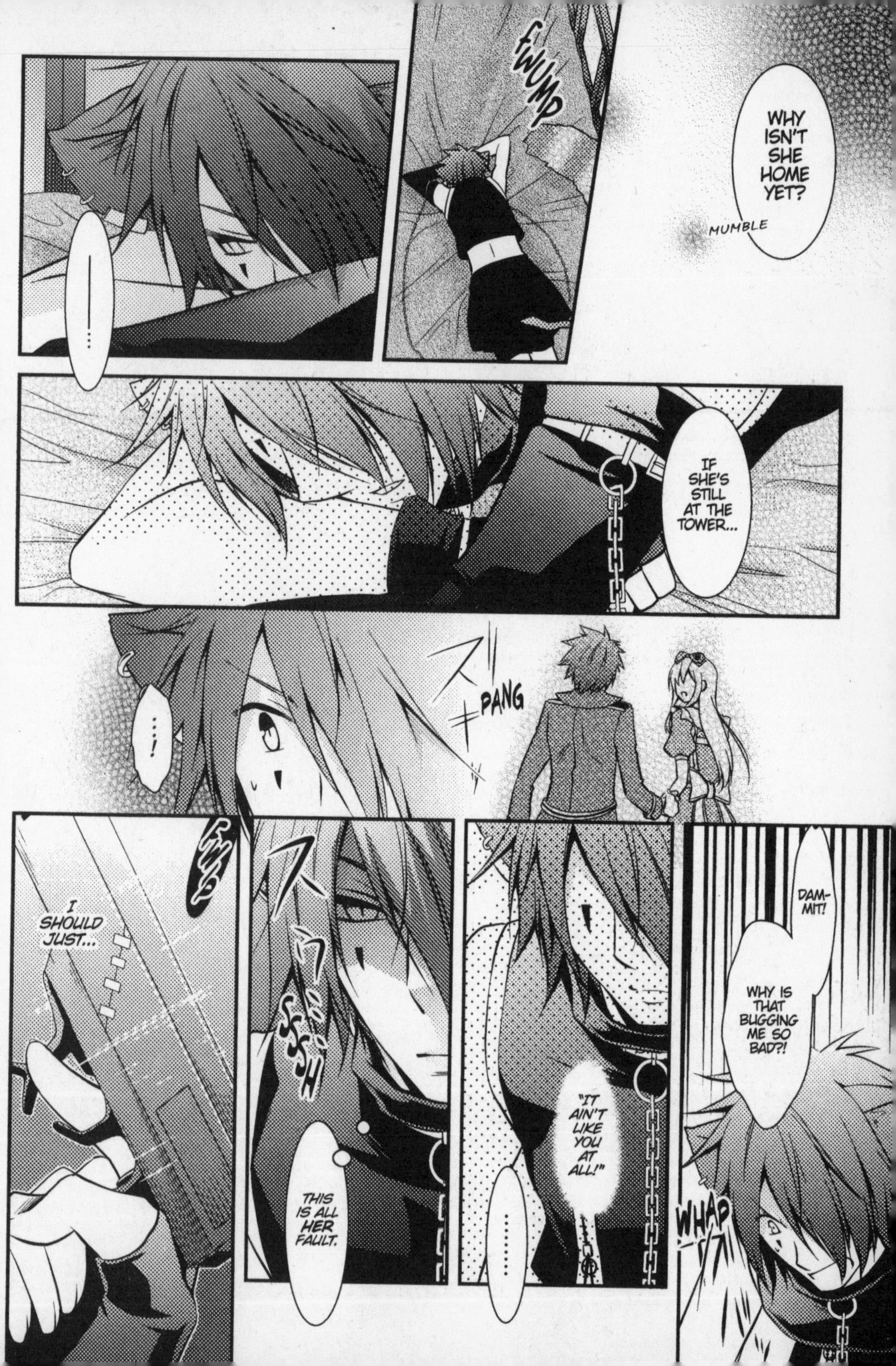
WHY ISN'T SHE HOME YET?
MUMBLE
FWUMP
......
IF SHE'S STILL AT THE TOWER...
PANG
...!
DAM-MIT!
WHY IS THAT BUGGING ME SO BAD?!
WHAP
"IT AIN'T LIKE YOU AT ALL!"
......
SSSH
THIS IS ALL HER FAULT.
I SHOULD JUST...

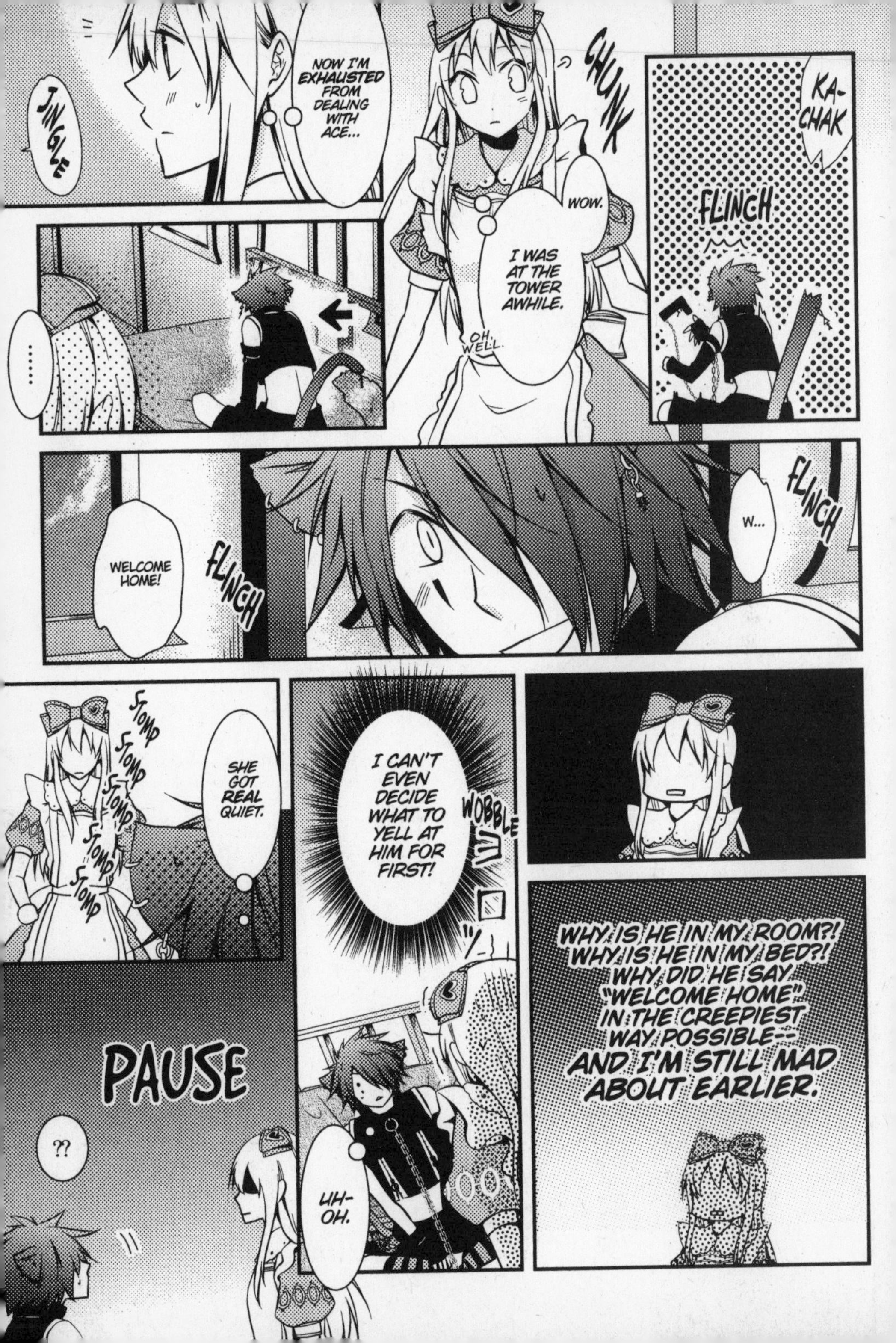

KA-CHAK
FLINCH
CHUNK
WOW.
I WAS AT THE TOWER AWHILE.
OH, WELL.
NOW I'M EXHAUSTED FROM DEALING WITH ACE...
JINGLE
......
W...
FLINCH
WELCOME HOME!
FLINCH
WHY IS HE IN MY ROOM?! WHY IS HE IN MY BED?! WHY DID HE SAY "WELCOME HOME" IN THE CREEPIEST WAY POSSIBLE-- AND I'M STILL MAD ABOUT EARLIER.
I CAN'T EVEN DECIDE WHAT TO YELL AT HIM FOR FIRST!
WOBBLE
UH-OH.
STOMP STOMP STOMP STOMP STOMP STOMP
SHE GOT REAL QUIET.
PAUSE
??

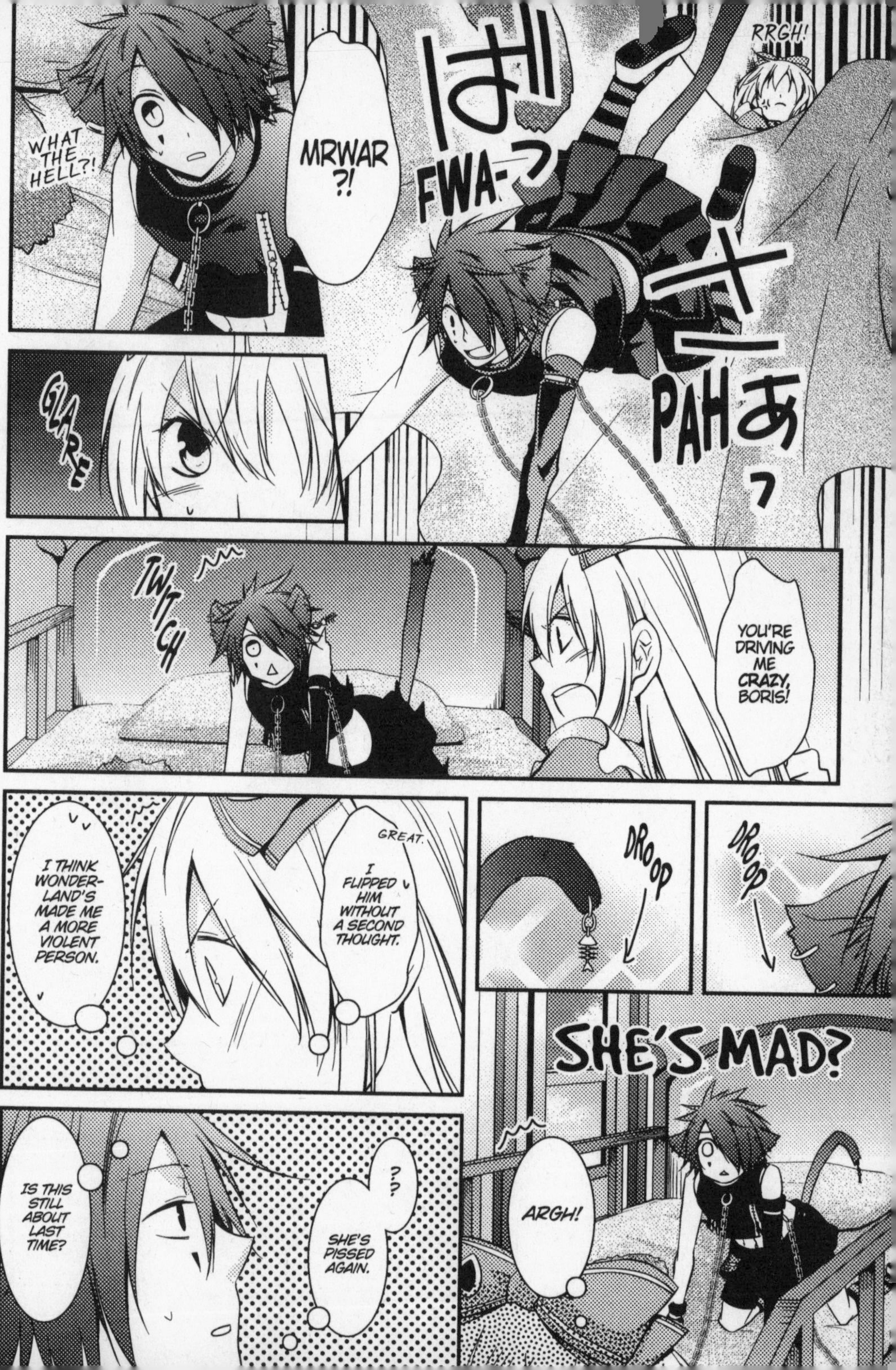
RRGH!
は FWA-っ
さ PAH あっ
MRWAR?!
WHAT THE HELL?!
GLARE
YOU'RE DRIVING ME CRAZY, BORIS!
TWITCH
DROOP
DROOP
GREAT.
I FLIPPED HIM WITHOUT A SECOND THOUGHT.
I THINK WONDER-LAND'S MADE ME A MORE VIOLENT PERSON.
SHE'S MAD?
ARGH!
??
SHE'S PISSED AGAIN.
IS THIS STILL ABOUT LAST TIME?

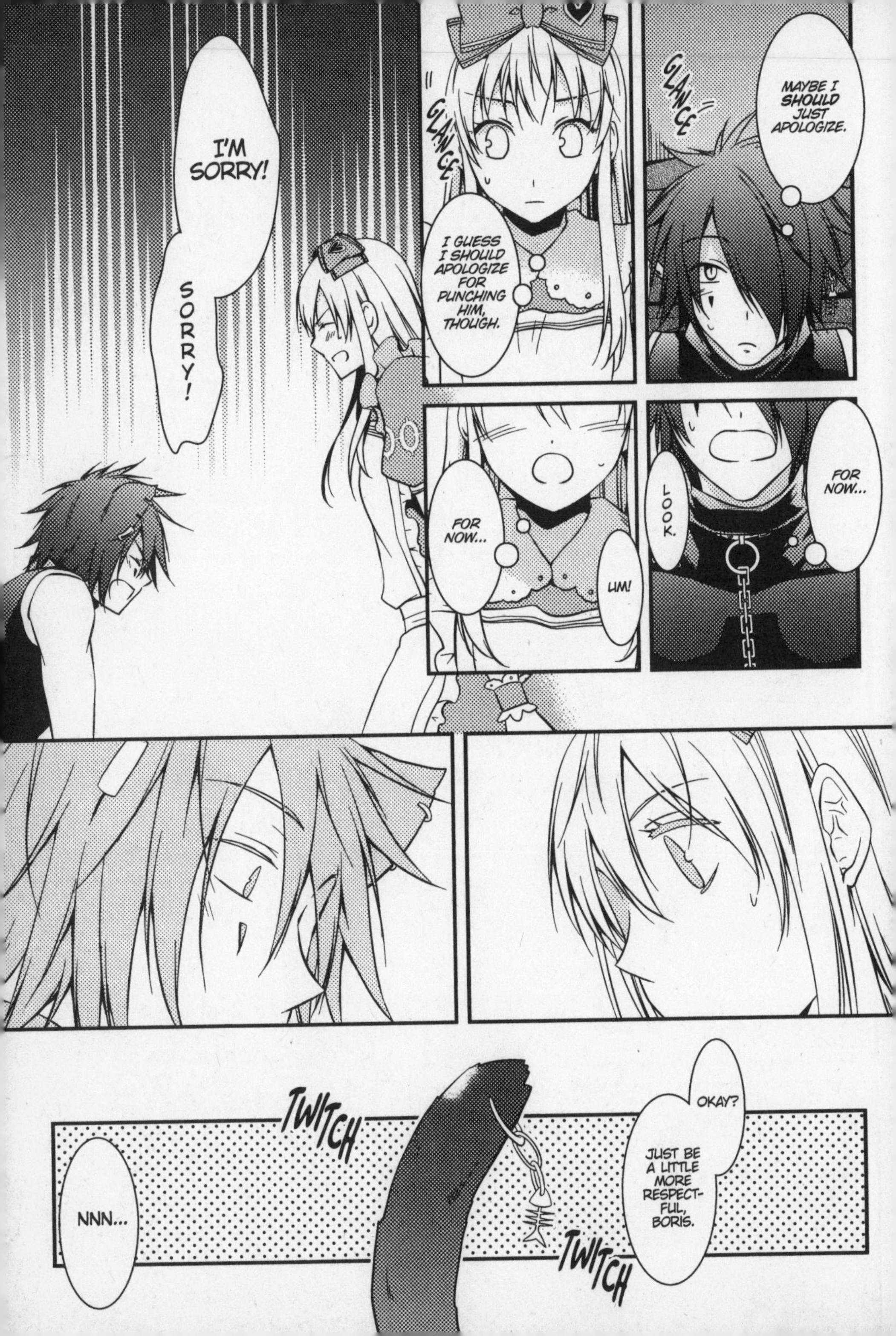
GLANCE
MAYBE I SHOULD JUST APOLOGIZE.
GLANCE
I GUESS I SHOULD APOLOGIZE FOR PUNCHING HIM, THOUGH.
FOR NOW...
LOOK.
FOR NOW...
UM!
I'M SORRY!
SORRY!
SORRY!
OKAY?
JUST BE A LITTLE MORE RESPECT-FUL, BORIS.
TWITCH
TWITCH
NNN...

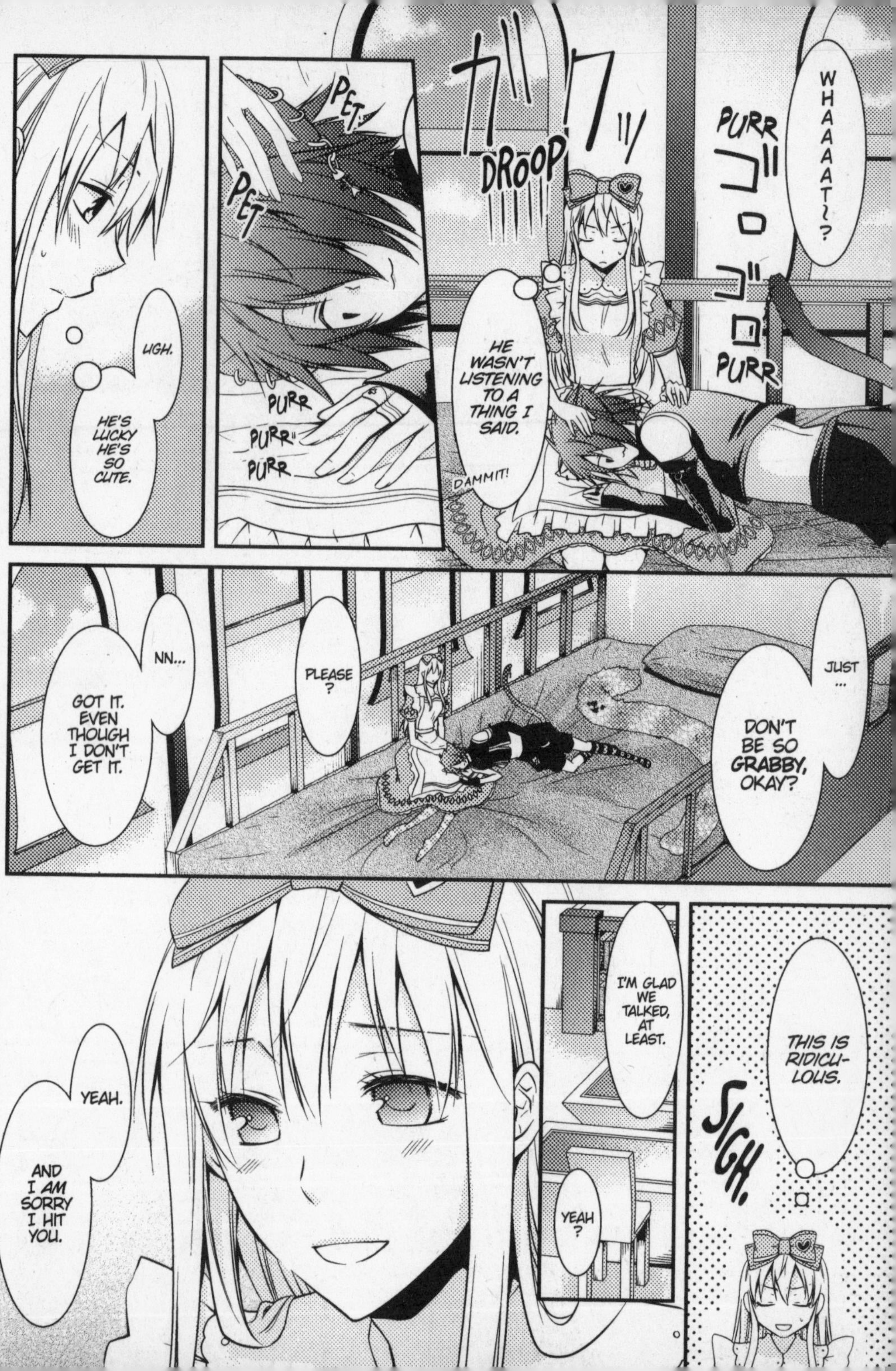
WHAAAAT~?
PURR
ゴロゴロ
PURR
カッ
DROOP
HE WASN'T LISTENING TO A THING I SAID.
DAMMIT!
PET
PET
PURR
PURR
PURR
UGH.
HE'S LUCKY HE'S SO CUTE.
JUST...
DON'T BE SO GRABBY, OKAY?
PLEASE?
NN...
GOT IT. EVEN THOUGH I DON'T GET IT.
THIS IS RIDICU-LOUS.
SIGH.
I'M GLAD WE TALKED, AT LEAST.
YEAH?
YEAH.
AND I AM SORRY I HIT YOU.

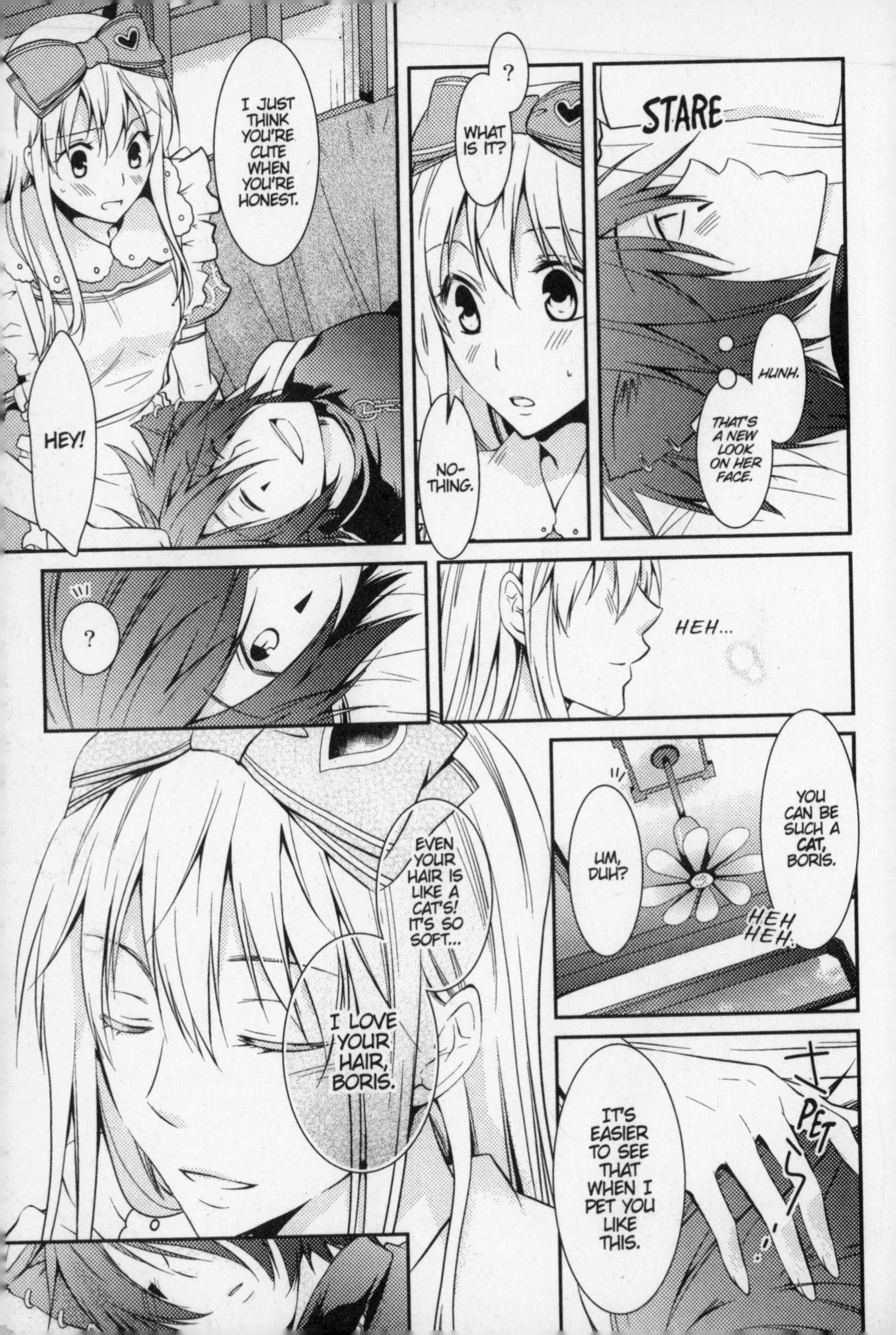
STARE
HUNH.
THAT'S A NEW LOOK ON HER FACE.
?
WHAT IS IT?
NO-THING.
I JUST THINK YOU'RE CUTE WHEN YOU'RE HONEST.
HEY!
HEH...
?
YOU CAN BE SUCH A CAT, BORIS.
HEH HEH.
UM, DUH?
IT'S EASIER TO SEE THAT WHEN I PET YOU LIKE THIS.
PET
EVEN YOUR HAIR IS LIKE A CAT'S! IT'S SO SOFT...
I LOVE YOUR HAIR, BORIS.

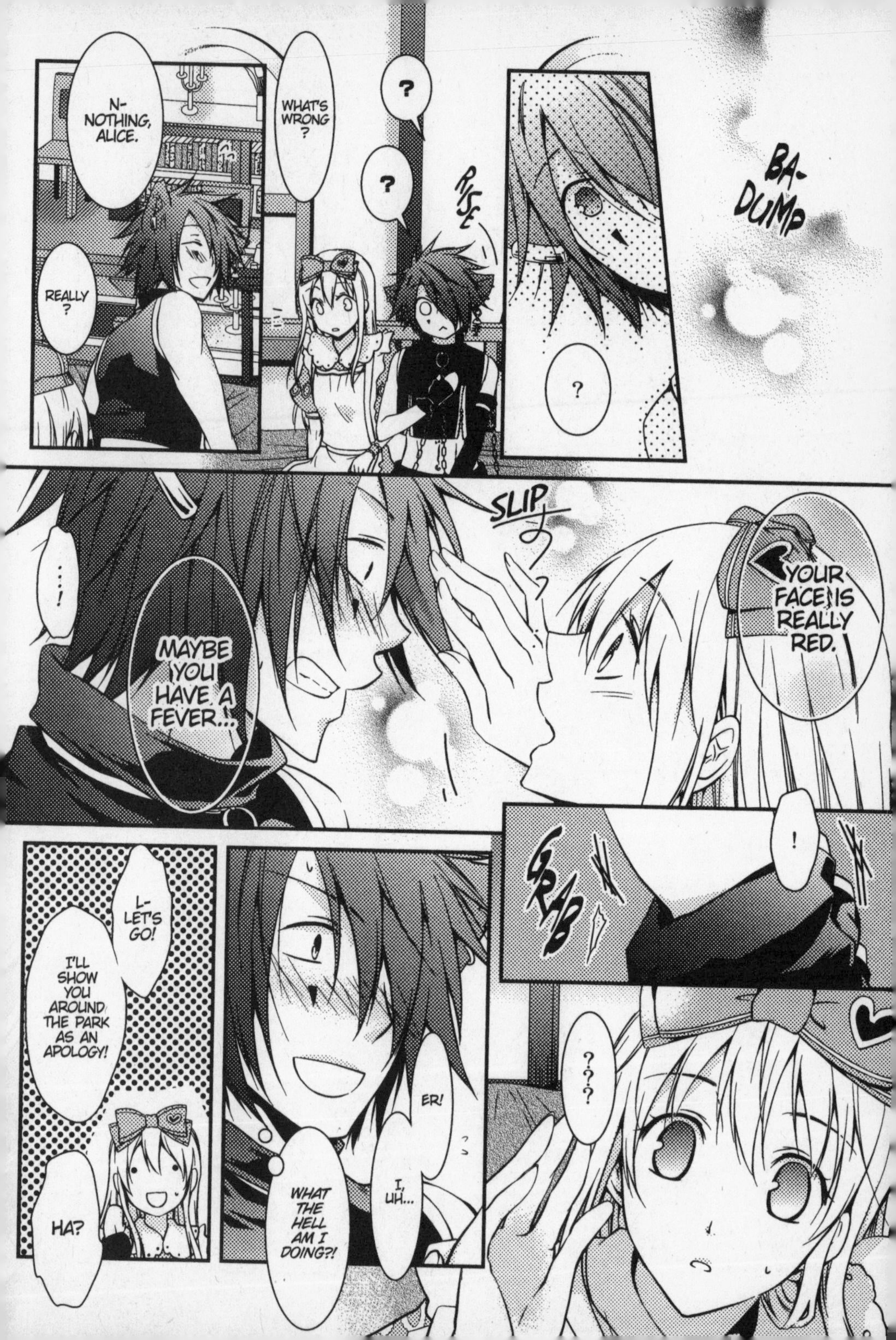
BA-DUMP
?
?
?
RISE
WHAT'S WRONG?
N-NOTHING, ALICE.
REALLY?
YOUR FACE IS REALLY RED.
SLIP
MAYBE YOU HAVE A FEVER...
...!
!
GRAB
???
ER!
I, UH...
WHAT THE HELL AM I DOING?!
L-LET'S GO!
I'LL SHOW YOU AROUND THE PARK AS AN APOLOGY!
HA?

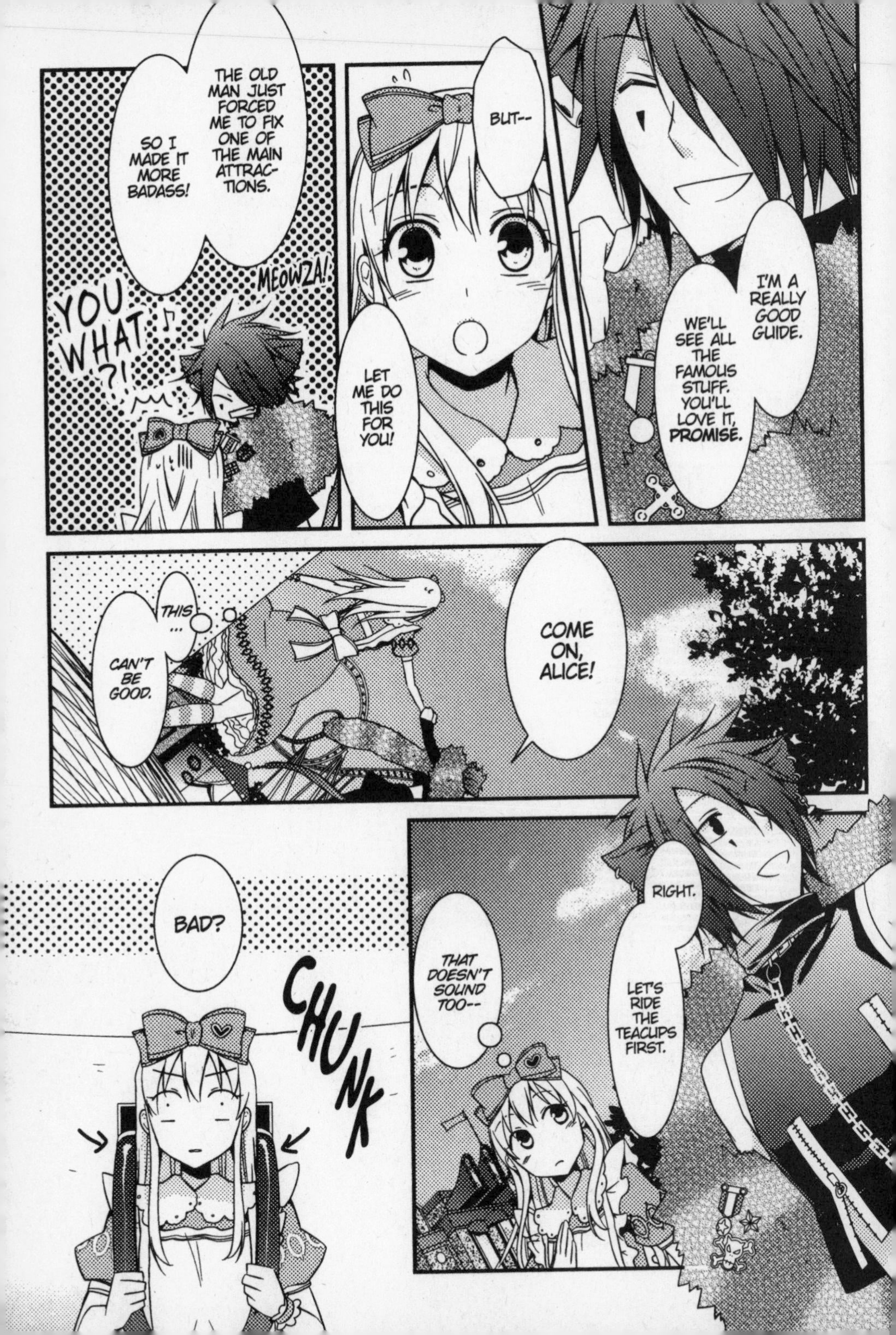

I'M A REALLY GOOD GUIDE.
WE'LL SEE ALL THE FAMOUS STUFF. YOU'LL LOVE IT, **PROMISE.**
BUT--
LET ME DO THIS FOR YOU!
THE OLD MAN JUST FORCED ME TO FIX ONE OF THE MAIN ATTRACTIONS.
SO I MADE IT MORE BADASS!
MEOWZA!
YOU WHAT?!
COME ON, ALICE!
THIS... CAN'T BE GOOD.
RIGHT.
LET'S RIDE THE TEACUPS FIRST.
THAT DOESN'T SOUND TOO--
BAD?
CHUNK

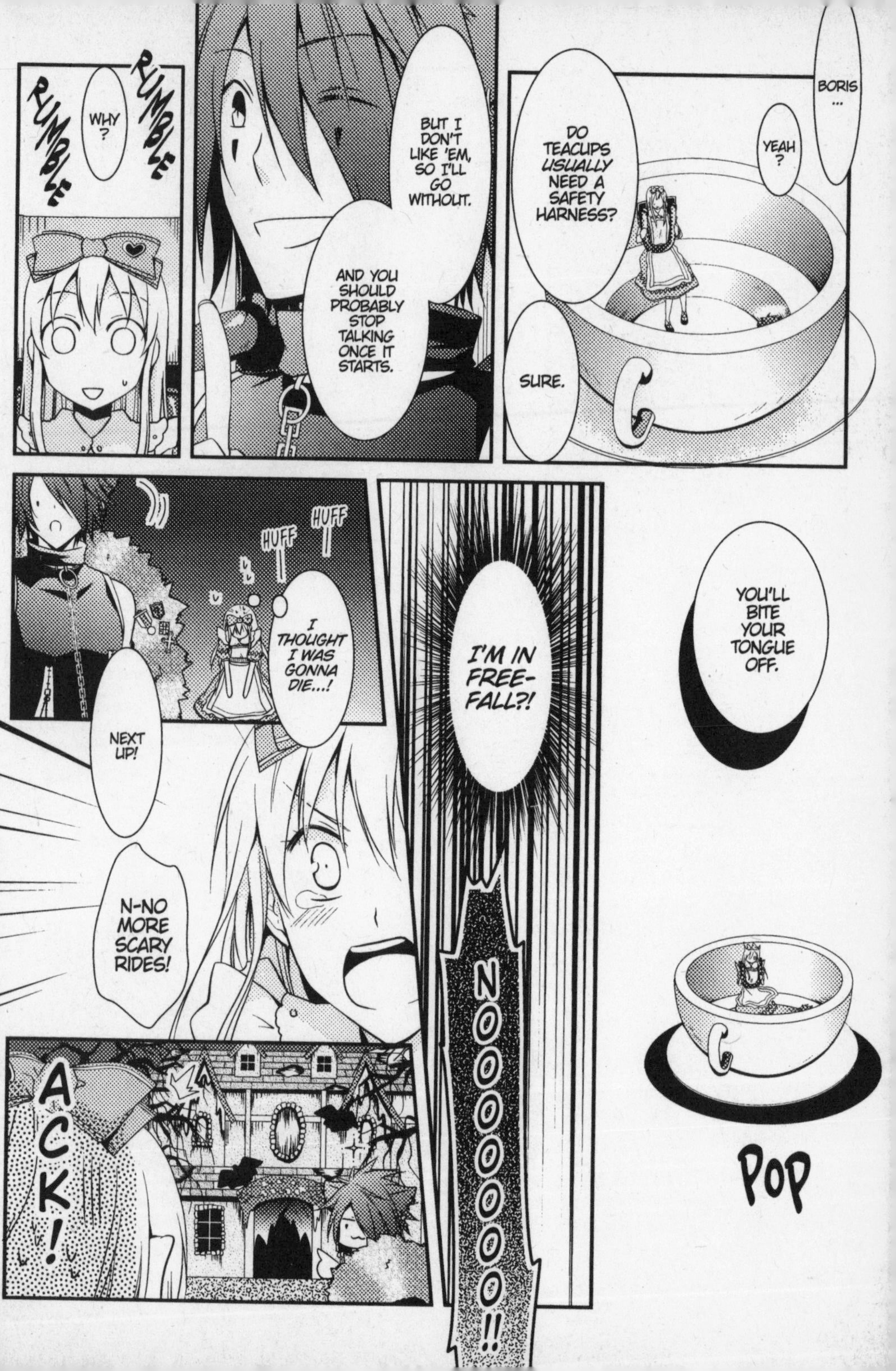
BORIS ...
YEAH ?
DO TEACUPS USUALLY NEED A SAFETY HARNESS?
SURE.
BUT I DON'T LIKE 'EM, SO I'LL GO WITHOUT.
AND YOU SHOULD PROBABLY STOP TALKING ONCE IT STARTS.
RUMBLE RUMBLE
WHY ?
YOU'LL BITE YOUR TONGUE OFF.
POP
I'M IN FREE-FALL?!
NOOOOOOOOO!!
HUFF HUFF
I THOUGHT I WAS GONNA DIE...!
NEXT UP!
N-NO MORE SCARY RIDES!
ACK!

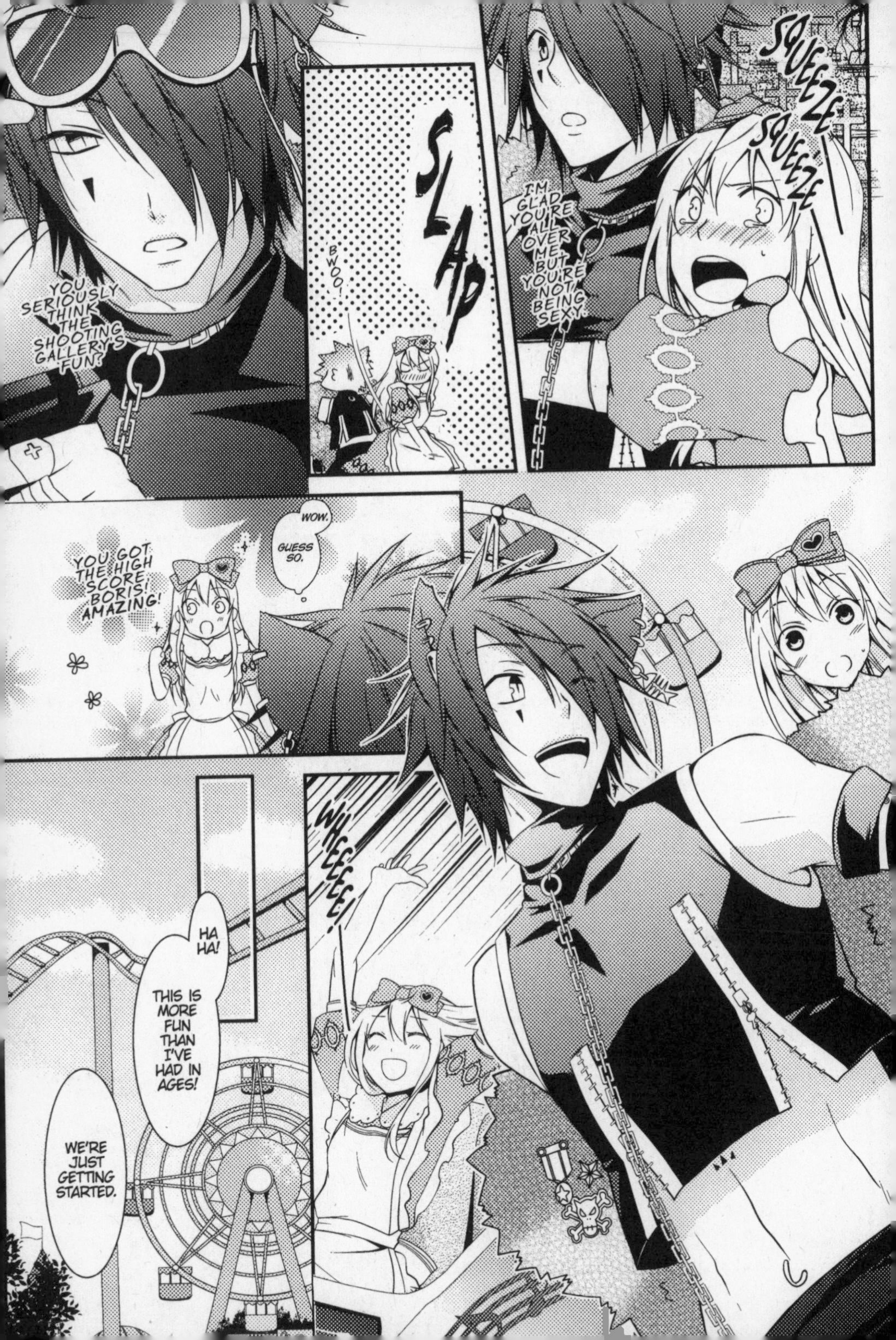
SQUEEZE
SQUEEZE
I'M GLAD YOU'RE ALL OVER ME, BUT YOU'RE NOT BEING SEXY.
SLAP
BWOO!
YOU SERIOUSLY THINK THE SHOOTING GALLERY'S FUN?
YOU GOT THE HIGH SCORE, BORIS! AMAZING!
WOW.
GUESS SO.
WHEEEEE!
HA HA!
THIS IS MORE FUN THAN I'VE HAD IN AGES!
WE'RE JUST GETTING STARTED.

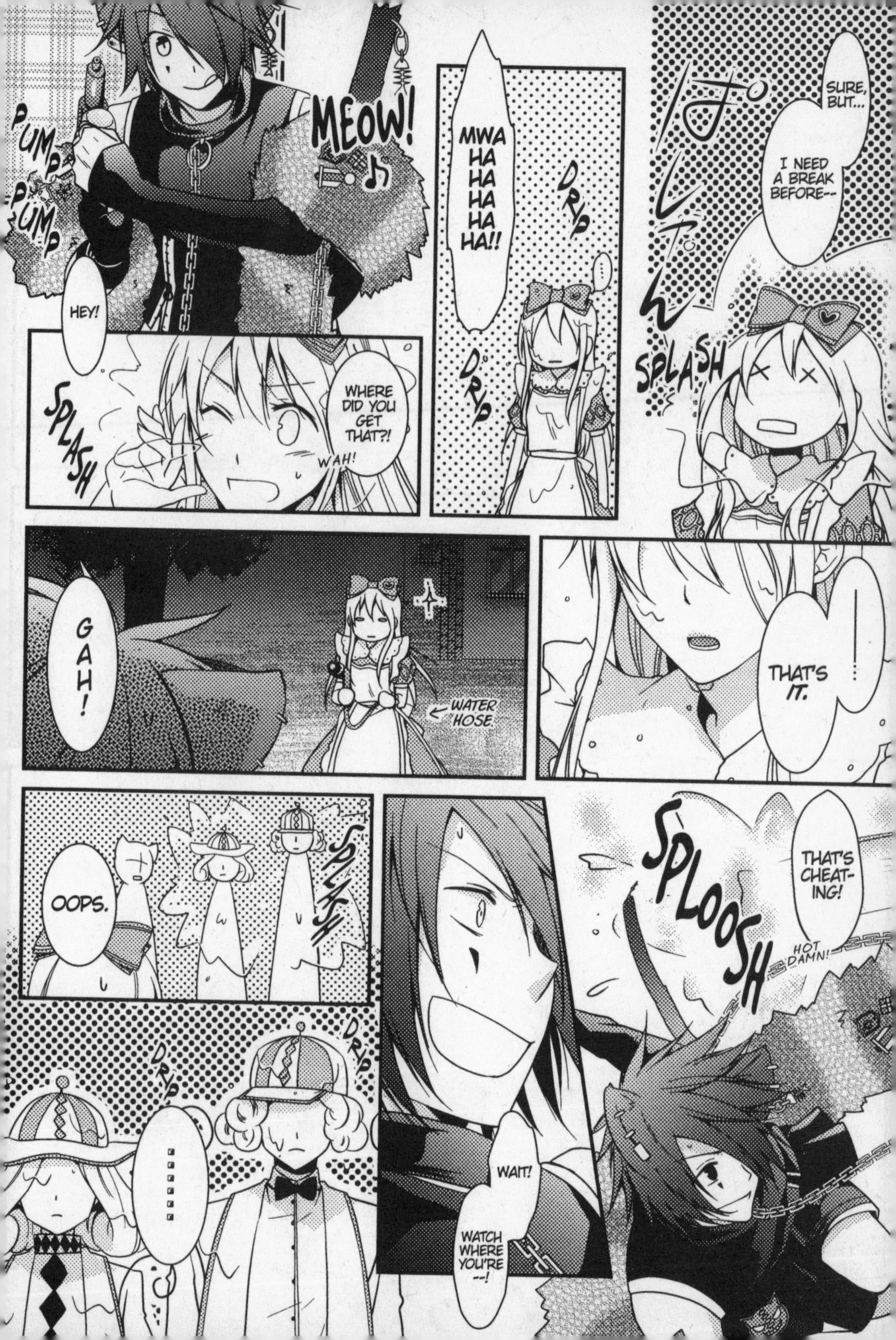
SURE, BUT...
I NEED A BREAK BEFORE--
SPLASH
MWA HA HA HA HA HA!!
DRIP
DRIP
...
PUMP PUMP PUMP
MEOW!
HEY!
SPLASH
WHERE DID YOU GET THAT?!
WAH!
...!
THAT'S IT.
GAH!
WATER HOSE.
THAT'S CHEATING!
SPLOOSH
HOT DAMN!
WAIT!
WATCH WHERE YOU'RE --!
SPLASH
OOPS.
DRIP
DRIP
......

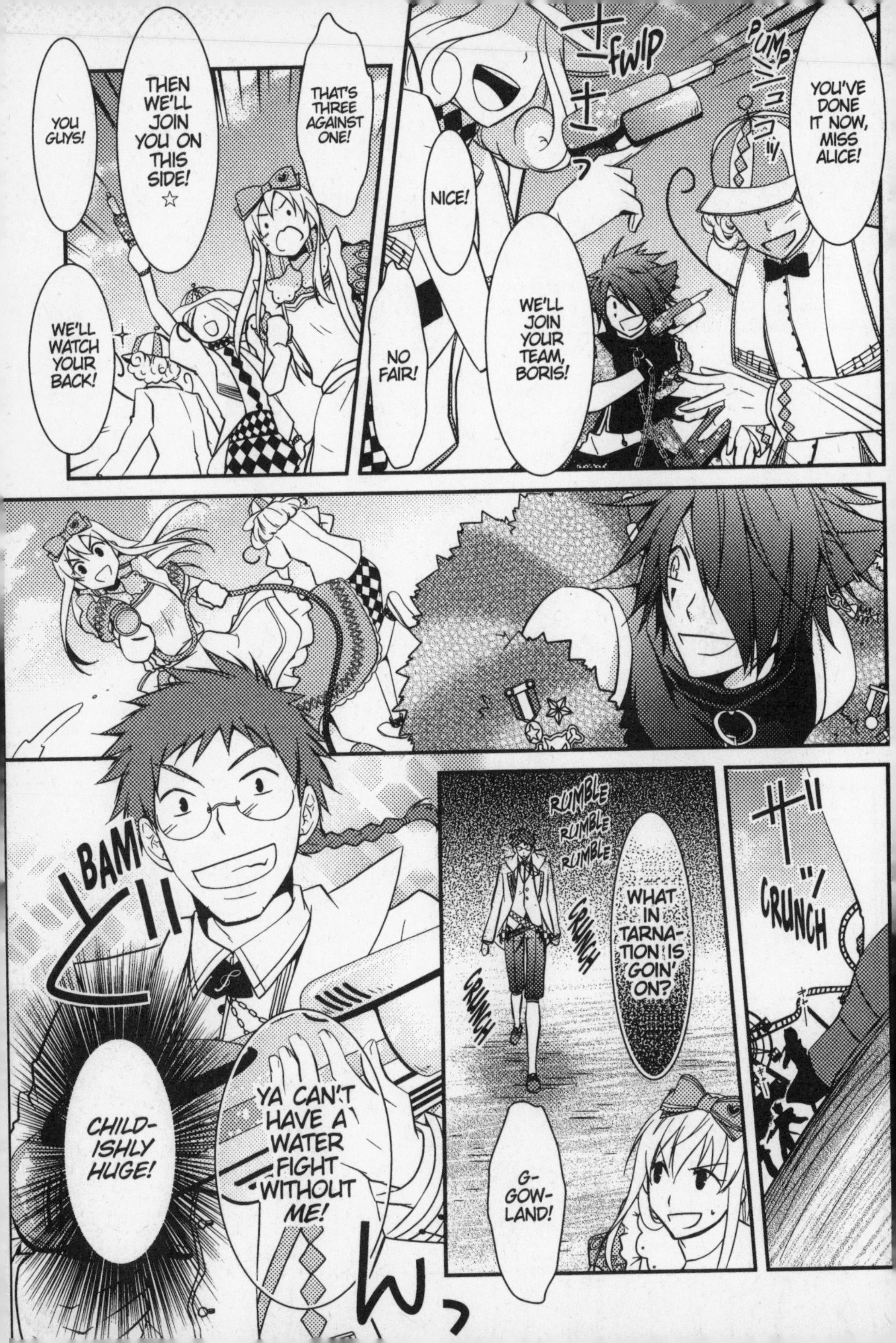
PUMP
YOU'VE DONE IT NOW, MISS ALICE!
FWIP
NICE!
WE'LL JOIN YOUR TEAM, BORIS!
NO FAIR!
THAT'S THREE AGAINST ONE!
THEN WE'LL JOIN YOU ON THIS SIDE! ☆
YOU GUYS!
WE'LL WATCH YOUR BACK!
CRUNCH
RUMBLE RUMBLE RUMBLE
WHAT IN TARNATION IS GOIN' ON?
CRUNCH
CRUNCH
G-GOWLAND!
BAM
YA CAN'T HAVE A WATER FIGHT WITHOUT ME!
CHILDISHLY HUGE!

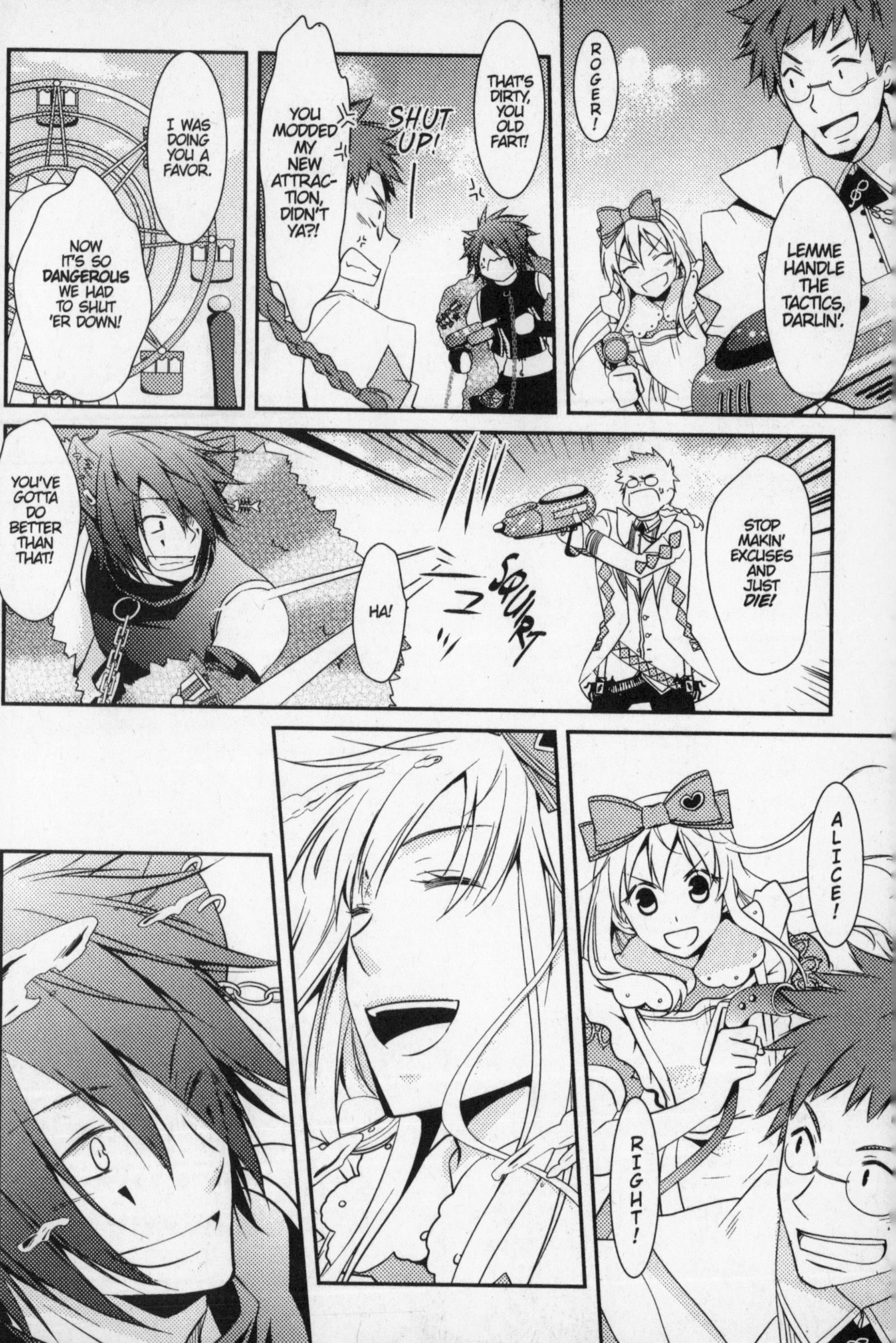
LEMME HANDLE THE TACTICS, DARLIN'.
ROGER!
THAT'S DIRTY, YOU OLD FART!
SHUT UP!
YOU MODDED MY NEW ATTRACTION, DIDN'T YA?!
I WAS DOING YOU A FAVOR.
NOW IT'S SO DANGEROUS WE HAD TO SHUT 'ER DOWN!
STOP MAKIN' EXCUSES AND JUST DIE!
SQUIRT
HA!
YOU'VE GOTTA DO BETTER THAN THAT!
ALICE!
RIGHT!

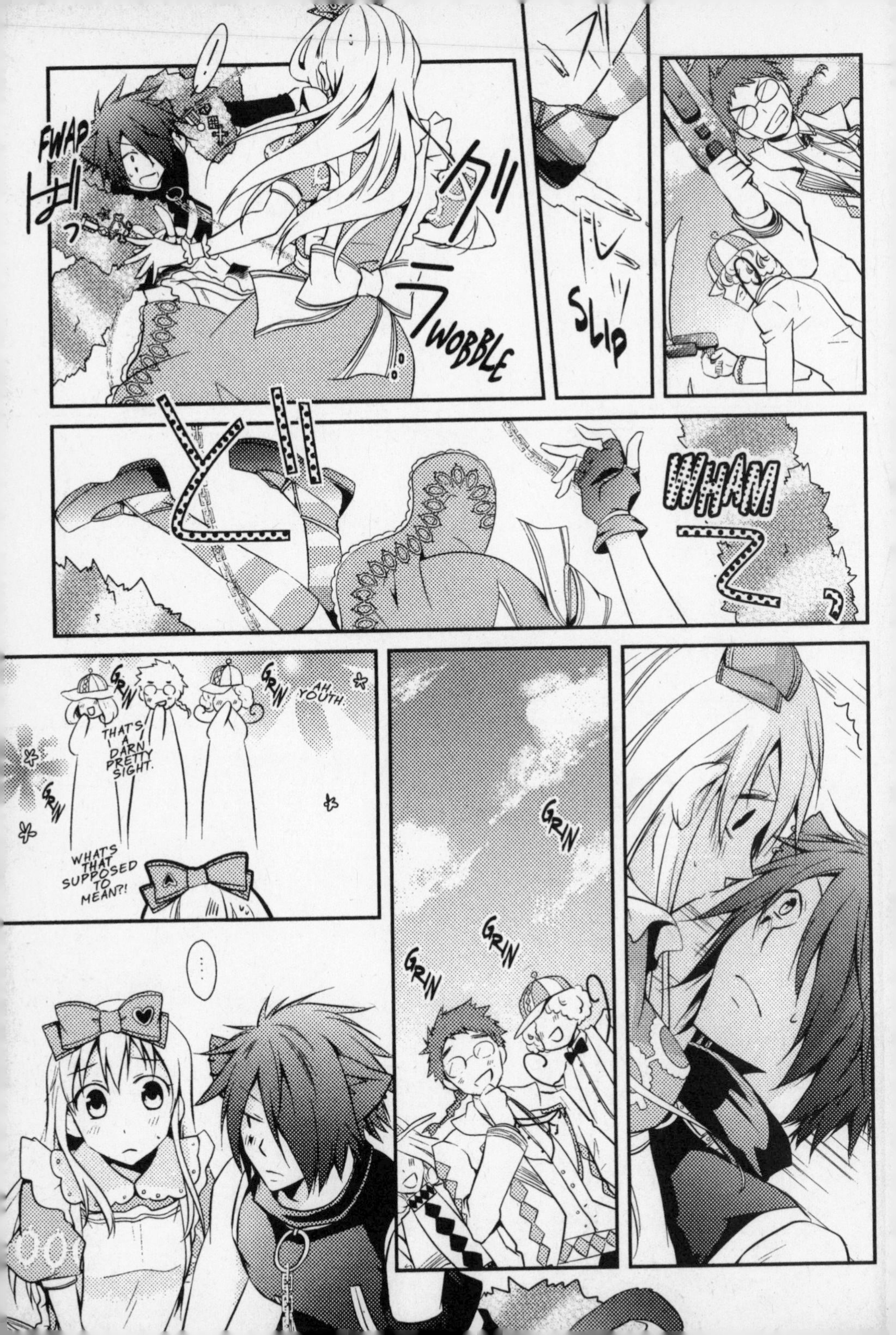
SLIP
!
FWAP
WOBBLE
WHAM
GRIN
GRIN
GRIN
AH, YOUTH.
GRIN
THAT'S A DARN PRETTY SIGHT.
GRIN
GRIN
WHAT'S THAT SUPPOSED TO MEAN?!
....

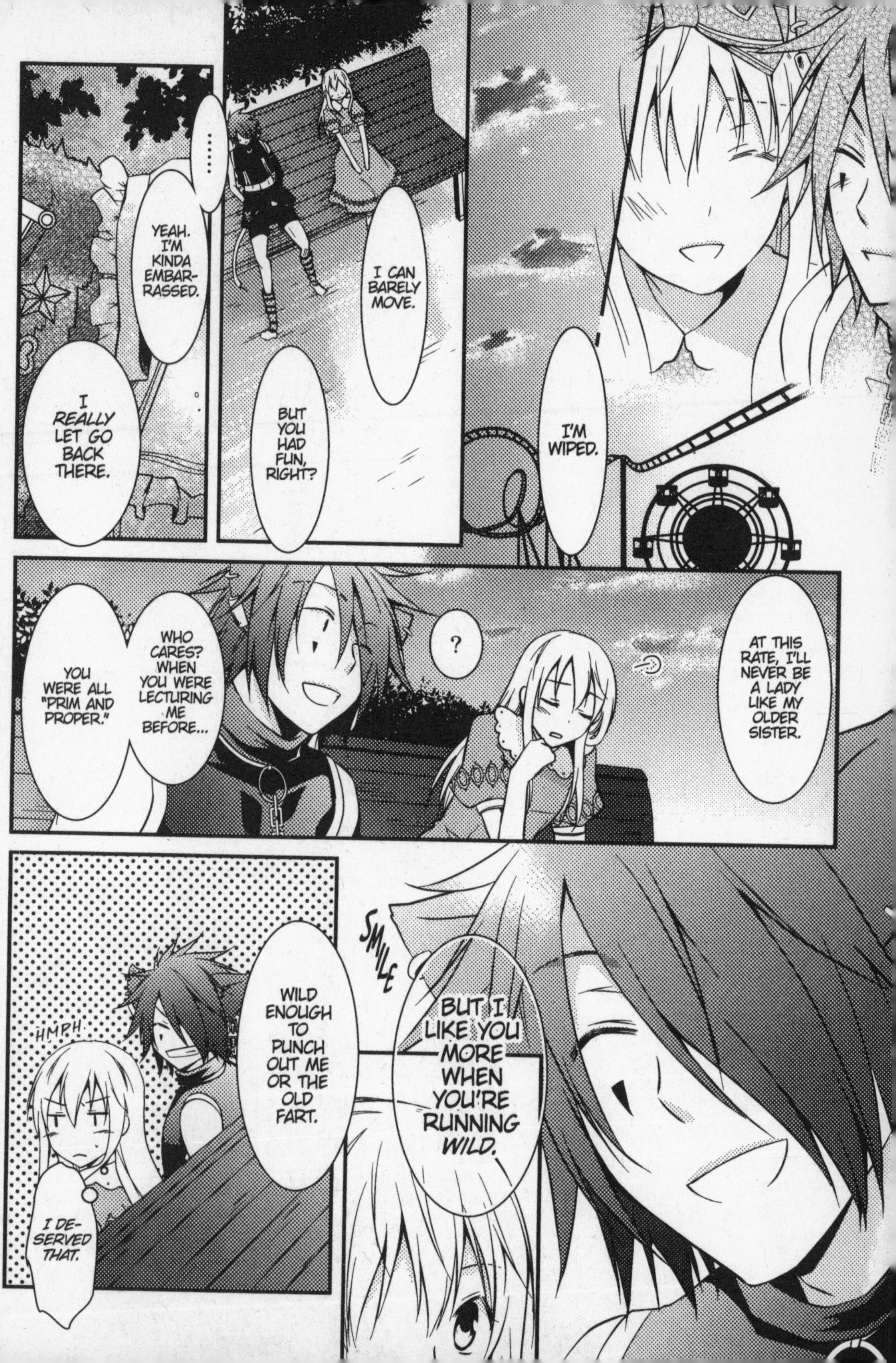
I'M WIPED.
I CAN BARELY MOVE.
BUT YOU HAD FUN, RIGHT?
......
YEAH. I'M KINDA EMBARRASSED.
I *REALLY* LET GO BACK THERE.
AT THIS RATE, I'LL NEVER BE A LADY LIKE MY OLDER SISTER.
?
WHO CARES? WHEN YOU WERE LECTURING ME BEFORE...
YOU WERE ALL "PRIM AND PROPER."
SMILE
BUT I LIKE YOU MORE WHEN YOU'RE RUNNING *WILD.*
WILD ENOUGH TO PUNCH OUT ME OR THE OLD FART.
HMPH
I DE-SERVED THAT.

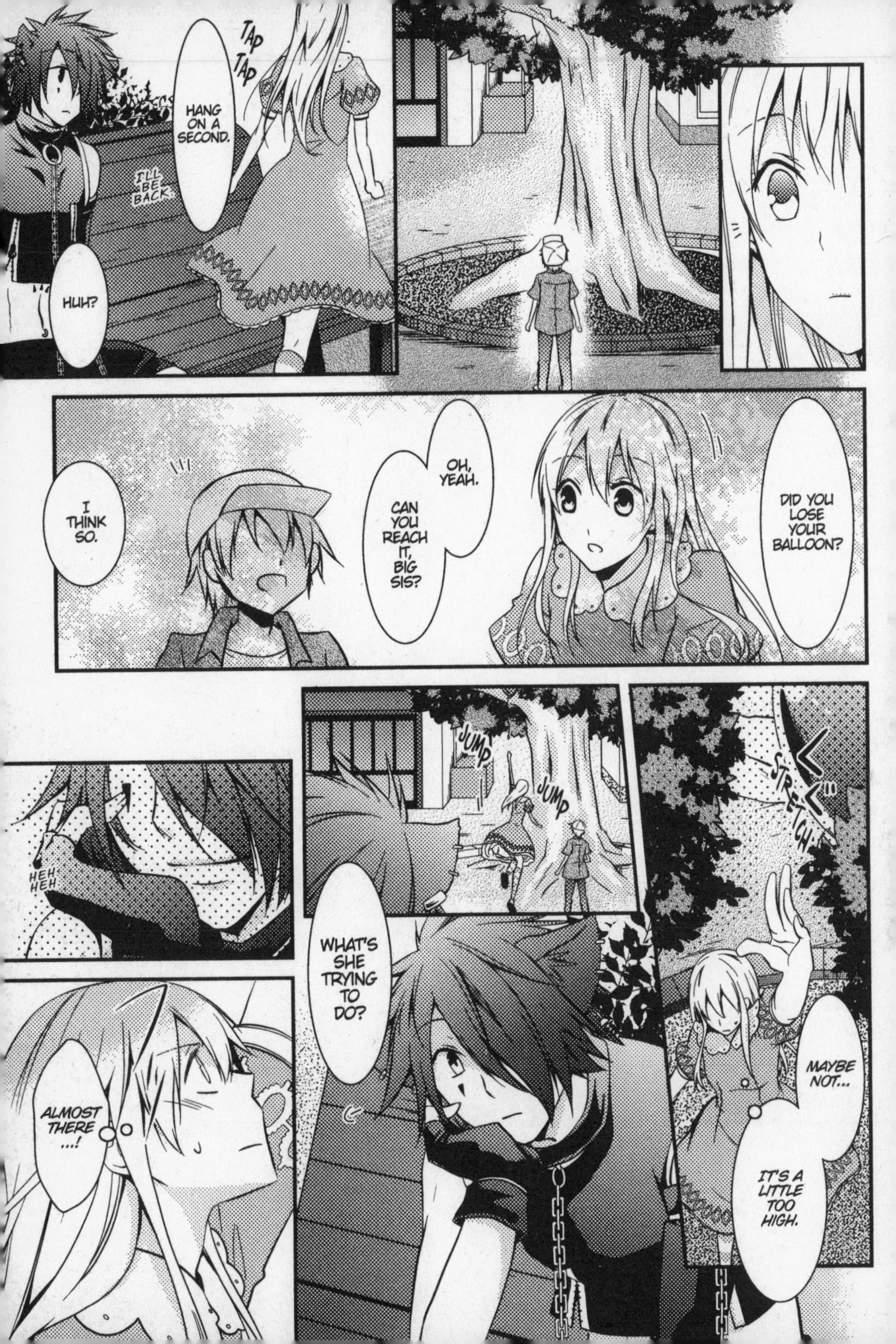
TAP TAP
HANG ON A SECOND.
I'LL BE BACK.
HUH?
DID YOU LOSE YOUR BALLOON?
OH, YEAH.
CAN YOU REACH IT, BIG SIS?
I THINK SO.
STRETCH
MAYBE NOT...
IT'S A LITTLE TOO HIGH.
JUMP
JUMP
WHAT'S SHE TRYING TO DO?
HEH HEH
ALMOST THERE ...!

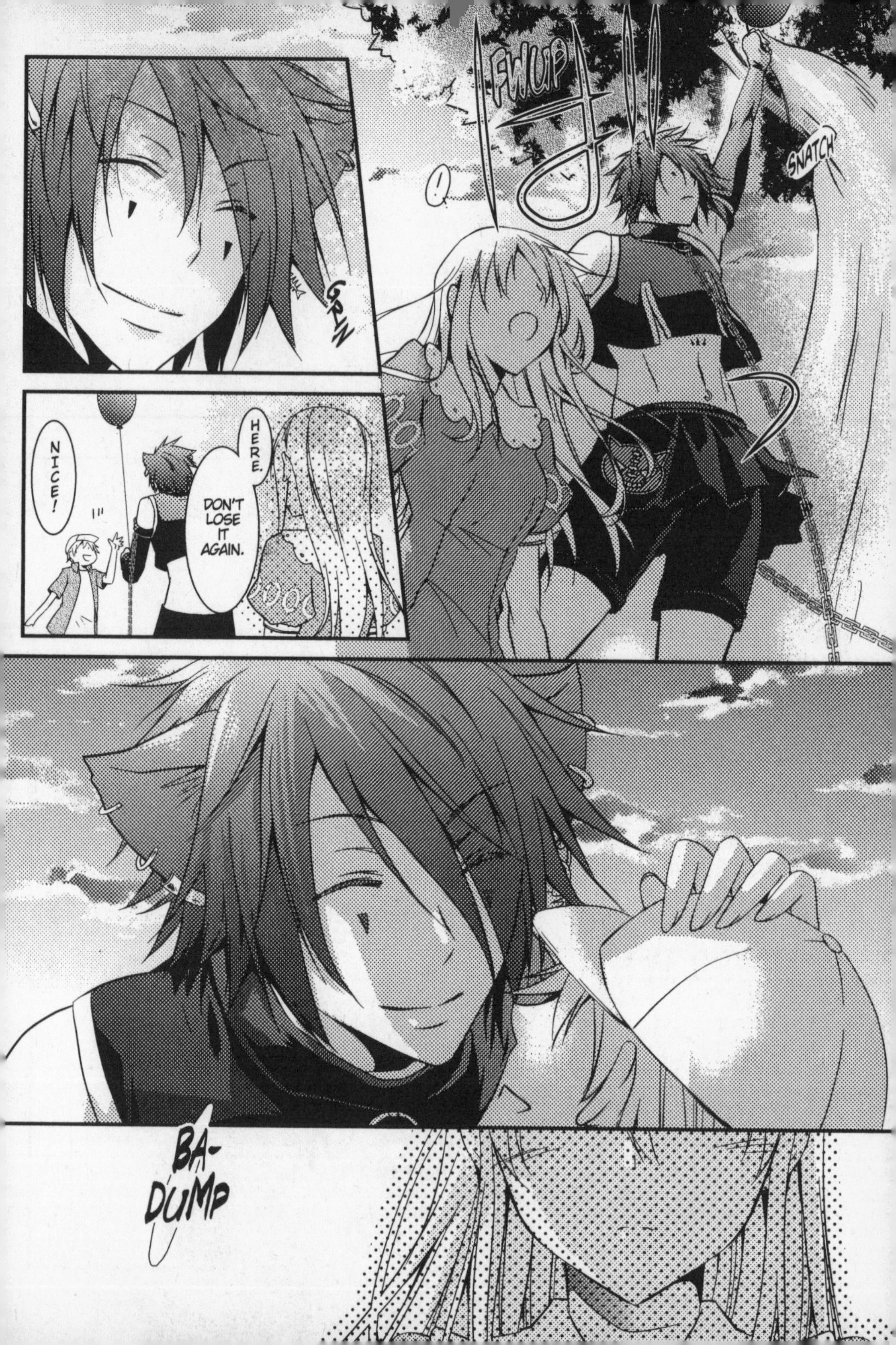
FWUP
SNATCH
!
GRIN
HERE.
DON'T LOSE IT AGAIN.
NICE!
BA-DUMP

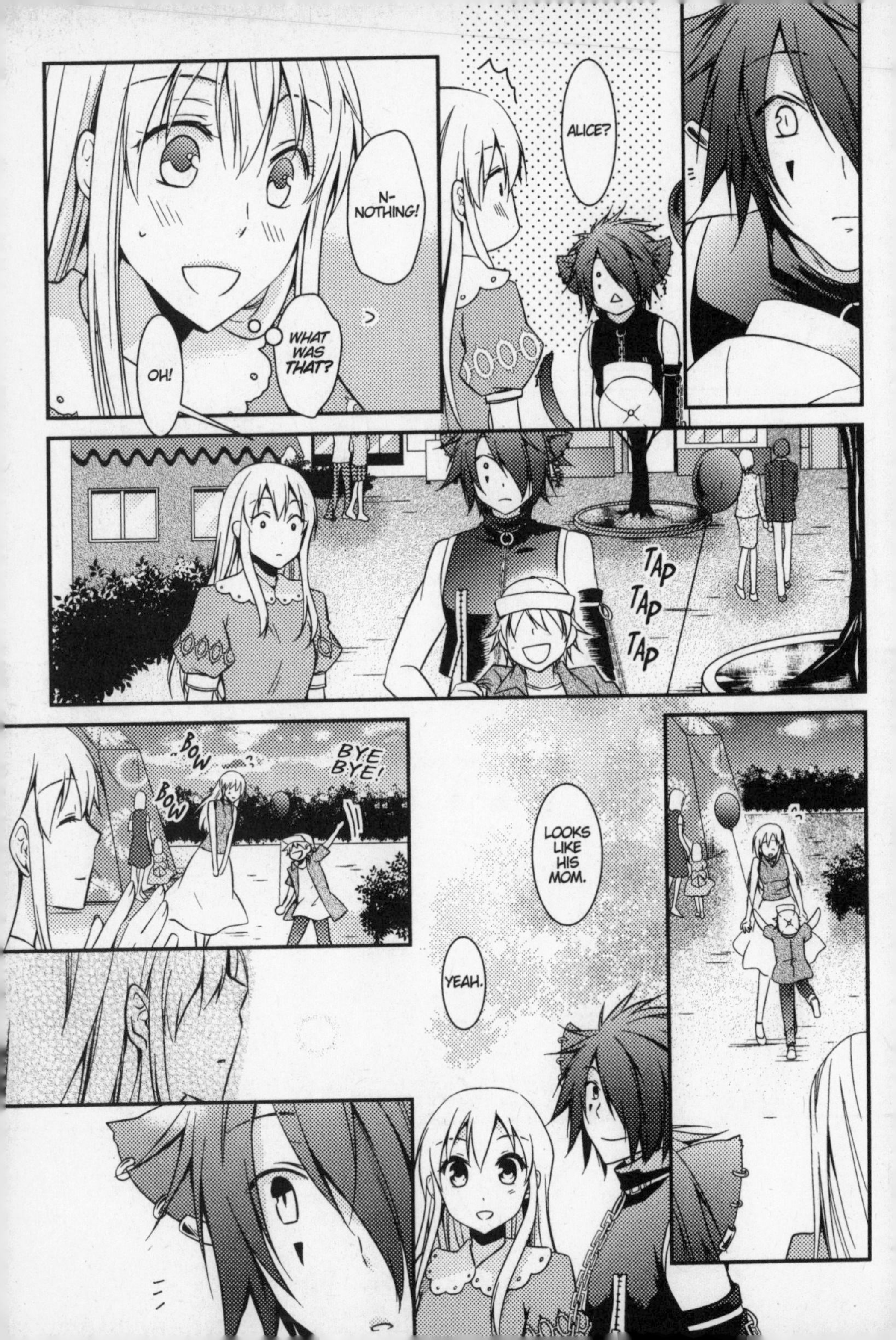
ALICE?
N-NOTHING!
WHAT WAS THAT?
OH!
TAP TAP TAP
BYE BYE!
BOW BOW
LOOKS LIKE HIS MOM.
YEAH.

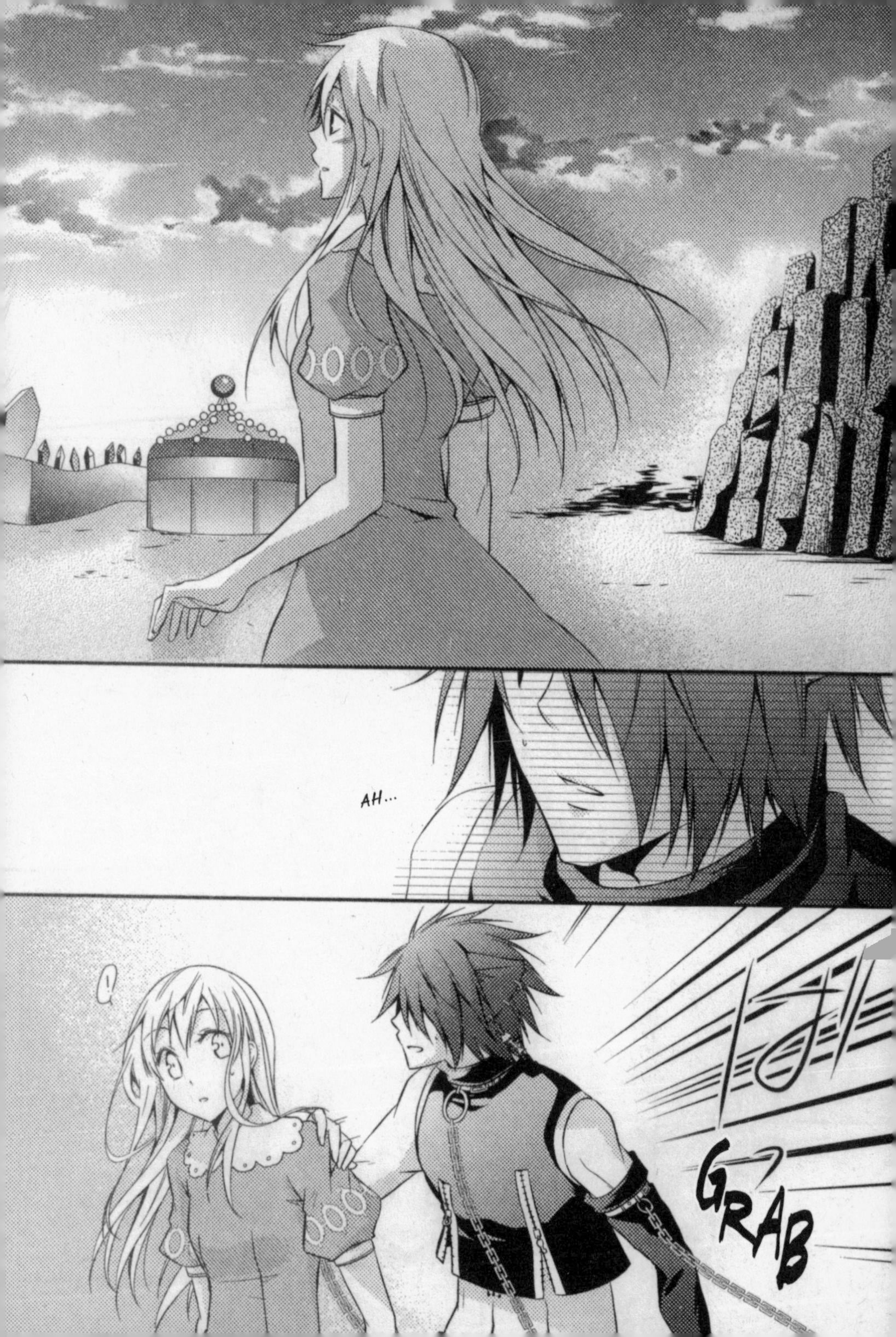
AH...
GRAB
!

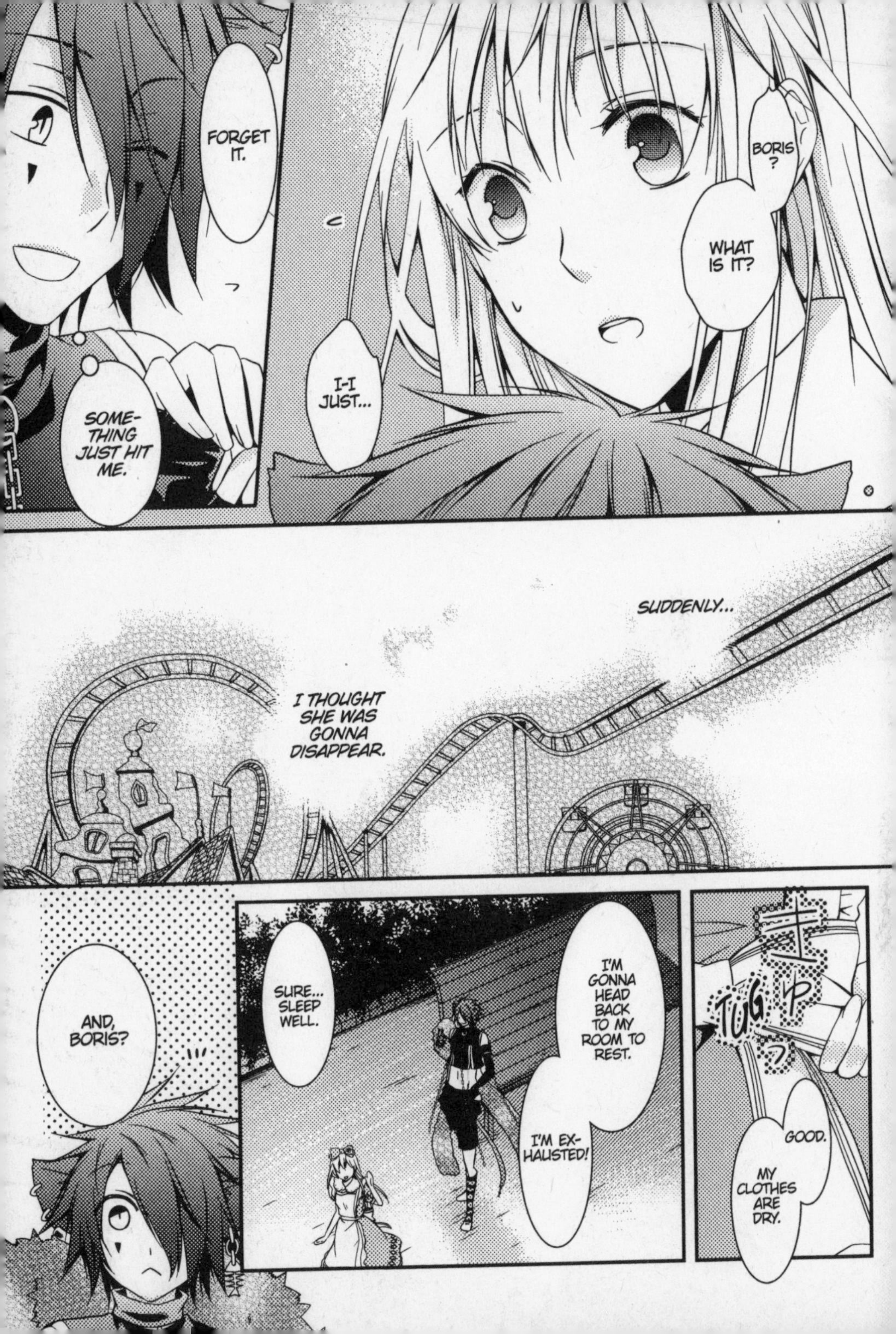
BORIS?
WHAT IS IT?
I-I JUST...
FORGET IT.
SOME-THING JUST HIT ME.
SUDDENLY...
I THOUGHT SHE WAS GONNA DISAPPEAR.
TUG
GOOD.
MY CLOTHES ARE DRY.
I'M GONNA HEAD BACK TO MY ROOM TO REST.
I'M EX-HAUSTED!
SURE... SLEEP WELL.
AND, BORIS?

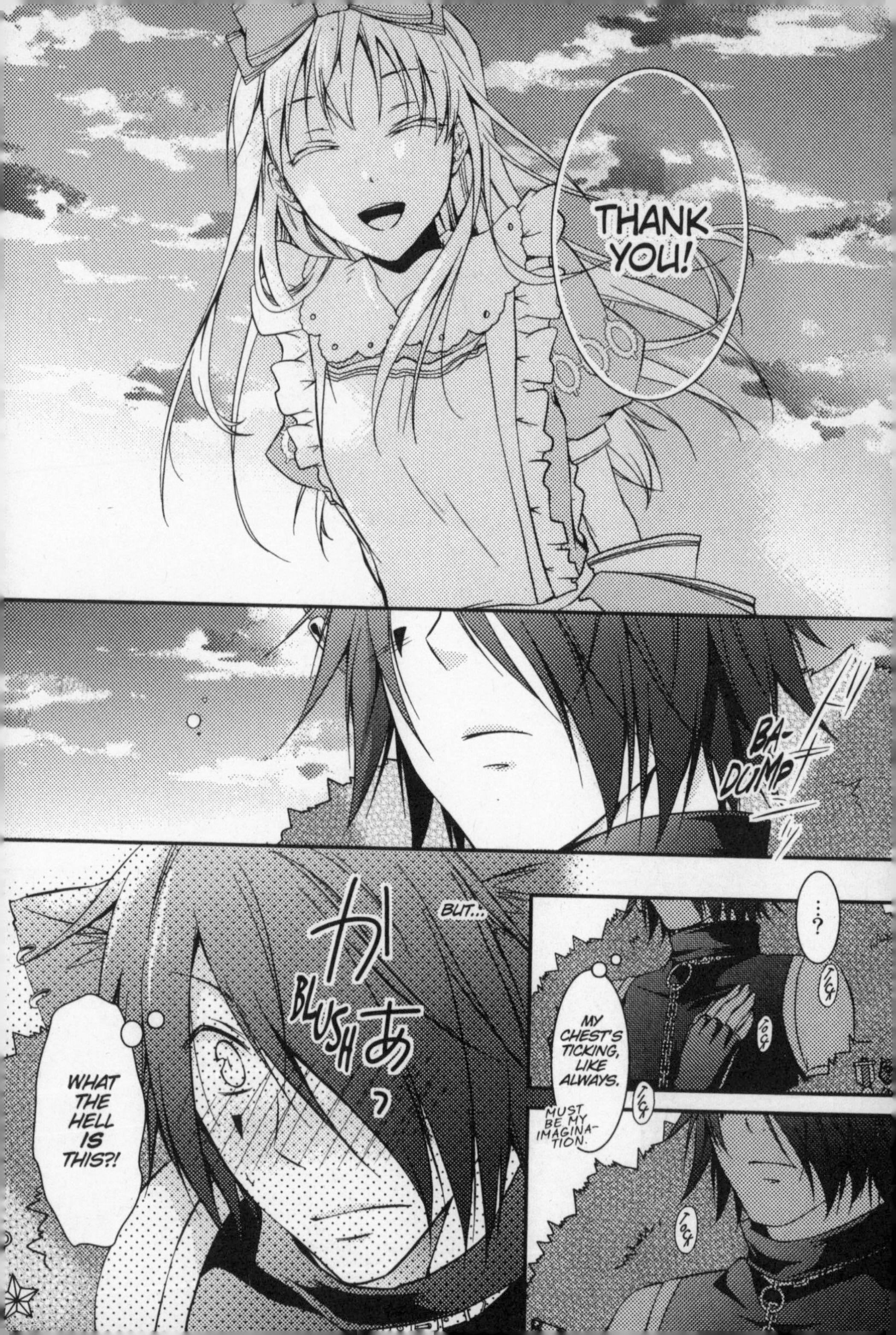
THANK YOU!
BA-DUMP
...?
TICK
TOCK
MY CHEST'S TICKING, LIKE ALWAYS.
TICK
MUST BE MY IMAGINATION.
TOCK
BUT...
かあっ
BLUSH
WHAT THE HELL IS THIS?!

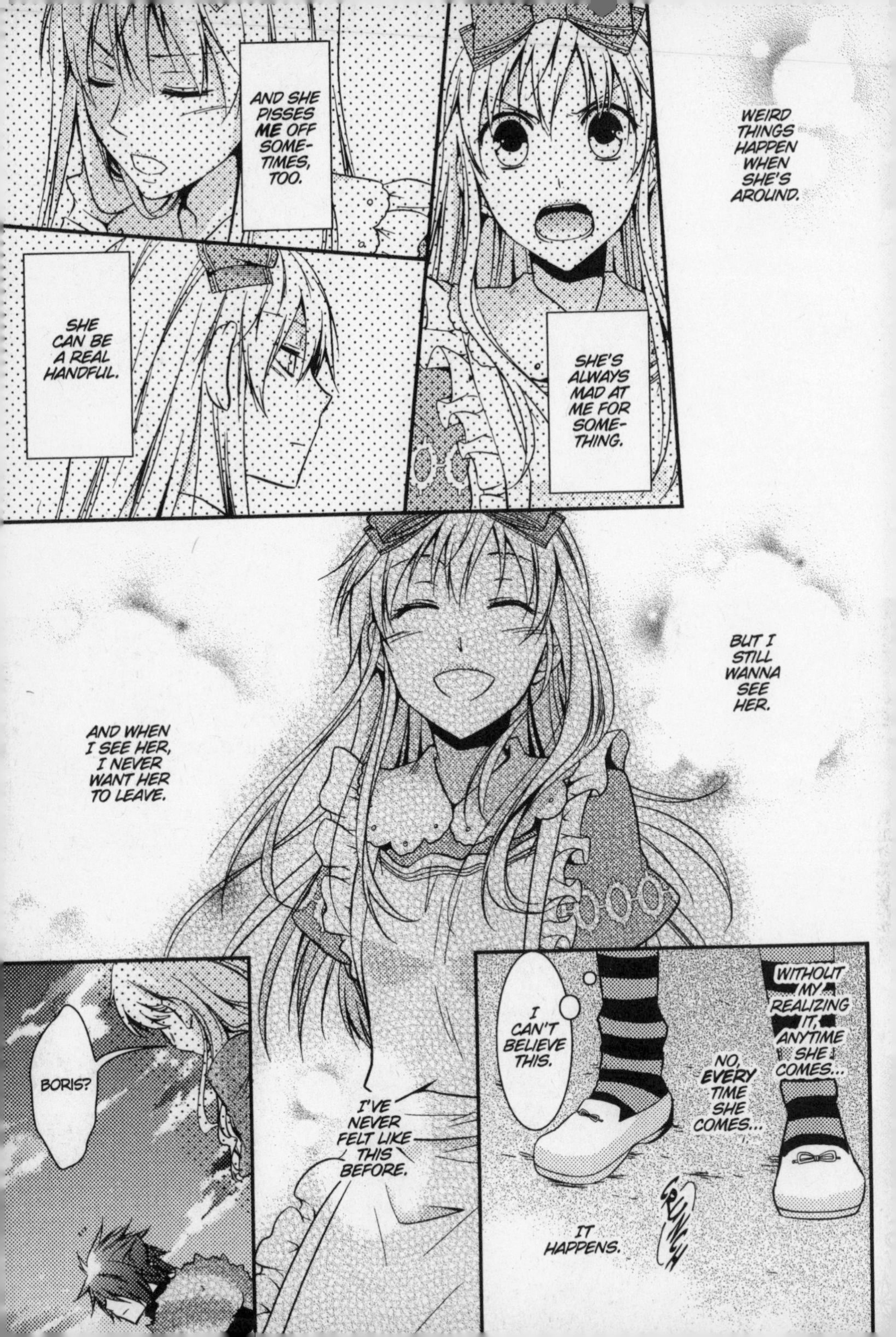
WEIRD THINGS HAPPEN WHEN SHE'S AROUND.
SHE'S ALWAYS MAD AT ME FOR SOME-THING.
AND SHE PISSES ME OFF SOME-TIMES, TOO.
SHE CAN BE A REAL HANDFUL.
BUT I STILL WANNA SEE HER.
AND WHEN I SEE HER, I NEVER WANT HER TO LEAVE.
WITHOUT MY REALIZING IT, ANYTIME SHE COMES...
NO, EVERY TIME SHE COMES...
I CAN'T BELIEVE THIS.
CRUNCH
IT HAPPENS.
I'VE NEVER FELT LIKE THIS BEFORE.
BORIS?

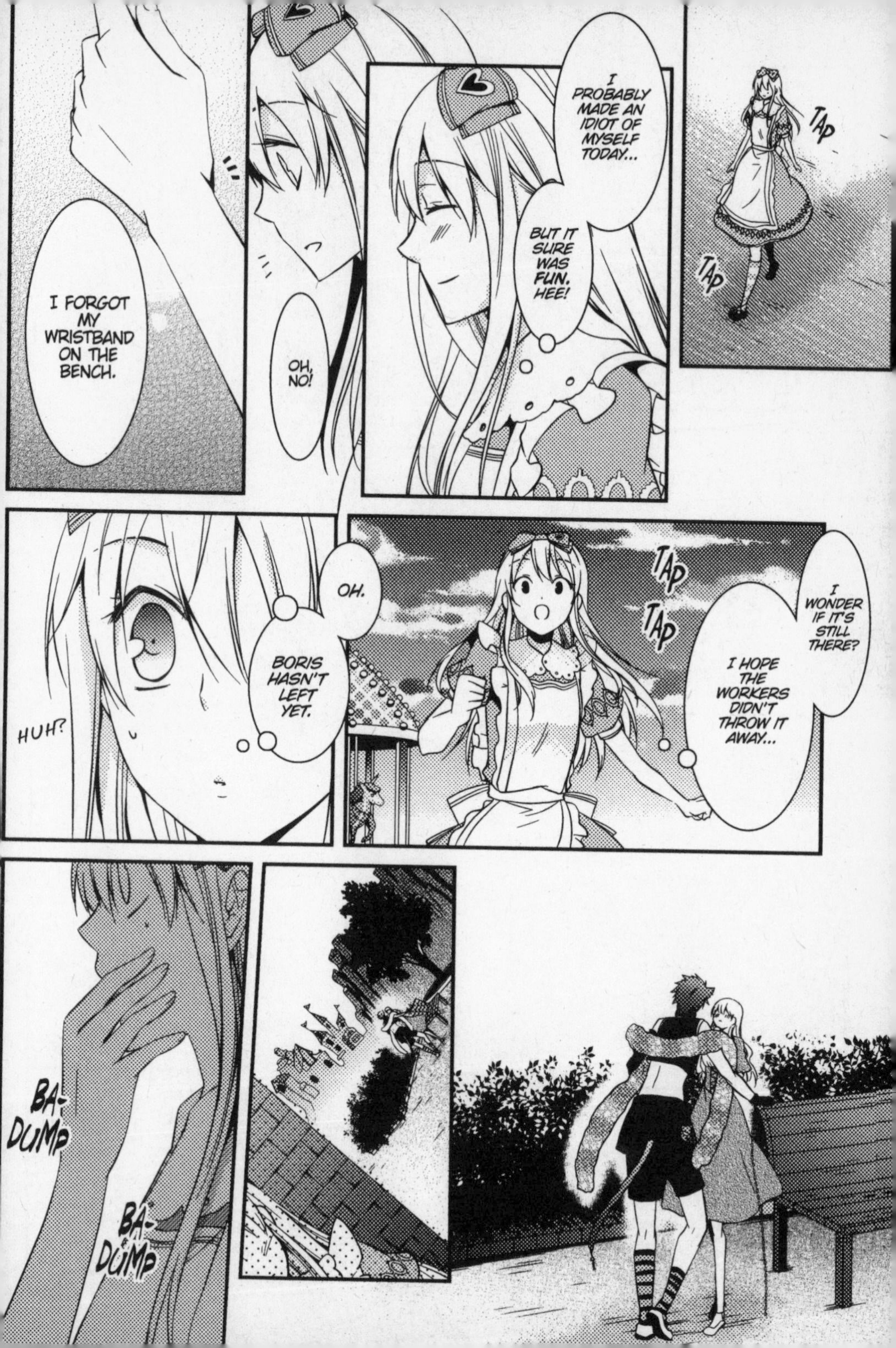
TAP
TAP
I PROBABLY MADE AN IDIOT OF MYSELF TODAY...
BUT IT SURE WAS FUN. HEE!
OH, NO!
I FORGOT MY WRISTBAND ON THE BENCH.
TAP
TAP
I WONDER IF IT'S STILL THERE?
I HOPE THE WORKERS DIDN'T THROW IT AWAY...
OH.
BORIS HASN'T LEFT YET.
HUH?
BA-DUMP
BA-DUMP

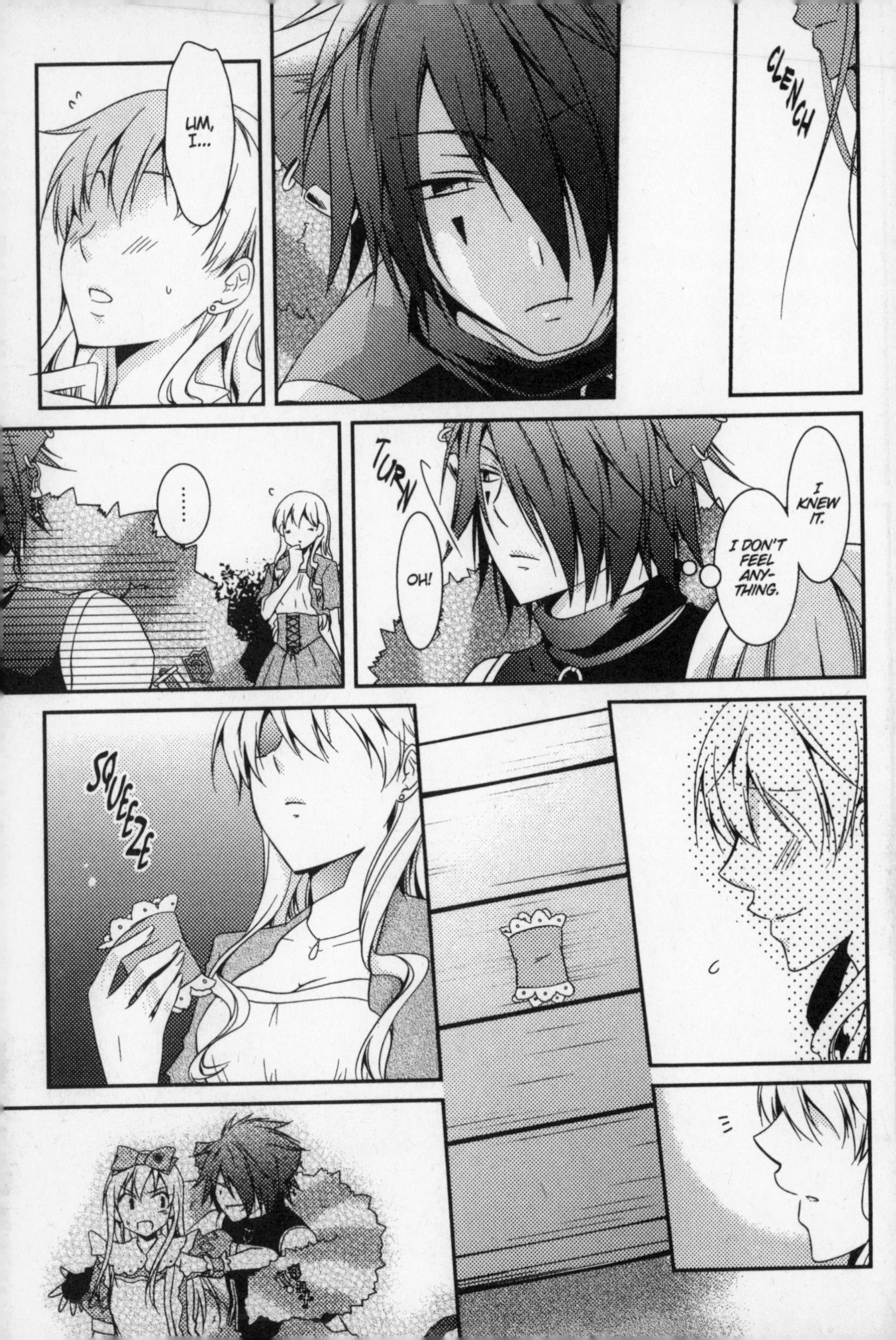
CLENCH
UM, I...
I KNEW IT.
I DON'T FEEL ANY-THING.
TURN
OH!
......
SQUEEZE

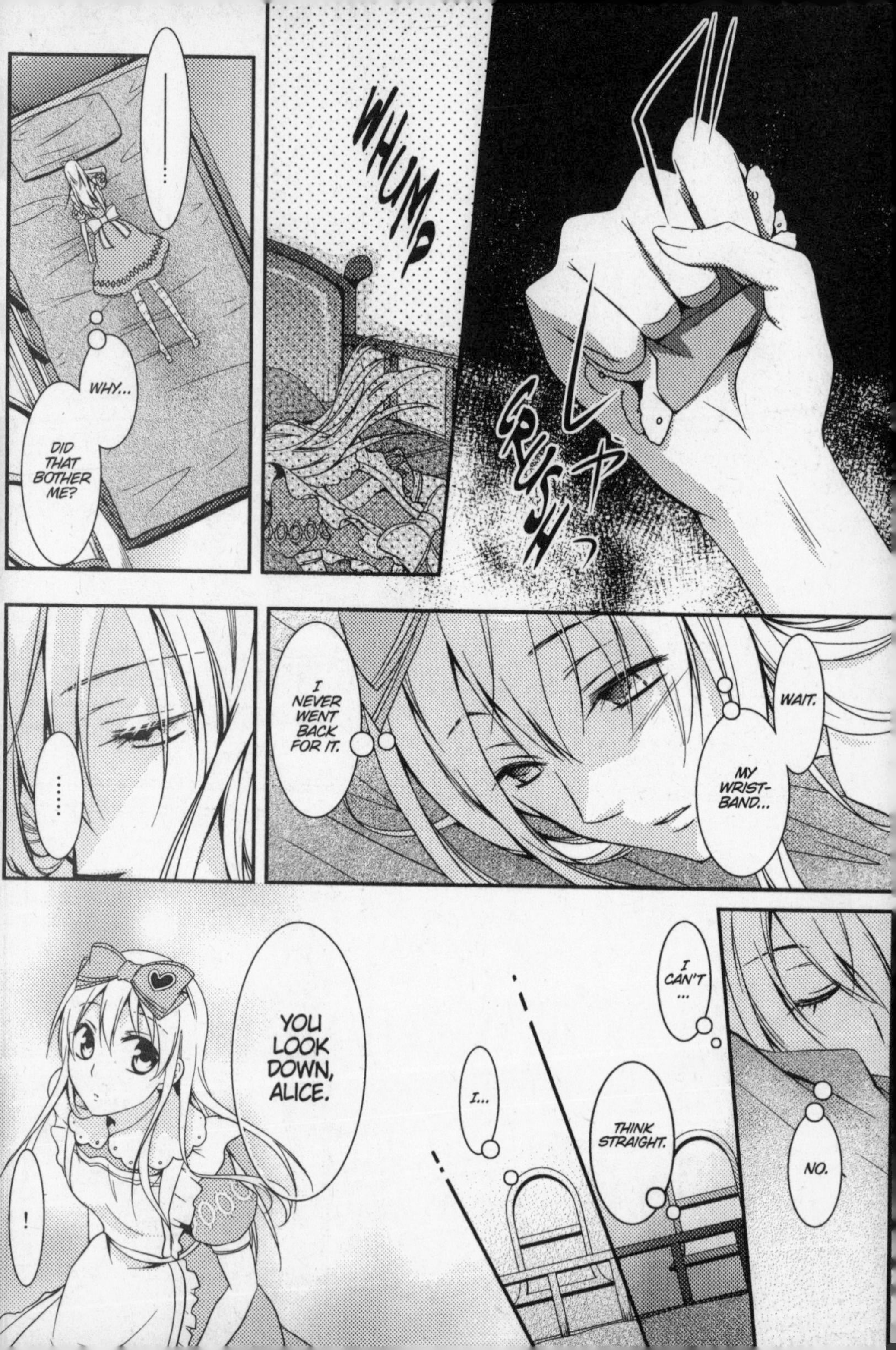
CRUSH
WHUMP
......
WHY...
DID THAT BOTHER ME?
WAIT.
MY WRIST-BAND...
I NEVER WENT BACK FOR IT.
......
NO.
I CAN'T ...
THINK STRAIGHT.
I...
YOU LOOK DOWN, ALICE.
!

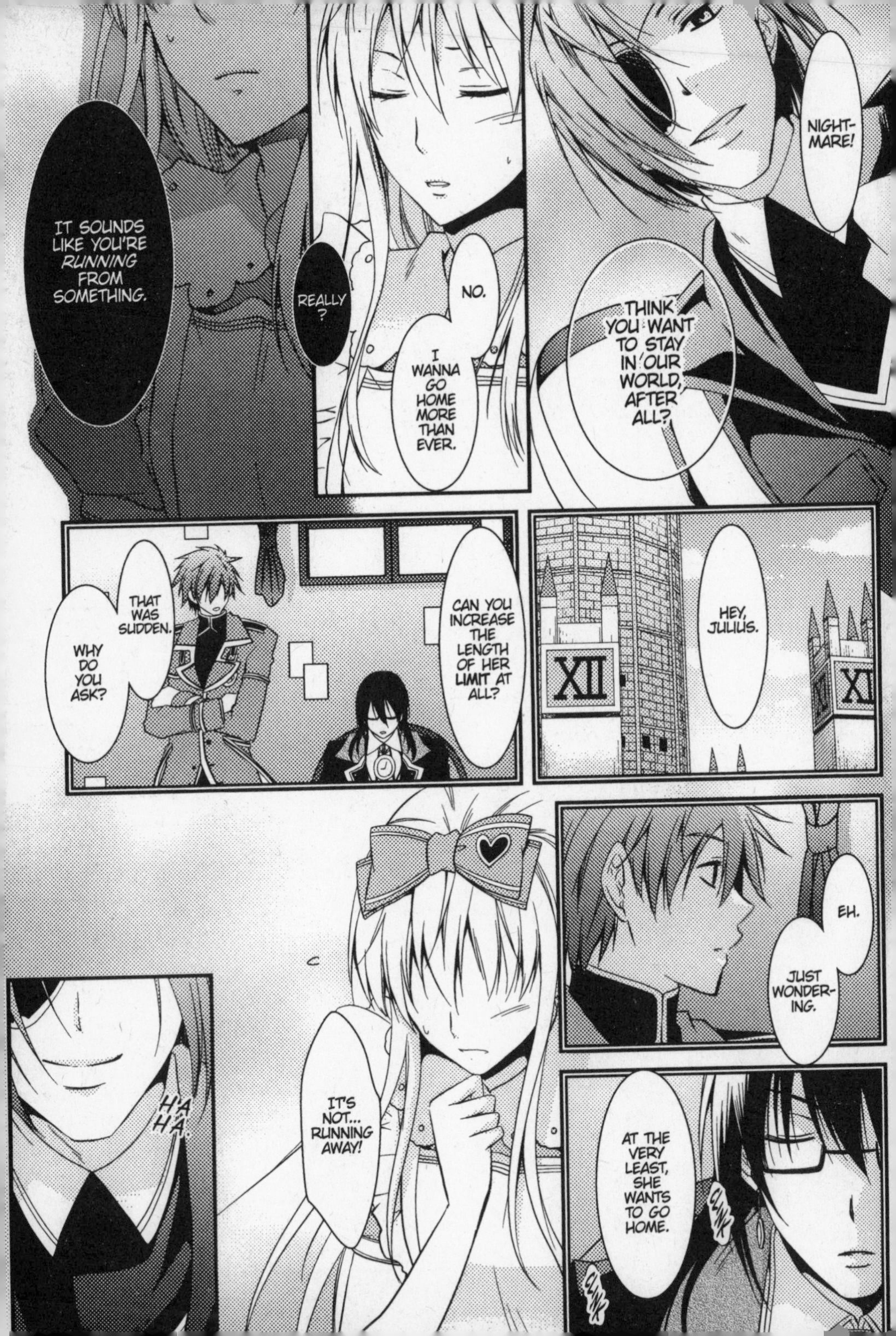
NIGHT-MARE!
THINK YOU WANT TO STAY IN OUR WORLD, AFTER ALL?
NO.
I WANNA GO HOME MORE THAN EVER.
REALLY?
IT SOUNDS LIKE YOU'RE *RUNNING* FROM SOMETHING.
HEY, JULIUS.
XII
CAN YOU INCREASE THE LENGTH OF HER LIMIT AT ALL?
THAT WAS SUDDEN.
WHY DO YOU ASK?
EH.
JUST WONDER-ING.
AT THE VERY LEAST, SHE WANTS TO GO HOME.
CLINK
CLINK
IT'S NOT... RUNNING AWAY!
HA HA.

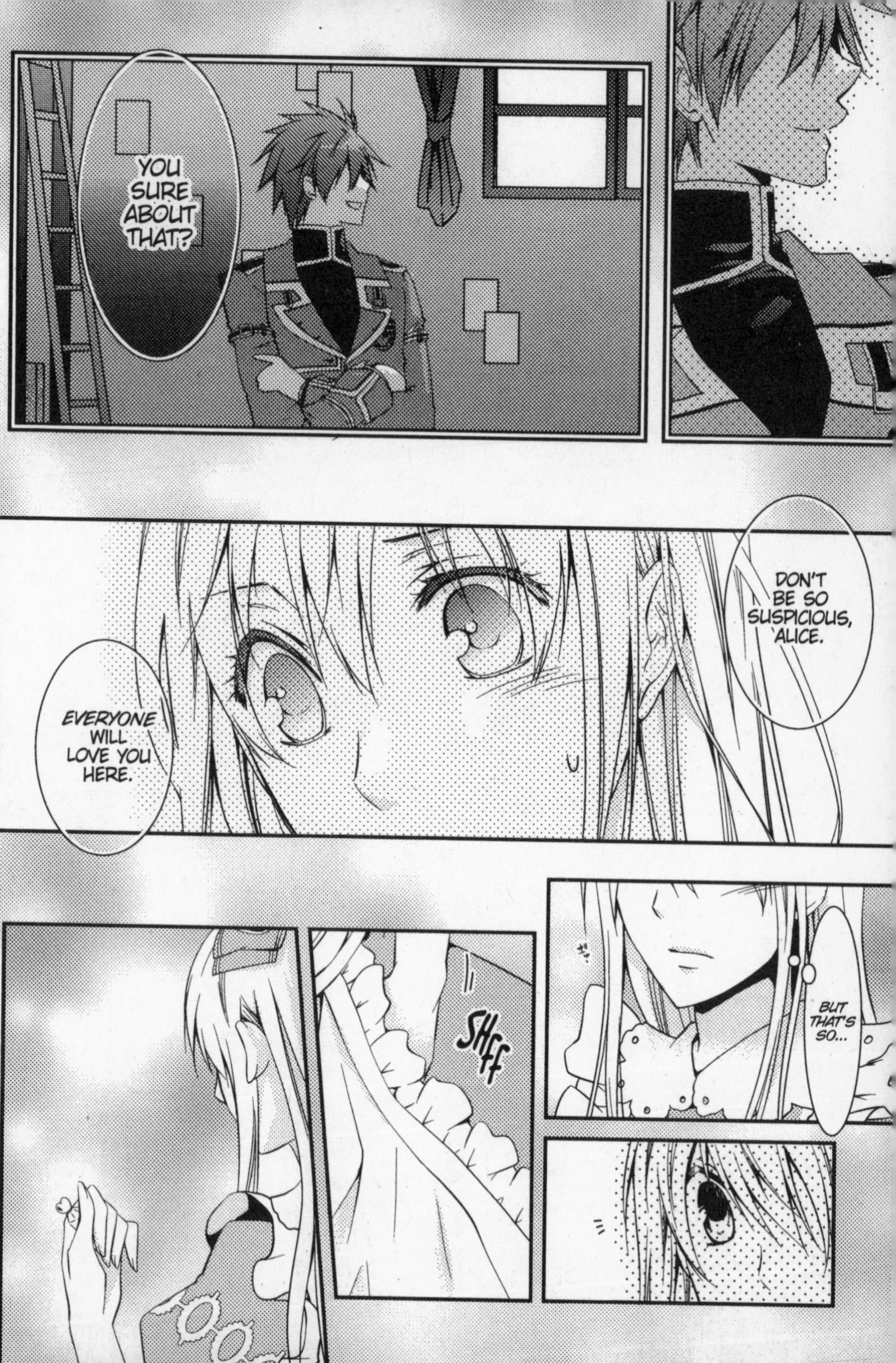
YOU SURE ABOUT THAT?
DON'T BE SO SUSPICIOUS, ALICE.
EVERYONE WILL LOVE YOU HERE.
BUT THAT'S SO...
SHFF

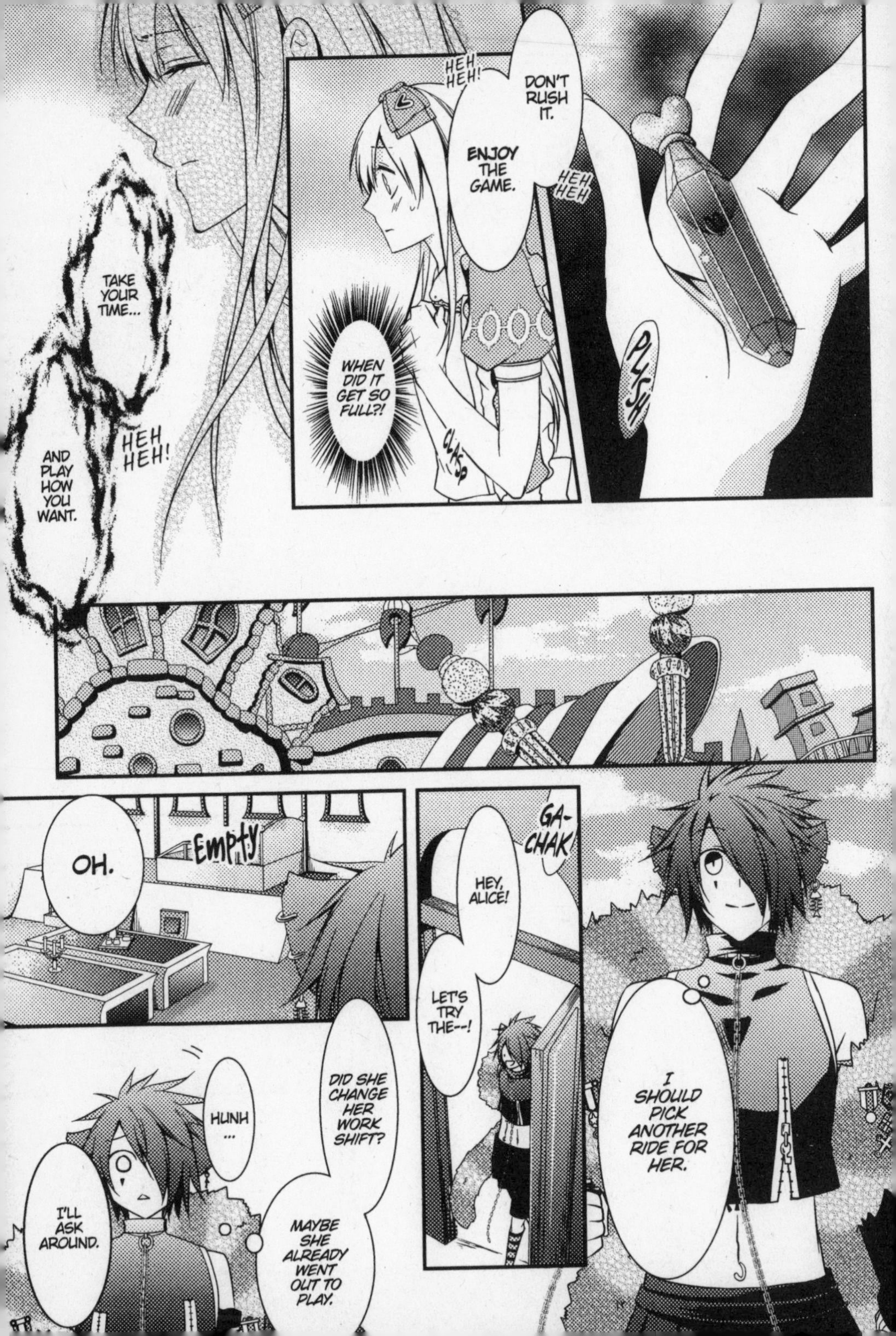
HEH HEH
PLYSH
HEH HEH!
DON'T RUSH IT.
ENJOY THE GAME.
WHEN DID IT GET SO FULL?!
CLASP
TAKE YOUR TIME...
HEH HEH!
AND PLAY HOW YOU WANT.
GA-CHAK
HEY, ALICE!
LET'S TRY THE--!
Empty
OH.
HUNH ...
DID SHE CHANGE HER WORK SHIFT?
MAYBE SHE ALREADY WENT OUT TO PLAY.
I'LL ASK AROUND.
I SHOULD PICK ANOTHER RIDE FOR HER.

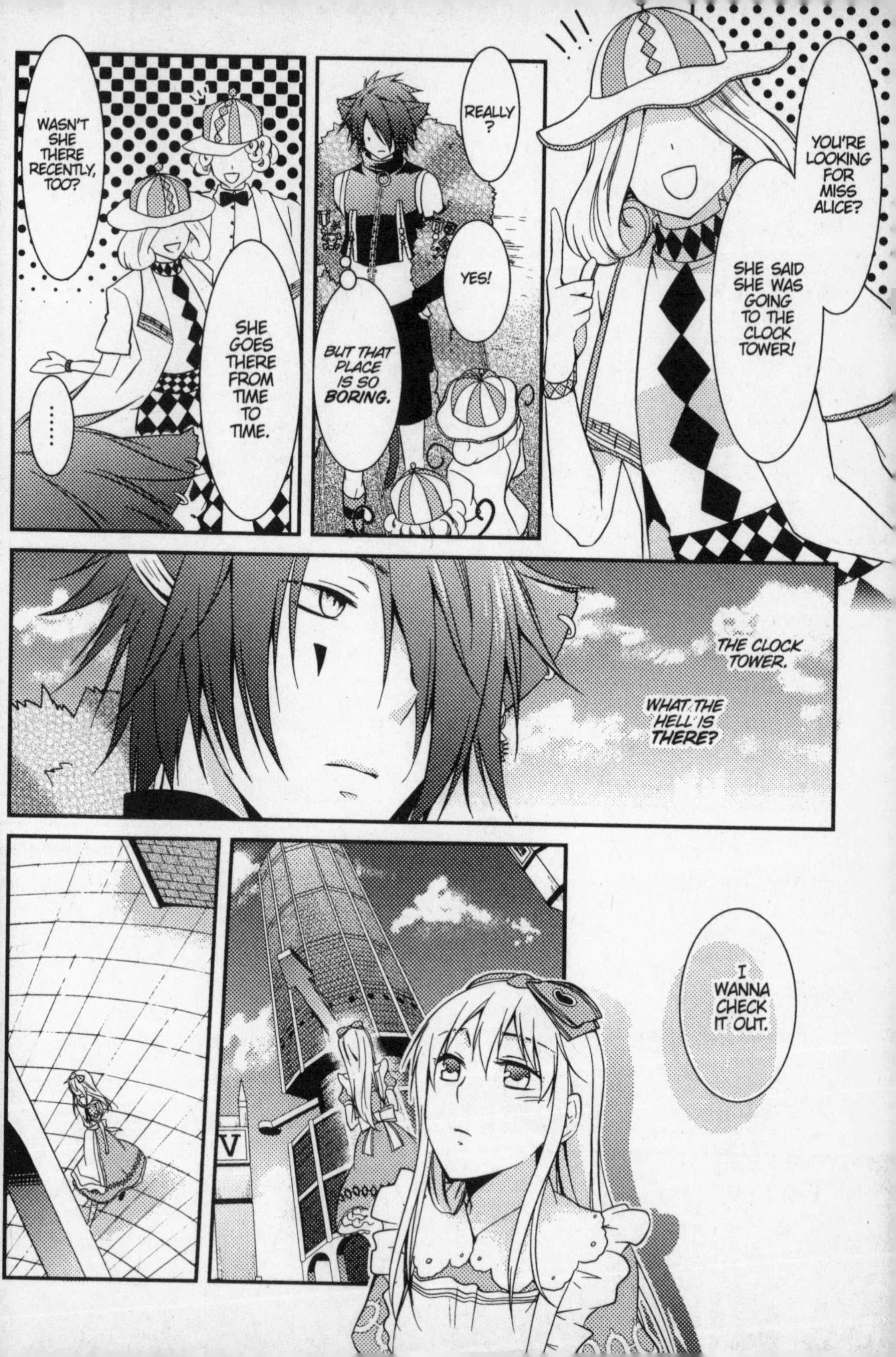
!!!
YOU'RE LOOKING FOR MISS ALICE?
SHE SAID SHE WAS GOING TO THE CLOCK TOWER!
REALLY?
YES!
BUT THAT PLACE IS SO BORING.
WASN'T SHE THERE RECENTLY, TOO?
SHE GOES THERE FROM TIME TO TIME.
......
THE CLOCK TOWER.
WHAT THE HELL IS THERE?
I WANNA CHECK IT OUT.

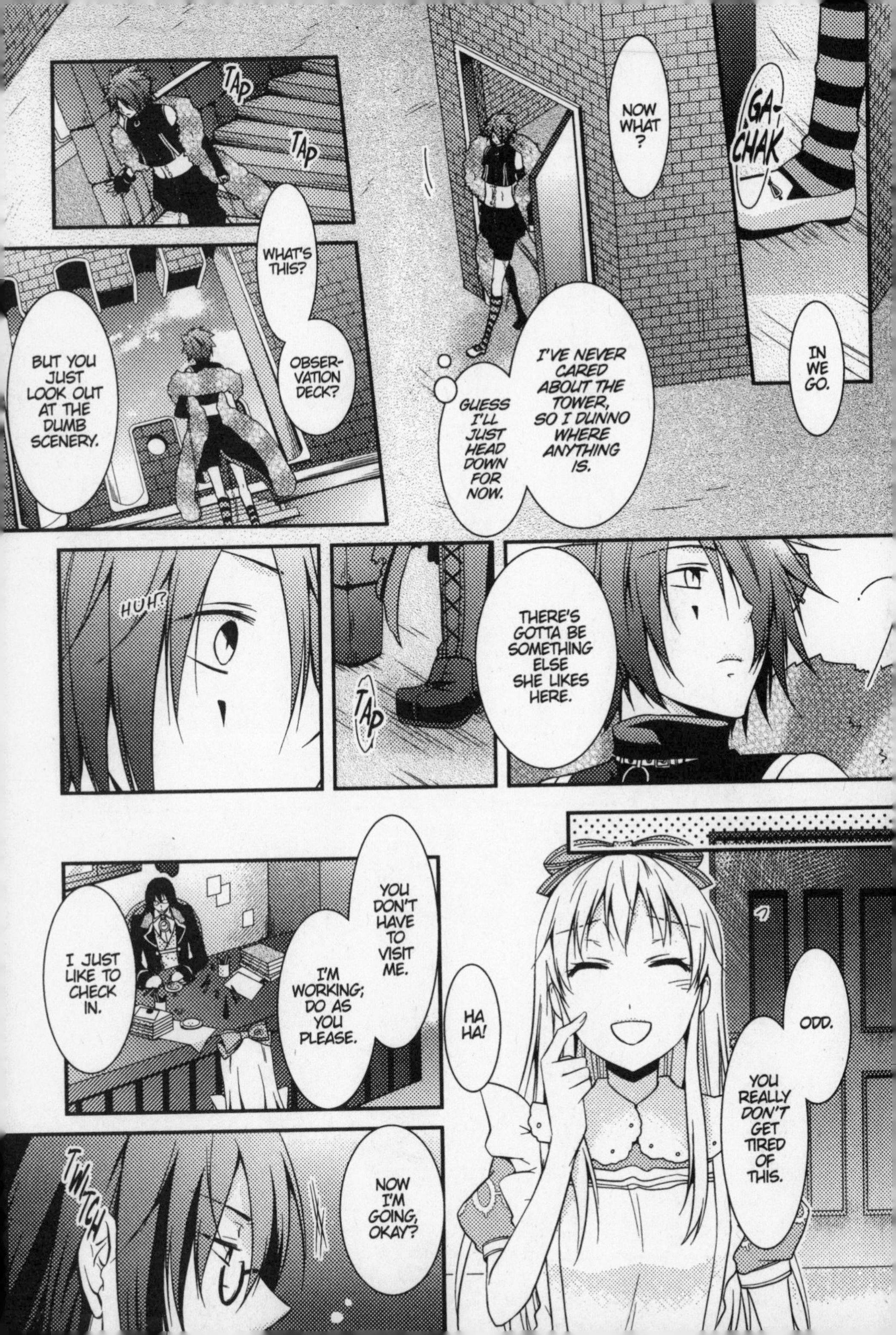
GA-CHAK
IN WE GO.
NOW WHAT?
I'VE NEVER CARED ABOUT THE TOWER, SO I DUNNO WHERE ANYTHING IS.
GUESS I'LL JUST HEAD DOWN FOR NOW.
TAP
TAP
WHAT'S THIS?
OBSERVATION DECK?
BUT YOU JUST LOOK OUT AT THE DUMB SCENERY.
THERE'S GOTTA BE SOMETHING ELSE SHE LIKES HERE.
TAP
HUH?
ODD.
YOU REALLY DON'T GET TIRED OF THIS.
HA HA!
YOU DON'T HAVE TO VISIT ME.
I'M WORKING; DO AS YOU PLEASE.
I JUST LIKE TO CHECK IN.
NOW I'M GOING, OKAY?
TWITCH

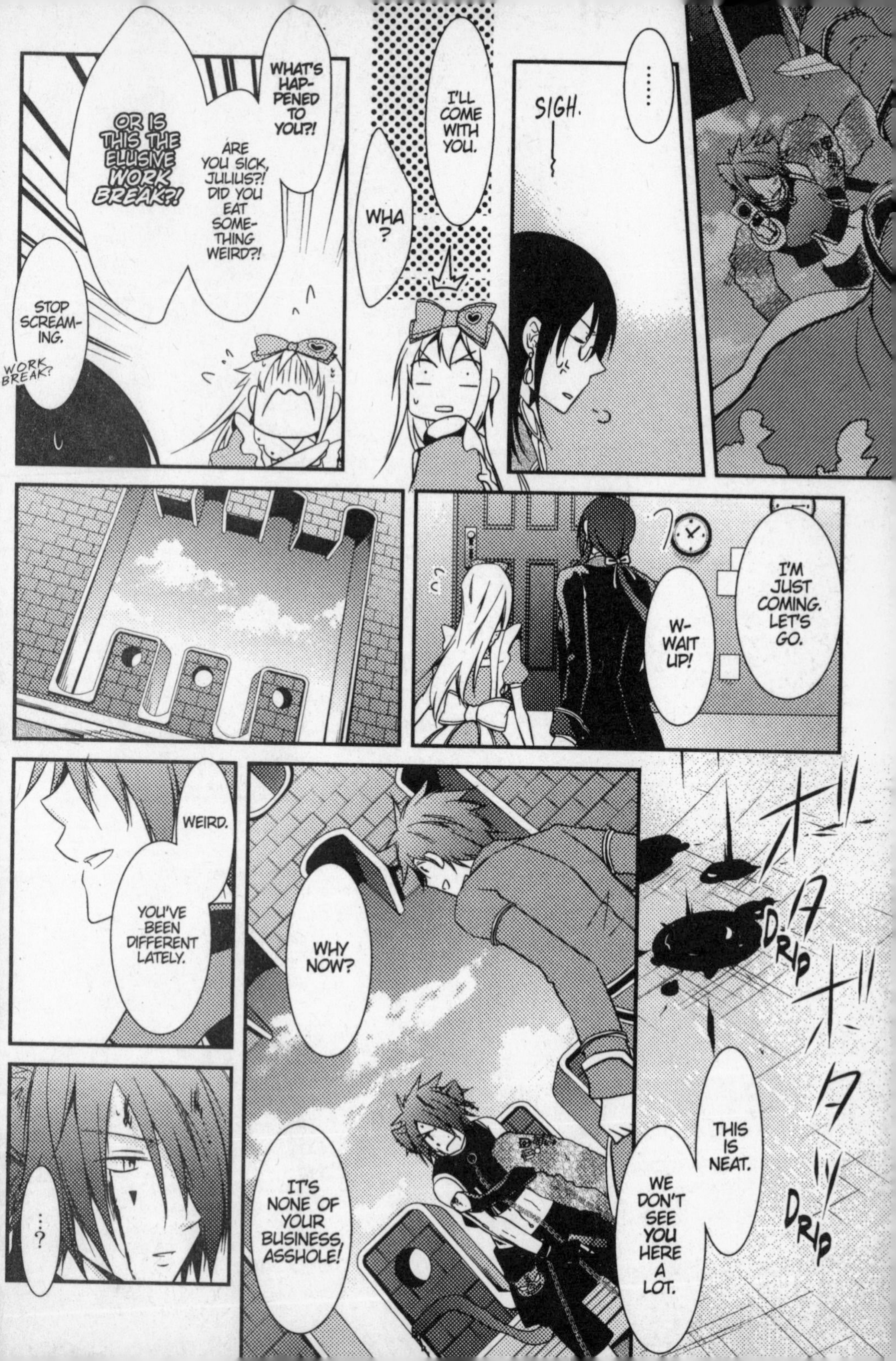
......
SIGH.
I'LL COME WITH YOU.
WHA?
WHAT'S HAPPENED TO YOU?!
ARE YOU SICK, JULIUS?! DID YOU EAT SOMETHING WEIRD?!
OR IS THIS THE ELUSIVE WORK BREAK?!
STOP SCREAMING.
WORK BREAK?
I'M JUST COMING. LET'S GO.
W-WAIT UP!
DRIP
DRIP
THIS IS NEAT.
WE DON'T SEE YOU HERE A LOT.
WHY NOW?
IT'S NONE OF YOUR BUSINESS, ASSHOLE!
WEIRD.
YOU'VE BEEN DIFFERENT LATELY.
...?

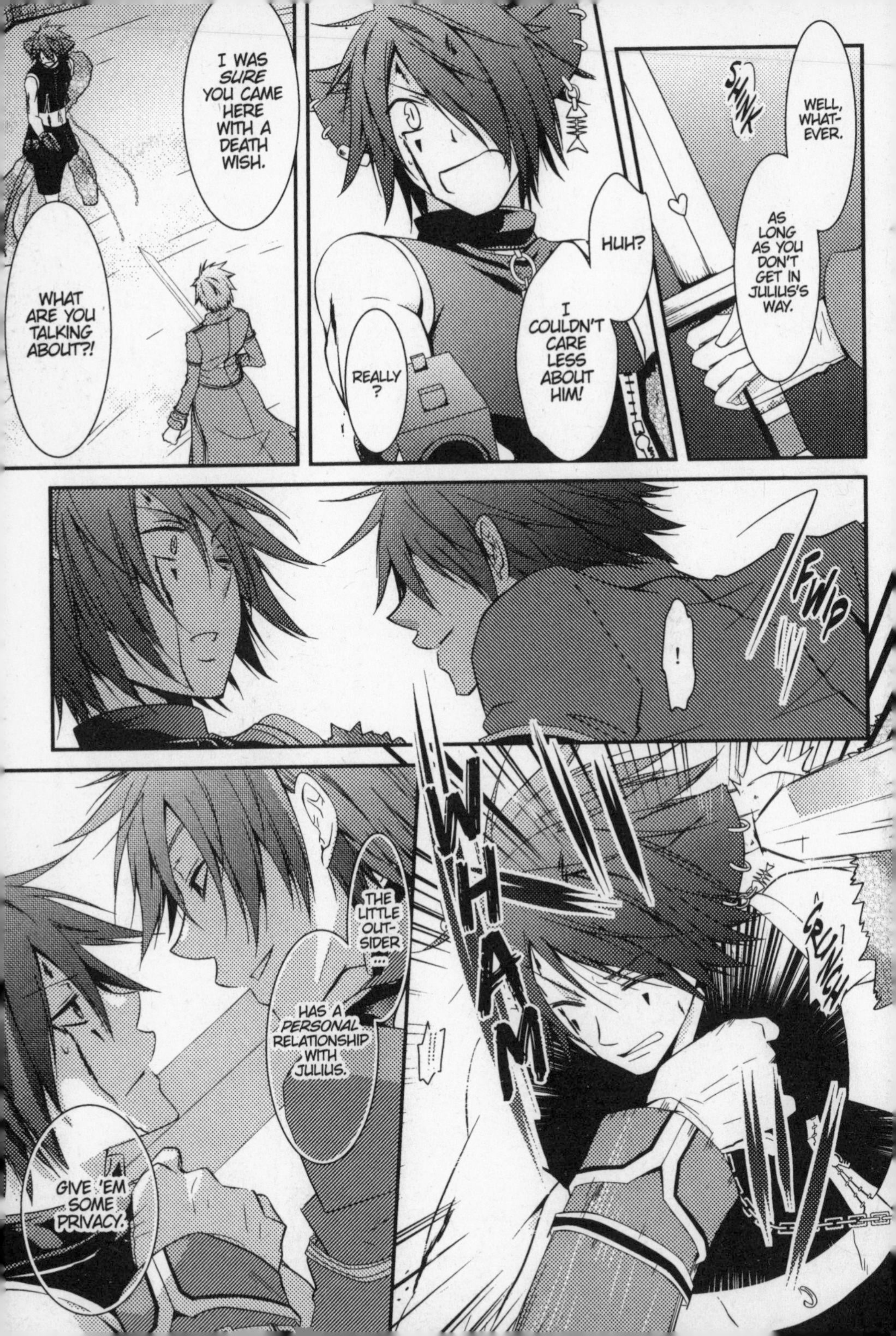
SHINK
WELL, WHAT-EVER.
AS LONG AS YOU DON'T GET IN JULIUS'S WAY.
HUH?
I COULDN'T CARE LESS ABOUT HIM!
REALLY?
I WAS *SURE* YOU CAME HERE WITH A DEATH WISH.
WHAT ARE YOU TALKING ABOUT?!
FWIP
!
WHAM
CRUNCH
THE LITTLE OUT-SIDER...
HAS A *PERSONAL* RELATIONSHIP WITH JULIUS.
GIVE 'EM SOME PRIVACY.

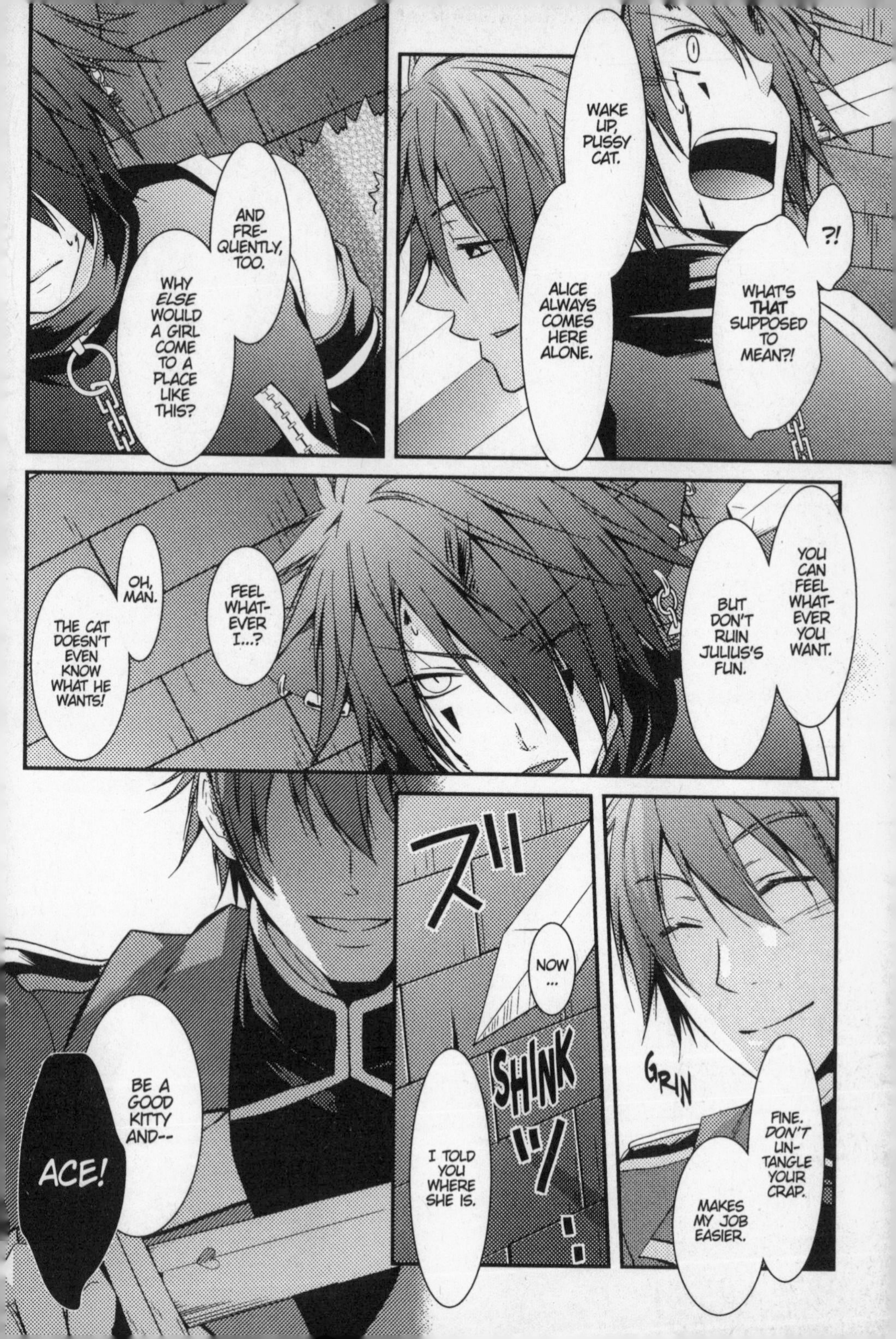
WAKE UP, PUSSY CAT.
ALICE ALWAYS COMES HERE ALONE.
?!
WHAT'S THAT SUPPOSED TO MEAN?!
AND FRE-QUENTLY, TOO.
WHY *ELSE* WOULD A GIRL COME TO A PLACE LIKE THIS?
YOU CAN FEEL WHAT-EVER YOU WANT.
BUT DON'T RUIN JULIUS'S FUN.
FEEL WHAT-EVER I...?
OH, MAN.
THE CAT DOESN'T EVEN KNOW WHAT HE WANTS!
FINE. *DON'T* UN-TANGLE YOUR CRAP.
MAKES MY JOB EASIER.
GRIN
ズ
NOW ...
SHINK
I TOLD YOU WHERE SHE IS.
BE A GOOD KITTY AND--
ACE!

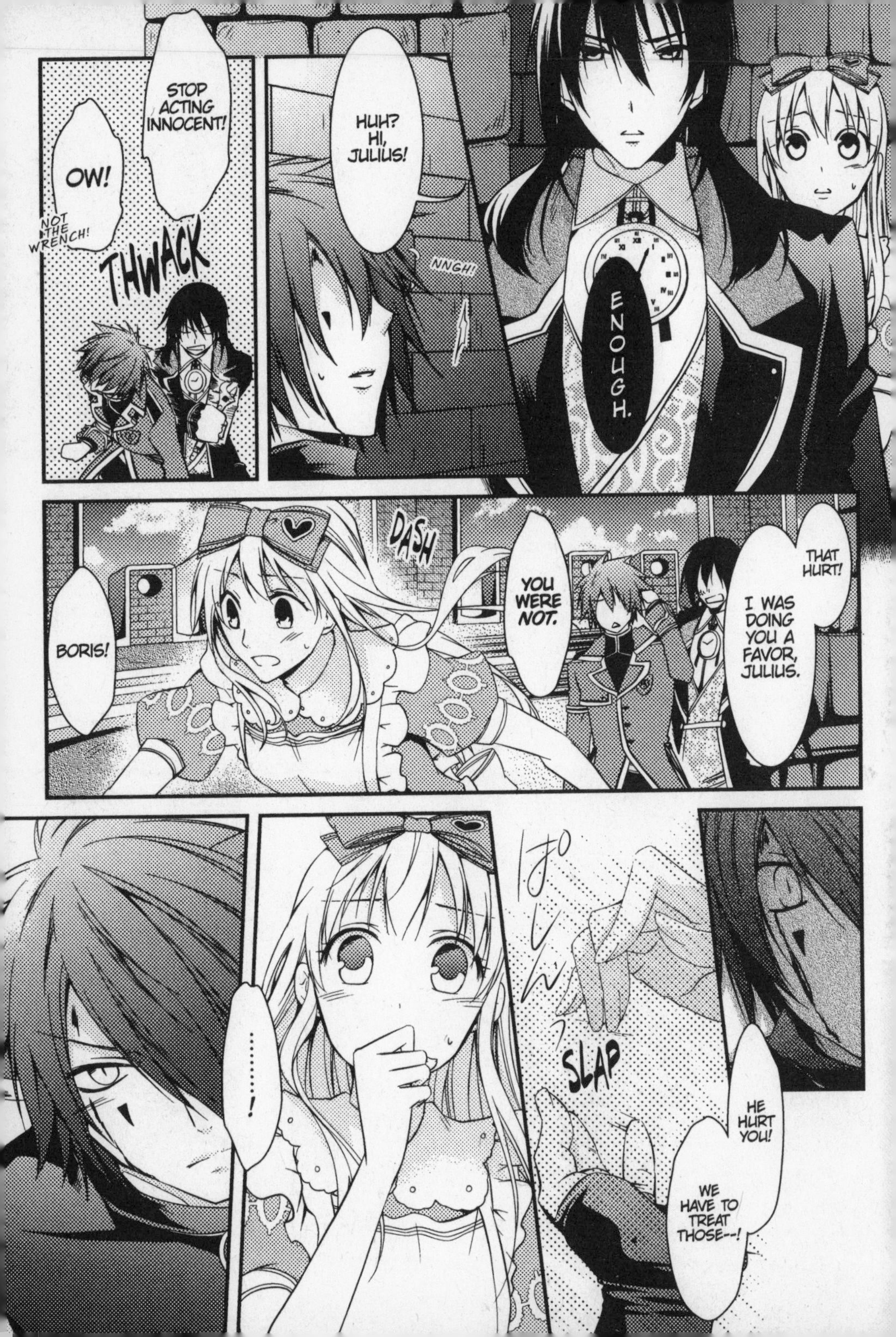
ENOUGH.
HUH? HI, JULIUS!
NNGH!
STOP ACTING INNOCENT!
OW!
NOT THE WRENCH!
THWACK
THAT HURT!
I WAS DOING YOU A FAVOR, JULIUS.
YOU WERE NOT.
DASH
BORIS!
HE HURT YOU!
WE HAVE TO TREAT THOSE--!
SLAP
......!

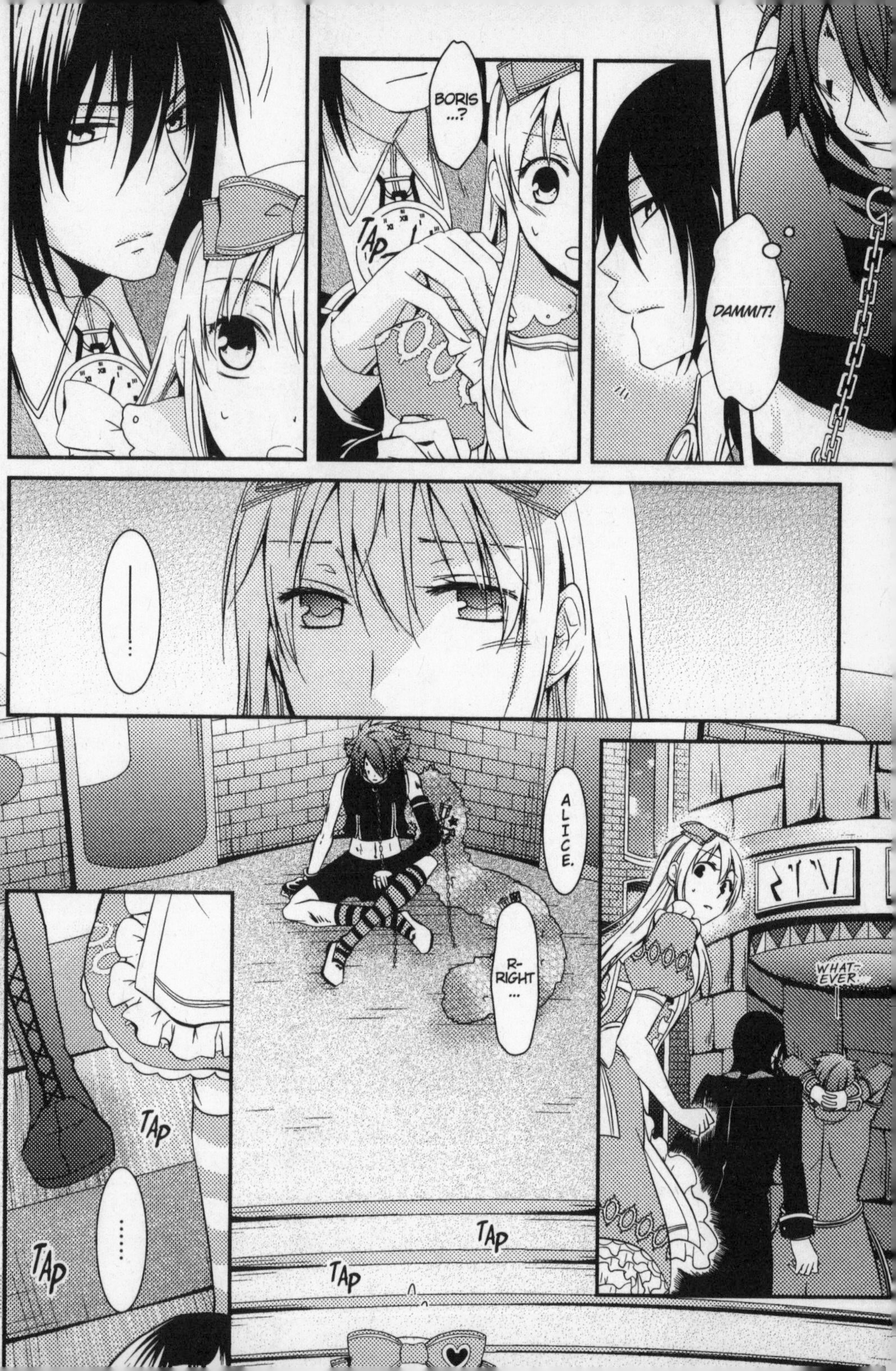
DAMMIT!
BORIS ...?
TAP
—...
WHAT-EVER.
ALICE.
R-RIGHT ...
TAP
TAP
TAP
......
TAP

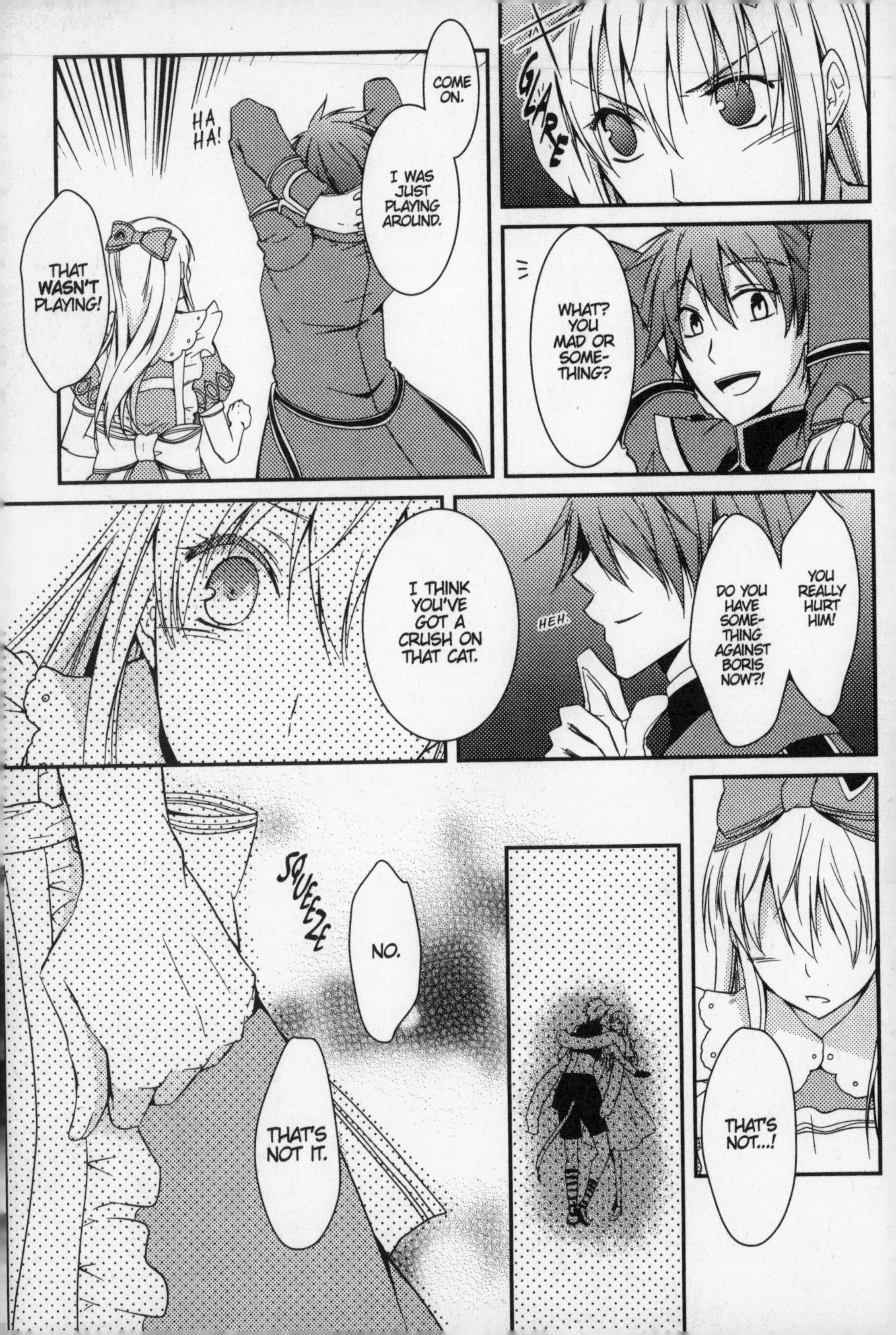
GLARE
WHAT? YOU MAD OR SOME-THING?
COME ON.
I WAS JUST PLAYING AROUND.
HA HA!
THAT WASN'T PLAYING!
YOU REALLY HURT HIM!
DO YOU HAVE SOME-THING AGAINST BORIS NOW?!
HEH.
I THINK YOU'VE GOT A CRUSH ON THAT CAT.
THAT'S NOT...!
SQUEEZE
NO.
THAT'S NOT IT.

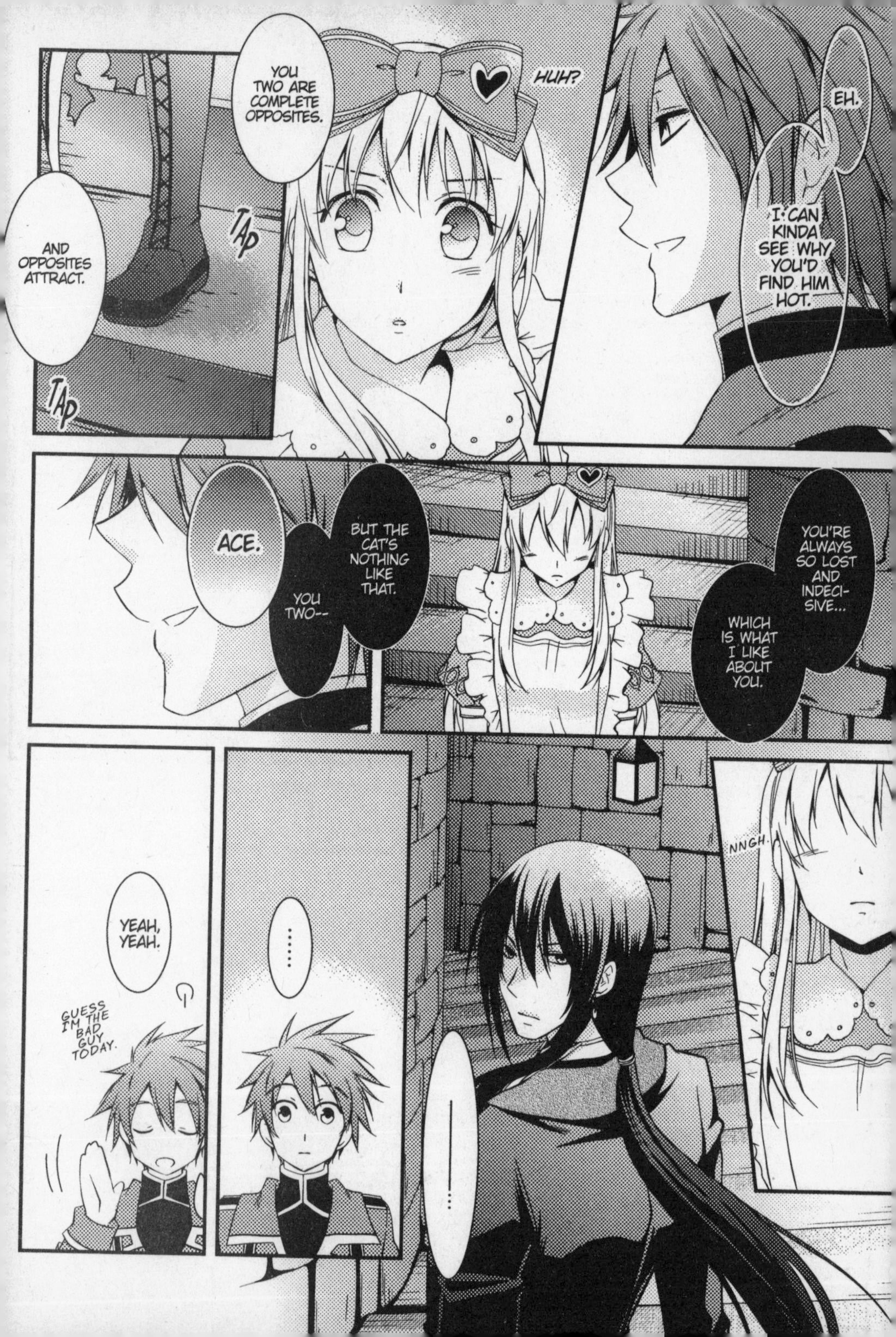

EH.
I CAN KINDA SEE WHY YOU'D FIND HIM HOT.
HUH?
YOU TWO ARE COMPLETE OPPOSITES.
AND OPPOSITES ATTRACT.
TAP
TAP
YOU'RE ALWAYS SO LOST AND INDECI-SIVE...
WHICH IS WHAT I LIKE ABOUT YOU.
BUT THE CAT'S NOTHING LIKE THAT.
YOU TWO--
ACE.
NNGH.
......
......
YEAH, YEAH.
GUESS I'M THE BAD GUY TODAY.

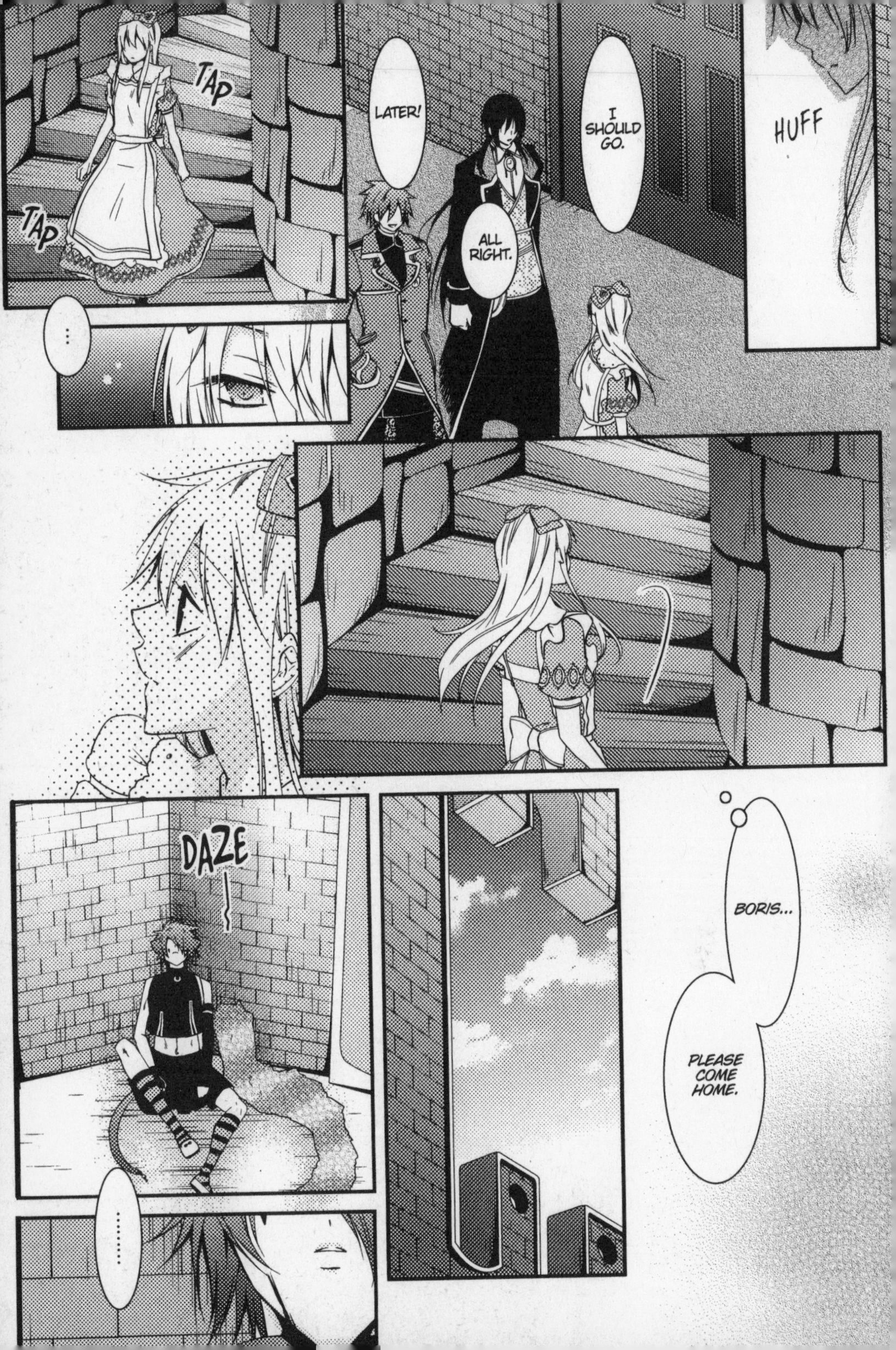
HUFF
I SHOULD GO.
LATER!
ALL RIGHT.
TAP
TAP
...
BORIS...
PLEASE COME HOME.
DAZE
......

"THE LITTLE OUTSIDER... HAS A PERSONAL RELATIONSHIP WITH JULIUS."

SQUEEZE

DAMMIT!

ROLL

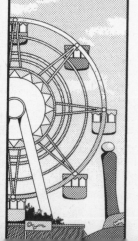

I'M SUCH A LOSER.

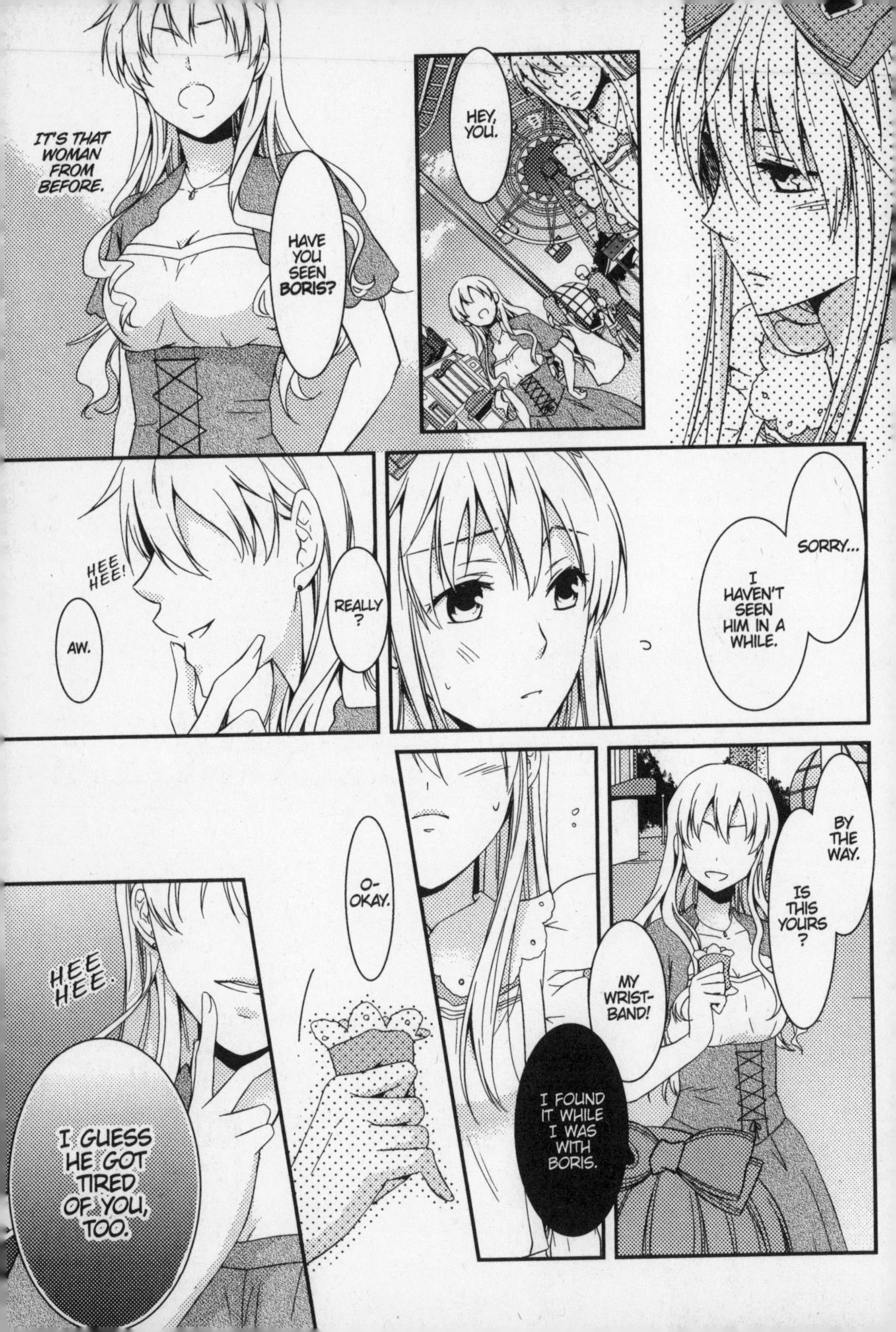
HEY, YOU.
IT'S THAT WOMAN FROM BEFORE.
HAVE YOU SEEN BORIS?
SORRY...
I HAVEN'T SEEN HIM IN A WHILE.
REALLY?
HEE HEE!
AW.
BY THE WAY.
IS THIS YOURS?
MY WRIST-BAND!
I FOUND IT WHILE I WAS WITH BORIS.
O-OKAY.
HEE HEE.
I GUESS HE GOT TIRED OF YOU, TOO.

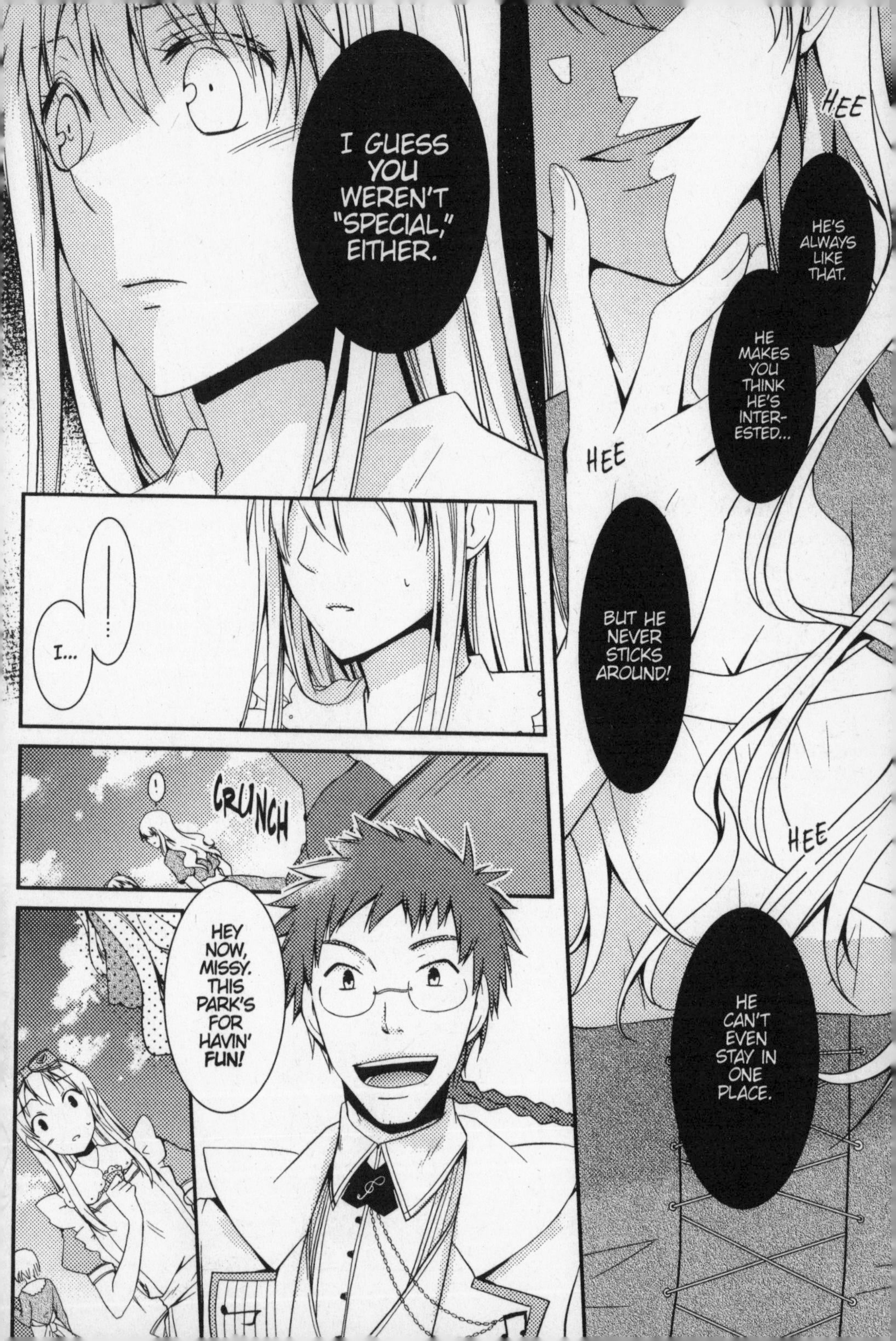
HEE
HE'S ALWAYS LIKE THAT.
HE MAKES YOU THINK HE'S INTER-ESTED...
HEE
BUT HE NEVER STICKS AROUND!
HEE
HE CAN'T EVEN STAY IN ONE PLACE.
I GUESS YOU WEREN'T "SPECIAL," EITHER.
...!
I...
!
CRUNCH
HEY NOW, MISSY. THIS PARK'S FOR HAVIN' FUN!

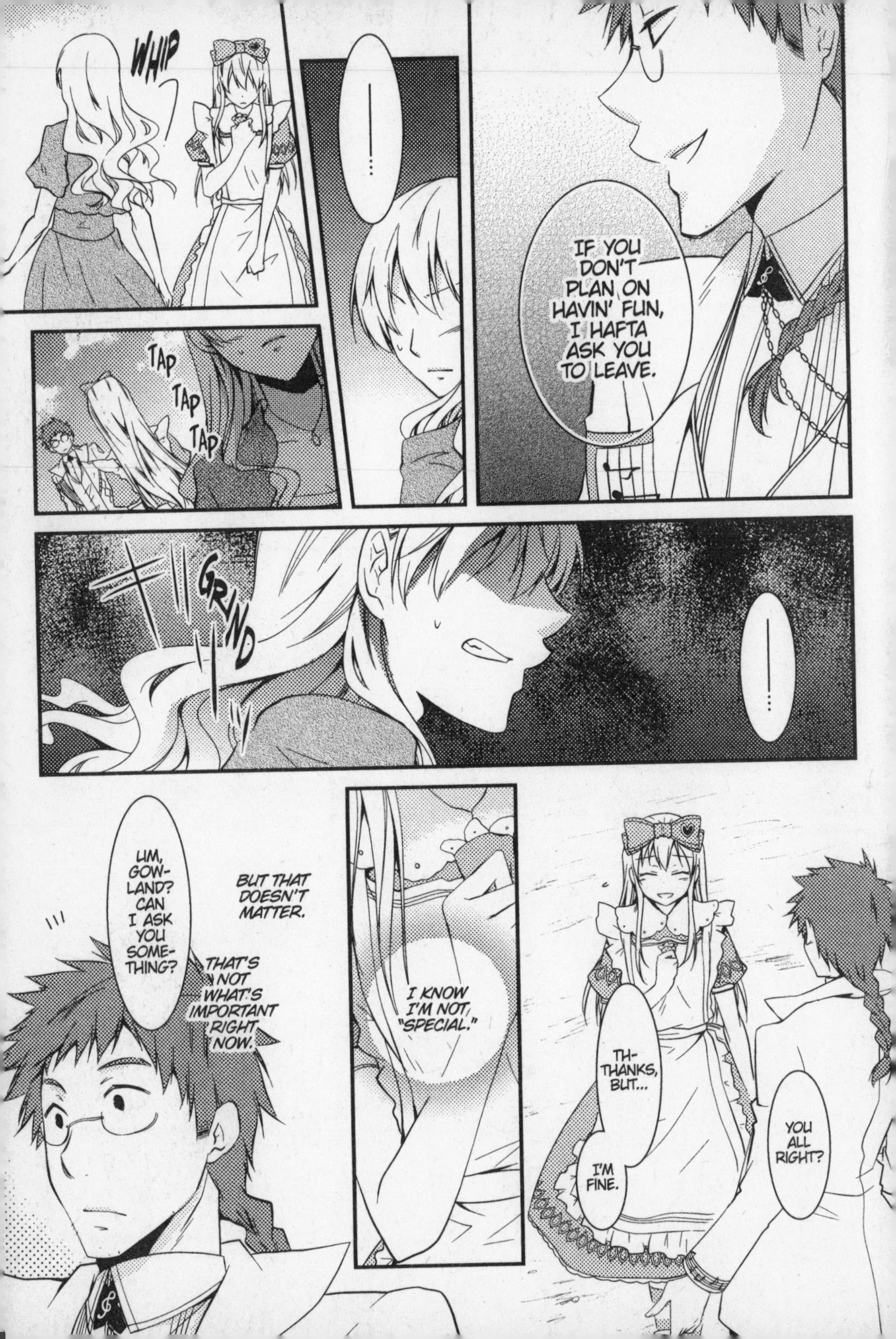
IF YOU DON'T PLAN ON HAVIN' FUN, I HAFTA ASK YOU TO LEAVE.
—......
WHIP
TAP TAP TAP
—......
GRIND
YOU ALL RIGHT?
TH-THANKS, BUT...
I'M FINE.
I KNOW I'M NOT "SPECIAL."
BUT THAT DOESN'T MATTER.
THAT'S NOT WHAT'S IMPORTANT RIGHT NOW.
UM, GOW-LAND? CAN I ASK YOU SOME-THING?

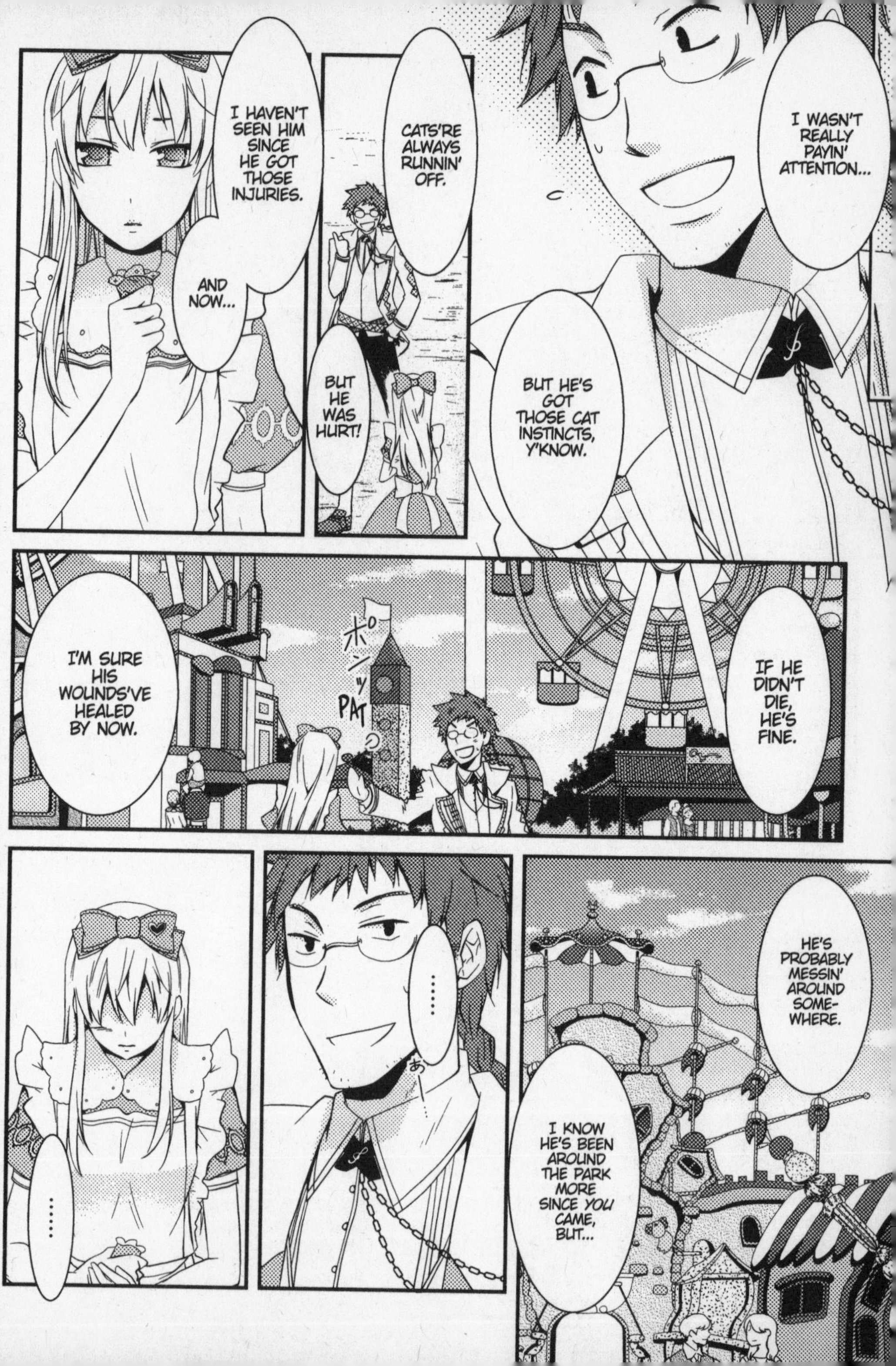
I WASN'T REALLY PAYIN' ATTENTION...
BUT HE'S GOT THOSE CAT INSTINCTS, Y'KNOW.
CATS'RE ALWAYS RUNNIN' OFF.
BUT HE WAS HURT!
I HAVEN'T SEEN HIM SINCE HE GOT THOSE INJURIES.
AND NOW...
IF HE DIDN'T DIE, HE'S FINE.
ポンッ
PAT
I'M SURE HIS WOUNDS'VE HEALED BY NOW.
HE'S PROBABLY MESSIN' AROUND SOME-WHERE.
I KNOW HE'S BEEN AROUND THE PARK MORE SINCE *YOU* CAME, BUT...
......
あ...
......

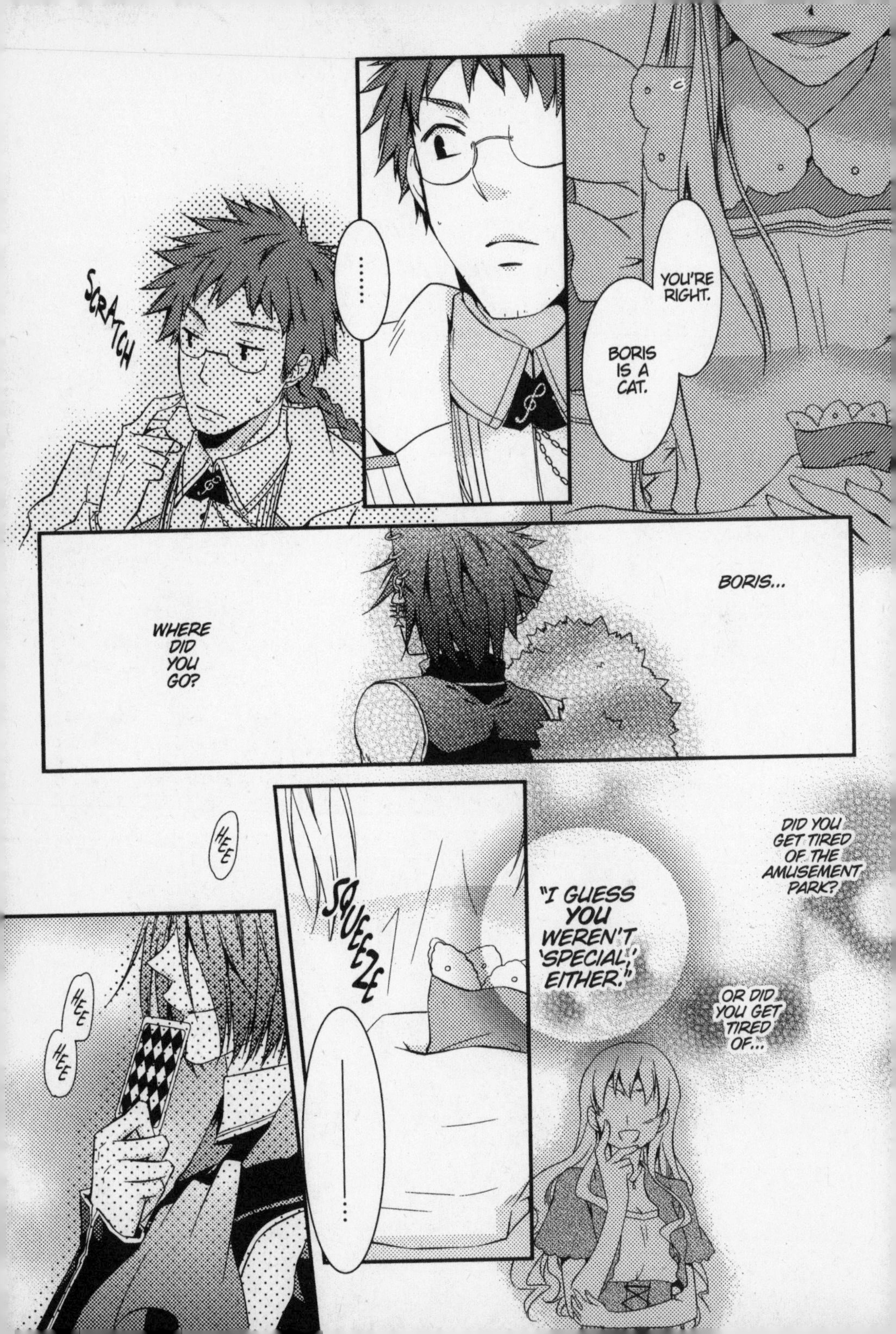
YOU'RE RIGHT.
BORIS IS A CAT.
......
SCRATCH
BORIS...
WHERE DID YOU GO?
DID YOU GET TIRED OF THE AMUSEMENT PARK?
"I GUESS YOU WEREN'T 'SPECIAL' EITHER."
OR DID YOU GET TIRED OF...
SQUEEZE
......
HEE
HEE HEE

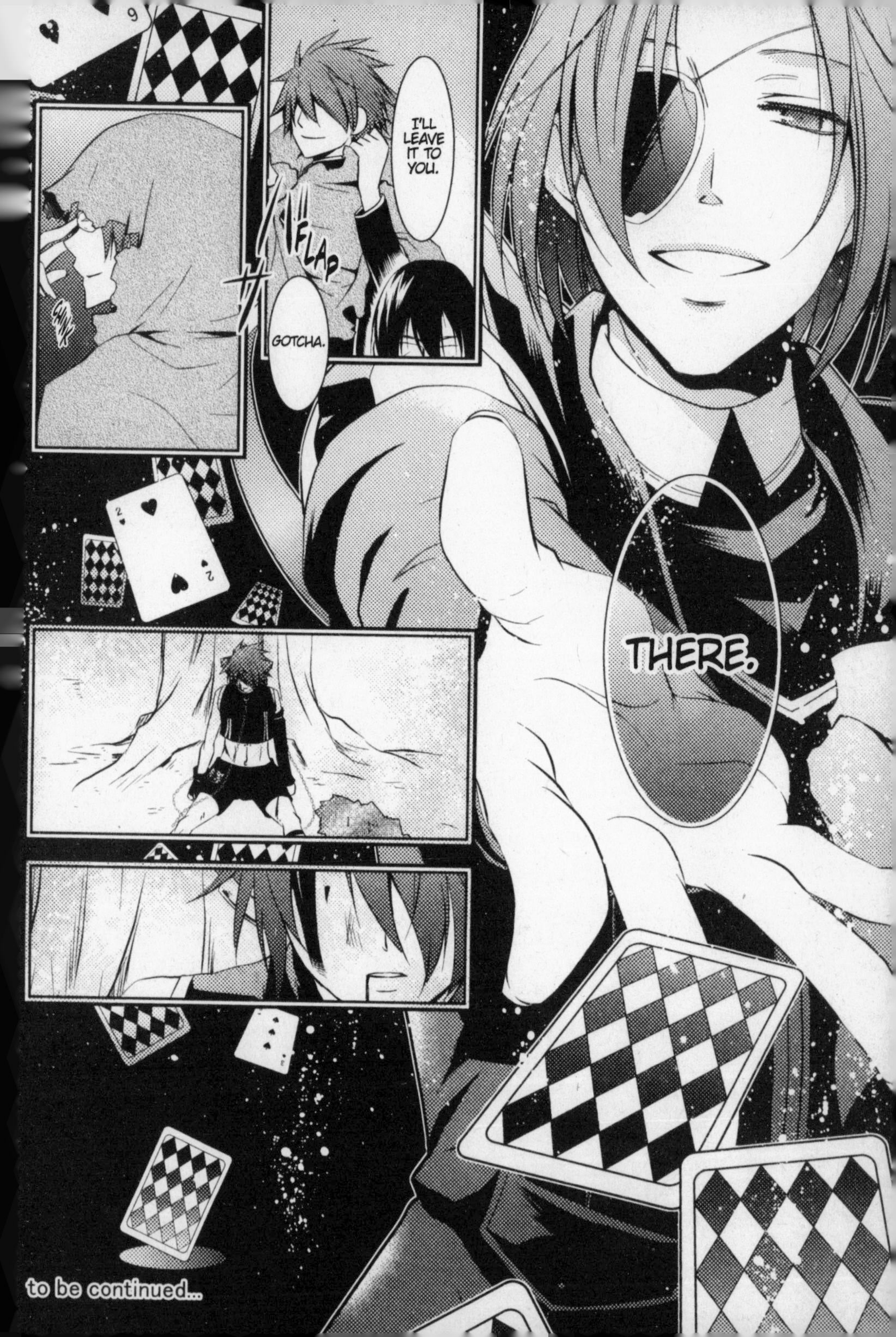
THERE.
I'LL LEAVE IT TO YOU.
FLAP
GOTCHA.
to be continued...

THANK YOU VERY MUCH!

THIS SIDE STORY WILL CONTINUE...
I HOPE YOU STAY WITH ME A LITTLE LONGER.

I'M TIRED OF ALL THE EVIL PARTS. WHAT DO I DO, PETER?
I DON'T KNOW.
SHOULD I ROAST YOU OR SIMMER YOU, PETER?

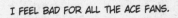

I FEEL BAD FOR ALL THE ACE FANS.

CHESHIRE CAT WALTZ VOL. 5 - POST-MORTEM

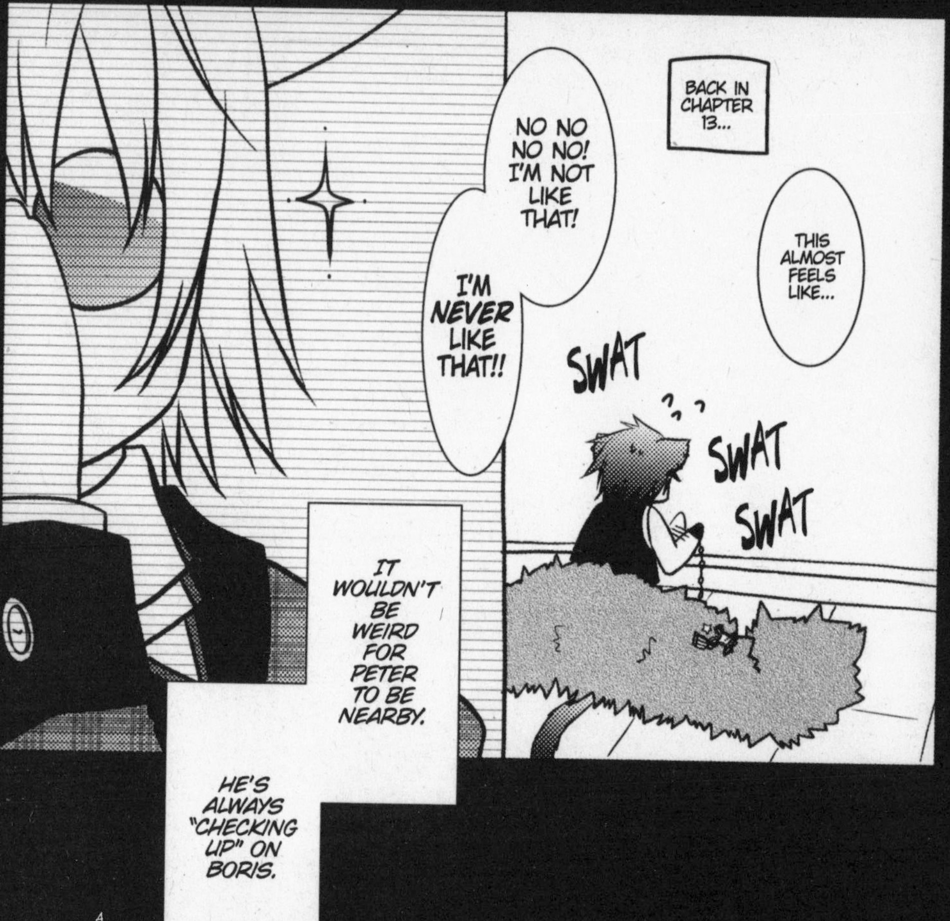
BACK IN CHAPTER 13...
THIS ALMOST FEELS LIKE...
NO NO NO NO! I'M NOT LIKE THAT!
I'M NEVER LIKE THAT!!
SWAT
SWAT
SWAT
IT WOULDN'T BE WEIRD FOR PETER TO BE NEARBY.
HE'S ALWAYS "CHECKING UP" ON BORIS.
A VICIOUS CONDITION.

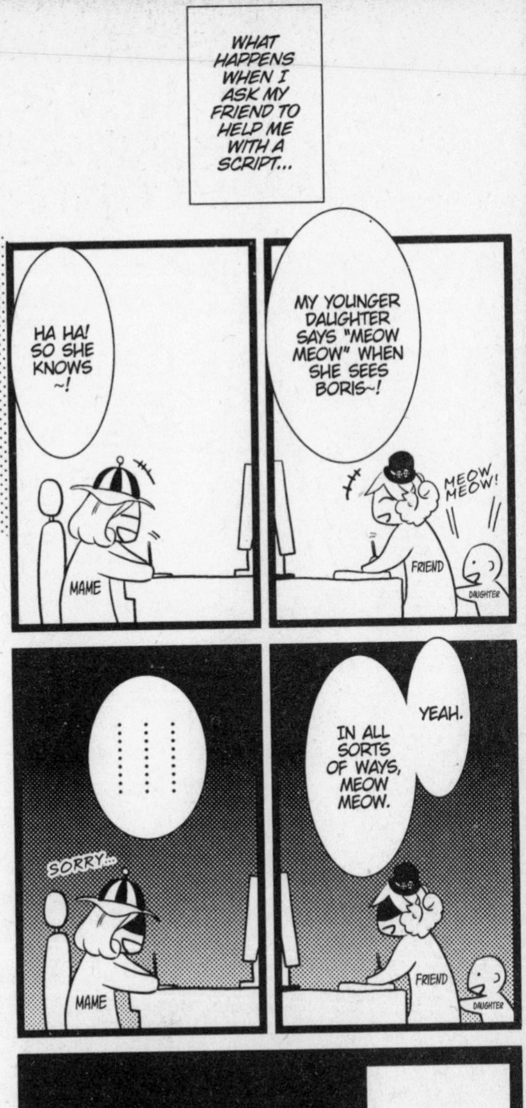
WHAT HAPPENS WHEN I ASK MY FRIEND TO HELP ME WITH A SCRIPT...
MY YOUNGER DAUGHTER SAYS "MEOW MEOW" WHEN SHE SEES BORIS~!
MEOW MEOW!
FRIEND
DAUGHTER
HA HA! SO SHE KNOWS ~!
MAME
YEAH.
IN ALL SORTS OF WAYS, MEOW MEOW.
FRIEND
DAUGHTER
......
SORRY...
MAME
"EMOTIONAL EDUCATION."
THAT VOCABULARY WORD POPPED INTO MY HEAD FOR A SECOND.

♣ Special Thanks! ♣

QuinRose
Everyone who helped make this book
Friends and acquaintances
My family who lives far away
And most of all, the readers!

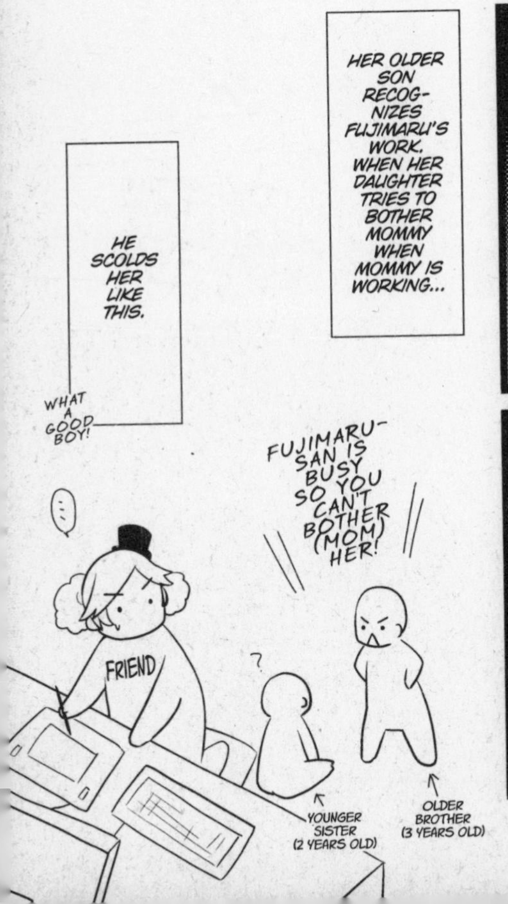
HER OLDER SON RECOGNIZES FUJIMARU'S WORK. WHEN HER DAUGHTER TRIES TO BOTHER MOMMY WHEN MOMMY IS WORKING...
HE SCOLDS HER LIKE THIS.
FUJIMARU-SAN IS BUSY SO YOU CAN'T BOTHER (MOM) HER!
WHAT A GOOD BOY!
...
?
FRIEND
YOUNGER SISTER (2 YEARS OLD)
OLDER BROTHER (3 YEARS OLD)

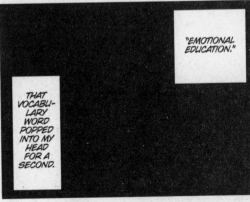

COMING SOON

AUGUST 2013

Alice in the Country of Hearts:
The Clockmaker's Story

SEPTEMBER 2013

Alice in the Country of Clover:
Cheshire Cat Waltz Vol. 6

OCTOBER 2013

Alice in the Country of Joker:
Circus and Liars Game Vol. 3

The Sacred Blacksmith

聖剣の刀鍛冶

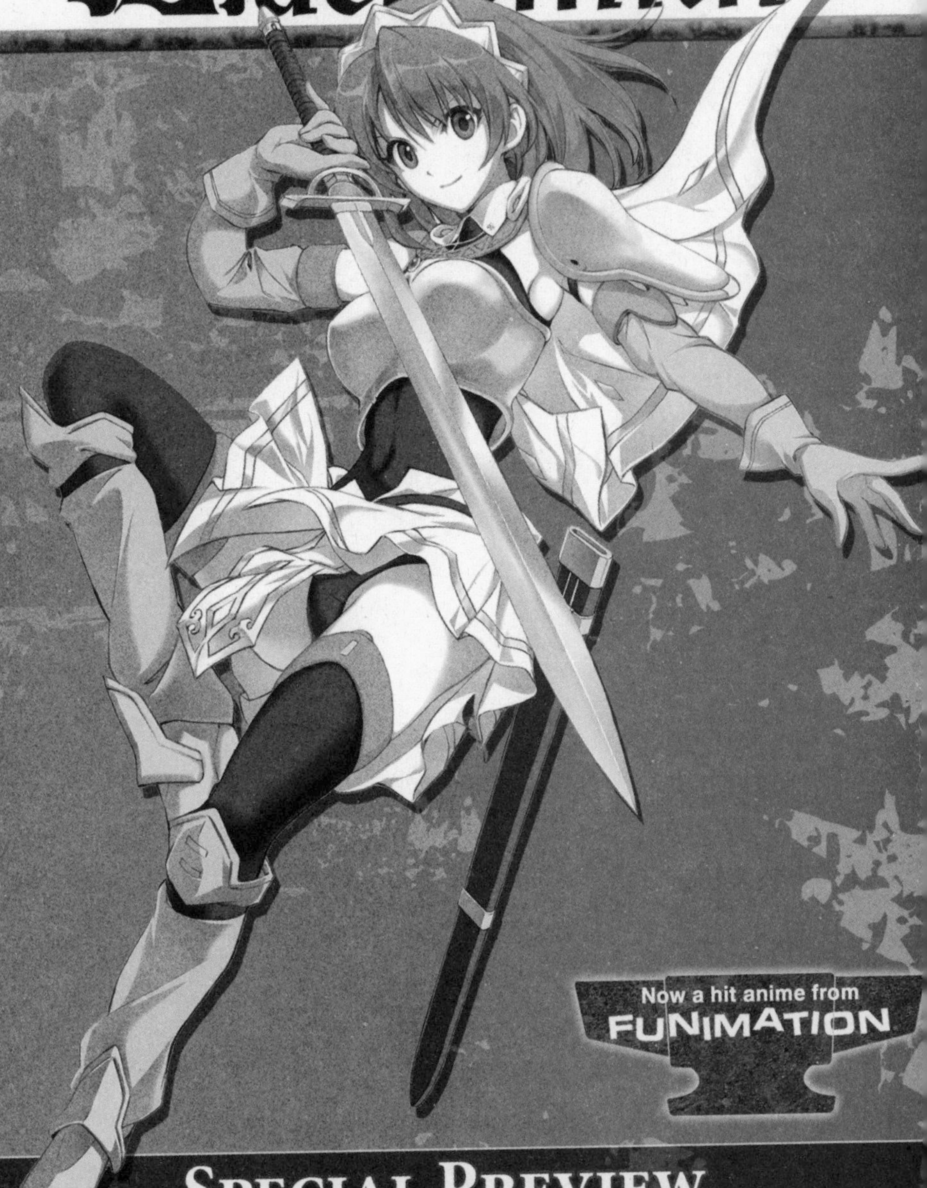
Now a hit anime from
FUNIMATION

SPECIAL PREVIEW

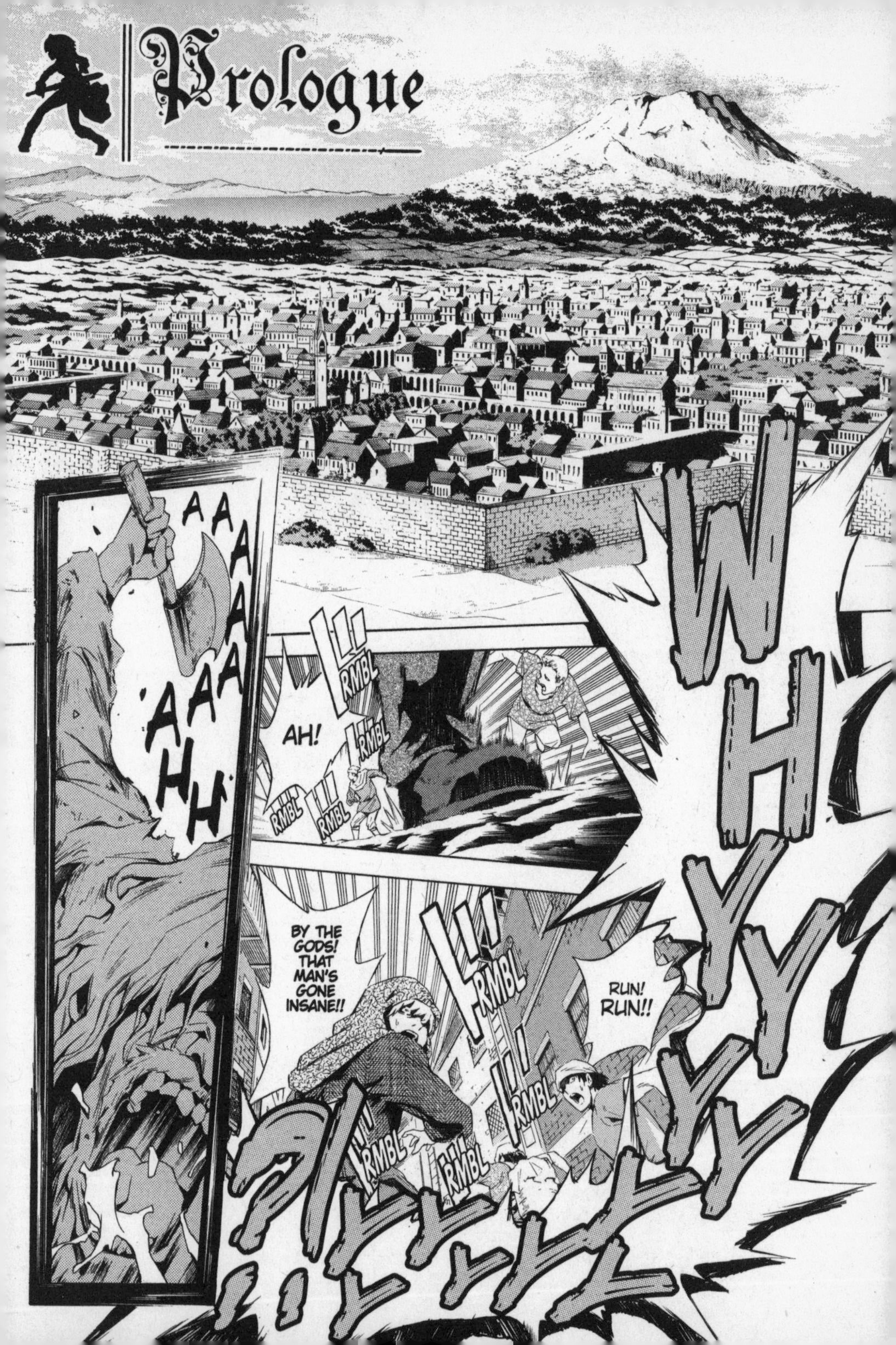
Prologue
RMBL
AH!
RMBL
RMBL
RMBL
RUN! RUN!!
BY THE GODS! THAT MAN'S GONE INSANE!!
RMBL
RMBL
RMBL
RMBL
AAAAAAAAAHH

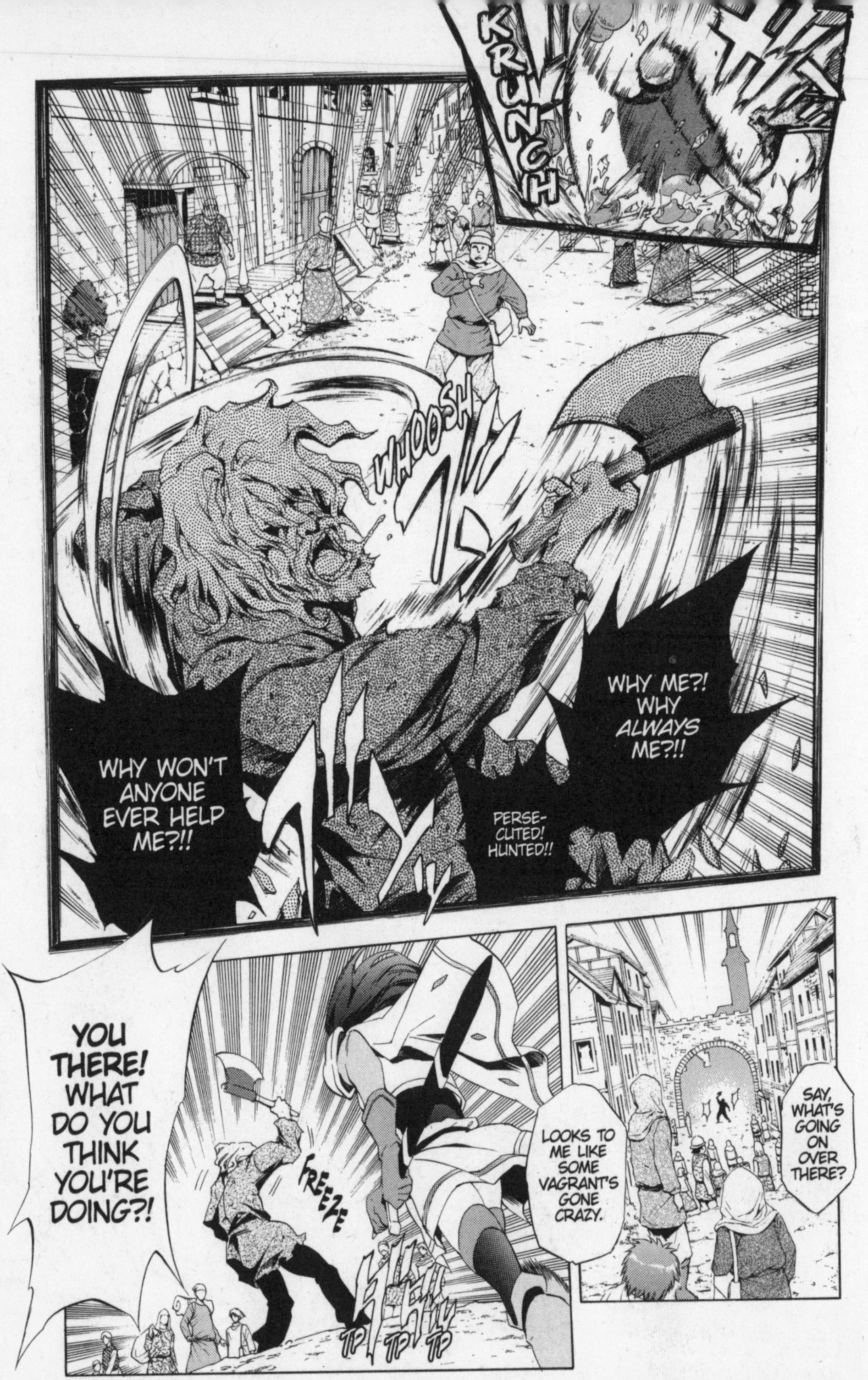
KRUNCH
WHOOSH
WHY ME?! WHY ALWAYS ME?!!
PERSE-CUTED! HUNTED!!
WHY WON'T ANYONE EVER HELP ME?!!
SAY, WHAT'S GOING ON OVER THERE?
LOOKS TO ME LIKE SOME VAGRANT'S GONE CRAZY.
YOU THERE! WHAT DO YOU THINK YOU'RE DOING?!
FREEZE
TP TP TP

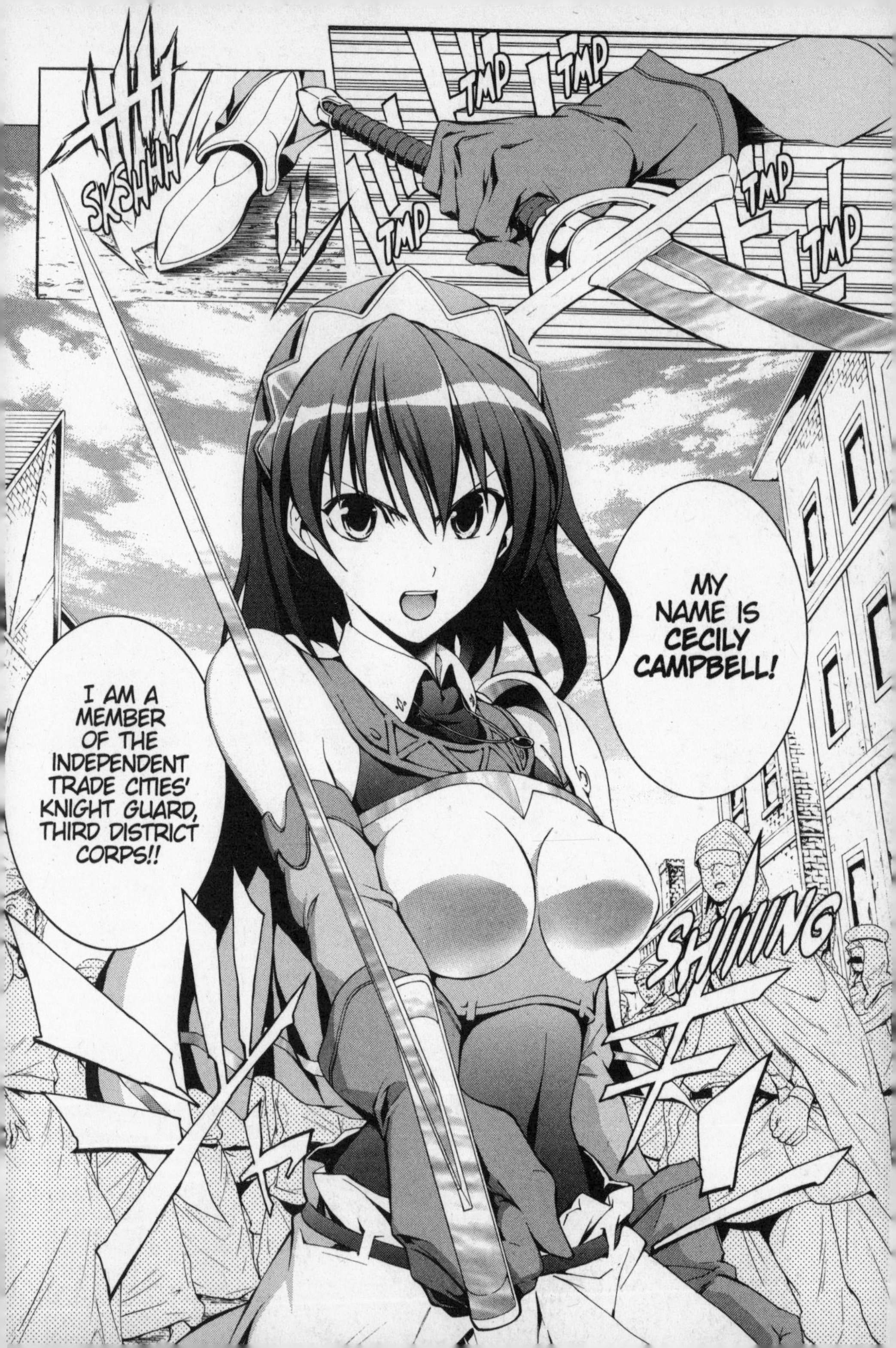
TMP
TMP
TMP
TMP
TMP
TMP
SKSHHH
MY NAME IS CECILY CAMPBELL!
I AM A MEMBER OF THE INDEPENDENT TRADE CITIES' KNIGHT GUARD, THIRD DISTRICT CORPS!!
SHIIING

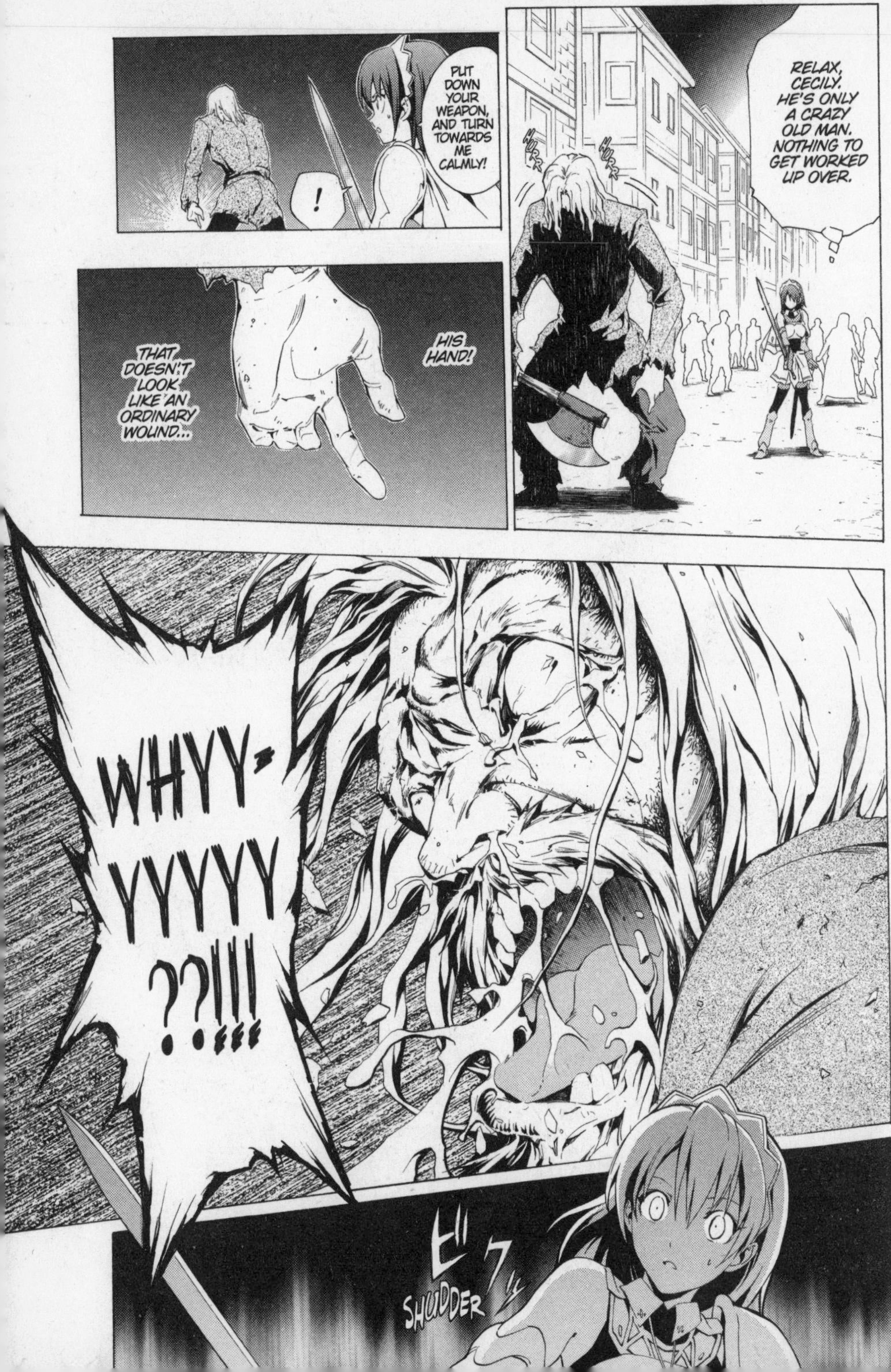
RELAX, CECILY. HE'S ONLY A CRAZY OLD MAN. NOTHING TO GET WORKED UP OVER.
HURR
HURR
PUT DOWN YOUR WEAPON, AND TURN TOWARDS ME CALMLY!
!
HIS HAND!
THAT DOESN'T LOOK LIKE AN ORDINARY WOUND...
WHYY-YYYYY??!!!!
ビクッ
SHUDDER

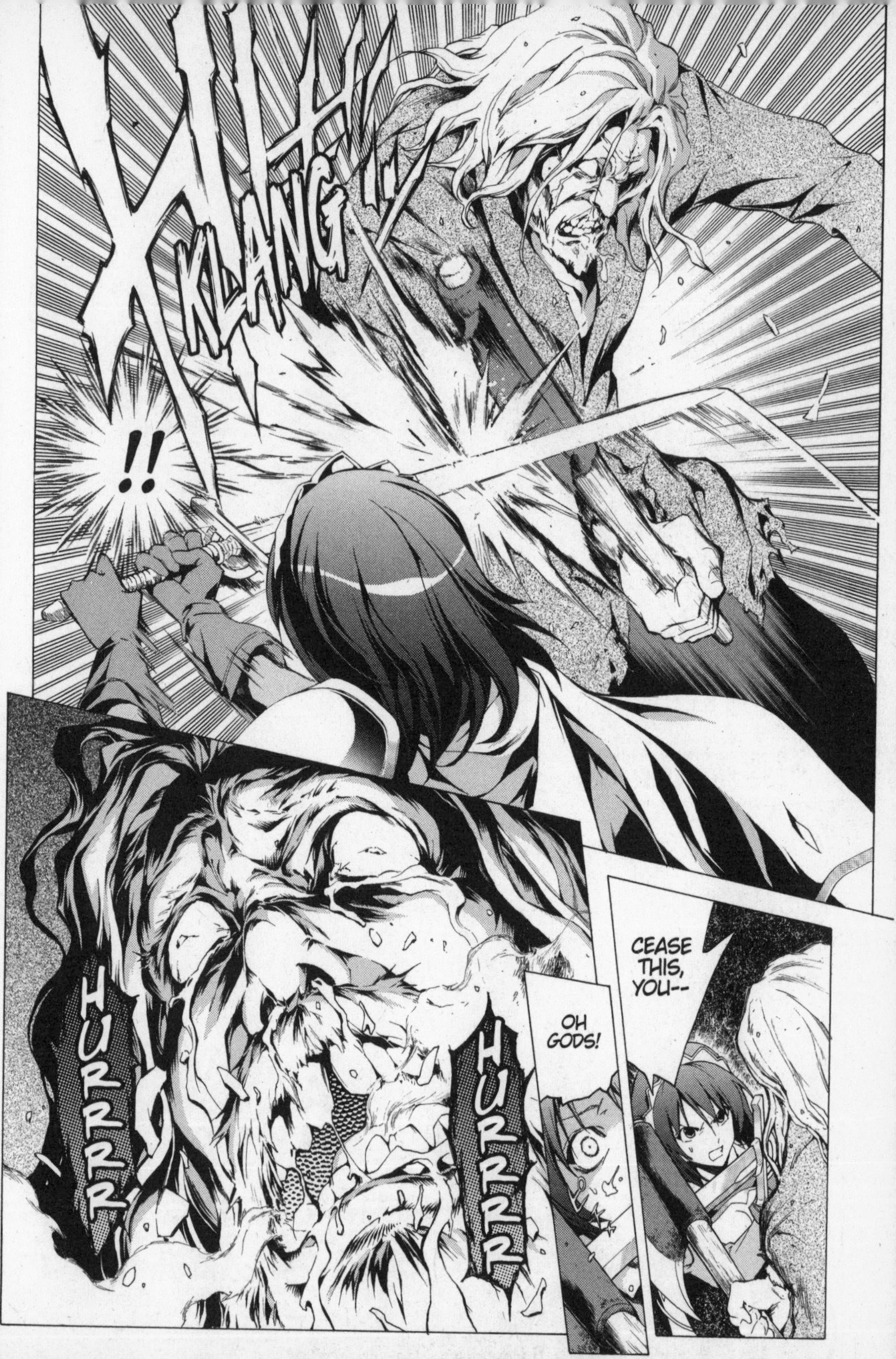
KLANG
!!
CEASE THIS, YOU--
OH GODS!
HURRRR
HURRRR

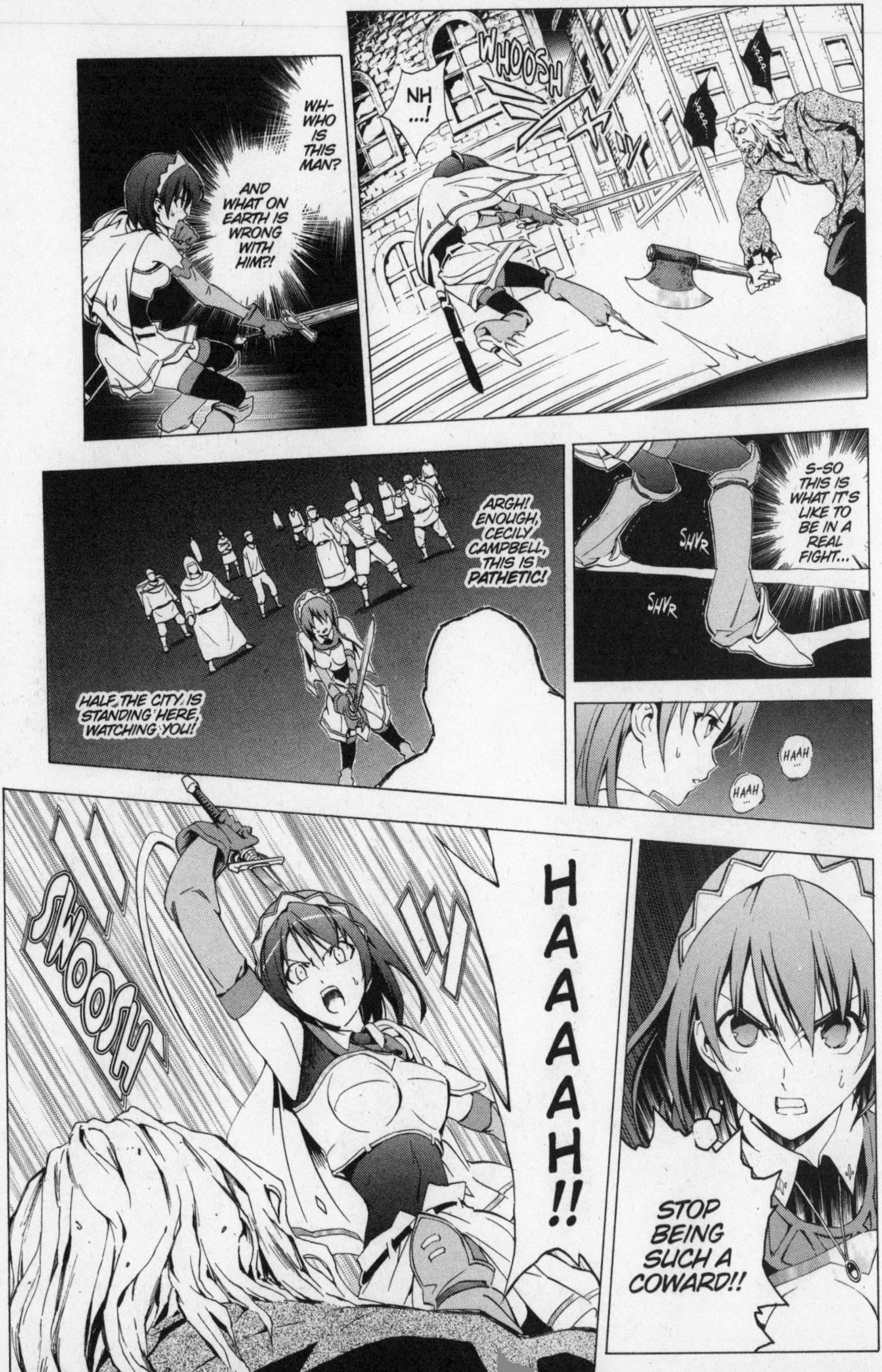
Hrrr...
Hrrr...
WHOOSH
NH ...!
WH- WHO IS THIS MAN?
AND WHAT ON EARTH IS WRONG WITH HIM?!
S-SO THIS IS WHAT IT'S LIKE TO BE IN A REAL FIGHT...
SHVR
SHVR
HAAH ...
HAAH ...
ARGH! ENOUGH, CECILY CAMPBELL, THIS IS PATHETIC!
HALF THE CITY IS STANDING HERE, WATCHING YOU!
STOP BEING SUCH A COWARD!!
HAAAAAH!!
SWOOSH

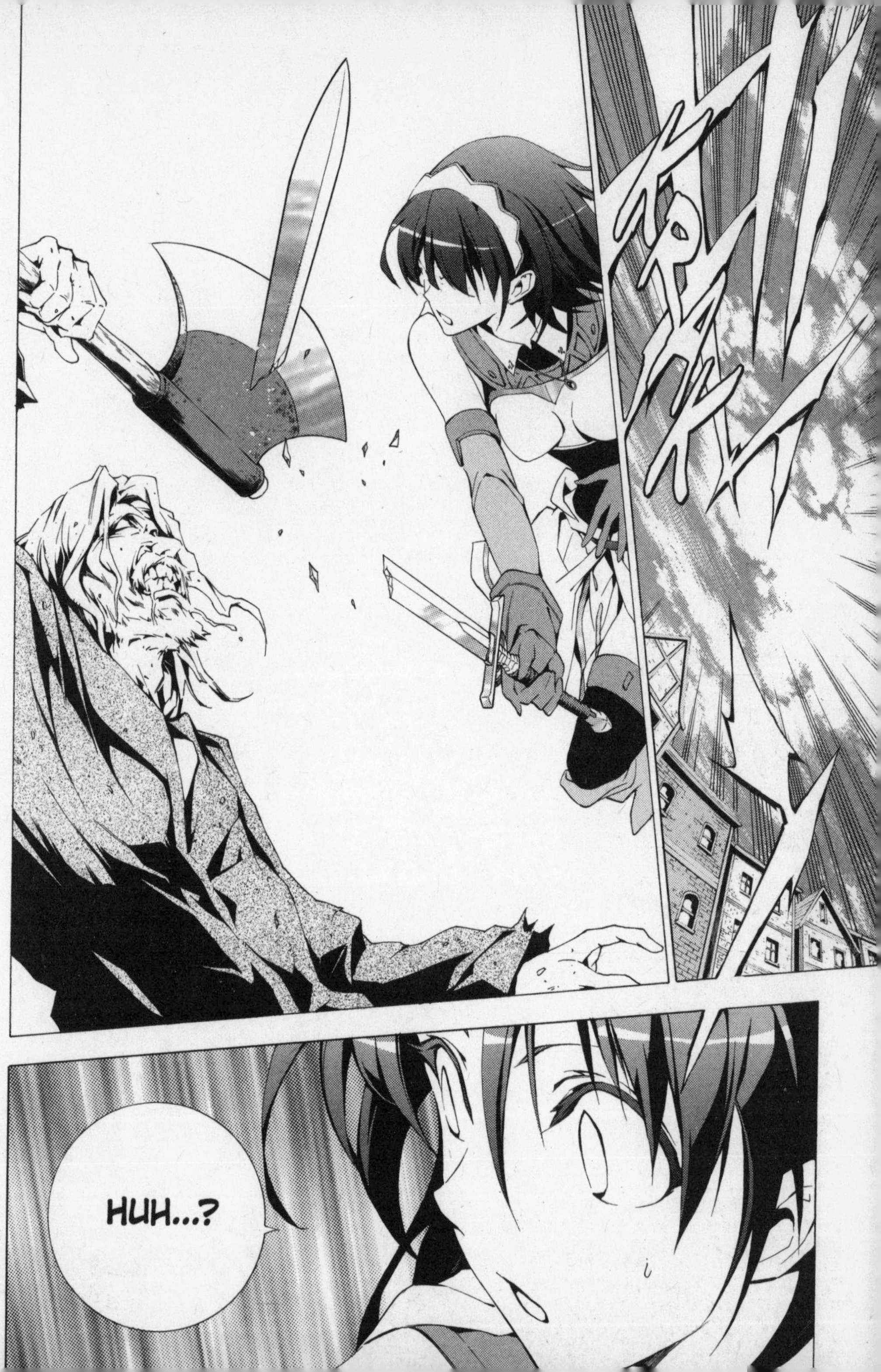
HUH...?

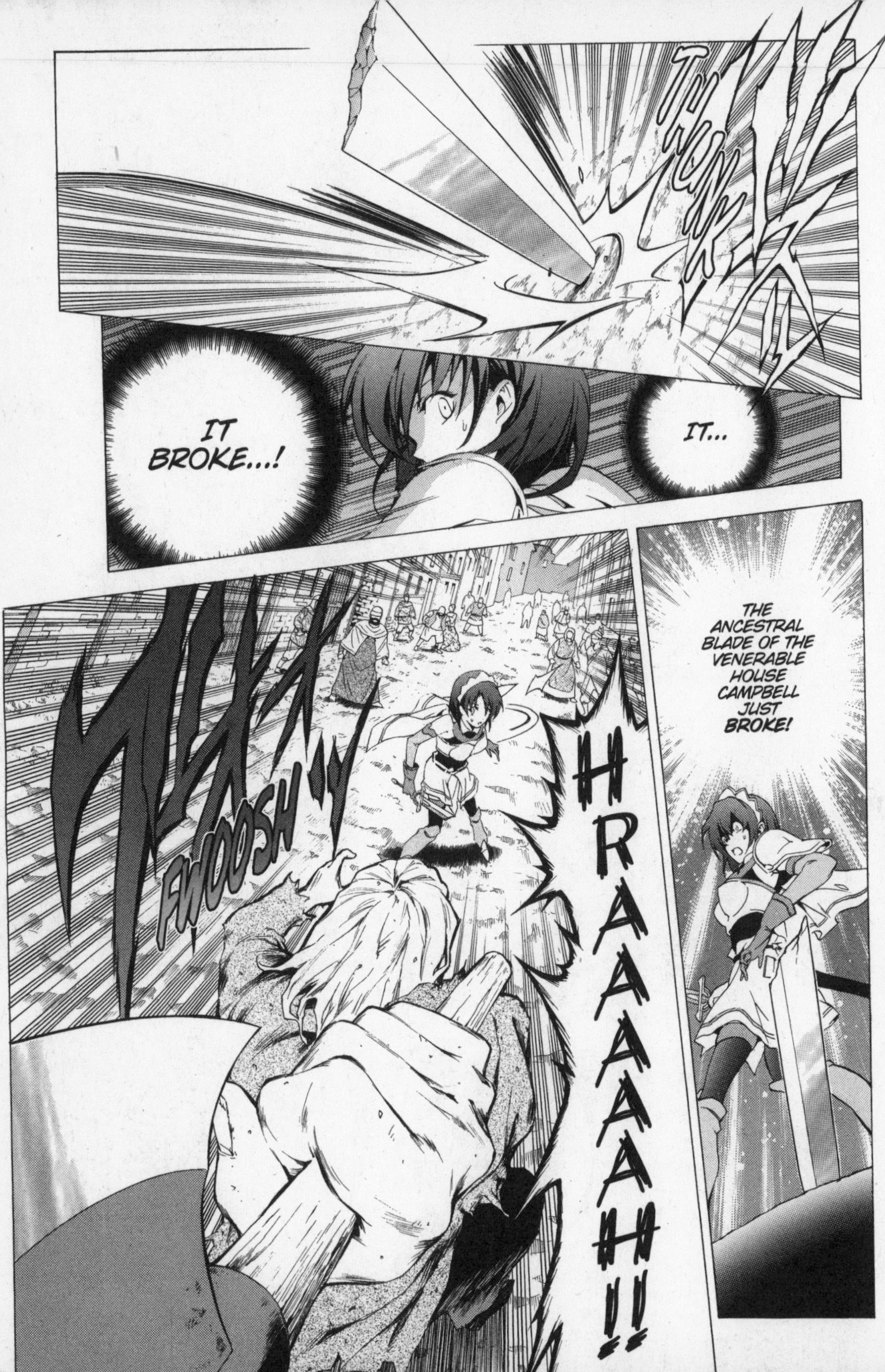
THUNK
IT...
IT BROKE...!
THE ANCESTRAL BLADE OF THE VENERABLE HOUSE CAMPBELL JUST BROKE!
FWOOSH
HRAAAAAAH!!

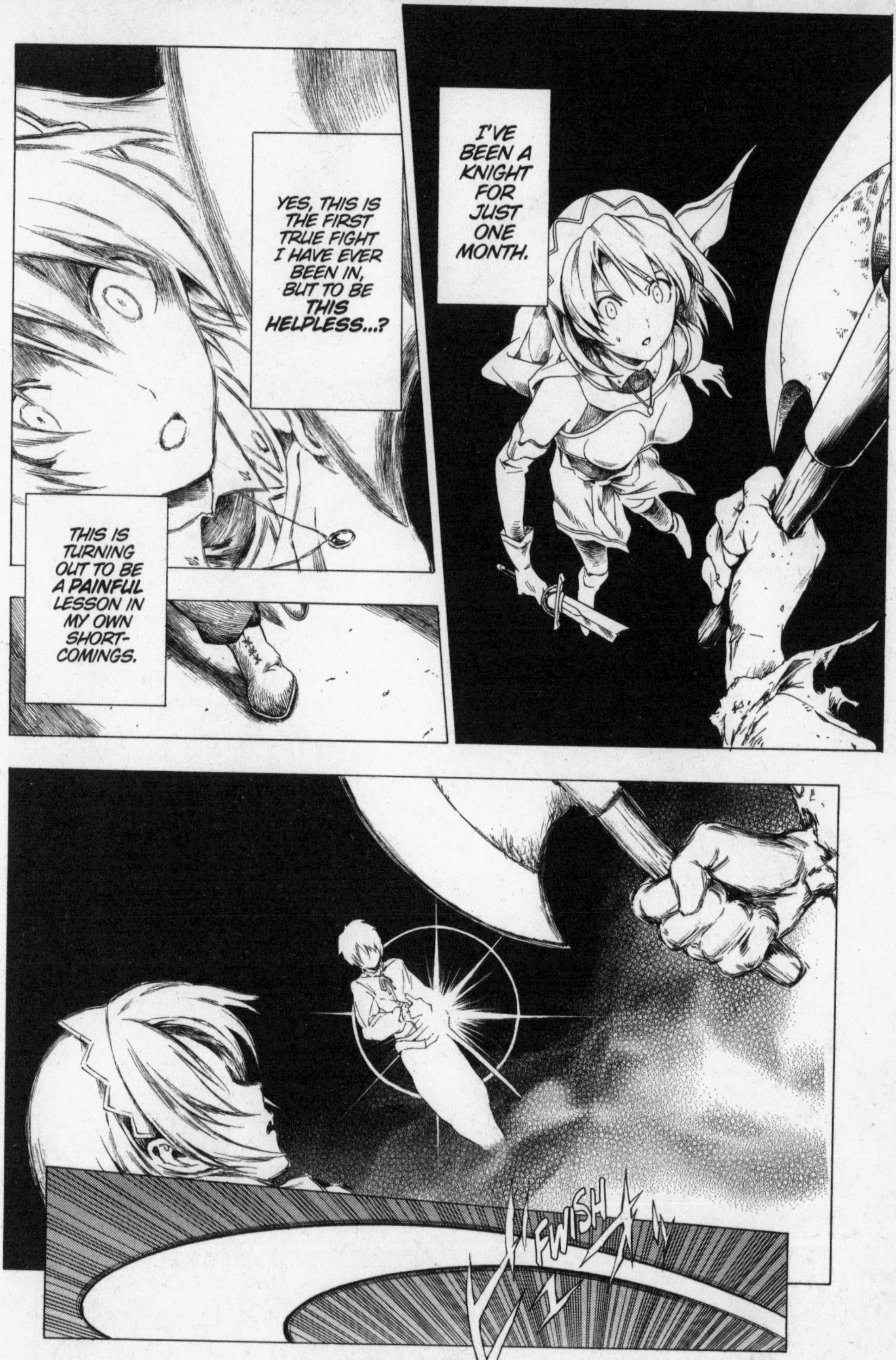
I'VE BEEN A KNIGHT FOR JUST ONE MONTH.
YES, THIS IS THE FIRST TRUE FIGHT I HAVE EVER BEEN IN, BUT TO BE THIS HELPLESS...?
THIS IS TURNING OUT TO BE A PAINFUL LESSON IN MY OWN SHORT-COMINGS.
FWISH

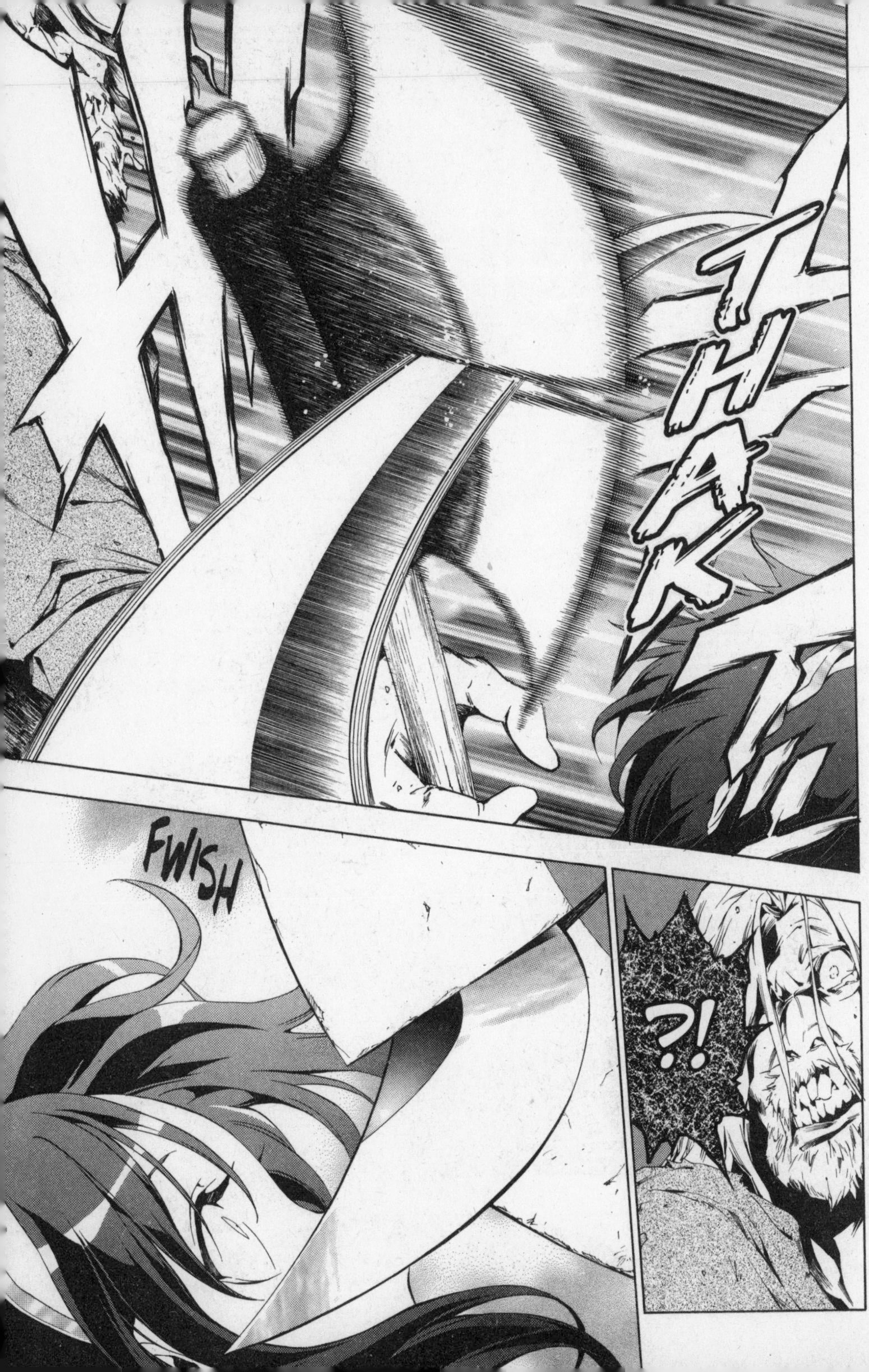
THAK
FWISH
?!

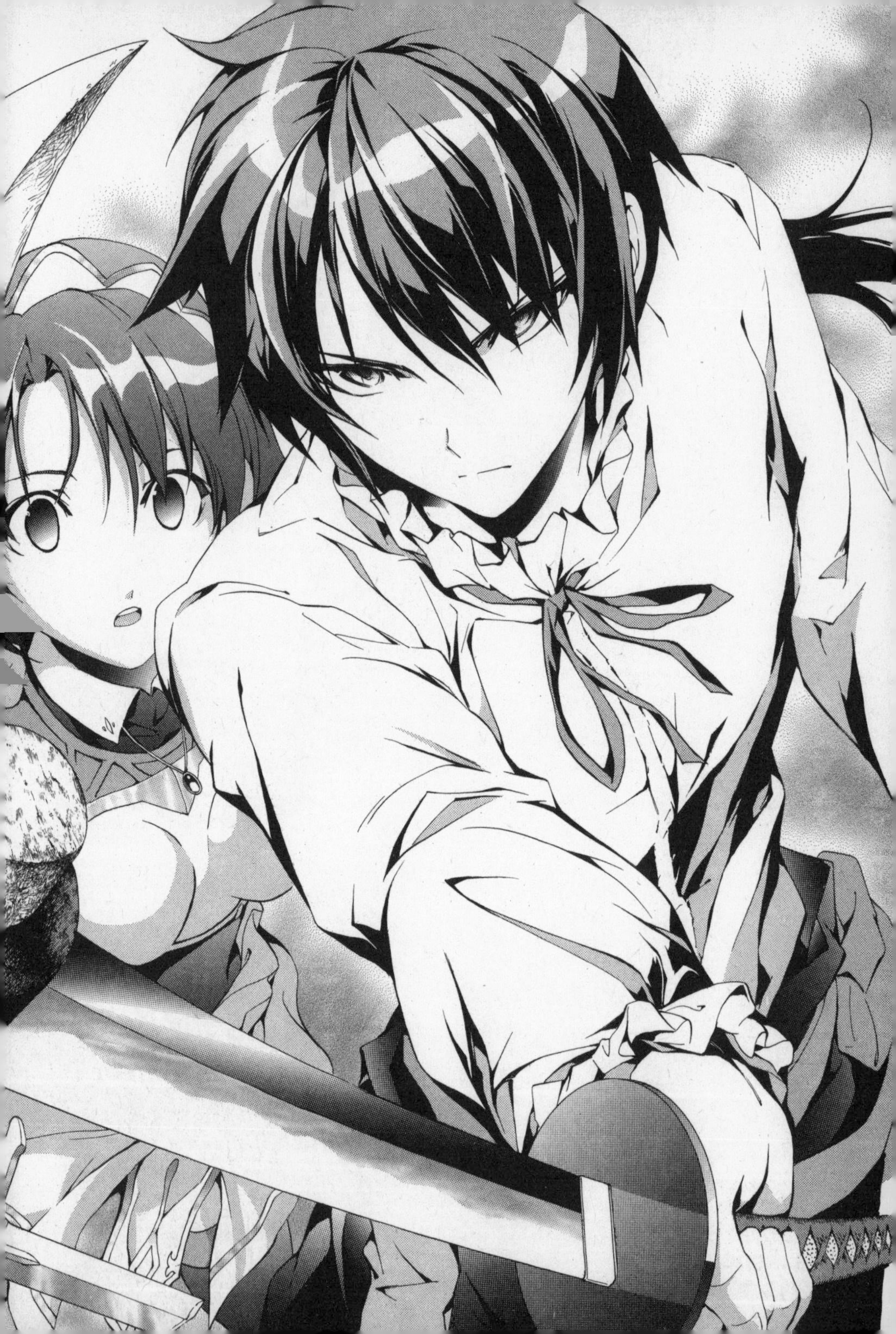